Asia
Pacific
in World
Politics

Asia Pacific
in
World Politics

Derek McDougall

LYNNE
RIENNER
PUBLISHERS

BOULDER
LONDON

Published in the United States of America in 2007 by
Lynne Rienner Publishers, Inc.
1800 30th Street, Boulder, Colorado 80301
www.rienner.com

and in the United Kingdom by
Lynne Rienner Publishers, Inc.
3 Henrietta Street, Covent Garden, London WC2E 8LU

Library of Congress Cataloging-in-Publication Data
McDougall, Derek, 1945–
    Asia Pacific in world politics / Derek McDougall.
        p.   cm.
    Includes bibliographical references and index.
    ISBN-13: 978-1-58826-194-6 (hardcover : alk. paper)
    ISBN-10: 1-58826-194-8 (hardcover : alk. paper)
    ISBN-13: 978-1-58826-170-0 (pbk. : alk. paper)
    ISBN-10: 1-58826-170-0 (pbk. : alk. paper)
    1. Asia—Foreign relations.   2. Pacific Area—Foreign relations.
3. Security, International. I. Title.
    JZ1980.M33 2006
    327.5—dc22
                                        2006020883

British Cataloguing in Publication Data
A Cataloguing in Publicastion record for this book
is available from the British Library.

Printed and bound in the United States of America

    The paper used in this publication meets the requirements
∞   of the American National Standard for Permanence of
    Paper for Printed Library Materials Z39.48-1992.

5   4   3   2   1

Contents

Preface

The focus of this book is Asia Pacific as one of the significant regions in world politics. It examines international politics within Asia Pacific on the assumption that developments in the region will in turn have an important impact on the world more generally. Most of the world's major powers are involved here: the United States, China, Japan, and Russia. India also has a role, and the various European powers (as well as the European Union itself) put some emphasis on their relations with Asia Pacific.

I give particular attention, in Part 1, to the roles of the United States, China, and Japan and the ways in which these three powers interact. This means a strong focus on Northeast Asia. Part 2, covering the Taiwan and Korea conflicts, also directs attention to Northeast Asia, although the significance of these conflicts goes well beyond their immediate context. The subject of Part 3 is Southeast Asia, with an emphasis on Indonesia; and in Part 4, I turn to the significance of Russia, Australia, and a range of regional and global international organizations.

Throughout, I give particular attention to the post–Cold War period, although the historical context is not neglected. While security issues feature prominently, economic issues are also covered, as are relatively new issues on the international agenda such as human rights and, of course, the impact of the September 11 terrorist attacks.

*   *   *

My debts in writing the book are many. I would like to thank Lynne Rienner for her encouragement and patience. I would also like to thank all of the people involved in the production process at Lynne Rienner Publishers. Some parts of the book draw on my earlier work, *The International Politics of the New Asia Pacific* (Boulder, CO: Lynne Rienner, 1997). The historical section in Chapter 1 is based on my contribution to Katherine Palmer Kaup, ed., *Understanding Contemporary Asia Pacific* (Boulder, CO: Lynne Rienner, forthcoming 2007).

Contrary to the perceptions of some, one of the best things about academia is the people you meet. My students and tutors in Asia Pacific International Politics at the University of Melbourne have been a constant stimulus, as have my many honors and graduate students. Tutors who worked with me in this area during the writing of the book were Daniel Bray, Tom Davis, Kingsley Edney, Manusavee Monsakul, Jemma Purdey, Kumuda Simpson, Matt Sussex, Dirk Tomsa, and Joanne Wallis. Jemma Purdey and David Envall helped by reading the chapters relating to their areas of expertise. Toshiya Nakamura facilitated my involvement with the Research Institute for Peace and Security in Tokyo. I am grateful for the supportive environment of the Department of Political Science at the University of Melbourne, and acknowledge the contributions of my heads of department, Brian Galligan and Ann Capling. The infrastructure provided by the general staff in the department has also been invaluable. In this respect I would like to acknowledge Rita De Amicis, Joanna Buckingham, Darren Smith, Natalie Reitmier, and Wendy Ruffles. Antigone Vasilopoulos and Erin Richardson have been a great help to me since their arrival in my department. I was able to complete the book during a period of study leave spent as a visiting fellow at Wolfson College, University of Cambridge.

I would like to thank my recently "retired" colleagues, Phillip Darby, Peter Shearman, and David Tucker, for the many and varied contributions they have made to my thinking about international politics. Among the next generation of scholars working on Asia Pacific, I have learned a lot from Michael Connors and Nick Bisley. The book has benefited from my interactions with many other people, encompassing a diverse range of views and expertise, including Amitav Acharya, Ron Anderson, Carl Bridge, Barry Buzan, Joseph Camilleri, Richard Chauvel, Hugh Collins, Michael Cox, Robyn Eckersley, Annmarie Elijah, Lawrence Freedman, Richard Herr, Helen Hill, Helen Hintjens, Brian Hocking, Leslie Holmes, John Langmore, Stephanie Lawson, Philomena Murray, Kim Nossal, Chengxin Pan, Tim Shaw, Gary Smith, Michael Smith, Adam Tarock, Ross Terrill, Effi Tomaras, William Tow, Russell Trood, Michael Wesley, Andrew Williams, Page Wilson, and Garry Woodard. The list could go on, and apologies if I have left anyone out.

Among the previous academic generation my debts are to W. Macmahon ("Mac") Ball, Lloyd Churchward, and Ralph Braibanti. I am particularly grateful for the way in which friends have given their support, whether emotional or academic (or both). Thanks especially to David

Dunt, Jeremy Salt, Neil Day, Margaret Hall, Katrina Gorjanicyn, Jacinta Sanders, and Sophie Chapman (and also Maureen Williams in Cambridge). Thanks also to my "fumily" (Kirsty, Ros, Anne), who have offered me plenty of distractions, some of which helped with the book!

I dedicate this book to my father, Jack. He has always been there for me.

—Derek McDougall

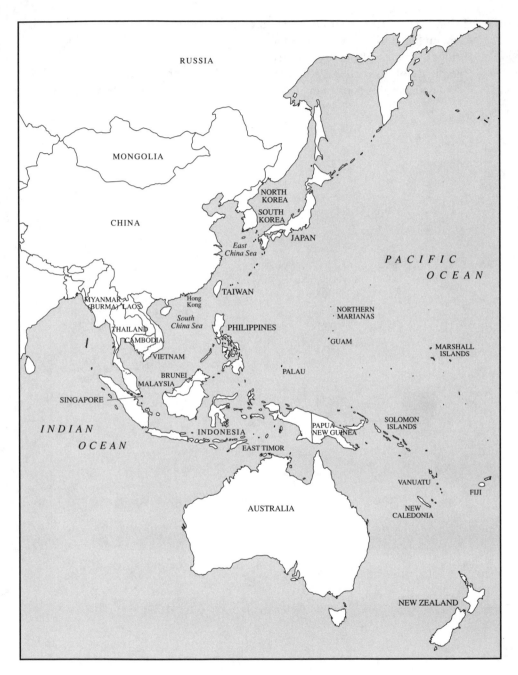

Asia Pacific

Understanding Asia Pacific International Politics

1

A s a significant component of world politics, Asia Pacific confronts many major issues. This is a region in which the United States, China, and Japan relate directly to one another. The United States has been the dominant power in the region in the post-1945 period, and this situation has been enhanced in the post–Cold War period. At the same time China, which embarked on an ambitious program of economic modernization in the late 1970s, has grown steadily stronger. Are China and the United States on a collision course or can they cooperate? Where does Japan, as the world's second largest economic power, fit in this picture? Japan has maintained its alliance with the United States, while also developing a more independent direction; it does not wish to see the region dominated by China. Tensions have continued throughout the early twenty-first century in relation to both Taiwan and Korea. Are these tensions likely to result in war at some point? In Southeast Asia the various states have faced numerous "nation building" challenges, none more so than Indonesia. Many groups oppose the authority of the existing states, and these tensions often spill over into the international arena. Throughout Asia Pacific one can also observe the expanding presence of regional and global organizations. Does this presence amount to much, and if so what? Are we moving into an era when states, both major and lesser powers, will become less significant for Asia Pacific international politics? This book is concerned with this whole range of issues and questions as they appear in the current phase of world politics in Asia Pacific.

In providing a study of international politics in Asia Pacific, we need to have working definitions of both "international politics" and "Asia Pacific." Both terms are often taken for granted but, in fact, both are open to debate. We will begin with a discussion of how the terms international politics and

1

Asia Pacific are used in this book, and then examine the historical context of international politics in Asia Pacific, and some of the major features of contemporary Asia Pacific. At the end of the chapter there is an overview of the plan of the book.

■ Defining International Politics and Asia Pacific

International Politics

An everyday definition of "international politics" encompasses political relationships transcending state boundaries. Political relationships concern the pursuit of power and influence. Often the focus is on the relationship between states. While this dimension is certainly a very important aspect of international politics, it would be an oversimplification to see this as the whole. A broader view allows scope for actors other than states. These include international organizations, transnational corporations, and nongovernmental organizations. Along with states, these actors seek to further their objectives in the global arena. The term "global politics" is emerging to denote the wide variety of actors involved and the range of issues that arise. International or global issues in the contemporary world cover not just traditional military security, but many other forms of security (defense against terrorism being the most obvious one in the post–September 11 world). There are also major questions concerning economics, culture and religion, the environment, human rights, and the movement of people (immigration, refugees), to mention some of the more significant. The term "globalization" suggests the way many of these issues are dealt with at a global level. At the same time there are also movements and processes countering globalization or attempting to point it in a different direction. The continuing role of states is relevant here, as are developments at the regional and substate levels. "Antiglobalization" movements are not necessarily opposed to globalization as such, but certainly argue in favor of giving greater attention to the social, political, and environmental impacts of the prevailing economic orthodoxy.

The different views on the nature of international politics are reflected in some of the important theoretical approaches. At one level these approaches can be distinguished on the basis of how they characterize the key actors and processes in international politics. There can also be differences relating to the significance and content of the moral dimension of international politics. During the Cold War the realist approach dominated the study of international politics. In the post–Cold War era this approach has been challenged by newer approaches such as liberalism (also referred to as liberal institutionalism) and globalization theory. Various critical approaches emphasize the importance of moral goals. There is also an issue about whether the major theories are too Western-oriented. Culturalistic approaches emphasize the way factors specific to particular states or societies (in this case in the Asian context) influence international behavior. We will briefly review some of the major theoretical approaches, since one needs to be aware of the assumptions underlying the analysis presented in this book.[1]

Mid-twentieth-century realism is associated with writers such as E. H. Carr and Hans Morgenthau.[2] Their focus was on the role of states in international politics, and how the behavior of states is motivated by power considerations. States sought to protect and advance their national interest. At a minimum national interest involved the protection of a state's territorial integrity, but broader strategic, economic, societal, and cultural dimensions were usually also involved. A state's ability to achieve its objectives was determined by its power, involving military, economic, political, and other dimensions. The balance of power was the most important feature in the functioning of international politics. In pursuing their objectives states sought to make common cause with other states having similar interests in a given situation. They would act to oppose states seen as threatening those interests. Traditional realists were opposed to moralism in international politics, that is, the belief that good would prevail through means such as international law and international organization irrespective of power realities. Morgenthau in particular was also critical of ideologically motivated crusades. Nevertheless Carr and Morgenthau, although differing in their approaches, both saw moral principles as a very important feature of international politics. The issue was to work out what those principles should be and how they should be implemented.

In the latter decades of the twentieth century an important development was the emergence of neorealism, associated in particular with Kenneth Waltz.[3] Waltz's key argument was that the international behavior of states derived from the anarchical character of international politics. States had to protect themselves in a situation where there was no overriding authority. Balancing behavior was the most obvious example of how states sought to achieve their security goals. In Waltz's view international politics was best explained in terms of the nature of the system as a whole, rather than by focusing on the characteristics of states or even human nature. He gave less explicit attention to moral issues than did Carr and Morgenthau. Nevertheless goals such as peace and security are important to Waltz. His concern is to show how the achievement of such goals is dependent upon understanding how states function in international politics.

Liberalism (or liberal institutionalism) provides an important alternative to the various versions of realism.[4] As an approach to international politics, liberalism places some emphasis on the role of states but also gives attention to other actors such as international organizations, transnational corporations, and nongovernmental organizations. Whereas realism focuses on the high politics of security issues, liberalism puts more emphasis on issues concerning economic and social interactions (low politics). The interdependence of all actors in the international domain is a particular theme. In general, liberalism is not explicitly concerned with moral issues. There is, however, an assumption that increasing interdependence will promote international peace and promote human welfare.

Some of the themes in liberalism are developed further in globalization theory.[5] Globalization as a theoretical approach is particularly important in fields such as sociology and international political economy, but it also has implications for understanding international politics. The key point is that increasingly political, economic, social, and cultural processes need to be understood on a global level. In the economic domain there is an assumption (no doubt oversimplified) that the global marketplace is dominant. Individual states have less control over their destiny in such a situation (although this can vary with the particular state, of course). From this perspective the high politics of realism is dealing with only one aspect of a very complex world, and is thus grossly oversimplified. While some globalization theorists see the phenomenon leading to a more cosmopolitan and fairer world, this is not necessarily the case. The antiglobalization movement is in some respects a misnomer as supporters of this movement are not necessarily opposed to globalization as such. What they are critical of is the idea that the global marketplace should be regarded as some kind of juggernaut that necessarily takes priority over other kinds of values articulated through various political means, whether states or groups based in civil society.

The emphasis on viewing international politics from the perspective of underlying values is a key feature of various critical approaches. Some of the approaches come under the general term of "critical theory," although there are also more specific formulations (e.g., the various feminist perspectives on international politics). Some of the critical approaches have distinctive views on the functioning of international politics. The most obvious example is the way in which feminist approaches see the various actors and processes of international politics as gendered, and with generally adverse effects on women. Irrespective of the interpretation of international processes, critical approaches share the view that it is necessary to discern the values implicit in international politics at various levels, and to subject those values to critical scrutiny. The complementary challenge is to develop and implement values that will more fully strengthen humanity than does existing international politics. An important issue here is whether priority should be given to participation in states (as argued by communitarians) or to the global arena (the cosmopolitan position).

All of the approaches that have been outlined so far are global in perspective but have been developed primarily in a Western context. The culturalistic approach argues that in explaining the dynamics of international politics one needs to give greater attention to factors that are specific to particular states and cultures. Lucian Pye suggests that contrary to the view that power is "a single basic phenomenon which operate[s] according to universal principles, regardless of time, place or culture . . . people at different times and in different places have had quite different understandings of the concept of power."[6] One needs to be aware of the specific and general values that people involved in international interactions (whether in a governmental role or otherwise) bring to their task, and of the factors affecting those values. These factors can include the impact of history, as well as more immediate considerations of economics and domestic politics. One cannot assume that factors operating at a global level necessarily determine the behavior of individual actors. Factors specific to particular actors also need to be taken into account. Different levels are relevant, and to focus simply on one level is to risk oversimplification of a complex reality. In terms of the moral dimension of international politics the culturalistic approach draws attention to the diversity of perspectives in the world. Samuel Huntington believes this diversity represents a fundamental "clash of civilizations."[7] An alternative view is that while there is clearly diversity, different manifestations of a considerable degree of underlying unity in humanity are represented.[8]

At one level the approach to international politics in this book is eclectic. The study is not intended as a theoretical work, but it draws on a number of approaches. There is a strong emphasis on the role of states, but not to the exclusion of other actors. While at a general level states as such might have declined in significance in international politics, they still play a dominant role in relation to many issues. This is particularly the case with the major powers in the region, but applies to other states too. The book has a major emphasis on strategic issues in Asia Pacific, but economic issues are also considered, and there is some attention to the "new international agenda." Taking up the argument of the culturalistic approach, there is a strong emphasis on the particular circumstances of the relevant actors. These circumstances cover not just culture in the general sense, but other more specific factors such as the impact of domestic politics and the economic environment. Moral issues emerge mainly through the analysis of the perspectives of key actors. Issues of peace, security, and justice are foremost. An important question concerns the extent to which states see these issues primarily in terms of national interests, as compared to broader conceptions of regional and global interests. The underlying motivation of other actors is also relevant in this context. An important consideration is the extent to which the processes of international politics in Asia Pacific limit the ability to achieve desired moral goals.

Asia Pacific

Having indicated the approach taken to international politics in this book, it is also necessary to define the use of the term "Asia Pacific." All regions are constructs. States generally promote definitions of regions to suit their own purposes. The concept of Asia Pacific dates from the 1960s and 1970s.[9] It was promoted by countries such as the United States, Japan, and Australia as a means of linking East Asia to the wider Pacific region. "Asia Pacific" highlights the Asian dimension in a way that "Pacific region" does not. "East Asia" is obviously more geographically limited and excludes powers such as the United States and Australia. "Far East" as a term is Eurocentric and historically dated. From a political perspective "Asia Pacific" legitimizes the involvement of the United States in East Asian affairs. The United States cannot describe itself as an Asian power but its extensive involvement in the Pacific justifies describing it as part of Asia Pacific. US support has been a major factor in enabling the concept to become established.[10] Although they do not carry the weight of the United States, Pacific-oriented Western countries such as Australia, Canada, and New Zealand have similar reasons for supporting the construct. In the case of Japan an important factor behind its support was that while the concept provided a justification for continued US involvement in East Asian affairs, it also multilateralized that involvement. From Japan's perspective this meant that if tensions arose in US-Japanese relations, there could be possibilities for defusing such tensions in wider regional settings.

As previously indicated, the term "Pacific region" does not contain any specific reference to Asia. The major alternative regional construct has been "East Asia," which excludes Western powers such as the United States. From the late 1980s the main advocate for this approach was Mahathir Mohamad, prime minister of Malaysia from 1981 to 2003. Although Malaysia became a member of Asia-Pacific Economic Cooperation (APEC), formed in 1989, Mahathir's preference was for an East Asian Economic Grouping or Caucus. The "East Asian" approach received a fillip at the time of the Asian economic crisis in 1997, with the subsequent emergence of ASEAN Plus Three (i.e., the members of the Association of Southeast Asian Nations, together with China, Japan, and South Korea). In December 2005 a new grouping, known as the East Asia Summit, emerged following a meeting in Kuala Lumpur.

The usual definition of "Asia Pacific," and the one used in this book, includes East Asia and the Western powers of the Pacific (the United States, Australia, Canada, New Zealand). East Asia can be divided into Northeast Asia and Southeast Asia. Northeast Asia covers China (including Hong Kong), Taiwan (claimed by China), Japan, South Korea (Republic of Korea, or ROK), North Korea (Democratic People's Republic of Korea, or DPRK), Russia (specifically the Russian Far East or Pacific Russia), and Mongolia. Southeast Asia comprises Brunei, Burma (known officially as Myanmar), Cambodia, East Timor, Indonesia, Laos, Malaysia, the Philippines, Singapore, Thailand, and Vietnam. Apart from East Timor, all of the Southeast Asian countries are members of the Association of Southeast Asian Nations (ASEAN). While Australia and New Zealand are the major powers of the South Pacific, the entire Pacific islands region comes within a definition of Asia Pacific. Together with Australia and New Zealand, the independent and self-governing island states constitute the Pacific Islands Forum. The most significant of the island states are Papua New Guinea and Fiji. It should also be pointed out that some definitions of Asia Pacific include not just the United States and Canada, but the Pacific seaboard countries of Latin America. Mexico, Peru, and Chile are members of APEC, for example. India also interacts with Asia Pacific in various ways.

There is some focus in this book on the major powers of Asia Pacific: the United States, China, and Japan. Because these powers are particularly engaged in Northeast Asia, there is a strong emphasis on that subregion. At the same time attention is also given to Southeast Asia as another significant subregion. While the role of the major powers receives special attention, lesser but still significant powers are also considered. These include Taiwan, the two Koreas, Indonesia, Russia, and Australia. Apart from the focus on states the regional dimension (both Asia Pacific and subregional in the case of Southeast Asia) is an important theme in the discussion of international organizations. Regional organizations play a significant role in giving substance to the Asia Pacific concept.

■ The Historical Context

While the focus in this book is on the contemporary era and the recent past, many of the issues we deal with have deep historical roots. Therefore it is helpful to provide an outline of some of the major phases in the history of Asia Pacific international politics. At this stage it is appropriate to provide an overview of the historical context in terms of the following phases: first, the era of traditional civilizations; second, the era of imperialism; and third, the 1945–1989 period.[11] Throughout the book there will be discussion of the historical context where this is relevant to the issue in question.

Traditional Civilizations

Contemporary Asia Pacific is organized as a system of states based on the Westphalian model developed in Europe in 1648. The shift to this model resulted from the impact of Europeans in the region, but the Westphalian system was not the prevailing model historically. China was the dominant force in Northeast Asia, but it functioned as a "civilization" rather than as a "state" or "sovereign power" in the modern Western sense. Viewing itself as the Middle Kingdom, China developed as a distinctive civilization over a period of thousands of years. Although there were periods of conflict and division within China, Chinese civilization also made significant contributions in the development of bureaucracy (the mandarin system), science and technology, the arts, agriculture and industry, commerce, and philosophy (particularly Confucianism and Taoism). While the writ of the emperors ran wide, China saw itself primarily as a model for others within its "civilization area" to follow. Chinese influence was particularly strong in Korea and Vietnam. This influence was not just cultural, as the leaders of these entities were also required to pay tribute to the Chinese emperor. China was also the dominant cultural influence in the development of Japan. In this case, however, Japan followed a policy of isolating itself from the outside world as much as possible. Hence Japanese civilization also developed along its own lines; Japanese rulers did not pay tribute to China. In the Chinese view of the world, people living beyond its civilizational influence were characterized as barbarians. There was minimal interaction.

In Southeast Asia the situation was even more complex. While China was an important influence in the northern part of Southeast Asia, particularly in Vietnam, Indian civilization also had a major impact. The term "Indo-China" originally covered the whole of mainland Southeast Asia and reflected the dual influences. Hinduism and Buddhism in Southeast Asia derive originally from India. Cambodia (Angkor) was one Southeast Asian empire where the influence of Indian civilization was strong. The survival of Bali as a predominantly Hindu island within a largely Muslim Indonesia is a reflection of earlier Indian influence. Traders brought Islam to maritime Southeast Asia (modern Indonesia, Malaysia, and the southern Philippines) from about the thirteenth century. No single empire dominated Southeast Asia. Significant political entities included Angkor, Champa (central and southern Vietnam), Srivijaya and Majapahit (successive states covering an extensive region of modern Indonesia), Pagan (Burma), and Sukhothai and

Ayutthya (successive states in the area of modern Thailand). Rather than using Western principles of sovereignty, these entities were based on a "mandala" (circle) system. Power was concentrated at the center of the entity but was more diffuse the further one moved from the center. This meant that between adjoining centers of power there would be grey areas where local leaders might hold sway or where there might be overlapping layers of authority.[12]

The Era of Imperialism

The advent of extensive European involvement in the region from the fifteenth century did not mean the immediate replacement of the existing international system by a Western-oriented one. Europeans were particularly interested in trade, and missionaries also became involved in some areas. Trade did not necessarily require the establishment of political control. It was generally preferable to have cooperative relationships with local rulers. One vehicle for European penetration was through mercantile companies such as the Dutch United East India Company (VOC). Trading centers and forts were established in some regions and these sometimes came under the political control of European powers. Portugal was the earliest European power to become involved in the region with a particular interest in the Spice Islands (later known as the Moluccas or Maluku). Malacca (in modern Malaysia) and Macau (China) were important Portuguese centers. Spain became involved in the Philippines but did not extend its interest much beyond there. Later the Netherlands superseded Portugal as the most active European power in the region. Its particular interest was in what later became the Netherlands East Indies (modern Indonesia). The Dutch were also the only outsiders allowed access to Japan after 1639, with a settlement at Nagasaki. The British and French were active in the so-called Far East from at least the eighteenth century.

The greatest external pressure on the existing international system in East Asia occurred during the nineteenth century. This pressure took different forms in Northeast Asia and Southeast Asia. In Northeast Asia the imperialist powers generally sought domination but, with some exceptions, did not emphasize the acquisition of territory. There were means other than annexation to ensure the achievement of strategic and economic objectives. The changing situation was most obvious in relation to China. Particularly from the time of the Opium War in 1842 (between Britain and China), China was forced to make a number of concessions to Western powers through a series of unequal treaties. Some of these concessions involved territory (Hong Kong being a notable example). Another sign of China's weakness was the imposition of a system of extraterritoriality, whereby

Westerners were generally subject to the laws of their own countries rather than those of China. Western powers established spheres of influence in different regions of China: Britain in the Yangtze valley and adjoining Hong Kong; France in Yunnan next to Indochina; Germany in the Shantung peninsula; and so on. The United States pursued an open-door policy with the aim of giving all external powers equal access to China. Russia put the most emphasis on territorial expansion at China's expense. This reflected Russia's economic weakness: annexation would allow Russians to be given preferential treatment in a way that was not possible when open competition prevailed. Its expansion into Siberia dated from the seventeenth century. During the nineteenth century it acquired parts of Central Asia from China, as well as the area adjacent to Vladivostok. Northern Manchuria became a Russian sphere of influence.

In Northeast Asia Japan was also subjected to strong Western pressures, but the outcome there was very different from that in China. In 1853–1854 Commodore Matthew Perry of the US Navy was instrumental in bringing Japan's self-imposed isolation to an end. Japan, too, faced unequal treaties and the imposition of a system designed to bring commercial advantages to Westerners. With the Meiji Restoration of 1868, however, Japan took steps to strengthen its political and economic system from within. The aim was to resist Western encroachments and to compete with the Western powers on their own terms. Japan achieved remarkable success in this respect. By the end of the nineteenth century Japan had joined the Western powers in making gains at China's expense and was also competing strongly with Russia in Northeast Asia. Following its success in the Sino-Japanese war of 1894–1895, Japan acquired Taiwan. Japan also won a stunning victory in the Russo-Japanese war of 1904–1905. Manchuria came predominantly under Japanese influence. Then, following a short period of Japanese "protection," by 1910 Korea was a Japanese colony.

During the 1930s and early 1940s the main territorial threat to China came from Japan. The inability of the Q'ing dynasty to resist imperialist encroachments had led to its downfall in the 1911 revolution. China remained weak, however. Warlords controlled important regions of the country. From 1927 conflict between the communists (led by Mao Tse-tung) and the ruling nationalists under Chiang Kai-shek contributed to China's weakness. In 1931 Japanese forces seized Manchuria and established the puppet state of Manchukuo. In 1937 war broke out between Japan and China, first in the north but extending subsequently to large parts of eastern China. From 1941 this conflict became the China theater of the Pacific War.

As compared with Northeast Asia, in Southeast Asia there was a stronger emphasis on territorial expansion by the Western powers. Japan did not become involved in this territorial expansion until the Pacific War. As previously indicated, up until the early nineteenth century the Western powers in Southeast Asia had established some centers and limited areas where they had political control. During the course of the nineteenth century there was greater competition among those powers, which encouraged the acquisition of colonies in certain regions. Colonial control took various forms, depending on the particular situation; local political factors were often important. The main changes in Southeast Asia involved Britain, France, and the Netherlands. Britain became the colonial power in Burma, the Malay Peninsula, Singapore, and northern Borneo. France acquired Indochina: Vietnam (administered as Tongking, Annam, and Cochinchina, running from north to south), Cambodia, and Laos. The Netherlands extended its control throughout the entire Indonesian archipelago to constitute the Netherlands East Indies. In addition to the three European powers, the United States became a colonial power when it acquired the Philippines from Spain following the latter's defeat in the Spanish-American War of 1898–1899. Within Southeast Asia only Thailand (then known as Siam) escaped colonial rule. This was largely due to the country's location as a buffer zone between the British and French spheres in mainland Southeast Asia.

During the early decades of the twentieth century, nationalist movements developed as a challenge to Western rule in a number of Southeast Asian countries. The most significant movements were in Vietnam and Indonesia. The greatest challenge to the existing colonial system, however, came with Japanese expansion into the region during the Pacific War. Japan wished to incorporate Southeast Asia into its Greater East Asia Co-Prosperity Sphere. In this scheme Southeast Asia would be a major source of raw materials for Japanese industry. Japan occupied all of the British, Dutch, and US possessions in Southeast Asia. In Indochina Japan had the cooperation of the Vichy French government in Indochina for much of the war, but took more direct control in the closing phases. Thailand also cooperated with Japan. Nationalist movements in Indonesia and Burma worked with Japan as a means of advancing their own goals. With Japan's defeat in 1945, clearly the reimposition of the previous colonial system would be no easy task.

The 1945–1989 Period

The main dimensions of international relations in Asia Pacific in the post–Cold War era emerged during the 1945–1989 period. This is sometimes referred to as the era of the Cold War, but to say that the Cold War was the dominant theme in the region's international relations would be an oversimplification. Important themes in the history of international relations in Asia Pacific during this period included the new international roles of China and Japan, the position adopted by the United States, the Cold War conflicts in the 1950s and 1960s, decolonization in Southeast Asia, the Sino-Soviet conflict, the Sino-American rapprochement of the 1970s, the emergence of Southeast Asian regionalism, and postcolonial conflicts in Southeast Asia. To appreciate the significance of these various themes and their interrelationships it will be helpful to focus on three key phases: the late 1940s, the 1950s and 1960s, and the 1970s and 1980s.

Late 1940s. The late 1940s laid the foundations for international relations in Asia Pacific for the entire postwar period. The United States occupied defeated Japan from 1945 to 1951. At first the United States was intent on democratizing and demilitarizing Japan. The aim was to ensure that Japan would never again become a threat. By 1947, however, the United States had shifted tack due to changes occurring at a global level. The onset of the Cold War meant that the containment of communism, and specifically of the Soviet Union, became its first priority, and the United States wished to ensure that Japan would be an ally in that struggle. Hence the radical objectives of the early occupation were superseded in favor of a more conservative policy. The United States concluded a lenient peace treaty with Japan in 1951; at the same time, a mutual security treaty linked Japan to the emerging US alliance system.

While developments in Japan were consistent with US Cold War objectives, developments in China were more of a setback. At the time of World War II the United States had expected China to play a major role as a replacement for Japan in East Asia. On that basis China became one of the permanent members of the United Nations Security Council. With Japan's defeat, however, full-scale civil war resumed between the communists and nationalists in China. Although the United States initially had hopes of effecting compromise, for the most part it favored the nationalists. However, the position of the nationalists had been weakened by the war with Japan and the communists extended their political support in many areas. Over the period 1945–1949 the communists advanced from their bases in northern China and by late 1949 controlled the whole of the mainland. The People's Republic of China (PRC) was proclaimed on 1 October 1949. Clearly this development had major implications for the international situation in Asia Pacific. The United States interpreted the emergence of the PRC as a fillip for the Soviet Union, and certainly a Sino-Soviet alliance was created in 1950. The Chinese revolution had received little support from Stalin, however, who maintained diplomatic relations with the nationalist government until well into 1949. Sino-Soviet tensions would remain largely hidden but by the 1960s there was open conflict.

In Southeast Asia in the late 1940s Cold War issues had some impact, but the major changes related to the issue of decolonization. With the defeat of Japan, the two colonial powers most intent on restoring their prewar positions were France and the Netherlands. In both cases conflict ensued with the relevant nationalist movements. In Vietnam, war between France and the communist-led Viet Minh lasted from 1946 to 1954. The Viet Minh's communist orientation made it suspect in the eyes of the United States. From the US perspective the success of the Viet Minh would bolster the position of China and the USSR in the region. In Indonesia the conflict was a more straightforward contest between colonialism and nationalism, and by 1949 the Netherlands had conceded independence. The United States granted independence to the Philippines in 1946, as did Britain in the case of Burma in 1948.

1950s and 1960s. In the 1950s and 1960s international relations in Asia Pacific were dominated by the confrontation between China and the United States. Direct conflict between the two powers occurred in the context of the Korean War of 1950–1953, which commenced with (communist) North Korea's attack on (anticommunist) South Korea on 25 June 1950. With UN authorization US forces (supported by forces from a number of other countries) had come to the assistance of South Korea. However, instead of stopping at the dividing line between the two Koreas (the 38th parallel), the United States decided to take the conflict into the north. China felt threatened, and Chinese "volunteers" entered the war from late 1950.[13] China had also been affected at the very start of the war when the sending of the US Seventh Fleet to the Taiwan Strait meant that Chinese communist forces could not liberate Taiwan from the nationalists. The nationalist government was able to consolidate its position as the Republic of China. US diplomatic relations continued with the nationalists and a mutual defense treaty was signed in 1954. The PRC became the main focus of the US containment strategy in Asia Pacific. The PRC saw US protection of Taiwan as unwarranted interference in the Chinese civil war. From the Chinese perspective the United States was attempting "encirclement" of China.

In the 1960s the emergence of the Vietnam War also highlighted the Sino-US confrontation. The United States interpreted the conflict between Vietnamese communist forces and the anticommunist Saigon government from the perspective of its global strategy of containment. Both the USSR and China were seen as supporting the Vietnamese communists. It was believed that the defeat of South Vietnam would mean an extension of Chinese power.

The United States slowly realized the significance of the emerging Sino-Soviet conflict. China and the USSR saw each other as rivals, not allies. There was an important element of "power politics" in this conflict and each country competed for influence in different regions of the world. In Vietnam, for example, China and the USSR did not engage in a cooperative endeavor, but instead vied for dominant influence. There were territorial differences, with their origins in earlier expansion by Tsarist Russia at China's expense. Racial tensions recalled the earlier imperialist era. The fact that both powers espoused communism added an important ideological dimension to the conflict. Irrespective of whether ideology was a fundamental cause of the rivalry, it certainly added to the bitterness of the exchanges.

During the 1950s and 1960s Japan gradually emerged once again as a major economic power in Asia Pacific. It relied on the United States for defense. There were significant US forces in Japan, and Okinawa remained under US control until 1972. Japan acted as a rear base for the United States during the Korean War, and also gave low-level support to the United States during the Vietnam War. Under the Yoshida Doctrine, dating from the early 1950s, Japan concentrated on its own economic development and spent no more than about 1 percent of gross domestic product (GDP) on defense. Under Article 9 of the 1947 "peace constitution" Japan had forsworn the use of force in its international relations, but this was subsequently interpreted to allow for self-defense. There was a mismatch between Japan's growing economic strength and its very limited international political role.

In Southeast Asia issues of decolonization continued to have an impact. From the Vietnamese communist perspective the Vietnam War was simply a continuation of the earlier struggle against the French for independence. Malaya became independent from Britain in 1957 and was joined in 1963 by Singapore and the northern Borneo territories in the new federation of Malaysia (Singapore separated in 1965). This development provoked a conflict with Indonesia. Sukarno, Indonesia's first president, saw the new federation as a neocolonial scheme to perpetuate British influence, and mounted an anti-Malaysia campaign known as "Konfrontasi" (Confrontation). Under Sukarno's leadership Indonesia had espoused an increasingly radical direction, but Sukarno himself fell following an attempted leftist coup in September 1965. The military regime or New Order that emerged under President Suharto was strongly anticommunist and, in fact, hundreds of thousands of alleged communists and their sympathizers were massacred. The changes in Indonesia brought an end to Confrontation. They also prepared the way for a new regionalism when the Association of Southeast Asian Nations (ASEAN) was founded in 1967. This was a way of strengthening the relations among the non-communist countries in Southeast Asia and of integrating Indonesia into regional affairs. Apart from Indonesia, the founding members were Malaysia, the Philippines, Singapore, and Thailand.

1970s and 1980s. During the 1970s and 1980s the most significant development in international relations at the broadest regional level was the emergence and development of the Sino-US rapprochement. The Nixon administration, which took office at the beginning of 1969, sought to achieve improved relations with both China and the USSR, thereby improving US leverage with both communist powers. China regarded its conflict with the USSR to be more threatening than its conflict with the United States. Improved US relations would enable China to focus its efforts on its issues with the USSR. This convergence in perspectives paved the way for a visit to China by President Richard Nixon in February 1972. In the Shanghai Communiqué, as signed by the two sides, the United States to all intents and purposes recognized the "one China" principle, while also maintaining its interest in a peaceful resolution of the Taiwan issue. The United States and the PRC did not establish formal diplomatic relations until 1979, at which point US recognition of the Republic of China (Taiwan) ceased and the mutual security treaty also ended. Taiwan became more isolated, although the United States provided for unofficial relations with Taiwan and continuing arms sales through the Taiwan Relations Act (1979). Apart from the changes in the US-China-Taiwan relationship, the effect of the Sino-US rapprochement was to end polarization in the region and to allow for greater fluidity in international relationships. There was added scope for regional countries to develop relations with both China and the United States and to pursue more independent policies.

From the US perspective the Sino-US rapprochement made withdrawal from the Vietnam conflict easier. It would have been much more difficult for the United States if it were presented as a boost for the major communist powers, and China in particular. Such an argument was difficult to sustain in light of the accommodation between China and the United States. US withdrawal was provided for in the Paris accords of 1973; by April 1975 the Saigon government had fallen. While Vietnam as a whole now came under communist rule, and communist governments also emerged in Cambodia and Laos, this did not bring peace to Indochina. The Khmer Rouge government in Cambodia pursued radical communist policies resulting in extensive loss of life. It was also strongly anti-Vietnamese. Vietnam intervened in Cambodia in late 1978 and deposed the Khmer Rouge government. The resulting conflict, lasting until 1991, was known as the Third Indochina War.

Vietnam installed a pro-Vietnamese government in Phnom Penh. Arrayed against Vietnam and its Cambodian supporters was the anti-Vietnamese resistance. While the Khmer Rouge was the strongest element in the resistance, rightist and royalist (Sihanoukist) groups were also involved. At the international level the strongest dimension of the conflict related to the Sino-Soviet conflict. China supported the anti-Vietnamese resistance while the USSR backed Vietnam. The ASEAN countries and the United States also supported the opposition to Vietnam.

A major development affecting the Third Indochina War was the Sino-Soviet rapprochement of 1989. While this had implications for international politics more broadly, in relation to Indochina it meant that the main external parties had agreed about a framework for resolving the conflict. Securing agreement among the Cambodian parties required a further two years, after which the UN became involved in a process of transition, culminating in elections in 1993.

The greater fluidity in international relations in Asia Pacific following the Sino-US rapprochement had implications for Japan, which was able to expand its international role. Okinawa reverted to Japanese rule in 1972, but it remained the major US base in the region. The United States encouraged Japan to expand its international role but Japan remained cautious. The "peace constitution" was a limitation, but it also reflected widely held Japanese sentiment. Neighboring countries, particularly China and South Korea, were suspicious of any moves by Japan to expand its security role. There was increased opportunity for Japan in terms of economic diplomacy and areas such as aid. Japan was active in the Group of 7 (the world's major economic powers, known as G7) and expanded its links with Southeast Asia. However, Japanese strength could also lead to resentment in many countries.

Japanese economic development provided a model for certain other East Asian countries to follow. The emergence of the Asian Tigers was a noteworthy development in the 1970s and 1980s. South Korea, Taiwan, Hong Kong, and Singapore were the main examples. They experienced very high growth rates and emphasized export-led industrialization. Governments often played an active role in stimulating the economy. In the case of South Korea its economic development contributed to tensions with North Korea. Whereas in the 1950s and 1960s the economic situation of the two countries was more comparable in terms of measures such as per capita GDP, by the 1970s and 1980s South Korea was economically more successful. This possibly contributed to various acts of terror undertaken by North Korea during these decades, including the assassination of members of the South Korean cabinet in Rangoon in 1983 and the destruction of a South Korean airliner in 1987.

Apart from the Third Indochina War, an important development in the international politics of Southeast Asia during the 1970s and 1980s was the strengthening of regionalism. ASEAN, founded in 1967, assumed a new importance after the Bali summit of 1976; it became the major regional focus for the non-communist countries in an increasingly significant way. This was related to the end of the Vietnam War. With the reduction of the US presence in the region the strategic landscape in Southeast Asia required reassessment. Ironically, the Third Indochina War contributed to the stronger ASEAN focus in the late 1970s and 1980s.

In the 1970s and 1980s East Timor was the major unresolved issue of decolonization in Southeast Asia. The Portuguese presence in this territory was a vestige of the colonial era dating back to the sixteenth century. Political changes in Portugal in 1974 raised the question of Portuguese Timor's future. Indonesia preferred to see East Timor become part of Indonesian territory, but was frustrated by the strong popular support for Fretilin, a radical nationalist movement. Indonesia invaded the territory in late 1975 and later incorporated it as the twenty-seventh Indonesian province. Resistance to Indonesian rule continued for some decades.

While East Timor was an issue relating to Western colonialism, the subsequent development of the conflict there highlighted how the postcolonial state system in Southeast Asia was often imposed against the will of significant groups. Many groups within Southeast Asian states saw themselves as nations in their own right and wished to establish their own states. In Indonesia, for example, there were significant separatist movements in Aceh and West Papua (at the western and eastern ends of the archipelago respectively). In the southern Philippines, Muslims resisted rule from Manila. In Burma the various hill peoples (the Karen, the Kachin, the Wa, and the Mon) had opposed the Rangoon government from the time of independence. These conflicts weakened the states in Southeast Asia. Separatist movements sought international support for their cause.

These various developments in Asia Pacific in the 1970s and 1990s indicate some of the main features of the regional context at the end of the Cold War. There is no precise date for this event, although the fall of the Berlin Wall in late 1989 is often regarded as of major symbolic importance. The end of the Cold War had a greater impact in Europe than in Asia Pacific. Europe was more polarized between East and West. The Sino-Soviet conflict had been a complicating factor in Asia Pacific in terms of any simple polarization. As far as the United States was concerned, the main contest in Asia Pacific had been with China, and that relationship had been transformed with the achievement of rapprochement in 1972. In Asia Pacific the major developments relating to the end of the Cold War concerned the Soviet Union. The achievement of Sino-Soviet rapprochement has already been noted. Soviet-Japanese relations did not change significantly. Soviet-US relations clearly changed at the global level and in Europe in particular but there were also implications in the North Pacific. Tensions relating to the opposing military deployments of the United States and the USSR in this region did ease at this time.

Major Features of Contemporary Asia Pacific

While understanding the historical background helps to put recent developments in the international politics of Asia Pacific into context, it is constructive to be aware of some of the key features of the polities of the region. It is often assumed that the actors composing a region have much in common. This can vary. In the case of the European Union a high level of integration exists compared to many other regions of the world. While there are differences among member states, there are also numerous common features in relation to political and economic systems, types of societies, cultures, and underlying values. Asia Pacific is at the opposite end of the spectrum. There is considerable diversity in all of these features. To put the substantive chapters of the book into context it will be useful at this point to remind ourselves of the existing diversity. This can be done in relation to the various features mentioned as points in common for the European Union; namely, political systems, economic systems, types of societies, cultures, and underlying values. Considering this diversity, it is useful to ask what gives Asia Pacific coherence as a region.

Political Systems

Asia Pacific encompasses a broad range of political systems. This is evident first of all in relation to the major powers. Both the United States and Japan have liberal democratic political systems. China on the other hand has an authoritarian political system under the leadership of the Chinese Communist Party. The term "communist" has become increasingly less relevant in the Chinese context; legitimacy is based more on nationalism and economic performance. The political spectrum is also broad when we consider powers other than the United States, Japan, and China. Along with the United States, Western powers such as Canada, Australia, and New Zealand are based on liberal democratic principles. Unlike the United States, these three states have parliamentary systems; Canada and Australia are similar to the United States in being federal in nature.

A number of the states in both Northeast and Southeast Asia are based on democratic principles; many have experienced democratization in recent times. In Northeast Asia, South Korea and Taiwan (claimed by China) have undergone democratization since the late 1980s. The Russian Federation (present in the region through the Russian Far East) has moved toward democratization since the collapse of the Soviet Union in 1991, but also retains some authoritarian features (some of which have strengthened under Vladimir Putin). In Southeast Asia the Philippines has followed a democratic model since independence in 1946, although martial law prevailed under President Ferdinand Marcos between 1972 and 1981, and patron-client relations have been a major feature of the system. In both Malaysia and Singapore the normal form of the political system has been democratic. In practice the Malay-dominated Barisan Nasional has ruled Malaysia. Under the People's Action Party Singapore has been essentially a one-party state. Indonesia's political system has passed through various phases. After a brief experience with parliamentary democracy in the early 1950s, it moved in an authoritarian direction under Sukarno's "guided democracy." Authoritarianism of a more anticommunist and promilitary orientation prevailed under Suharto's New Order beginning in 1965–1966. But following Suharto's fall in May 1998 Indonesia too has moved in the direction of democratization. This has brought to the fore a number of issues, such as the role of regions within Indonesia, the position of Islam, and the role of the military. Thailand, another Southeast Asian state dominated by the military, has been engaged in democratization since the early 1990s. Cambodia under "strong man" Hun Sen is democratic in form but also employs authoritarian practices. After a period of United Nations tutelage from 1999, East Timor achieved independence in 2002 on the basis of democratic institutions.

Apart from China, there are communist-oriented authoritarian governments in North Korea, Vietnam, and Laos. While there have been moves toward reform in Vietnam, North Korea remains as the world's sole remnant of Stalinism. Burma is the main instance of a military-dominated regime in the region, and Brunei is ruled by a sultanate.

As this survey makes clear it is necessary to look behind a state's proclaimed principles to see how it functions in practice. Usually there are particular groups that are advantaged and others that are disadvantaged within any political system. The degree of real competition can vary. In an authoritarian system a particular group attempts to preserve its privileged position by minimizing competition from potentially rival groups. Among the Pacific islands some states have verged on the brink of becoming "failed states." The major example is the Solomon Islands where ethnic rivalry brought the virtual breakdown of government and Australia led international intervention in 2003; Fiji also has faced issues relating to ethnic conflict although the impact has been less than in the Solomons. Papua New Guinea, too, has faced problems in achieving effective government, experiencing a fragmented society and widespread corruption. Among the larger states of the region it is North Korea that has the greatest potential to fail. Indonesia is also facing severe problems in achieving a balance between democratization and effective government.

Economic Systems

In terms of economic systems most Asia Pacific countries are broadly capitalist, but that term allows for considerable diversity. Capitalism assumes that the private sector plays a central role in economic dynamics, but normally governments attempt to manage the environment in which that sector functions. Variation can occur at a number of levels. The private sector can encompass a range of large, middle-sized, and small organizations; the mix can vary from country to country. Even within a predominantly capitalist economy, government enterprises can play a key role in some situations. The direct involvement of governments in managing national economies can vary; some governments are more interventionist than others. Globalization means that the ability of governments to control economic developments within their respective borders has become more limited. Major economic powers can clearly have greater influence in these circumstances than smaller powers. Even where an economy is predominantly capitalist many people are engaged in a subsistence sector, simply producing enough food to meet their own requirements. People involved in a subsistence economy might concurrently have some involvement in the capitalist sector.

The two major economic powers of Asia Pacific are the United States and Japan; the United States has the world's largest GDP, Japan has the second largest. Both countries have advanced industrial economies, and the United States is also a major agricultural producer. The Japanese version of capitalism is much more controlled than the US version. The Japanese government acts to ensure the achievement of preferred social goals. A good example is in relation to agriculture. Japan restricts agricultural imports in order to protect rural society, even though this policy means much higher prices for Japanese consumers. Although the United States also has protective measures in place, in theory at least it is much more "free trade" in orientation.

Among the other industrial powers of the region the range in types of capitalism is similar to that between the United States and Japan. In Northeast Asia South Korea and Taiwan, two of the "newly industrializing countries" (NICs), are close to the Japanese model. Australia and Canada are closer to the United States in approach; both countries are also leading agricultural producers. New Zealand is a smaller version yet. China is an emerging economic power, with a significant private sector, an extensive but contracting (and sluggish) state sector, and a large peasant-based subsistence economy.

In Southeast Asia Singapore has the most advanced economy (and the highest living standards), based largely on its role as a center for international finance and as a transshipment hub. Prior to the Asian economic crisis of 1997, Thailand, Malaysia, and Indonesia experienced significant economic growth through the development of their manufacturing sectors. Traditionally these countries (and the Philippines) were exporters of agricultural produce (and minerals in some cases). All three were adversely affected by the economic crisis, with Indonesia most so. The newer members of ASEAN (Vietnam, Laos, Burma, Cambodia) and also newly independent East Timor have essentially Third World economies: large subsistence sectors, with primary produce as the main export earner. Brunei is a small oil-rich state. Vietnam and Laos have communist-style centralized economies, but with reforms enabling the private sector to play an increasingly important role. The main example of an unreformed communist command economy is outside Southeast Asia: North Korea. North Korea has experienced significant economic decline, including periods of famine.

Types of Societies

The types of societies in Asia Pacific display considerable variation. At one end of the spectrum are the advanced industrialized countries such as the United States, Japan, Canada, and Australia. These countries typically have small rural populations and are highly urbanized. Most people identify as middle class. Changes in the nature of manufacturing industry have meant the decline of the traditional working class. At the other end of the spectrum there are societies that might be described as Third World. They have large peasant populations, and small urban elites concentrated in cities that function as transport and administrative centers. The newer ASEAN members (Vietnam, Burma, Laos, Cambodia) typify this type of society. In the middle of the spectrum of societies we have several countries that have emerged or are emerging from Third World status to take on some of the characteristics of the advanced industrialized countries. Usually these countries will still have large peasant populations, but increasing urbanization is an important feature. The development of manufacturing industry encourages the emergence of a working class. Many people are attracted to the cities from the countryside, irrespective of whether they are engaged in manufacturing. An underclass of slum dwellers can develop. Probably China is the major example of this type of society, but the older ASEAN members (Indonesia,

Malaysia, Thailand, the Philippines) have many of the characteristics indicated. South Korea and Taiwan have moved further in the direction of the advanced industrialized countries.

Ethnic divisions play a role in a number of Asia Pacific countries. As immigrant societies, the United States, Canada, and Australia have an important multicultural dimension. Immigration from Asian countries has played a role in this development; in the case of the United States an increasing proportion of the population is of Hispanic background (13.3 percent in 2002 according to the US Census Bureau).[14] New Zealand is sometimes described as bicultural, with about 80 percent of its population of European background, and the rest mainly Maori and other Pacific islanders. Japan is a relatively homogeneous society, with over 99 percent of the population ethnic Japanese (Koreans are the most significant minority). Korea (both North and South) is also ethnically homogeneous. China is more than 90 percent Han Chinese, but there are significant minorities such as the Muslims of the northwest, the Tibetans, the hill peoples of the southwest, the Mongolians, and the Manchu. Most Southeast Asian countries have important ethnic divisions. Ethnic Chinese are a significant minority throughout the region; ethnically Singapore is predominantly a Chinese city-state. Chinese are the largest minority in Malaysia (about one-third). Javanese are the single biggest ethnic group in Indonesia but there are many different ethnic groups throughout the archipelago. Divisions between Burmans and hill peoples are important in Burma. There is a similar, although less significant, division between Vietnamese and hill peoples in Vietnam. In the Philippines most people are of Malay background but there is a wide variety of languages spoken; the position of the Muslim peoples in the south represents one key division. In Thailand about three-quarters of the population are ethnically Thai, with Chinese as the most significant minority. Ethnic divisions also play a role throughout the Pacific islands region, most notably between Indo-Fijians and indigenous Fijians in Fiji, among the hundreds of tribal groupings in Papua New Guinea and among the island-based groups in Solomon Islands.

Cultures and Underlying Values

Ethnic divisions frequently involve differences in culture. Cultural diversity within Asia Pacific can be examined in terms of particular countries, as well as at a region-wide level. While culture can refer to the assumptions underlying how people live, here we will focus primarily on religious beliefs and worldviews. This approach directs us also to the underlying values governing the conduct of the various societies in the region. Asia Pacific includes a number of the world civilizations or their representatives. Using Samuel Huntington's categories, the civilizations represented in Asia Pacific are Western, Sinic or Chinese, Japanese, and Islamic.[15] Hindu or Indian civilization is also an influence, and Orthodox Russian civilization might also be included in the case of the Russian Far East. While Huntington's approach is oversimplified in many respects, these categories do give us a starting point for reviewing the region's cultural diversity. It should not be assumed, however, that "diversity" necessarily results in clashes.

The United States, Canada, Australia, and New Zealand might be seen as national embodiments of Western civilization in the region. In the eastern Pacific, Western civilization is also an influence in Latin America (described by Huntington as either a separate civilization or a subcivilization of Western civilization). More broadly Western civilization has had an effect on most Asia Pacific countries both in the era of imperialism and more recently through the economic, technological, political, and cultural influence of Western powers (particularly the United States). Western civilization is based on the Judeo-Christian religious heritage. While religious beliefs remain important (most obviously in the United States), the Enlightenment also powerfully affected Western societies. The emphasis on science and rationality has had a secularizing effect. Although the practice can vary, the separation of church and state is the norm in the Western societies of Asia Pacific. The rule of law and institutions based on liberal democracy are also of great significance.

Certain of the civilizations identified by Huntington are based on China, Japan, and India. This does not mean that the influence of these civilizations is restricted to these countries alone. Chinese civilization has been an influence on neighboring countries such as Korea and Vietnam, and in the more distant past on Japan. Indian civilization has been an important influence in several Southeast Asian countries. Japan's cultural impact has been more limited although it was a colonial power in both Korea and Taiwan in the first part of the twentieth century; the Taiwanese are generally more positive about this experience than are the Koreans. These three nation-based civilizations involve a range of religions and worldviews: Confucianism and Taoism in China, Shintoism in Japan, and Hinduism and Buddhism in India. Each of these approaches is quite complex. A common feature is the way they attempt to integrate the whole of life, rather than thinking in terms of separate spheres. They are often conservative in the sense of upholding the existing order rather than encouraging questioning and change.

Another great civilization in Asia Pacific is Islam. Indonesia has more Muslims than any other country in the world. Muslims (mostly the indigenous Malays) are a majority in Malaysia. There are Muslim minorities in some Asia Pacific countries: the Philippines, Burma, Thailand, Cambodia, Singapore, and China. There are also many Muslims to be found in the Western countries of the region as a result of immigration (not to mention the Black Muslims in the United States). Like the other Asian civilizations Islam has an integrated approach whereby the basic principles of the religion are related to all areas of life, including politics. However, within Islam there is great diversity, not just in terms of the understanding of the underlying religious principles, but also in areas such as politics. Thus some Muslims in countries such as Indonesia and Malaysia wish to see the establishment of Islamic states, whereas others adhere to the more liberal view that Muslims need to accept pluralism and be tolerant of other views.

While diversity is certainly the dominant impression one has in any survey of the main features of contemporary Asia Pacific, there are also some unifying themes. The most notable are the dominance of democracy in the sphere of political organization and capitalism as a mode of economic organization. Clearly, however, there is a great range covered by each term, and there are instances that go against the norm. Asia Pacific does not gain its coherence from the dominance of certain political and economic norms within the region. As indicated earlier, a major factor in the development of the Asia Pacific concept has been that it legitimizes the involvement of the United States in East Asian affairs. This particular regional definition has therefore been promoted strongly by the United States. That this is a context where a number of major powers (United States, China, Japan) interact is significant. As a region Asia Pacific is also significant in terms of the world economy; in 2000 East Asia's share of world product was 26 percent, the United States 22 percent, and Western Europe 18 percent.[16] In global economic forums Asia Pacific countries generally favor greater liberalization (but not invariably); working together strengthens their bargaining power. Nevertheless regional organizations play a more limited role compared with a number of other regions of the world. Relatively speaking the international politics of Asia Pacific retains a strong emphasis on state-centered approaches.

■ Plan of the Book

A book on Asia Pacific in world politics, focusing specifically on the international politics of the region, can only deal with some aspects of the whole. At the end of the earlier defining sections on international politics and Asia Pacific I indicated the sense in which those terms are used in this book. The focus is on particular aspects of Asia Pacific international politics, but without losing sight of the area's many other aspects. All that is claimed here is that the issues dealt with in subsequent chapters are important in themselves and highlight the dynamics of international politics in the region.

The underlying assumption is that to understand the dynamics of international politics in Asia Pacific, one needs to focus first on the interaction of states and, in particular, on the interaction of its major powers (United States, China, Japan). This point applies most strongly to Northeast Asia. In Southeast Asia the situation is more complex. There are more states involved, and they often have weak foundations; the major powers have an influence but they are less significant than in Northeast Asia. In Northeast Asia the significance of nonmajor powers, particularly the two Korean states and Taiwan, needs to be taken into account, as does Russia (still a major power in some respects, but of declining significance). A more comprehensive approach would take account of the role of Russia in Asia Pacific, as well as of the role of middle powers such as Australia and Canada. India, although not normally defined as an Asia Pacific power, can have an impact on the international politics of the region too. Considerations of space mean that not all of these actors can be examined in detail. They are referred to in the context of some issues, with Russia and Australia the subject for one chapter. Apart from the focus on the major powers in Northeast Asia, and on the more complex situation in Southeast Asia, there is some attention to the role of international organizations, both regional and global, as actors of growing importance for Asia Pacific international politics. While the most significant actors provide the structure of the book, the role of these actors is elaborated in relation to the issues of greatest significance in the region. This means a strong emphasis on security issues, of both the traditional political-military kind and the newer comprehensive approach, including human security. The new security issues are most obvious in Southeast Asia. A second emphasis is on the range of economic issues affecting international politics in the region. A third emphasis is on some of the issues in the "new international agenda," again most obviously in Southeast Asia, but also in the context of the role played by international organizations.

We begin in Part 1 with an examination of the roles of the United States, China, and Japan, the region's major powers, focusing on both the factors influencing their policies and the general approach they have adopted. The first point covers such factors as historical experience, ways governments have interpreted their roles, and domestic politics. The second point deals with political-strategic, economic, and other issues of concern to the various powers in relation to their regional involvement. Having examined the main features of the roles of the United States, China, and Japan, we then focus on the ways these powers have interacted with each other. There are chapters on the relationships between Japan and the United States, China and the United States, and China and Japan. The major emphasis is post–Cold War but relevant background on the post-1945 context is also provided.

Part 2 turns to two of the key conflicts of the region: Taiwan and Korea. While the major powers are involved in these conflicts (China and the United States most obviously in relation to Taiwan, and all three in the case of Korea), there is also an attempt to highlight the significance of political developments in both Taiwan and the two Koreas.

Part 3 looks at Southeast Asia. Chapter 10 provides an overview of international politics in this subregion and highlights the often tenuous basis of the local states, while also drawing attention to the emergence of a number of new international issues such as unregulated people movements and HIV/AIDS. Chapter 11 is devoted to Indonesia as the most important of the Southeast Asian states and highlights the impact of domestic developments on Indonesia's international position.

Part 4 examines some of the other actors playing a role in Asia Pacific international politics. Chapter 12 focuses on the involvement of Russia and Australia in the region. Both states are on the edge of the region in some senses, while also aspiring to have an influence over developments affecting their own interests. Chapter 13 examines international organizations as yet another type of actor in the international politics of Asia Pacific. The underlying theme is the relationship between states and governmental international organizations, giving attention to the role of both regional and global organizations in the region. Southeast Asia's ASEAN is covered, as well as Asia Pacific and East Asia dimensions, and various organizations of the United Nations system are discussed.

Part 5, with its concluding chapter, suggests some of the themes that are emerging as leading aspects of international politics in Asia Pacific in the early twenty-first century. Based on the analysis presented I will consider whether major changes are occurring or are likely to occur in terms of the types and importance of actors and of key issues.

▪ Notes

1. A useful overview of major theories of international politics is Burchill et al., *Theories of International Relations*.

2. Carr, *The Twenty Years' Crisis, 1919–1939;* Morgenthau, *Politics Among Nations.*

3. Waltz, *Theory of International Politics.*

4. See in particular Keohane and Nye, *Power and Interdependence.*

5. See Held et al., *Global Transformations.*

6. Pye, *Asian Power and Politics,* p. 19. On the culturalistic argument, see also Kang, "Getting Asia Wrong."

7. Huntington, *The Clash of Civilizations and the Remaking of World Order.*

8. On the impact of culture on international politics, see Solomon, "Political Culture and Diplomacy in the Twenty-first Century."

9. For a critical perspective, see Dirlik, ed., *What Is in a Rim?*

10. Buzan, "The Asia-Pacific," p. 84.

11. Useful historical texts include Murphey, *A History of Asia;* Mackerras, *Eastern Asia.* For a more contemporary focus, emphasizing the links between economics, society, and politics, see Tipton, *The Rise of Asia.* On the history of international politics in Asia Pacific, covering the Cold War and post–Cold War periods, see Yahuda, *The International Politics of the Asia-Pacific.*

12. See Acharya, *The Quest for Identity,* pp. 18–29.

13. "Volunteers" was the term used by China for the forces it sent into the Korean War.

14. US Census Bureau, "The Hispanic Population in the United States: March 2002," (issued June 2003), www.census.gov/prod/2003pubs/p20-545.pdf (accessed 14 September 2005).

15. Huntington, *The Clash of Civilizations and the Remaking of World Order.*

16. Philip Dorsey Iglauer, "An Asia Pacific World," *Korea Times,* 21 April 2005, http://times.hankooki.com/lpage/opinion/200504/kt2005042116243854300 .htm (accessed 15 September 2005). The shares of world product in 1950 were: East Asia 10 percent, United States 27 percent, and Western Europe 18 percent.

Part 1

The Major Powers
in the Region

The United States | 2

The theme of Part 1 of the book is the role of the major powers in Asia Pacific, giving particular attention to Northeast Asia: the United States, China, and Japan. We examine the major factors affecting the role of each power and the general approach they have taken toward the region. Chapters on the Japanese-US, Sino-US, and Sino-Japanese relationships highlight how the major powers have interacted with each other.

In this chapter we examine the position of the United States as one of the three major powers in the Asia Pacific region. We focus first on the range of factors influencing the approach of the United States, giving particular attention to the historical experience of the country in the region, the interpretation of US national interests, and the impact of domestic politics. We then examine the general approach adopted by the United States toward Asia Pacific during the post–Cold War era, with reference to the three relevant presidential administrations: George H. W. Bush (1989–1993), William Jefferson Clinton (1993–2001), and George W. Bush (2001–). The aim is to indicate the overall direction taken by each administration. Later chapters provide a more detailed examination of US relationships with key countries in the region.

■ Factors Influencing US Policies in Asia Pacific

Historical Experience of the United States in Asia Pacific

Although we have a particular concern with the post–Cold War period, the involvement of the United States in the region we now know as Asia Pacific dates back to the early years of the Republic. Americans were active as traders in the Far East. The region almost became another chapter in the saga of westward expansion. In 1853–1854 Commodore Matthew Perry of the US Navy took the lead in forcing the opening of Japan to the outside world. In China the United States played a secondary role in relation to Britain. It was mainly intent on protecting and expanding its trading opportunities. Following a policy known as "me-tooism," the United States insisted that any privileges granted to Britain in China should also be extended to the United States. As a strong economic power, the United States preferred the open-door policy to any territorial division of China among the imperialist powers (whether through annexation or spheres of influence). The open door meant that all powers should have equal access to China (the same approach could be extended to other regions of the world).

In Southeast Asia the United States did become a colonial power following its defeat of Spain in the Spanish-American War of 1898–1899. While this war focused on the Caribbean, and particularly Cuba (a Spanish possession up to that time), the United States acquired the Philippines as one of the consequences of the Spanish defeat. Generally speaking, however, Northeast Asia was the main focus for the United States. At the time of the Russo-Japanese War in 1904–1905 President Theodore Roosevelt became involved in facilitating a settlement between the two countries. The Treaty of Portsmouth (1905) acknowledged the gains made by Japan as a result of the war.

Although the Pacific was not a major theater in World War I (which the United States entered in 1917), the aftermath of that conflict saw the United States, Japan, and the British Empire as the major powers in the region. The Washington Conference of 1921–1922 attempted (among other things) to stabilize the existing power relationships in the region. By the 1930s, however, Japanese expansionism was a major concern for the United States. China suffered most, first with the loss of Manchuria to Japan in 1931, and then the onset of the Sino-Japanese war in 1937. Japan's plans for a Greater East Asia Co-Prosperity Sphere would have violated the open-door principles of the United States. Japan acted first, with its attack on Pearl Harbor on 7 December 1941. Henceforth the United States entered World War II, and the campaign in the Pacific culminated in the dropping of atomic bombs on the Japanese cities of Hiroshima and Nagasaki in August 1945, with Japan surrendering shortly thereafter.

From the late 1940s to the late 1980s the Cold War dominated the international policies of the United States.[1] In Japan the United States was the occupying power, but by 1947 the direction of US policies there shifted to ensure that Japan would become an ally of the United States. There was a shift to a more lenient approach, reflected above all in the 1951 peace treaty with Japan. In the 1945–1949 Chinese civil war the United States had initially favored a settlement based on a coalition of nationalists and communists, but then gave support to the nationalists. The proclamation of the People's Republic of China in October 1949 was hence a major setback for the United States. Nevertheless the United States did not give overt support to the nationalist government that had established itself in Taiwan until the outbreak of the Korean War in June 1950. Although this conflict had an important intra-Korean dimension, the United States saw it in Cold War terms as part of communist expansionism. Under United Nations auspices, the United States made a major commitment to fighting this war until an armistice reflecting the military stalemate was concluded in 1953.

While the United States was preoccupied with Cold War concerns, decolonization was a major theme in Southeast Asia from the 1940s to the 1960s. Independence came to the Philippines in 1946, although close ties remained with the United States. The United States was generally sympathetic to the Indonesian struggle for independence from the Netherlands in the late 1940s. Where communist elements were involved in a nationalist movement, the Cold War concerns of the United States generally dominated US policies. This was most obviously the case in Vietnam where the United States was providing significant support to France by the early 1950s. The United States was reluctant to accept the success of the communist-dominated Viet Minh in 1954. This was the background to US support for the anticommunist government that emerged in South Vietnam, leading eventually to the Vietnam War during the 1960s and early 1970s. With the US withdrawal from Vietnam, communist forces there had triumphed by 1975.

This development did provide the context for the emergence of a new phase in US involvement in Asia Pacific. The rapprochement or accommodation between the United States and China in 1972 brought an end to the confrontation that had dominated the relationship between the two powers in the 1950s and 1960s. US involvement in the region henceforth saw greater fluidity and less polarization than had previously been the case. The relationship with Taiwan was effectively downgraded, and this was confirmed with the establishment of diplomatic relations between the United States and the People's Republic of China in 1979. The relationship with Japan, central to US involvement in the 1950s and 1960s, remained important to the United States, but there were now important opportunities for the United States to cooperate with China on various issues, not least against the Soviet Union.

In Southeast Asia in the post–Vietnam War period the United States put more emphasis on the role of the Association of Southeast Asian Nations (ASEAN), originally formed in 1967. With the Vietnamese intervention in

Cambodia in late 1978, the United States, ASEAN, and China found themselves aligned in opposition to Vietnam (supported in this instance by the Soviet Union). The United States supported ASEAN as a grouping of noncommunist Southeast Asian states. Among them the US relationships with Indonesia, the Philippines, and Thailand were the most significant.

Given the changes arising from the Sino-US rapprochement, one can ask whether the end of the Cold War had the same significance in Asia Pacific as it did in Europe. Although there had been important changes in Europe too, it remained more polarized in the 1970s and 1980s than was the case in Asia Pacific. From the US perspective the main point in common between Asia Pacific and Europe was that the Soviet Union was a rival in both regions. Cold War tensions were an important element of international politics in Asia Pacific, even if the tensions in Europe were on a grander scale. With the development of a more normal relationship with the USSR (and Russia after 1991), a significant source of tension in Asia Pacific came to an end. One consequence of the easing of tensions was how China and the USSR achieved an accommodation in 1989, in turn paving the way for a resolution of the Cambodian conflict. Of course, from the viewpoint of the United States, the end of the Cold War also meant that it no longer needed to win support from China in terms of the Soviet-US contest. Hence there were more possibilities for tensions between the two to arise.

The Interpretation of US National Interests

How the United States has interpreted its national interests in Asia Pacific may be seen in the context of how its involvement in the region has developed historically. Two dimensions of national interests stand out: the political-strategic and the economic. To these might be added an ideological dimension, relating to how the United States has sought to defend and extend liberal-democratic values.

Over the past century US policies in Asia Pacific have aimed to prevent the region from coming under the domination of any rival power. Such domination would not necessarily threaten the US mainland itself, but would make it more difficult for the United States to pursue more specific political and economic objectives in the region. To counter any possibility of domination by a rival power the United States has sought to develop a countervailing balance. This might be on a regionwide basis or it might relate to specific subregions. Thus, at the time of the 1904–1905 Russo-Japanese War it was in US interests to support a balance between Russia and Japan rather than to see one or the other completely dominant. In the context of the 1921–1922 Washington Conference, the aim was to foster a means for restraining the further development of Japanese power. Effectively the United States aligned with the British Empire against Japan. In the Pacific War of 1941–1945, the United States pursued a maritime strategy to fight Japan (supported by allies such as Australia), while Japan was simultaneously engaged in other theaters such as China and Burma (against British forces in the latter case). During the Cold War the United States developed a series of mostly bilateral alliances (Japan, the Philippines, Thailand, South Korea, Taiwan, Australia, New Zealand) to counter China in particular, although the Soviet Union was also a concern. In the period since the Sino-US rapprochement (reinforced by the end of the Cold War) the framework of bilateral relationships has remained (Taiwan ceased being an official ally in 1979), although there has also been some attention given to developing stronger multilateral frameworks. With some qualifications in relation to North Korea, the United States no longer sees particular states as enemies; there is, however, a network of aligned states that can be invoked should a problem arise. There is also a sense in which the United States now works as part of a concert of powers in the region. Rather than seeing certain powers as necessarily rivals, the United States can develop a cooperative framework with all of the major powers for dealing with the important issues in the region. In some respects the United States combines elements of both the balancing and the concert approaches in its strategy for protecting its political-strategic interests in Asia Pacific.

In terms of economic interests we have seen already how the United States developed the open-door policy by the late nineteenth century. Seeking to maximize its trading opportunities in the region, much of its attention focused on Japan. There were also great hopes (never fully realized) of expanding trade with China. In the post-1945 period Japan again emerged as the most important trading partner for the United States. As various Asian economies achieved significant economic growth their trade with the United States developed. The significance of a particular country for US trade could vary of course (see Table 2.1).

With the exceptions of Singapore, Hong Kong, and Australia, the individual trade balances were against the United States. This situation was particularly stark in the case of China. US exports to Asia Pacific (excluding Canada and the Latin American countries with a Pacific seaboard) made up over one-fifth of the total US exports in 2004. US imports from Asia Pacific were over one-third of the total US imports in 2004.

The generally unfavorable trade balance sometimes became a political issue within the United States. In general Asian countries exported manufactured goods such as electrical machinery and office equipment to the

Table 2.1   Major US Trade Partners in Asia Pacific, 2004 (US$ millions)

Trade Partner	Exports from the United States	Imports to the United States
China	34,721	196,698
Japan	54,400	129,594
South Korea	26,333	46,162
Taiwan	21,730	34,617
Malaysia	10,896	28,185
Singapore	19,600	15,305
Thailand	6,362	17,577
Hong Kong	15,809	9,313
Australia	14,270	7,544
Philippines	7,071	9,144
Indonesia	2,669	10,811

Source: International Trade Administration, US Department of Commerce, "TradeStats Express—National Trade Data," http://tse.export.gov/NTDMap.aspx?UniqueURL=ydynie 2r0h3or5fliu2ejwr4-2005-10-5-10-47-12, accessed 5 October 2005.

United States; China was a major supplier of clothing and footwear. The United States provided manufactured goods (such as electrical machinery, aircraft, transport equipment), chemicals, and agricultural products to Asian countries.

In addition to its political-strategic and economic interests in Asia Pacific, the United States has also had an ideological interest there consistent with the impact of its liberal democratic tradition on US foreign policy more generally. Wherever possible it has sought to promote democracy in Asia Pacific. Problems have arisen when there have been tensions between this objective and US political-strategic and economic objectives. Sometimes Asian countries or political movements have seen the ideological dimension of US foreign policy as an attempt to impose Western values. US opposition to the widely supported communist (but also nationalist) movement in Vietnam (most obviously during the Vietnam War) is an example. In other situations the United States has played down its democratic objectives in order not to undermine an authoritarian but pro-US government, as illustrated, for example, in its support for the martial law regime of President Marcos in the Philippines (1972–1986).

The Impact of Domestic Politics

In discussing US national interests in Asia Pacific the emphasis has been on the interpretation of those interests. The assumption is that national interests do not have an objective character but relate to the way in which the dominant groups in society perceive those interests. This raises the issue of how domestic politics in the United States affects the pursuit of US policies in Asia Pacific. At least three levels of domestic politics might be seen as relevant. These concern the respective roles of public opinion, interest groups, and the formal governmental structures.

Public opinion on foreign policy is not necessarily well formed. According to Gabriel Almond's classic study on *The American People and Foreign Policy,*[2] public opinion takes the form of a "foreign policy mood." This mood derives from the underlying international orientations that have developed historically within the United States. They indicate a certain general direction rather than suggesting specific policies. For the most part the foreign policy elite works within the broad parameters established by the foreign policy mood, but has considerable flexibility in working out the details of specific policies. In some situations, however, there can be strong pressures placed on the elite (and specifically the US government) to take certain kinds of actions. The role of the media can be important here. Some commentators talk about the "CNN factor." This has been an influence on US support for and involvement in humanitarian interventions in the post–Cold War era (for example, Somalia). Another example is the public response to the September 11 Al-Qaida attacks on the World Trade Center in New York and on the Pentagon in Washington. Public pressure meant that the US government was impelled to respond militarily.

In terms of more specific influences on US policies in Asia Pacific, there is a range of interest groups. These can vary depending on the specific issue but we might distinguish between economic and more ideologically oriented groups. Economic interest groups are concerned about how US policies in Asia Pacific affect them. Business or farm groups might see opportunities in expanding trade with Asia Pacific countries. From another perspective such expansion of trade might provide competition for certain business or farm groups within the United States. If Asian countries have lower labor costs, then such competition will be castigated as unfair. Ideological groups offer support or opposition to particular countries in Asia Pacific on the basis of the political features of those countries. Issues of democracy and human rights can be important in this respect. Churches, student groups, and human rights groups can become involved in the Asia Pacific policies of the United States on this basis.

At a more specific level, the US government is responsible for formulating the Asia Pacific policies of the United States. However, the term "US government" suggests a monolithic approach when this is not necessarily the case. At one level one has to keep in mind that the United States has a separation of powers system. This means that the president, as the head of the executive branch, and the Congress, as the legislative branch, are elected separately. The Congress is divided into the Senate and the House of Representatives, with the former as the more prestigious of the two chambers. Unlike the Westminster system, control of the executive is not dependent on having a majority of members in the House of Representatives. The president appoints cabinet members and retains ultimate responsibility. Cabinet members cannot be members of Congress. The separation of powers system is designed to prevent excessive concentration of power. Congress has to pass necessary legislation and authorize expenditure. There is a complex committee system designed to provide oversight of the executive branch. Treaties require a two-thirds vote by the Senate. This is an example of the checks and balances system that complements separation of powers as an underlying principle of the US Constitution.

Despite these constitutional arrangements the executive branch plays a dominant role in relation to foreign policy, including issues relating to Asia Pacific. This situation is particularly true with diplomatic and security issues. Economic issues provide more scope for congressional influence. The key government departments involved in diplomatic and security issues are the departments of state and defense, headed respectively by the secretary of state and the secretary of defense. Within the Department of State the assistant secretary of state for East Asian and Pacific affairs (a political appointee) normally has special responsibility for Asia Pacific issues. The president's national security adviser (head of the National Security Council, bringing together the heads of various security-related departments and agencies) is also important. The Central Intelligence Agency (headed by a director) is another body within the executive branch that can play a role in relation to Asia Pacific security. In terms of economic issues, whether in Asia Pacific or elsewhere, departments such as Commerce, Treasury, and Agriculture (all led by cabinet-level secretaries) can play a significant role. These various departments and agencies can have different perspectives on issues that arise. Hence politics within the executive branch, as well as between the executive and Congress, is an important aspect of how domestic politics relates to US policies toward Asia Pacific.

▦ The General Approach of the United States in Asia Pacific

In the post–Cold War era, successive US administrations have placed considerable emphasis on the development of Asia Pacific policies.[3] Here we provide an overview of how each administration since 1989 has approached the region. There were significant elements of continuity in US policy toward Asia Pacific throughout the post–Cold War era. At the same time there were some differences of emphasis depending on the administration in office. The two Republican administrations (George H. W. Bush and George W. Bush) were more strongly realist than the Democratic administration of Bill Clinton, in the sense that they put a stronger emphasis on military power as a tool of US policy. This is not to say that realism in this sense was not a strong focus under Clinton but, comparatively speaking, his administrations did provide more scope for liberal institutionalism. Similarly, while bilateralism was an important focus for US policy in Asia Pacific under all three administrations, the Clinton administration also allowed more scope for multilateralism to develop. Again, this is not to say that multilateralism was not of some significance for the two Bush administrations. Under George W. Bush the events of September 11 strengthened the trend toward renewed realism and a more assertive US posture. A moral dimension was present with all three administrations. Under George H. W. Bush the circumstances of the 1991 Gulf War led to a strong emphasis on the need to establish a "new world order" to uphold international law. During the Clinton period particular attention was given to the extension of democracy and human rights. Under George W. Bush, September 11 led not just to a strengthening of realism but to an assertion of the US role as the defender of liberty. Charles Krauthammer has described the combination of a moral imperative with realist means as "democratic realism."[4]

The George H. W. Bush Administration (1989–1993)

Under George H. W. Bush the United States faced a situation in Asia Pacific where the USSR (and Russia after 1991) no longer posed a threat. Nevertheless the United States saw the bilateral alliance that had emerged during the Cold War as having continued utility. This was sometimes characterized as a "hub" (United States) and "spokes" (US allies) arrangement. In an article in *Foreign Affairs* in 1991, Secretary of State James Baker described the structure as a "fan":

> To visualize the architecture of US engagement in the region, imagine a fan spread wide, with its base in North America and radiating west across the Pacific. The central support is the US-Japan alliance, the key connection for the security structure and the new Pacific partnership we are seeking. To the north, one spoke represents our alliance with the Republic of Korea. To the south, others extend to our treaty allies—the Association of Southeast Asian [Nations] (ASEAN) countries of the Philippines and Thailand. Further south a spoke extends to Australia—an important, staunch economic, political and security partner. Connecting these spokes is the fabric of shared economic interests now given form by the Asia-Pacific Economic Cooperation (APEC) process. Within this construct, new political

and economic relationships offer additional support for a system of cooperative action by groups of Pacific nations to address both residual problems and emerging challenges.[5]

Baker wrote of "the multiplicity of security concerns that differ from country to country and within the subregions of this vast area."[6] In this respect, the flexibility of US strategy in the region was seen as an advantage. Nevertheless, as the center of the fan, the United States was still regarded as its linchpin.

Whereas Baker's presentation outlined a general plan, the more specifically military aspects of security were examined in two studies entitled *A Strategic Framework for the Asian Pacific Rim,* produced by the US Department of Defense in 1990 and 1992 in the context of its East Asia Strategy Initiative (EASI). Shifting the strategic focus away from the USSR, the 1990 study predicted that the United States, as a balancing and deterring factor, would continue to contribute to stability within the region. In light of easing tensions, US forces in Japan, South Korea, and the Philippines were reduced by about 10 percent by 1993.[7]

The 1992 study continued the same line of thinking, reinforced now by the collapse of the USSR. With the demise of the Soviet threat, "the United States' regional roles, which had been secondary in our strategic calculus, have now assumed primary importance"; preventing "the rise of any hegemonic power or coalition" in the region was a major goal for the United States.[8] The planned reduction in US forces in Asia by 1993 was augmented by the unanticipated loss of 8,300 military personnel resulting from the closure of US bases in the Philippines. This meant that between 1990 and 1993 US forces were reduced by nearly 20 percent. A further reduction of 6.5 percent was planned for the period 1993–1995.[9]

The Clinton Administration (1993–2001)

It is not surprising that, having been elected on a platform emphasizing the centrality of US economic concerns, Bill Clinton focused on the relationship between those concerns and the involvement of the United States in political and security issues in the Asia Pacific region. On 31 March 1993, Winston Lord gave an early indication of the administration's approach in his Senate confirmation hearings to become assistant secretary of state for East Asian and Pacific affairs. Lord spoke of the need for the United States to "integrate our economic, political, and security policies" toward the Asia Pacific region. In the context of a more favorable attitude toward multilateralism, the building of "a new Pacific community" was to be encouraged.

The integration of the different facets of US policy can be seen in the ten goals set out by Lord. The highest priority was to be given to the pursuit of a "comprehensive, durable partnership with Japan." The strengthening of APEC "as the cornerstone of Asian-Pacific economic cooperation" and the development of multilateral forums for security consultations "while maintaining the solid foundations of our alliances" were also important. The other goals were as follows:

- Erasing the nuclear threat and moving toward peaceful reconciliation on the Korean Peninsula
- Restoring firm foundations for cooperation with a China where political openness catches up with economic reform
- Deepening our ties with ASEAN as it broadens its membership and scope
- Obtaining the fullest possible accounting of our missing in action as we normalize our relations with Vietnam
- Securing a peaceful, independent, and democratic Cambodia
- Spurring regional cooperation on global challenges like the environment, refugees, health, narcotics, nonproliferation, and arms sales
- Promoting democracy and human rights where freedom has yet to flower[10]

The emphasis on democracy and human rights is another point that needs to be considered when evaluating the direction of US involvement in Asia Pacific. During its first year, the Clinton administration articulated the goal of enlarging market democracies as an underlying rationale for its foreign policy. Winston Lord saw US policy in the Asia Pacific region as based on the three pillars of economic prosperity, security, and democracy:

> Economic prosperity is a powerful force for democratic change. But economies need a stable, secure environment to grow and develop. We have long worked with our allies and friends in Asia to provide that environment, to our mutual benefit. We are now reaping the fruits of that stability in the form of growing markets and flourishing trade. Likewise, we know that open, democratic societies make better trading partners and more peaceful neighbours.[11]

Clinton indicated his own priorities when he made his first official visit to Asia (to Japan and South Korea) in July 1993. He spoke of a "new Pacific Community" that would be based on "a revived partnership between the United States and Japan. . . . On progress toward more open economies and greater trade and on support for democracy. Our community must also rest on the firm and continuing commitment of the United States to maintain its treaty alliances and its forward military presence in Japan and Korea and throughout this region."[12]

During 1995, the Clinton administration attempted to make clear that it foresaw long-term US involvement in the security of the Asia Pacific region. Perhaps the clearest statement in this respect was *United States Security Strategy for the East Asia-Pacific Region* (EASR I), issued by the Department of Defense in February 1995. This document is also known as the Nye Report, after Joseph Nye, assistant secretary of defense for international security affairs. Unlike the defense department documents of 1990 and 1992, EASR I did not envisage any further reductions in US forces in the region; a force structure of about 100,000 was to be maintained.[13] According to Nye, US security strategy in East Asia was based on three elements: the strengthening of alliances, the maintenance of a forward military presence, and the development of regional institutions such as APEC and the ASEAN Regional Forum.[14]

In the second Clinton administration (1997–2001), key figures for Asia Pacific policy were Secretary of State Madeleine Albright and Secretary of Defense William S. Cohen. Stanley O. Roth was assistant secretary of state for East Asian and Pacific affairs. At a formal level, key documents issued early in the administration attempted to establish a coherent framework for US security policy in Asia Pacific. These documents suggested more emphasis on comprehensive security. While the Clinton administration continued to give particular attention to key bilateral relationships, it also supported the strengthening of multilateralism in the region. Whatever the formal approach, however, the administration had to contend with particular crises in Asia Pacific as they arose.

The two documents establishing the framework for security policy in the second Clinton administration were *A National Security Strategy for a New Century* and the *Report of the Quadrennial Defense Review* (QDR 1997), both issued in May 1997. The former was a presidential document; the latter came from the secretary of defense. Both dealt with US security policy at a global level, but with implications for and reference to Asia Pacific. The discussion of threats to US interests included not just "regional or state-centered threats" and "threats from weapons of mass destruction," but also "transnational threats." Transnational threats covered issues such as "terrorism, the illegal drug trade, illicit arms trafficking, international organized crime, uncontrolled refugee migrations, and environmental damage."[15] In relation to East Asia and the Pacific, Clinton wished to build on his vision of a new Pacific community. This meant affirming security and other forms of cooperation with Japan, developing "a productive relationship" with China, and dealing with the tensions on the Korean peninsula that were "the principal threat to the peace and stability of the East Asia region." Given the role of ASEAN, both multilateral and bilateral relations were important with the Southeast Asian countries.[16]

In QDR 1997 the key tenets of the defense strategy of "shaping, responding and preparing" were mostly expressed at a general level, but had implications for Asia Pacific. "Shaping the international environment" included "promoting regional stability," "preventing or reducing conflicts and threats," and "deterring aggression and coercion." "Responding to the full spectrum of crises" covered "deterring aggression and coercion in crisis," "conducting small-scale contingency operations," and "fighting and winning major theater wars." The 1998 version of *The United States Security Strategy for the East Asia–Pacific Region* (EASR II)[17] focused more specifically on Asia Pacific, although it was essentially a continuation of the strategy articulated in EASR I in 1995. The US military presence was to be maintained at 100,000 personnel. In addition to maintaining US bilateral alliances, support for the development of "security pluralism" indicated an important multilateral dimension in US strategy. The impact of "comprehensive security" was evident in the discussion of the challenges posed by terrorism, environmental degradation, infectious diseases, drug trafficking, energy issues, and humanitarian relief.

While these various documents indicated the underlying strategy of the second Clinton administration in Asia Pacific, one also needs to consider how its policy developed in practice. A strong focus for the administration was Northeast Asia. The 1997 US-Japan Defense Guidelines (following the US-Japan Joint Declaration on Security of 1996) were an attempt to consolidate and strengthen the security relationship with the main US ally in the region. At the same time Clinton sought to pursue a policy of engagement with China. In relation to the Korean peninsula, the 1994 Accords continued to provide a framework for dealing with North Korea. In Southeast Asia the major concern for the United States was Indonesia. A major consequence of the Asian economic crisis that arose in 1997, the authoritarian rule of the New Order gave way to democratization after the fall of Suharto in May 1998.

Initially the primary countries affected by the Asian economic crisis were South Korea and Thailand. Many financial institutions had been extending credit on terms that were too generous. The economies of these countries were not sufficiently productive to sustain this type of arrangement in the long term. Many financial institutions collapsed, and national production fell. This problem also affected Japan but its economy was sufficiently strong for it to be able to cope. In Southeast Asia the problems spread to other countries, most particularly Indonesia. It was this situation that led to the collapse of the Suharto government. The United States took the lead in responding to the Asian economic crisis, with Treasury Secretary Robert Rubin being the most prominent official involved. As the major contributor to the bailout of the affected economies, the United States worked primarily through the International Monetary Fund (IMF). The IMF insisted that those governments it was assisting commit to the principles of market liberalization. The United States opposed Japanese proposals for an Asian Monetary Fund that would have made assistance available on more generous terms more compatible with the East Asian pattern of close government involvement in the economy.

In Indonesia, the United States had had close relations with Suharto's New Order, while also being critical of human rights abuses such as the Dili massacre of 1991. Nevertheless, the United States welcomed the move toward democratization after Suharto's downfall. This was consistent with the Clinton administration's strategy of "democratic enlargement." The United States was the major contributor to the IMF's assistance package to Indonesia. From a strategic perspective, the United States was concerned about the instability occurring in Indonesia in the context of democratization. In 1999 it welcomed the attempt to resolve the conflict over East Timor through a ballot conducted by the United Nations. In September 1999 the United States became involved in pressuring Indonesia to accept international intervention to restore order in East Timor after Indonesian forces and their militia allies embarked on a campaign of wanton destruction in response to the proindependence vote. The United States provided some logistical and communications support for the intervention force led by Australia.

The George W. Bush Administration (2001–)

During the 2000 presidential election campaign Condoleezza Rice, the foreign policy adviser to George W. Bush, indicated that realism would form the basis for US security policies in Asia Pacific in an incoming Republican administration.[18] She argued for the elaboration of "key priorities" within a renewed focus on the "national interest" of the United States. In relation to US military power the focus should be on having forces "able to meet decisively the emergence of any hostile military power in the Asia-Pacific region, the Middle East, the Persian Gulf, and Europe." In Asia Pacific the main challenges were China and North Korea. China's desire to alter the balance of power in the region made it a "strategic competitor" to the United States. North Korea was a "rogue regime" with whom the United

States should deal "resolutely and decisively," but on the basis of deterrence. The United States had to be "resolute" in upholding peace in the Taiwan Strait. The relationships with Japan and South Korea needed to be strengthened; India's role in the regional balance relating to China was also important.

With the inauguration of the George W. Bush administration in January 2001, there was a shift toward the more realist agenda that Rice (the new national security adviser) had outlined. At cabinet level the key personnel in implementing US security policies in Asia Pacific were Secretary of State Colin Powell and Secretary of Defense Donald Rumsfeld. Richard Armitage was deputy secretary of state, and James Kelly was assistant secretary of state for East Asian and Pacific affairs. The new administration gave a higher priority to relations with US allies in the region, particularly Japan and South Korea. It was more cautious about China and, while officially maintaining support for the "one China" policy, also appeared more committed to the defense of Taiwan.

The Bush administration continued and strengthened the development of an anti-missile defense system in East Asia. There was a merger between the programs of national missile defense (NMD) and theater missile defense (TMD). NMD focused on the US homeland whereas TMD was regionally oriented. These developments in missile defense led to US withdrawal from the Anti-Ballistic Missile (ABM) Treaty that had been concluded in 1972 with the Soviet Union. In Asia Pacific there were implications for China, which feared that missile defense would neutralize its second strike capability. At a budgetary level the renewed focus on missile defense was reflected in the request of the Missile Defense Agency for US$8.3 billion in fiscal year 2003.[19] Most of this funding was for research and development.

At one level the response to the September 11 attacks on New York and Washington indicated a considerable strengthening in the realist approach of the Bush administration. Nevertheless the priorities as indicated earlier by Rice were also considerably revised. There was now a stronger moral orientation in US policies, with Bush portraying the "war on terrorism" as a contest between good and evil. There was a greater assertiveness in the use of US military power. There was a stronger unilateralist emphasis. The United States sought allies and international support for its stated objectives in the war on terrorism, but it was less constrained by these considerations than had previously been the case. At a military level, the immediate response to September 11 was the attack on Afghanistan and the deposing of the Taliban regime.[20] The new political situation made it easier for the Bush administration to use US military power in the more assertive way it thought desirable. In Bush's State of the Union address in February 2002 the focus shifted to the "axis of evil," a term denoting certain "rogue states" that were alleged to be developing nuclear weapons and other weapons of mass destruction (WMD). In Asia Pacific the focus was on North Korea; in the Persian Gulf region the concern was with Iraq and Iran.

In the aftermath of September 11 the Bush administration sought to enlist the support of allies and other powers in Asia Pacific for its war on terrorism. An early opportunity came at the meeting of APEC heads of government in Shanghai in October 2001.[21] Australia and New Zealand sent forces to assist the United States in Afghanistan; Japan sent vessels to the Indian Ocean in a support role. China indicated that it would support the anti-terrorist coalition, while also using the situation to crack down on Muslim separatists in Xinjiang. In relation to the war in Afghanistan, the United States had to shore up its relations with Pakistan and also established bases in Central Asia. In the context of the antiterrorist strategy, Southeast Asia assumed greater importance to the United States. Some US forces were sent to the Philippines to assist in the campaign against the Abu Sayyaf group. Indonesia was a particular concern. Although most Muslims in that country were moderates, there were also more radical elements, some of which were prepared to use violence (as reflected in the Bali bombings of October 2002). Although North Korea was part of Bush's axis of evil, Northeast Asia was generally less significant as a center for terrorism.[22]

Major US documents issued in 2001 and 2002 were consistent with these trends affecting US security policy in Asia Pacific. Much of the work for the *Quadrennial Defense Review Report* (QDR 2001) issued by the Department of Defense on September 30, 2001, would have been done before the September 11 attacks. Among the US goals for QDR 2001 was "Precluding hostile domination of critical areas, particularly Europe, Northeast Asia, the East Asian littoral, and the Middle East and Southwest Asia."[23] The four defense policy goals were: "assuring allies and friends; dissuading future military competition; deterring threats and coercion against US interests; and if deterrence fails, decisively defeating any adversary."[24] Among the strategic tenets relevant to Asia Pacific were those of "strengthening alliances and partnerships" and "maintaining favorable regional balances."[25] The force planning construct included the principle of forward deterrence. This involved maintaining "regionally tailored forces forward stationed and deployed in Europe, Northeast Asia, the East Asian littoral, and the Middle East/Southwest Asia to assure allies and friends, counter coercion, and deter aggression against the United States, its forces, allies, and friends."[26]

The National Security Strategy of the United States of America, as issued by President Bush in September 2002, involved a series of principles, many of which were relevant to Asia Pacific. The underlying moral dimension was explicit. The aim was "to help make the world not just safer but better," with particular goals being "political and economic freedom, peaceful relations with other states, and respect for human dignity."[27] The influence of the September 11 experience is clear in the emphasis on countering "global terrorism" and countering "weapons of mass destruction." In working with others "to defuse regional conflicts" reference is made to the opportunities that exist for US assistance to Indonesia.[28] The Asian alliances of the United States feature prominently in the goal of developing "agendas for cooperative action with the other main centers of global power." The document refers specifically to the alliances with Japan, South Korea, and Australia. US forces would continue to be maintained in the region. In addition to these bilateral alliances, the United States would work with regional institutions such as ASEAN and APEC "to develop a mix of regional and bilateral strategies."[29]

Since 2003 a major US preoccupation has been the war in Iraq. While Saddam Hussein was quickly toppled, a Sunni-led insurgency also developed. This made it difficult for the United States to achieve its objective of "democratic stability" in Iraq, and to withdraw its forces. US policy in all regions of the world, including Asia Pacific, was affected. With Iraq as the major preoccupation, other issues were generally assigned a lower priority. In Asia Pacific this included such major concerns as future US relations with China and Japan. The exception was any situation that might have immediate implications for the United States, North Korea being the main example in Asia Pacific. In relation to Taiwan the US emphasis was on maintaining the status quo. The major complication for the United States in Asia Pacific as a result of the Iraq war was with the Muslim majority states of Indonesia and Malaysia in Southeast Asia. Both South Korea and Japan contributed forces to the occupation, with the South Korean contingent being the third largest in Iraq; Thai and Filipino forces were withdrawn from Iraq during 2004. In the context of changes in US military strategy at the global level, but affected also by the Iraq experience, the United States announced in June 2004 that it would be withdrawing 12,500 troops from South Korea. This amounted to about one-third of the US deployment there. The reduction was originally to be effected by the end of 2005, but the withdrawal date was later changed to 2008.[30]

With the inauguration of the second George W. Bush administration in January 2005, there were some changes in personnel relating to Asia Pacific policy but no major change in direction was portended. Condoleezza Rice replaced Colin Powell as secretary of state, and Robert Zoellick became deputy secretary of state instead of Richard Armitage (Zoellick resigned in

July 2006). Donald Rumsfeld continued as secretary of defense. Christopher Hill, former US ambassador to South Korea, became the new assistant secretary of state for East Asian and Pacific affairs.

The *Quadrennial Defense Review Report* issued in February 2006 (QDR 2006) reflected a continuing preoccupation with the war on terror and the need for flexibility in meeting that challenge. Four strategic objectives were identified: defeating terrorist networks; defending the homeland in depth; shaping the choices of countries at strategic crossroads; and preventing hostile states and nonstate actors from gaining or using weapons of mass destruction.[31] Australia (along with the United Kingdom) was described as a model ally for its support in Iraq and Afghanistan, but the bilateral alliances with Japan and South Korea were also valued highly.[32] These links were relevant to the ability of the United States to have "forward-deployed forces and flexible deterrent options."[33] North Korea was one of the states causing concern on the issue of WMD proliferation.[34] Influencing "countries at strategic crossroads" was particularly important in Asia Pacific where China loomed large, although US relations with India and Russia were also relevant to this region. While China had "the greatest potential to compete militarily with the United States," it was the US aim to encourage China "to play a constructive, peaceful role in the Asia-Pacific region and to serve as a partner in addressing common security challenges, including terrorism, proliferation, narcotics and piracy."[35]

Comparing the Asia Pacific policies of Bill Clinton and George W. Bush, we can see a shift toward democratic realism under the latter. Both administrations gave attention to the moral dimension of foreign policy but each leader's emphasis was different. For Clinton the focus was on democracy and human rights. For George W. Bush, particularly following the events of September 11, the priority has been the protection of the values embodied in the United States itself, with world politics often portrayed as a contest between the forces of good and evil. Another point of comparison concerns the relationship between bilateralism and multilateralism in US strategies in Asia Pacific. While all administrations in the post–Cold War era have maintained the hub and spokes approach to US allies in the region, multilateralism did receive more attention during the Clinton period. Clinton did not neglect the role of military power (a key point in the realist approach), but liberal institutionalism was also seen as appropriate in many circumstances. This aspect has been relatively less important during the era of George W. Bush. Some observers see a shift toward unilateralism. Again this is a matter of emphasis. The United States under George W. Bush has been more assertive about advancing its perceived interests, but still needs the cooperation of its allies and other countries on many matters. Throughout the post–Cold War era the United States has sought to play a hegemonic role in Asia Pacific. There has been some variation in the strategies employed, but generally this has been a matter of emphasis rather than sudden changes from one approach to another.[36]

Notes

1. A good overview of US involvement in Asia Pacific since 1945 is Buckley, *The United States in the Asia-Pacific Since 1945.*

2. Almond, *The American People and Foreign Policy.*

3. See Buckley, *The United States in the Asia-Pacific since 1945,* chapters 6–7. For strategic aspects, see Tow, *Asia-Pacific Strategic Relations,* chapter 6; Weeks and Meconis, *The Armed Forces of the USA in the Asia-Pacific Region* provides details of US military involvement in the region. For a radical critique of the US role, see Johnson, *Blowback.*

4. Krauthammer, "Democratic Realism."

5. Baker, "America in Asia," pp. 4–5.

6. Ibid., p. 5.

7. See Kreisberg, "The U.S. and Asia in 1990," p. 7; Crowe and Romberg, "Rethinking Security in the Pacific," p. 125.

8. *A Strategic Framework for the Asian Pacific Rim,* p. 2.

9. Ibid., pp. 16, 22.

10. Lord, "A New Pacific Community," pp. 49–50.

11. Winston Lord, "Prosperity in the Pacific," *Far Eastern Economic Review,* 11 November 1993, p. 23.

12. Jonathan Friedland, Shim Jae Hoon, and Susumu Awanohara, "Clinton's Clarion Call," *Far Eastern Economic Review,* 22 July 1993, p. 10.

13. *The United States Security Strategy for the East Asia–Pacific Region 1995,* p. 24.

14. Nye, "East Asian Security," pp. 94–95. A subsequent evaluation is Nye, "The 'Nye Report.'"

15. *A National Security Strategy for a New Century,* p. 7.

16. Ibid., pp. 28–29.

17. United States, Department of Defense, *The United States Security Strategy for the East Asia–Pacific Region 1998.*

18. Rice, "Campaign 2000."

19. *The Military Balance 2002–2003,* p. 242.

20. The Bush administration had been attempting to isolate the Taliban regime well before 9/11. See Ahmed Rashid, "The Taliban: First the War," *Far Eastern Economic Review,* August 2, 2001, p. 26.

21. See McDougall, "Asia-Pacific Security Regionalism," pp. 130–131.

22. See Campbell and Tatsumi, "In the Aftermath of the Storm."

23. United States, Department of Defense, *Quadrennial Defense Review Report,* September 30, 2001, p. 2. The East Asian littoral is "the region stretching from south of Japan through Australia and into the Bay of Bengal."

24. Ibid., p. 11.

25. Ibid., pp. 14–15.

26. Ibid., p. 20.

27. *The National Security Strategy of the United States of America,* p. 1.

28. Ibid., p. 10.

29. Ibid., p. 26.

30. Pollack, "The United States and Asia in 2004," pp. 7–8.

31. United States, Department of Defense, *Quadrennial Defense Review Report,* February 2006, p. 3. www.defenselink.mil/pubs/pdfs/QDR20060203.pdf (accessed 20 February 2006).

32. Ibid., pp. 6–7.

33. Ibid., p. 14.

34. Ibid., p. 32.

35. Ibid., p. 29.

36. For an overview of US hegemonic strategy in Asia Pacific, see Mastanduno, "Incomplete Hegemony and Security Order in the Asia-Pacific."

China 3

This chapter focuses on China as another of the major powers in Asia Pacific.[1] In the first part of the chapter we examine the major factors that influence Chinese policies in the region. These factors cover China's historical experience, its worldview, the impact of domestic politics, and China's power. In the second part of the chapter we provide an overview of China's policies in Asia Pacific, with reference to political-strategic and economic dimensions.

◼ Factors Influencing China's Policies in Asia Pacific

China's Historical Experience

A major underlying factor influencing China's involvement in the world, including Asia Pacific, is its sense of itself as a civilization with some five thousand years of history. The Chinese heartland is centered in eastern China, including the Yangtze valley. Although divided at various times, this area has also experienced long periods of unity under different dynasties. The most recent dynasty was the Q'ing or Manchu dynasty, which ruled China from 1644 to 1911. It was during this time that China experienced its greatest territorial expansion, incorporating not just Manchuria but also vast areas to the west. The term used to denote China's sense of its centrality was "Middle Kingdom." A tribute system encompassed neighboring countries such as Korea and Vietnam. Japan was not part of this system but its culture also derived originally from China. Areas such as Tibet and large parts of Central Asia were within the Chinese zone of influence. With the emperor at the apex, a bureaucratic elite known as

mandarins ran the Chinese system of government. Mandarins were selected on a meritocratic basis through an examination system. While mandarins commanded considerable prestige, scholars were also an esteemed
group in China. China made many advances in the arts and sciences. Important philosophical and religious systems, of which Confucianism and
Taoism were the most notable examples, also developed. Most people
were engaged in agriculture as peasants, but industry and commerce were
also significant.

China was aware of parts of the world beyond its own immediate
sphere; however, contact was generally minimal. One early encounter with
Europeans was the visit of Marco Polo in the thirteenth century. More constant contact with Europeans developed from about the sixteenth century,
with traders and missionaries becoming active. The Portuguese were
prominent in this development, particularly at Macau. While Europeans
were clearly outside the Chinese culture area, the Chinese regarded them
as inferior in civilization and attainments.

Despite this attitude, there was one area where Westerners were clearly
superior in relation to the Chinese. Europeans (and Americans) possessed
more powerful technology and were also better organized on the whole to
deploy that technology in pursuit of their ends. This situation became most
evident in the course of the nineteenth century. China's weakness was
amply demonstrated when it was defeated in the Opium War with Britain in
1842. China also lost in another war with Britain from 1856 to 1860. During the mid- and late nineteenth century China ceded some ports to foreign
powers, most notably Hong Kong in the case of Britain. It also lost large
swaths of territory in the north to Russia. Britain, Russia, France, and Germany all had spheres of influence in China. In the treaty ports, foreign powers had special concessions to further their commercial interests. Most foreign nationals came under a regime of extraterritoriality whereby they were
subject not to Chinese laws but to the laws of their own country. By the end
of the nineteenth century Japan had joined the Western powers in making
depredations at China's expense. With China's defeat in the Sino-Japanese
war of 1894–1895, the Chinese province of Taiwan became a Japanese
colony. The United States followed an open-door policy, aimed not at territorial concessions from China but parity of treatment with other powers in
the development of trade and investment.

The treatment meted out to China by the Western powers led to considerable resentment among Chinese. It also undermined the position of the
Q'ing dynasty. Any ruler who could not defend China was said to have lost
the mandate of heaven. Chinese resentment was heightened by the perception that it was a superior civilization, but had proved inadequate in defend-

ing itself against the barbarians. Various movements to strengthen China's position developed. Some focused on the reform of the imperial system, but found it difficult to overcome its rigidities. The Taiping Rebellion (1848–1864), while ultimately suppressed, was a sign of internal weakness. In 1900 the Boxer Rebellion was motivated by anti-foreigner sentiment. In the early twentieth century the nationalist movement, of which Sun Yat-sen was the leading figure, sought the overthrow of the Q'ing dynasty and its replacement by a new political system. In the 1911 revolution the dynasty did fall, and a republic came into being. The aim remained that of giving China its proper place in the world. But China was internally riven, with warlords controlling large parts of the country. At the time of World War I Japan attempted to make gains at China's expense; Japan was the major concern for China up to the 1940s.

Following the death of Sun Yat-sen in 1925 the Chinese Nationalists or Guomindang (Kuomintang) were led by Chiang Kai-shek. The Chinese Communist Party (CCP) was formed in 1921 and initially worked in conjunction with the Nationalists. In 1927, however, Chiang Kai-shek turned on the Nationalists in the major urban centers. The communists under Mao Tse-tung retreated into the countryside and in 1934–1935 undertook the Long March to Shaanxi province in northwestern China. Civil war between nationalists and communists continued to undermine China's ability to rebuild itself. In 1931 Japan occupied Manchuria, and in 1937 war engulfed the whole country. While there was nominal cooperation between nationalists and communists in fighting Japan, in practice tensions (if not open conflict) continued. At issue was the question of which group could provide the leadership to enable China to regain its rightful place in the world.

This was the issue that was central in the resumption of the civil war after the defeat of Japan in 1945. By 1949 Chiang Kai-shek had retreated to Taiwan, and the People's Republic of China had been proclaimed as a communist state. Mao believed that communist ideology, adapted to Chinese circumstances, was the way for China to overcome the humiliation of the imperialist era and to become strong once again. In practice Mao oscillated between a pragmatic and a more revolutionary approach toward China's reconstruction. In the 1950s the former predominated, whereas in the 1960s the latter took hold in the form of the Cultural Revolution. In the Chinese context pragmatism meant allowing a role for experts in promoting economic development, and subordinating the demands of ideology if they impeded it. During the Cultural Revolution, on the other hand, ideological demands were very much to the fore, with the focus on "red" rather than "expert." Apart from the devastating impact of the Cultural Revolution on individual lives, this approach also undermined the Chinese economy. By the early 1970s there was a reversion to the pragmatic approach, and this continued and accelerated after Mao's death in 1976.

At the international level, pragmatism led China to seek allies and countries sharing common interests. Initially the focus was on the Sino-Soviet alliance as established in 1950. China also promoted links with leading countries in the nonaligned world such as India and Indonesia. The shift to a more revolutionary approach in the 1960s exacerbated tensions with the Soviet Union, leading in turn to the Sino-Soviet conflict, a major feature of international politics up to the late 1980s. There was more focus on "people's war" as a model of revolution for Third World countries. China became more isolationist, generally eschewing links with nonaligned countries. Pragmatic interests could contribute to tensions, as in the case of India, where the border dispute led to a Sino-Indian war in 1962. As a democratic country India also represented a different model for Third World countries to follow. The Chinese reversion to pragmatism by the early 1970s was accompanied by a rapprochement with the United States. In the 1960s China had regarded both the United States and the USSR as enemies. By 1972 it had concluded that the USSR was the greater threat and that China could strengthen its position by coming to an accommodation with the United States. China also made efforts to strengthen its relations with a range of Western and Third World countries at this time.

After 1976 Deng Xiaoping emerged as China's leader, continuing in that role until his death in 1997. His leadership during this period reinforced the focus on pragmatism as the way for China to strengthen itself and become a major force in world politics. During the Maoist period Deng had frequently encountered difficulties because of his revisionist tendencies. As leader he was able to give those tendencies full rein. His focus was on reforming the economic system so that China could maximize its economic growth. Deng's program was expressed in the "four modernizations," covering agriculture, industry, science, and defense. Communal ownership was to be modified in agriculture to encourage peasants to produce for profit and thus enhance productivity. Industry was to be restructured along capitalist lines even though a state sector would continue; private investment (including foreign investment) would be encouraged. Improvements in technology would also help in the quest for economic growth. Defense would take a lower proportion of the national budget, but spending in absolute terms would still be high because of the expanding economy. China's defense forces would be modernized and make more use of advanced technology. Deng's program was very successful in making China stronger economically.

The main problem with Deng's rule was that the authoritarian political system continued alongside the introduction of economic capitalism. Economic changes meant that the pressures within the political system also changed. New organizations and groupings wanted to influence the system in their own favor; the educated middle class sought to express itself politically. Pressures for democratic change built up. Reaction came in the form of the Tiananmen Square massacre in June 1989 when hundreds of prodemocracy demonstrators were killed. Although there had been liberal elements in the leadership favoring concessions, the majority believed that the authoritarian system had to continue. The question remained as to whether the political system would be sufficiently adaptable to deal with the vast economic and social changes that were occurring in China. If the political system was not strong in this way then this would impede the goal of restoring China's position as a major influence in world affairs.

At an international level China under Deng sought to develop those relationships that would be most beneficial in terms of their reform program. Any pretensions to act as a beacon of revolution in the Third World were abandoned. The focus was on countries that could assist China in terms of trade, investment, and access to technology. The United States, Japan, and the Western world more generally were particularly important in this respect. Within China's immediate region there was a continuing concern with issues that affected China's security: Taiwan, the Korean peninsula, Indochina, and the South China Sea in particular. At the same time, however, regional relationships that involved tangible economic benefits grew in importance. South Korea was prominent in this respect, and economic ties also put the relationships with both Hong Kong and Taiwan in a different light. In Southeast Asia countries experiencing significant economic growth, such as Thailand, Malaysia, and Singapore, became more important to China. With communist ideology declining in importance, relationships with other communist countries also changed. Rapprochement with the USSR was achieved in 1989. China was concerned that the collapse of communism in both Eastern Europe and the USSR would undermine its own authoritarian political system. With the disintegration of the USSR at the end of 1991, China also had to contend with the emergence of new states in Central Asia.

China's Worldview

Whereas communism had been a major influence on China's worldview in the 1950s and 1960s, since Mao's death in 1976 the influence of this ideology has steadily declined. Increasingly the major emphasis in China's worldview, affecting both domestic and foreign policies, has been nationalism. Communism was one response to the challenge of empowering China to take its "rightful" place in the world. The shift to more pragmatic ways of achieving economic modernization has been accompanied by focus on a more broadly based nationalism as the ideological justification for the role China aspires to in the world. In both cases, perceptions of the injustice of China's treatment at the hands of the Western powers and Japan have been a powerful motivation.

A foreign policy framework that emerged early in the PRC era, and that has continued to exert an influence, has been the "five principles of peaceful coexistence." These cover "mutual respect for sovereignty and territorial integrity, mutual non-aggression, non-interference in each other's internal affairs, equality and mutual benefit, and peaceful coexistence."[2] While originally the five principles were agreed to in 1954 as the basis for the relationship between China and India, they have had a continuing relevance during both the Mao and post-Mao periods. The principles were important whenever China aimed for normal relations with other states. This was less the case during revolutionary phases in the Mao period but has been the primary focus at all other times.

Revolutionary emphases came to the fore in periods such as the Cultural Revolution of the 1960s. At that time China emphasized its support (essentially ideological) for revolutionary forces in different parts of the world. Vietnam was particularly important. It was argued that the doctrine that underpinned the Chinese revolution could be applied on a world scale. According to Lin Biao in "Long Live the Victory of People's War!" the revolutionary forces of the world could emulate the role of the countryside in the Chinese revolution and surround the reactionary forces of advanced capitalism (which paralleled the role played by the cities in the Chinese revolution).[3]

During the 1970s, and continuing into the 1980s, the dominant doctrine was that of "three worlds." This reflected the pragmatic emphasis that emerged during the final part of the Mao period and was taken further by Deng. Under this doctrine China was classified as part of the "third world." The United States and USSR constituted the "first world"; the "second world" consisted of capitalist, industrialized powers other than the United States. The main problem for China was the hegemonism of the USSR. In terms of the so-called three worlds, China developed a strategy that involved strengthening links with the United States and the second world to counter the threat posed by Soviet hegemonism.[4]

During the Deng era nationalism emerged as the dominant influence on the way China relates to the world. Communism in China had been fueled by strongly nationalist sentiments, but increasingly communism lost its role as the ideological underpinning for Chinese foreign policy. General statements on foreign policy took nationalism as their basis without any reference to communist formulations. Realism was an important influence on the Chinese approach. China upheld a traditional view of sovereignty. It approached issues in terms of what was judged best for the Chinese national interest. The concept of comprehensive national power involves using all relevant instruments of power to advance those interests.[5]

In the security realm a "new security concept" has emerged. This concept expresses support for the development of a multipolar world involving "mutual security and common trust," and in opposition to "hegemonism and power politics."[6] A multipolar world in which China played a significant role was clearly preferred to a situation where the United States exercised overriding power. The official view is elaborated in defense white papers issued in 1998, 2000, 2002, and 2004.

The Impact of Domestic Politics

Domestic politics is another area that is significant in determining the role China plays in the world. While China's historical experience exerts an influence at a broad level on China's contemporary situation, one also has to look more precisely at the interplay of domestic forces. Similarly the emergence of general frameworks or worldviews relating to foreign policy is also shaped by domestic politics. In assessing this dimension of Chinese foreign policy there are two major areas to keep in mind. One involves the broad forces underlying Chinese politics and society. The other concerns the nature of the foreign policy making process itself. We will consider each of these areas in turn.

China occupies an extensive territory and has a large population to support. In terms of area, China ranks behind Russia and Canada, and just ahead of the United States. With a population of over 1.2 billion people at the start of the twenty-first century, China has more people than any other country. Most of these people live in eastern China; the western provinces are much more sparsely inhabited. Maintaining territorial integrity has been a key objective for China. This issue features in many of the relationships with the fourteen countries that share land borders with China (not to mention the Taiwan issue). It should also be noted that the minority peoples are mainly located in outlying areas, and sometimes pose issues relating to territorial integrity. Some of these people, such as the Uighurs in Xinjiang, reject or question Chinese rule. They see China as an empire.[7]

Ensuring basic living standards for China's large population is a major objective for the Chinese government. With an ever-increasing population this is part of the explanation for the emphasis on achieving economic growth during the Deng and post-Deng eras. Since 1980 growth rates have been at least 7–8 percent each year.[8] Much of this growth has been within China's private sector. Reforming the large state sector has been an issue, with the leadership proceeding cautiously because of the large number of people employed in it. Increasing divisions within Chinese society raise questions of stability. These divisions exist not just between state and private sectors, but also between rural and urban areas, and between coastal and inland provinces. Most Chinese are still peasants, but have lower living standards than urban dwellers. This encourages people to move to the cities, where there is not necessarily employment or infrastructure to accommodate them. Coastal provinces have generally done better from China's recent economic growth than have provinces further inland. These inequalities can have a destabilizing effect.[9] The benefits of economic growth need to be spread sufficiently to counter widespread dissatisfaction. While average living standards in China appear to be at Third World levels, the situation is different when one takes into account relative costs and the level of provision in areas such as health and education. On this basis it is more appropriate to place China among the middle range of countries.[10]

These underlying issues are a major consideration in the way China relates to the rest of the world. However, the decisionmaking process itself has an important bearing on how they are interpreted and dealt with. Many of these issues arise as matters of domestic policy. They are also important in foreign policy, however, and increasingly domestic and foreign issues overlap. In this discussion we focus on foreign policy decisionmaking, while keeping in mind the wider political context. An essential point is that the Chinese political system, while it might have downgraded communism as an ideology, remains Leninist in nature. This means that power is concentrated in the higher levels of the Chinese Communist Party. At the same time China's opening to the world has put more pressure on the political system. Different institutions within the system vie with each other to gain access to the benefits of economic growth. Private sector organizations are in a position to exert more influence, and there is a growing middle class that might seek political expression.

Discussions of the Chinese political process[11] often focus on the role of the leader. In the cases of Mao and Deng the leader did not necessarily have a formal title. Irrespective of the formalities, being in a commanding position in relation to the levers of power in China provided the basis of leadership in each case. Mao was head of state during the 1950s and was also chairman of the CCP. For both Mao and Deng, chairing the Central Military Commission was an important source of power since this body provided direction for the People's Liberation Army (PLA). In the post-

Deng era leadership has become more formalized, with Jiang Zemin (1997–2002) and Hu Jintao (2002–) occupying the key state role of president and the key party role of general secretary.

The overall political direction in China—a Leninist system—is provided by the CCP, and its upper echelons in particular. This applies to foreign policy as much as to other areas of policy. At the top level the key body is the Politburo Standing Committee. The most significant leaders in China are members of this committee. It determines China's position on major foreign policy issues. The Standing Committee is supported in turn by the Party Secretariat. Below the Standing Committee are the Politburo itself and the Central Committee. A party congress meets every few years.

In relation to the institutions of the state the most important body is the State Council, which in turn has a smaller cabinet. The premier heads the State Council. The State Council deals with the more routine matters of foreign policy, and provides advice to the Party Secretariat. The scope of the council's involvement in foreign policy has expanded in recent years. The State Council also supervises a number of ministries involved in foreign policy: the Ministry of Foreign Affairs (MFA), the Ministry of Defense, the Ministry of Foreign Trade and Economic Cooperation (MOFTEC), and the Ministry of State Security. The National People's Congress, the main legislative body, is formally responsible for choosing both the State Council and the PRC president.

The PLA's role in Chinese politics, including its influence on foreign policy, is also important. The PLA's main link to the political system is through the Central Military Commission, a party body that reports directly to the general secretary. The Ministry of Defense provides a formal link to the state apparatus but is not a controlling body. Senior PLA figures also participate directly in the ruling bodies of the CCP. The Chinese leadership has been able to call on the PLA at various times to uphold the party's authority; the Tiananmen Square massacre in 1989 was the most obvious example. Jiang Zemin made use of his position as chairman of the Central Military Commission to reinforce his authority as both state and party leader. In fact, when Jiang Zemin stepped down as general secretary in 2002, he retained his role as chairman of the Central Military Commission. This situation lasted until September 2004 when Hu Jintao assumed the position.[12] As well as indicating Jiang Zemin's desire to retain influence, this transitional arrangement might have reflected Hu Jintao's lack of experience in dealing with the PLA, and the limited respect for him among military leaders.[13]

While the formal framework of an authoritarian system remains in place in China, it is clear that the leadership has to contend with an increasing range of pressures within the system. Zhao Quansheng portrays the situation in terms of a shift from "vertical authoritarianism" to "horizontal authoritarianism."[14] Rather than the political system being organized in terms of a top-down hierarchy, there are now numerous groups attempting to advance their objectives. At one level this is more pluralistic, but the groups still have to win the support of a top leadership that has achieved its position through the processes of the CCP rather than being elected. The groups vying for influence are not normally democratically chosen but represent different levels of government and various bureaucratic and economic interests.

David Lampton sees the trend toward an increasing range of actors in Chinese foreign policymaking as driven by "professionalization, corporate pluralization, decentralization, and globalization."[15] Professionalization refers to the greater emphasis on expertise in foreign policy decisionmaking. The effect is to bring in a range of agencies and people who might not otherwise be engaged in the policy process. Corporate pluralization refers to the way in which the increasing complexity of government requires consultation with a wide range of officially sanctioned bodies if decisions are to be legitimate and effective. In the area of foreign economic policy in particular, many groups outside the central institutions have an influence on decisionmaking. This situation is accentuated by globalization, which enables greater interaction between external and internal economic groups, with central institutions having less control than would previously have been the case.

Within the broad framework of the foreign policy making process, it is often possible to draw a distinction between conservative and liberal tendencies. These are not necessarily well-organized factions but represent different emphases in terms of the foreign policy issues that China faces. Conservatives tend to be more strongly nationalist and concerned about too much interaction with the outside world leading to an undermining of Chinese sovereignty. They favor a strong and continuing role for the state sector in China's economy. Liberals also wish to advance China's interests, but believe that increased interaction with the outside world can facilitate this goal. They focus in particular on the promotion of relations with countries that can assist China's economic development. They are more sympathetic to economic and political reform within China itself.

China's Power

Whatever the goals China sets itself in foreign policy, its ability to achieve those goals is strongly influenced by its power position. China's power can be assessed in terms of military, economic, and qualitative dimensions.

Power is also relative. China's power needs to be compared to that of potential adversaries. China could be seen as powerful in absolute terms while at the same time remaining inferior in important respects to other major Asia Pacific powers such as Japan and the United States. In this discussion the focus will be on the "absolute" dimensions of China's power. We will examine the military, economic, and qualitative strengths that underpin China's attempts to advance its foreign policy objectives. In any given situation, however, the ability of China to prevail will be determined by the way in which its assets are deployed in comparison with the assets of other relevant actors. This latter point will emerge in the discussion of China's policies in Asia Pacific, and in subsequent chapters dealing with the Sino-US and Sino-Japanese relationships, and the Taiwan and Korean issues.

Assessments of "hard power" usually focus in the first instance on the military dimension. China is one of the world's major military powers. It is difficult to estimate Chinese defense spending accurately. Some areas of military spending are not covered in the official defense budget. It is also necessary to estimate how much value China obtains for the money it spends through "parity purchasing power" (PPP). When making international comparisons one has to consider that goods bought in one country might be cheaper than in another country. On a PPP basis and taking into account extra-budgetary spending, the International Institute of Strategic Studies estimates that China spent US$62.5 billion on defense in 2004.[16] Defense spending accounted for 3.9 percent of GDP in 2003.[17] David Shambaugh places China third in the world for military spending, behind the United States and Russia, and just above France, Japan, the United Kingdom, and Germany.[18] It should be noted that China's defense spending has been increasing, with an estimated doubling in real terms in the last decade of the twentieth century.[19] China's economic growth means that this increase can be absorbed without putting excessive strain on the economy.

A major reason for the increase in defense spending is China's attempts to modernize its armed forces. Defense doctrine has changed considerably since Mao's time when the main emphasis was on "people's war" as a means of providing "defense in depth" should China be attacked. This called for the PLA to merge with the people to fight foreign invasion through guerrilla methods. Under Deng there was a shift to a doctrine of "people's war under modern conditions." This reflected an attempt to equip the PLA with weapons and equipment relevant to situations in which China might find itself. This has been taken further from the 1990s in the doctrine of "limited war under high-technology conditions."[20] Since the United States is a potential adversary, China has attempted to learn the lessons of

the 1991 Gulf War and the various other conflicts in which the United
States has been involved. Essentially this means putting more emphasis on
the acquisition of technology that would be relevant to conflicts in which
China might become engaged.

This shift in defense doctrine is reflected in the changing structure of
China's armed forces.[21] Traditionally China has placed its main emphasis
on its ground forces. These remain as the main component but are being reduced in size. Between 1985 and 2005 the number of military personnel
(covering all components) fell from 3.9 million to about 2.3 million. Of this
latter figure, about 1.6 million were in the army, about 255,000 in the navy,
and about 400,000 in the air force. The army had over 8,580 tanks and over
4,500 armored personnel carriers and armored infantry fighting vehicles.

Modernization means not only providing technological enhancement
for the ground forces, but also improving the capabilities of the naval and
air forces. China does not have a "blue water" navy (i.e., a force capable
of operating in areas distant from China). At most it has a "green water"
navy (one that can be deployed in China's coastal waters), and even then
there are significant limitations. China would be very restricted in using its
naval forces against Taiwan.[22] Russian arms sales have assisted China in
upgrading its air and naval forces. In 2003 there were about 150 advanced
Russian fighter aircraft in the air force, with those numbers expected to
more than double under coproduction plans over the next several years.
The acquisition of *Sovremenny*-class destroyers (two initially and two on
order) and four *Kilo*-class submarines from Russia similarly boosted
China's navy.[23]

A final element of China's military power to note is its possession of
nuclear weapons. China first acquired such weapons in 1964. In 2005 the
main elements of its nuclear forces were 46 intercontinental ballistic missiles, 35 intermediate-range ballistic missiles, one Xia-class submarine
armed with 12 submarine-launched ballistic missiles, and 725 short-range
ballistic missiles.[24] China claims that its weapons are for defensive purposes and would not be used first. However, there is also an argument that
in certain circumstances China would be prepared to use some elements of
its forces (such as the short-range missiles) in more localized contexts.[25]

While defense forces might be the most obvious dimension of a state's
hard power, military power derives ultimately from a country's economic
strength. Hence it is important to delineate the main aspects of China's economic power. A basic measure is of the country's gross domestic product.[26]
In 2004 China's GDP was estimated at US$1.68 trillion. This compares
with US$11.7 trillion for the United States, and US$4.66 trillion for Japan.
Among the major European powers, Germany's GDP for the same year was

US$2.16 trillion, the United Kingdom US$2.13 trillion, and France US$2.0 trillion; Russia's GDP was US$1.4 trillion. At US$1,293, China's per capita GDP, however, was far less than for any of these other powers.

Overall statistics provide only one indication of China's economic power. It is also helpful to examine how the Chinese economy is structured and how it relates to the rest of the world. During the post-Mao era China has focused on the development of its industrial sector and particularly those areas where it has a comparative advantage. With its low labor costs, China is a leading world exporter of goods such as toys, textiles, and clothing. Much of the new industrial development has occurred within the expanding private sector and in the coastal provinces. The state sector employs large numbers of people but is more sluggish in its performance; the inland provinces are generally poorer than their coastal counterparts. Increased productivity in agriculture has helped sustain the large number of people who remain in the countryside.

While China is not a high technology economy, its economic development has been facilitated by improved access to technology. Foreign investment has fueled China's high growth rates, with Hong Kong, Taiwan, the United States, and Japan being important sources (see further below). China's involvement with the international economy has been furthered through its membership of the International Monetary Fund and the World Bank since 1980, and of the World Trade Organization (WTO) since 2001. Its main trading partners in 2004 were (in order) the United States (21.1 percent), Hong Kong (17.0 percent), Japan (12.4 percent), and South Korea (4.7 percent) for exports, and Japan (16.8 percent), Taiwan (11.5 percent), South Korea (11.1 percent), and the United States (8.0 percent) for imports.[27]

There is a question as to whether China's increasing links with the international economy enhance or weaken its influence in world politics. On the one hand the trade and investment links that many countries have with China are important for the economies of those countries. They develop a stake in China's continued economic growth. Economic ties with China can nevertheless adversely affect particular interests within some countries, and large trade deficits can also lead to political controversy. From China's perspective, attempts to exert power in the international arena need to keep in mind consequences for countries with which it has important economic ties. Despite the benefits China's opening to the world has brought in terms of economic growth, it should also be noted that China's sheer size does make it more self-sufficient than most countries. Increased economic interaction with the outside world encourages pluralization within China. Both governmental organizations (central and provincial) and private sector organizations have more scope and need to relate to international companies and investors. The development of such relationships in turn weakens the authoritarian political system in China.

A third dimension of China's power focuses on qualitative aspects. This covers issues such as leadership and the political system, as well as the phenomenon of "soft power." While the foreign policy making process in China has been discussed previously, there is also the question of whether the overall political system detracts from or enhances China's power. Leadership is one aspect of this issue. Broad judgments are possible on the basis of assessing how well the Chinese leadership responded to key episodes in the PRC's history. Thus Mao is generally judged negatively in relation to the Cultural Revolution. Deng might be assessed more positively in relation to China's economic modernization, but more negatively in relation to Tiananmen Square. A key question for the political system is how well it copes with meeting the needs of the Chinese people. One official justification for the authoritarian system in China is that stability is necessary to provide for those needs. A more democratic system would be destabilizing and make the achievement of economic and social objectives more difficult. On the other hand, it might be argued that authoritarianism is becoming increasingly brittle given the pluralization occurring within the economy and society. If new demands cannot be accommodated within the system, then it is likely to destabilize, with a corresponding impact on China's power. Should there be a period of upheaval during transition to a new political system, this would also undermine China's power. The mobilization of nationalist sentiment is one way that the Chinese leadership has attempted to counter demands that political modernization should accompany economic modernization.

Among the various elements of soft power, culture and ideas are of particular significance. A country has soft power insofar as other countries see it as a model to follow. At various times China has portrayed itself as a model for Third World or developing countries to follow. It is debatable, however, whether the Dengist model, combining political authoritarianism (notionally communist) and economic capitalism, has exerted much influence elsewhere. Culturally China has some influence through overseas Chinese. There is some cultural affinity with Vietnam, North and South Korea, Taiwan, and Singapore, although this does not necessarily translate into political influence.

In general terms China's power derives primarily from its growing economy and the way this affects its region and the world. China's defense forces give its power a hard edge, but this should not be overestimated given the power available to potential adversaries. Qualitative aspects of power, including soft power, are relevant but not of decisive influence in China's case.

▪ An Overview of China's Policies in Asia Pacific

China's historical experience, its worldview, and its domestic politics all contribute to the direction taken by Chinese foreign policy. The nationalism underlying China's approach derives from the country's historical experience at the hands of Western (and later Japanese) imperialism during the nineteenth and early twentieth centuries in particular. What this means in terms of policies is determined within the framework of Chinese domestic politics, with a range of possibilities from liberal or reformist to conservative. China's ability to achieve whatever objectives emerge from the political process is related to the power assets it has available, taking into account that power is not absolute but relative to the position of other states and actors.

Keeping this background in mind it is possible to describe certain general objectives underlying Chinese foreign policy. These objectives derive from the worldview of Chinese nationalism but are more focused. The objectives give particular attention to China's region while also being broader in scope. A primary objective for China is to have the status of a major power. This does not necessarily mean that China wants to dominate East Asia but it does wish to have a major influence throughout the region. The corollary is that China does not wish to be dominated by other powers. Closely related to China's quest to seek and maintain major power status is its aim of maintaining territorial integrity. Although China had expanded beyond its core area over a period of many centuries, during the nineteenth and early twentieth centuries it suffered territorial losses or reduced influence in territories that were nominally part of China. This is an important factor in explaining why China wishes to regain Taiwan. It also helps explain Chinese sensitivity to separatism in Xinjiang and Tibet. The return of Hong Kong to Chinese sovereignty in 1997 was also important in terms of this objective.

Another broad Chinese objective is to use foreign policy to facilitate the achievement of stability and economic growth within China itself. With the world's largest population and average living standards that put China in the middle range of countries at best, there is a great challenge just to provide for the basic needs of the people in terms of employment, food, housing, health, and education. This is why the post-Mao leadership has put so much emphasis on economic modernization. From the perspective of foreign policy there is an argument that China should focus on those international relationships that are going to be most helpful for the country's economic growth. Underlying this focus on economic goals is also the concern that failure to make progress will undermine the existing political system. China will be politically more stable if the economy continues to grow. Gross economic inequalities could contribute to instability even if growth is achieved.

Keeping in mind these general objectives, we can now focus on China's policies in the Asia Pacific region. We will give attention in the first instance to the political-strategic dimension, and then turn to the economic dimension. Some of the issues raised will be examined in more detail in subsequent chapters. The aim at this stage is to provide an overview. Among other things, this will be helpful in placing subsequent chapters into a broader context.

Political-Strategic Dimensions

The first two of China's foreign policy objectives are clearly political-strategic in nature. The goals of achieving and maintaining major power status and upholding China's territorial integrity are central to the relationships and issues that engage China in the Asia Pacific region. Because China has concerns in all of its neighboring regions we will extend the definition of Asia Pacific to encompass not just Northeast and Southeast Asia, but also Central Asia and South Asia. We can see how the objectives of major power status and territorial integrity underlie China's relationships with the United States and Japan, but they are also pivotal in each of these four regions.

In terms of China's goal of major power status, the United States is the main state with which China must contend in Asia Pacific. The United States has alliance relationships with both Japan and South Korea, extending to the stationing of military forces in these countries. Although the United States gives diplomatic recognition to the PRC, it also has close political relations with Taiwan. In effect US support underpins the defense of Taiwan. Clearly US involvement in Northeast Asia limits Chinese influence. China has often regarded US regional involvement as amounting to "containment." On the other hand, one could argue that the US role in the region does not detract from China's major power status as such. While China does not dominate the region it exerts a strong influence. On some issues China's role is indispensable. It would be difficult to conceive of issues concerning North Korea being handled without significant Chinese involvement. On the issue of territorial integrity, China's main concern in relation to the United States involves the issue of Taiwan. From China's perspective Taiwan should be integrated into the PRC, and US policy is one of the main constraints limiting a more forceful Chinese policy.

Japan also acts as a constraint on the Chinese role in Northeast Asia. Despite China's strong economic growth, Japan remains much stronger as an economic power. Despite spending only about 1 percent of GDP on defense, Japan is also significant as a military power (see Chapter 4). Japan thus appears as a significant power China has to deal with in relation to Northeast Asian issues. Japan is not necessarily a rival, but could be in certain circumstances. China views the Japanese alliance with the United States as bolstering the US position in Asia Pacific, and thereby limiting Chinese influence. There is also the argument that the US-Japan alliance constrains Japan. The likelihood of Japan assuming a more nationalist orientation would be greater if the US-Japan alliance were not in place. A more nationalist Japan in turn would be more likely to see itself as a rival to China for influence in Northeast Asia and beyond than is currently the case. On the issue of territorial integrity, China is sensitive to the relationship Japan has with Taiwan. As with the United States, Japan recognizes the PRC but also has close unofficial political relations with Taiwan. China's attitude is also colored by the fact that Taiwan was under Japanese colonial rule from 1895 to 1945. Unlike the situation with Japanese colonial rule in Korea, the Taiwanese have a more positive memory of that period. A specific Sino-Japanese territorial dispute that should be noted concerns their competing claims to the Diaoyu or Senkaku Islands in the East China Sea.

While the United States and Japan are the major powers China has to contend with in Northeast Asia, there are also issues concerning Taiwan, Korea, and Russia that have a bearing on China's objectives of achieving and maintaining major power status, and protecting its territorial integrity. For China, Taiwan is most clearly an issue relating to territorial integrity. The loss of this province to Japan after the Sino-Japanese war in 1894–1895 was symptomatic of China's weakness during the imperialist era. This humiliation can only be overcome when the province is restored to China. At the same time this division of China undermines China's claim to major power status. A major power would be expected to exercise sovereignty over all territories regarded as properly its own.

In the case of Korea, issues of territorial sovereignty are not directly involved for China. At the same time the memory of how China felt threatened by US forces (under the auspices of the United Nations) when they took the conflict right to the Yalu River dividing northern Korea and Manchuria in 1950 remains an influence on Chinese perceptions of the peninsula's strategic significance. In general China views the Korean situation as one occurring within its own immediate region. As well as the strategic implications of proximity for China, there are also important economic interests involved. From the early 1990s South Korea has become an important economic partner for China in terms of trade and investment.

With North Korea, China is concerned that any collapse would lead to a great burden for China itself. China would be expected to contribute to economic recovery and could also have to provide for refugees. For these reasons China believes it should play a major role in dealing with the Korean issue. Major power status is involved but it is not status alone that determines how China develops its policy in relation to this issue.

Russia's position in Northeast Asia (and, before 1991, the position of the USSR) has also been a matter bearing on the pursuit of political-strategic objectives by China in Asia Pacific and beyond. Russia can have influence on a number of issues that are important to China in Northeast Asia, most notably Korea. Russian influence in Central Asia is relevant to the relationships that China has attempted to develop in that region since 1991. Russia's relationship with both Japan and the United States can either diminish or contribute to the power that China can exert in the area. If Russia is on good terms with both Japan and the United States, then that can be a constraining factor for China. In certain circumstances China might look to alignment with Russia as a means of bolstering its position in relation to Japan and the United States. Normally the situation is more fluid than this, but there is clearly a range of possibilities for China. Russia is also a very important consideration in terms of upholding China's goal of maintaining territorial integrity. Large areas of the Russian Far East and parts of Siberia were once part of China. While China does not aim to regain these territories, their loss is part of the Chinese historical memory. Mongolia, once part of China, became an independent state through the support of the USSR. Historically the antecedent states of post-1991 Russia have exerted influence in Manchuria and Xinjiang at various times. Russia has not supported separatism or a weakening of Chinese influence more recently, but the fact that Tsarist and Soviet governments did play such a role at various times colors the way China views contemporary Russia.

In Southeast Asia, China's concern is to exert an influence commensurate with the status of a major power. It is particularly interested in the northern tier countries of Indochina (Vietnam, Cambodia, Laos), Thailand, and Burma. China shares borders with Vietnam, Laos, and Burma. In the past China has seen developments in Indochina threatening its security. This was particularly the case in the first, second and third Indochina wars, covering the periods 1946–1954, early 1960s–1975, and 1978–1989 respectively. In the first war the threat came from France supported by the United States; in the second war the United States was the problem; in the third war China believed Vietnam's alignment with the USSR was contributing to Soviet encirclement of China. In the post–Cold War era China has attempted to ensure that none of the northern tier countries adopt policies detrimental to Chinese interests.

Another important issue for China in relation to Southeast Asia is the South China Sea. This is not strictly a matter of upholding China's territorial integrity. Rather, China believes that it has a claim to this area as "historic waters." China's claim (supported by Taiwan) brings it into conflict with a number of Southeast Asian states: Vietnam, the Philippines, Brunei, Malaysia, and Indonesia. While China believes it has strong grounds for its claim, its ability to maintain its position in the South China Sea is also a good test of its status as a major power.

In both the so-called northern tier and in maritime Southeast Asia, the position of the overseas Chinese is of concern to China. This group is a significant minority in virtually all of the countries of the region, and Singapore is overwhelmingly ethnic Chinese. China has to avoid policies and actions that give substance to allegations that overseas Chinese act as a "fifth column" within Southeast Asian countries. At the same time China wishes to ensure that these people are not victimized, as is sometimes the case. This issue could be seen as another test of China's status as a major power. Cultural affinity in this instance, however, could also be an influence in its own right on Chinese policy.

While South Asia and Central Asia are not normally considered part of Asia Pacific, it is helpful to examine their role in China's political-strategic policies. Both regions are very important in Chinese foreign policy. The policies China has pursued in relation to these regions also help to put China's Asia Pacific policies into a broader context. In the case of South Asia, this is again a region that borders China. China has seen India as a major rival. India also has aspirations to major power status and this in turn can limit China's influence in various ways. In terms of the regional balance within South Asia, China has generally given its support to Pakistan. At one level China's achievement of nuclear status was a way of enhancing its power in relation to India; India has now countered this by also becoming a nuclear power. It should be noted that China has border disputes with India, manifested most obviously in the 1962 Sino-Indian border war. China also sees India as giving succor to Tibetans who aspire to independence.

In the case of Central Asia there has been a significant change in China's approach since 1991. Before 1991 Central Asia was part of the USSR. After 1991 independent states emerged in this region: Uzbekistan, Kazakhstan, Tajikistan, Turkmenistan, and Kyrgyzstan. China shares borders with Kazakhstan, Tajikistan, and Kyrgyzstan, and has a short border with Afghanistan. At one level the weakening of Russian influence in this area provided more opportunities for Chinese influence and thus enhanced China's status as a major power. At another level the breakup of Soviet Central Asia meant there was more instability in the region. This was relevant to China's goal of upholding its territorial integrity. The part of

China that borders Central Asia is Xinjiang where there is a separatist movement based on the Uighurs. Turkic peoples, including Uighurs, are to be found on both sides of the border. East Turkestan is the preferred term for people claiming independence for Xinjiang. In the case of Afghanistan, China saw the pre-2001 Taliban regime as a source of support for separatists in Xinjiang. The fall of the Taliban was therefore in China's interests. However, the war against the Taliban also led the United States to establish bases in Uzbekistan (withdrawn in 2005), which added to Chinese fears of US containment, as well as complicating China's own involvement in Central Asia.

Economic Dimensions

When we turn to the economic dimension of China's involvement in Asia Pacific, there is some overlap with the relationships and issues that are important at a political-strategic level, but also some differences in emphasis. The United States and Japan are important to China not just because of their strategic role in Asia Pacific, but also because of their role as trading partners and sources of investment. In Northeast Asia China has also developed significant economic ties with both Taiwan and South Korea. Tables 3.1 and 3.2 indicate the general pattern concerning China's trade and sources of investment. The impact of these patterns on China's policy toward the United States, Japan, Taiwan, and South Korea merits comment.

The United States and Japan are clearly important to China's goal of maintaining economic growth. The United States is China's most important export destination, with items such as toys, sporting goods, and footwear being among the leading exports. These commodities take advantage of the ready availability of cheap labor in China. Low labor costs are also a factor making China attractive to US companies that invest in China. The trade balance being very much in China's favor attracts some negative attention in the United States. In 2004 US imports from China amounted to US$196.7 billion; US exports to China were worth US$34.7 billion.[28] From the US perspective China was its second most important source of imports, amounting to 13.4 percent of total imports in 2004.[29] While China is thus a significant source of US imports, the United States continues to have a range of sources. Apart from trade and investment, China's relationship with the United States has been important for Chinese participation in the major institutions of global economic governance. Chinese entry to the International Monetary Fund and the World Bank dates from the early 1980s; membership in the World Trade Organization was achieved in 2001. As the world's leading economic power, the United States plays a

Table 3.1   China's Principal Trade Relationships, 2004 (percentages)

Export Destinations		Import Sources	
United States	21.1	Japan	16.8
Hong Kong	17.0	Taiwan	11.5
Japan	12.4	South Korea	11.1
South Korea	4.7	United States	8.0
Germany	4.0	Germany	5.4

Source: Australian Department of Foreign Affairs and Trade, "China Fact Sheet," www .dfat.gov.au/geo/fs/chin.pdf, accessed 6 October 2005.

key role in all of these institutions, and hence the position adopted by the United States has major implications for China.

Japan also is very important for China's economic objectives. Japan is China's third most important export destination, and its single most important source of imports. The trade balance is in China's favor, but not to the same extent as between China and the United States. Even though China is Japan's second most important export destination (13.1 percent of exports in 2004), and its most important source of imports (20.7 percent in 2004),[30] Japan's trade remains diversified and it is by no means dependent on China. Japan is also a prominent source of foreign investment in China, with cheap labor again being a major attraction.

Apart from Japan, in Northeast Asia China's links with South Korea and Taiwan also contribute to the achievement of its economic objectives.

Table 3.2   Sources of Foreign Investment in China, January–September 2002

	Amount Contracted (US$ millions)	Percentage of Total
Hong Kong	20,950.1	30.0
Virgin Islands	10,187.5	14.6
United States	7,332.1	10.5
Taiwan	5,716.0	8.2
Japan	4,555.6	6.5
South Korea	4,035.4	5.8
Singapore	2,612.4	3.7
Cayman Islands	1,779.5	2.5
United Kingdom	879.2	1.3
Germany	690.8	1.0

Source: US-China Business Council, "Foreign Investment in China," www.uschina.org/ statistics/2003foreigninvestment.html, accessed 16 July 2006.

Hong Kong is another element in this situation, although since the "one country, two systems" settlement of 1997 it is part of the PRC rather than a foreign relations issue. As Tables 3.1 and 3.2 indicate, both South Korea and Taiwan are important trading partners and sources of investment for China. Taiwan ranks second for China's imports; South Korea is fourth for exports and third for imports. For both South Korea and Taiwan, China is significant as a trading partner without being dominant. In the case of South Korea, China took 19.6 percent of exports in 2004, and provided 13.2 percent of imports.[31] With Taiwan, China took 19.5 percent of exports in 2004, and provided 9.9 percent of imports.[32] Hong Kong's situation in relation to China is complex. While Hong Kong appears as the second most important export destination for China, many of these exports would then be transshipped. Similarly investment could be channeled through Hong Kong without necessarily originating there.

Maintaining and developing ties with its various economic partners facilitates China's ability to achieve its economic goals. If China sees an economic relationship as particularly important then that can have some impact in relation to the pursuit of political-strategic objectives. Economic links with the United States and Japan might lead to some modification in Chinese political-strategic policies toward those countries. On the other hand, if a political-strategic objective is assumed to be of fundamental importance in certain circumstances, then this can override whatever priority is placed on economic objectives. Economic ties with Taiwan are becoming increasingly important to China, but it is debatable whether or not these ties would lead to a modification in the Chinese goal of bringing about reunification.

▨ Notes

1. Recent books on China's foreign relations include Kornberg and Faust, *China in World Politics;* Deng and Wang, ed., *China Rising;* Sutter, *China's Rise in Asia;* Goldstein, *Rising to the Challenge;* Zhao, ed., *Chinese Foreign Policy.*
2. Chan, *Chinese Perspectives on International Relations,* p. 146.
3. Lin Piao, "Long Live the Victory of People's War!"
4. Roy, *China's Foreign Relations,* pp. 30–31.
5. See Zheng, *Discovering Chinese Nationalism in China,* pp. 114–122.
6. Quoted in Tow, *Asia-Pacific Strategic Relations,* p. 32.
7. See Terrill, *The New Chinese Empire.*
8. Nathan and Ross, *The Great Wall and the Empty Fortress,* p. 17. For post-2000 figures, see Australian Department of Foreign Affairs and Trade, "China Fact Sheet," www.dfat.gov.au/geo/fs/chin.pdf (accessed 6 October 2005).
9. See Shambaugh, ed., *Is China Unstable?*

10. Nathan and Ross, *The Great Wall and the Empty Fortress,* p. 17.

11. For brief assessments of the foreign policy making process in China, see Nathan and Ross, *The Great Wall and the Empty Fortress,* chapter 7; Roy, *China's Foreign Relations.* A useful text on Chinese politics is Saich, *Governance and Politics of China.*

12. Lam, "Hu Jintao's Move to Consolidate Power," p. 1.

13. See Shambaugh, *Modernizing China's Military,* p. 32.

14. Quansheng, "Domestic Factors of Chinese Foreign Policy."

15. Lampton, "China's Foreign and National Security Policy-Making Process," p. 4.

16. *The Military Balance 2005–2006,* p. 270.

17. *The Military Balance 2004–2005,* p. 355.

18. Shambaugh, *Modernizing China's Military,* p. 222.

19. Ibid., p. 223.

20. Ibid., pp. 69–93.

21. 1985 figures are from *The Military Balance 2002–2003;* other figures are from *The Military Balance 2005–2006.*

22. See Shambaugh, "A Matter of Time."

23. "China's Military Modernisation."

24. *The Military Balance 2005–2006,* p. 270.

25. Shambaugh, *Modernizing China's Military,* pp. 91–93.

26. Figures are from *The Military Balance 2005–2006.*

27. Australian Department of Foreign Affairs and Trade, "China Fact Sheet," www.dfat.gov.au/geo/fs/chin.pdf (accessed 6 October 2005).

28. International Trade Administration, US Department of Commerce, "Trade Stats Express—National Trade Data," http://tse.export.gov/NTDChart.aspx?Unique URL=2oa3bai50dlk5y5523dmet55-2005-10-6-8-22-11 (accessed 6 October 2005).

29. Australian Department of Foreign Affairs and Trade, "United States Fact Sheet," www.dfat.gov.au/geo/fs/us.pdf (accessed 6 October 2005).

30. Australian Department of Foreign Affairs and Trade, "Japan Fact Sheet," www.dfat.gov.au/geo/fs/jap.pdf (accessed 6 October 2005).

31. Australian Department of Foreign Affairs and Trade, "Republic of Korea Fact Sheet," www.dfat.gov.au/geo/fs/rkor.pdf (accessed 6 October 2005).

32. Australian Department of Foreign Affairs and Trade, "Taiwan Fact Sheet," www.dfat.gov.au/geo/fs/taiw.pdf (accessed 6 October 2005).

Japan | 4

A long with the United States and China, Japan also has the status of a major power in Asia Pacific. As with the previous two chapters, we focus in the first section on the factors that have influenced Japanese policies in Asia Pacific, with reference to Japan's historical experience, interpretation of its national interests, domestic politics, and the bases of Japan's power. The second section of the chapter provides an overview of Japan's policies in Asia Pacific, covering both political-strategic and economic aspects.

■ Factors Influencing Japan's Policies in Asia Pacific

Japan's Historical Experience

Japan has played a significant role in the history of Northeast Asia, but without having China's sense of itself as the center of a civilization. While Japan as a distinct polity can claim an existence dating back to at least the eighth century, its cultural roots in fact derive from China. From this starting point Japanese civilization developed its own characteristics in the succeeding centuries. However, Japan's geographical position as a group of islands some distance from the Asian mainland meant that China's influence was less there than in the case of Korea and Vietnam, which are territorially adjacent to China. Geography also enabled Japan to isolate itself from the rest of the world to a large extent periodically. Following the failure of an attempt at the end of the sixteenth century to invade Korea as a stepping-stone toward dominating China, Japan restricted contact with the external world. The Dutch and Chinese were allowed to trade from Dejima island, Nagasaki, and the Koreans through Tsushima.[1] From this time until 1868 Japan was under the rule of the Tokugawa shoguns or military leaders based at Edo (Tokyo); the emperor, who lacked political power, lived in Kyoto.

This system changed as the result of external pressure. In 1853 Commodore Matthew Perry of the US Navy appeared in Tokyo Bay with his squadron of black ships. Japan was compelled to end its isolation and open to trade with Western countries. Faced with the challenge of adjusting to this new situation, a group of samurai (warriors) overthrew the Tokugawa shogunate in 1868. Claiming to act in the name of the emperor, this development was known as the Meiji Restoration or Renewal. The emperor moved from Kyoto to Tokyo, and was used to give legitimacy to the changes that were effected by the group of oligarchs surrounding him. The thrust of the changes was to strengthen Japan so the country would not become subordinate to Western powers, as China had. Japan embarked on a course of rapid industrialization and the development of the infrastructure of a modern state. The economic resources necessary for these changes were developed from within. Japan attempted to learn from the Western countries without being dominated by them. At a political level the main model was Bismarck's Germany, as reflected in the Meiji Constitution of 1889. This constitution was based on the principle of executive dominance, with popular representation occurring through a parliament with limited powers. The emperor had not just a legitimizing role, but became a focus for national loyalty.[2]

By the late nineteenth century Japan was becoming a significant power in Northeast Asia. This was demonstrated most clearly in Japan's victory in the Sino-Japanese war of 1894–1895, when Taiwan became a Japanese colony. The world took even more notice when Japan defeated Russia in the Russo-Japanese war of 1904–1905. Korea became a Japanese protectorate (and then a colony in 1910), and Japanese influence in Manchuria expanded greatly. Clearly Japan was now competing strongly with the Western powers and was intent on asserting itself in relation to China. In 1902 Japan had allied itself with Britain, and entered World War I on that basis. Its hopes of making significant gains in China in the conflict's aftermath were not realized. In the 1930s, when military influence in Japan assumed new dimensions, Japan acquired Manchuria (1931) and then embarked on war in China (1937). Most significantly of all, Japan decided to launch preemptive war to overcome differences between itself and the United States in East Asia. Japan was intent on establishing a Greater East Asia Co-Prosperity Sphere, whereas the United States upheld an open-door policy. Japan attacked Pearl Harbor, Hawaii, on 7 December 1941.

The Pacific war, incorporating the previous Sino-Japanese conflict, became a major theater of World War II. At the height of the war Japan controlled Southeast Asia, eastern China, and much of the western Pacific. However, US military power eventually turned the tide, and Japan's fate was sealed with the dropping of atomic bombs on Hiroshima and Nagasaki in August 1945.

This second shock administered to Japan by the United States in 1945 had effects that were just as profound as the first one when Commodore Perry arrived on the scene in 1853. The US occupation of Japan, led by General Douglas MacArthur, lasted from 1945 to 1951. Initially the United States was intent on transforming the political system that had taken Japan into war. While the emperor remained, he became essentially a constitutional monarch rather than having a quasi-religious status. Democratization and demilitarization favored the forces on the left of Japanese politics. Under Article 9 of the Japanese Constitution, as enacted in 1947, the Japanese people renounced "war as a sovereign right of the nation and the threat or the use of force as means of settling disputes . . . land, sea, and air forces [would] never be maintained." In terms of foreign policy, it was envisaged that Japan would maintain neutral status as the "Switzerland of Asia." These emphases all changed with the onset of the Cold War, and particularly after the announcement of the containment doctrine by President Truman in March 1947. Henceforth the focus was on ensuring that Japan would be a US ally in the Cold War. Domestically this meant that there was less emphasis on promoting fundamental social, political, and economic changes. The forces on the right of Japanese politics were now favored. The new direction promoted by the United States was confirmed in 1951 with the conclusion of a relatively soft peace treaty with Japan and the simultaneous signing of the US-Japan Mutual Security Treaty. The latter treaty confirmed Japan's role as the major US base in the western Pacific. Japan provided a rear base for the United States during the Korean War (1950–1953), and was strategically well positioned in relation to both China and the USSR (the Soviet Far East), the major US rivals in Northeast Asia.

Under the 1951 settlement Japan became essentially a junior ally of the United States. In addition to providing base facilities for US forces, Japan developed its own Self-Defense Forces (SDF). Article 9 of the constitution was interpreted to allow Japan to develop forces for the defense of Japan itself. However, defense spending was limited to about 1 percent of GDP. Japan relied on the United States to provide a defense (including nuclear) umbrella. This arrangement also had the advantage that it allowed Japan to concentrate its resources on economic development. This general approach was termed the Yoshida Doctrine after Yoshida Shigeru, prime minister of Japan from 1946 to 1947 and from 1948 to 1954. It was reinforced by the consolidation of conservative groups into the Liberal Democratic Party (LDP) in 1955. The LDP was the basis of all governments up to 1993, after which it was out of office for about nine months, and then returned as the major group in a number of coalition governments.[3]

In 1960 Japan signed a revised version of the mutual security treaty with the United States. Although concessions were made to Japan, giving it equal status with the United States, the treaty was widely criticized, especially by the left wing, which resented Japan's continued role in the US Cold War strategy. Japan later gave passive support to the United States in the Vietnam War but did not become directly involved. The United States continued to occupy Okinawa during the war and made use of its facilities for long-range bombing missions in Vietnam. This, too, caused widespread criticism in Japan and reinforced the campaign for Okinawa to revert to Japanese sovereignty. The United States finally agreed to reversion in 1971.

By the 1970s, Japan's security environment was becoming more complex. Although the Sino-Soviet conflict continued as before, the hostility between China and the United States was replaced by the rapprochement of 1972. Japan had previously traded with China and now followed the United States in pursuing its own rapprochement with that country (Japan established diplomatic relations with the PRC in 1972). Japan's mutually hostile relationship with the USSR continued as before; a particular point of contention was the control of the Soviet-occupied Northern Territories (four islands immediately north of Hokkaido).

By this stage, too, Japan was emerging as one of the world's major economic powers. It has been calculated that, on the basis of purchasing power parity (PPP), Japan's per capita GNP rose from 56.2 percent of US per capita GNP in 1970, to 66.6 percent in 1980, and 73.1 percent in 1988.[4] Japan's industrial output was 29.3 percent that of the United States in 1975 and 31.9 percent in 1988.[5]

In the 1980s Japan was being increasingly pressured by the United States to assume a more significant defense role. Burden sharing was one way that Japan responded. Although the limit for defense spending had been set at 1 percent of GNP in 1976, this limit was removed in 1987.[6] Japan's economic growth meant that, even though defense spending remained at around 1 percent of GNP, the total Japanese defense budget was still quite large. According to NATO criteria, by 1988 Japan had the third highest defense budget in the world.[7] Prime Minister Suzuki Zenko stated in 1981 that Japan's SDF would undertake the protection of sea lanes up to one thousand nautical miles from Japan.

Japan's international role over the past 150 years has been largely the consequence of the external shocks of 1853 and 1945. In the first instance Japan modernized itself and attempted to compete with the Western powers at their own game. Although there was not necessarily a direct trajectory from the Meiji Restoration to the Pacific War of 1941–1945, the modernization undertaken did have a strongly authoritarian dimension and enhanced the role of the military. In post-1945 Japan the influence of the military was stripped away. While democratization was the goal of the United States, what emerged was "an amalgam of Occupation reformism and a kind of statist approach inherited from before the war."[8] What was clearly different about Japan at this stage was that its international role was subordinate to that of the United States. Within that framework, however, Japan has also focused on its own economic development and increasingly the articulation of a strategic role that puts more emphasis on its own distinctive interests.

Interpretation of Japan's National Interests

In Japan the impact of perceptions of national interests is reflected particularly in arguments about Japan's international role. In the post–Cold War era there have been significant debates and discussions about the continuing relevance of the Yoshida Doctrine. Three general positions can be discerned. A mainstream position supports the continuation of the Yoshida Doctrine, suitably modified to reflect more accurately changes in the international environment and Japan's position within that environment. From this perspective the alliance with the United States should remain central in Japanese foreign policy, although Japan should also be able to have more influence within that relationship. The nationalist right represents a second position. It wishes to see Japan behaving as a "normal state," including having the full range of defense forces. Some people associated with this position also support Japan's development of nuclear forces. Japan should become more independent of the United States, as reflected in the title of Shintaro Ishihara's book, *The Japan That Can Say No* (to the United States).[9] The pacifist left occupies a third position in this continuing debate. It is anti-US in the sense of generally being critical of the US role in the world and wanting to end the stationing of US forces on Japanese territory. Japan should not maintain defense forces and should contribute to international peace missions only at a nonmilitary level. The pacifist left strongly supports the retention of the existing Article 9 in the Japanese constitution.

While attitudes about the United States and Japan's defense clearly occupy a central place in the debate about Japan's international role, the different perspectives can also be discerned in relation to a number of other key issues.[10] These issues include attitudes toward the United Nations (UN), multilateralism, and Asia. Among the three perspectives there is general agreement that Japan should play a prominent role in the UN. But there are differences about what this should entail. One focus for discussion has been the proposal that Japan should become a permanent member of the UN Security Council. The foreign policy mainstream sees such a change as recognition of the place that Japan now occupies in world affairs. It would complement rather than contradict the security relationship with the United States. The nationalist right would also see such a change as a long overdue acknowledgment of Japan's place in the world. Supporters of this approach, however, generally see themselves as realists and do not give a high priority to international organizations as such, nor, by definition, do they place the same store in Japan's relationship with the United States. The pacifist left is also attracted to the proposal that Japan become a permanent member of the UN Security Council. Its reservations relate to a concern that holding such a position would put pressure on Japan to assume more international responsibilities, including military ones. Such a development would run counter to the strict constructionist interpretation of Article 9 of the constitution that is upheld by the pacifist left. Generally, however, the issue of expanding the permanent membership of the UN Security Council has been stalemated within the UN, most recently in the context of proposals for reform in 2005.

A particular issue relating to the UN concerns Japanese participation in peacekeeping operations. Irrespective of whether Japan is a permanent member of the UN Security Council, there has been pressure to take part in the peacekeeping operations that have burgeoned during the post–Cold War era. In terms of the three general perspectives, the mainstream position has favored some Japanese involvement in these operations. This is consistent with the belief that Japan should play a more prominent international role but should also strengthen its relationship with the United States. The nationalist right takes the position that Japan should behave as a "normal country" in relation to peacekeeping operations as with other international activities. However, also from their perspective, the focus of Japan's military forces should be on traditional defense rather than peacekeeping. The concern of the pacifist left is that Japan only makes nonmilitary contributions to UN peacekeeping. This is consistent with their view of Article 9.

In the late 1980s, Japan made significant financial contributions to a number of UN peacekeeping missions, including the Good Offices Mission in Afghanistan and Pakistan (UNGOMAP), the Iran-Iraq Military Observer Group (UNIIMOG), the Interim Force in Lebanon (UNIFIL), the Disengagement Observer Force between Syria and Israel (UNDOF), and the Transition Assistance Group in Namibia (UNTAG). Japanese noncombatant personnel participated in UNGOMAP, UNIIMOG, and UNTAG, as well as the UN Observer Mission in Nicaragua (ONUVEN) during the February 1990 elections.[11]

Japan came under pressure to contribute to the US-led coalition that acted under UN authority in the Gulf conflict of 1990–1991. On this occasion Japan's contribution was mainly financial, amounting to some US$13 billion overall, although in April 1991 (after hostilities had ceased) the Japanese government committed itself to sending six minesweepers to the Persian Gulf.[12] In the context of the Gulf conflict the Kaifu government introduced a peace cooperation bill in the Diet in August 1990 with a view to authorizing the involvement of the SDF in UN peacekeeping operations (PKOs) and in measures of "collective security" (as opposed to the "collective defense" barred by Article 9). Widespread opposition led to the bill's abandonment.[13] In June 1992 the upper house of the Diet approved the bill (officially titled the Law on Cooperation in UN Peacekeeping and Other Operations), which did allow the involvement of the SDF in peacekeeping operations but in heavily circumscribed conditions.[14] Following the passage of the PKO bill some six hundred members of the SDF undertook engineering duties with the UN Transitional Authority in Cambodia (UNTAC).[15] Subsequently SDF personnel took part in such operations as the UN Operation in Mozambique (ONUMOZ) from 1993 to 1995, the UN Disengagement Observer Force (UNDOF) in the Golan Heights from 1996, and the UN Mission in Kosovo (UNMIK) after 1999.[16] In May 2002 the Japanese government decided to send 690 SDF members to take part in the UN Mission of Support in East Timor (UNMISET).[17]

The Koizumi government introduced amendments to the Law on Cooperation in UN Peacekeeping and Other Operations, which were then enacted in December 2002. These provided for SDF participation in "core" peacekeeping activities, rather than being in a support role with the likelihood of involvement in conflict minimized.[18] Without specific UN authorization the SDF could not participate in the Iraq war in March–May 2003. The government did introduce legislation to enable the SDF to protect Japanese ships (mainly oil tankers) in the Persian Gulf, and to provide for SDF participation in the postconflict situation.[19]

While issues concerning the UN and peacekeeping have played an important part in the Japanese foreign policy debate in recent years, there has also been argument about how Japan should relate to multilateralism more generally. Japan has played a prominent role in the various institutions of global economic governance: the International Monetary Fund, the World Bank, and the World Trade Organization. It has also been involved in the G7 (G8 since Russia joined in 1998), the summit organization of leading economic powers. In the regional context Japan played an important role in the establishment of APEC in 1989. It was also a strong supporter of the ASEAN Regional Forum, a grouping for discussing regional security issues, which commenced in 1994. In the aftermath of the Asian economic crisis of 1997–1998 Japan has been involved in the meetings of ASEAN Plus Three (i.e., the ASEAN members plus China, Japan, and South Korea). Involvement in multilateralism is consistent with the three general perspectives on Japanese foreign policy. In terms of the mainstream approach multilateralism can complement a strong focus on the US relationship. It is also consistent with the argument that Japan should play a more significant international role. By placing Japan in a wider arena multilateralism can help in defusing tensions that might arise in US-focused bilateralism. Multilateralism can also enhance Japan's bargaining power in its relationship with the United States. These possibilities might appeal to the nationalist right, even though that group has a more traditional view of state behavior and does not particularly emphasize the role of international organizations. The pacifist left, although isolationist in some respects, is also attracted to the concept of Japan as a civilian power. Multilateral contexts can be useful as an arena for Japan to advance its international objectives.

Attitudes toward Asia provide another fulcrum for the different foreign policy perspectives that contend with each other in contemporary Japan. Although this might seem strange to people outside Japan, the Japanese do not necessarily think of themselves as Asian. From the time of the Meiji Restoration Japan aimed to compete with the Western powers and saw itself as distinct from the rest of Asia. Asia became an arena where Japan could assert its credentials as a great power. Although Japan no longer engages in military expansion, Asia is clearly important as a region where Japan can exert political influence and where it has important economic ties. From the perspective of the foreign policy mainstream, Japanese influence in Asia might be a means for enhancing the relationship with the United States. The idea of Japan as a bridge between the United States and Asia has some currency among adherents of this perspective. At the same time the mainstream perspective does not wish to present Japan as an "Asian power" intent on excluding the United States from Asian affairs. Among the nationalist right Asia is an important focus for the way they view Japan's role. The region is often seen as a source of threats, as the issue of North Korean nuclear weapons has made clear. The nationalist right views China as a potential rival. Japan's situation in the Asian region provides clear justification for Japanese rearmament. Attempts by China and both Koreas to portray such a development as presaging a revival of Japanese militarism are just a smokescreen to conceal their own interests. The pacifist left by definition is against Japanese rearmament, and portrays itself as sensitive to the views of Japan's neighbors. It is aware of the impact of past Japanese expansion in the region. By the same token the pacifist left is not necessarily Asianist. It is their underlying views on pacifism and antimilitarism that are foremost, rather than Japan's regional location.

The Impact of Domestic Politics

The debate about Japan's international role and its national interests takes place within the context of Japanese domestic politics. While the role that Japan assumes is strongly influenced by external factors, domestic politics is also a factor. Therefore it is useful to provide an overview of those factors in Japanese politics that bear most directly on foreign policy.[20] At a very broad level it is necessary to have some understanding of the underlying dynamics of Japanese politics. Then one can focus on more specific aspects, such as the role played by political parties and the bureaucracy, and influences that emanate from Japanese society.

The political system that prevailed in Japan from the mid-1950s through to 1993 is usually referred to as the "1955 system." The LDP was formed in 1955 and held government until 1993. Since Japan has a Westminster system this position was based on the LDP having clear majorities in the House of Representatives (lower house) of the Diet (parliament). Government worked through a tripartite system involving the LDP, the bureaucracy, and business interests. The policy momentum derived primarily from the bureaucracy, which in turn had close links to business. Politicians generally deferred to the bureaucracy in policy matters; they were mostly preoccupied with internal factional matters and the cultivation of support in their constituencies. In August 1993 the LDP lost office to an anti-LDP coalition, a situation that lasted until June 1994. Subsequently the LDP has been the largest party in a series of coalition governments. This new situation is far more fluid than was previously the case, and has been characterized as regime shift.[21] Glenn Hook and his colleagues argue that in these new circumstances a wider range of actors influences policymaking, and that a pluralistic and polyarchical model is more appropriate than focusing solely on the tripartite elite.[22]

Despite these changes political parties remain a crucial element of Japanese politics and thus crucial to understanding domestic influences on Japanese foreign policy. The LDP was the dominant party under the 1955 system and remains as the major party. It has a strong influence on the direction of policy and determines access to positions of power. Factions play an important role within the party as a means for allocating patronage. They are often associated with key political leaders. Another important organizational feature of the party is the *zoku* or "policy tribes." These are groupings of parliamentarians relating to particular areas of policy, including foreign policy. They can have a strong influence on the direction of policy, and are often linked to outside interests. In relation to foreign policy, the LDP has been identified with the mainstream position as previously outlined. The relationship with the United States has been central, but the LDP has also favored the development of a more significant international role for Japan. At times there can be intraparty conflict on foreign policy within the LDP; the competing arguments about the merits of the relationships with China and Taiwan provide a good example.

Alongside the LDP there has been a complex array of other parties. These parties are not necessarily distinct from the LDP in policy terms. In some cases they are, but quite often there is overlap between some non-LDP parties and the LDP, or at least sections of it. On the left of the political spectrum the main opposition to the LDP under the 1955 system came from the Japan Socialist Party (JSP). It articulated the pacifist left position in relation to foreign policy. A major change came when, following the collapse of the anti-LDP coalition government in June 1994 (in which the JSP had been a member), the JSP entered a coalition government with its old rival, the LDP. The JSP leader, Murayama Tomiichi, became prime minister. In relation to foreign policy the consequence of this change was that the JSP abandoned its pacifist left position in favor of the LDP's mainstream position. From 1996 (or 1991 with the English title) the JSP became known as the Social Democratic Party of Japan. The party split in 1996 with some elements joining the Democratic Party, which became the strongest left-center party. The Japan Communist Party (JCP) continued its adherence to the pacifist left position. However, with the abandonment of the JSP's earlier foreign policy stance and the general weakening of the party, it became easier for advocates of Japan as a "normal state" to advance their case.

While Japanese parties have not generally been strongly programmatic in orientation, one advocate of reorganization along such lines is Ozawa Ichiro. Ozawa's position can be characterized as center-right. In foreign policy he has been an active supporter of the argument that Japan should become a so-called normal state. Having been prominent in the LDP, including holding the position of secretary-general (1989–1991), Ozawa subsequently took a leading role in the formation of the non-LDP coalition government in 1993–1994. At a party level Ozawa has been the key figure in the Japan Renewal Party (1993–1994), the New Frontier Party (1994–1997), and the Liberal Party (1998–2003). The Liberal Party was the main alternative to the LDP on the right of Japanese politics, although the differences were not stark; the Liberal Party was in coalition with the LDP from January 1999 to April 2000. After leaving the coalition, the party continued alone before merging with the Democratic Party in October 2003.

A party of a different type is the Clean Government Party or Komeito, formed in 1964. It has close links with Soka Gakkai, a Buddhist organization. Although generally centrist in orientation, it has moved to the right in recent years. The more fluid political situation in Japan from the 1990s has given Komeito opportunities to enter coalition governments. In such circumstances it has generally supported mainstream foreign policy approaches, but some of its ideas are associated with the pacifist left; for example, it generally prefers nonmilitary approaches and multilateralism, including a focus on the United Nations.

Under the 1955 system the bureaucracy was generally the driving force for government policy, including foreign policy. As a measure of this situation, Japan has sometimes been characterized as a bureaucratic polity.[23] Since 1993 the bureaucracy has remained important, even though the policy process has become more complex. It remains important to consider the main sources of bureaucratic influence on Japanese foreign policy. Among the various government departments, the most significant are the Ministry of Foreign Affairs (MOFA), the Ministry of Finance (MOF), and the Ministry of International Trade and Industry (MITI). MITI was renamed the Ministry of Economy, Trade, and Industry (METI) in 2001. In addition the Japan Defense Agency (JDA), the Prime Minister's Office, and various other government departments also play some role in relation to foreign policy formulation.

The Ministry of Foreign Affairs is a significant influence on Japanese foreign policy but not a dominating one. The ministry is divided into various functional and regional bureaus, and also administers Japan's network of overseas embassies. In 2000 the functional bureaus were the Minister's Secretariat, the Foreign Policy Bureau, the Economics Bureau, the Economic Cooperation Bureau, the Treaties Bureau, and the International Information Bureau. The regional bureaus are the North American Affairs Bureau, the Asian Affairs Bureau, the Latin American and Caribbean Affairs Bureau, the Europe and Oceanic Affairs Bureau, and the Middle East and African Affairs Bureau.[24] A key bureau is the North American Affairs Bureau, which focuses on strengthening the bilateral relationship with the

United States. Tensions sometimes exist between this bureau and the Asian Affairs Bureau given that the focus of the latter is on promoting Japan's relations with the various countries of Asia.

Japan's role as an economic power, including its strong emphasis on economic diplomacy, helps to explain the influence of MOF and MITI/METI. In any government, the ministry concerned with the formulation of the budget and raising revenue exerts a strong influence in all areas of policy, including foreign policy. This is also the case in Japan. The Ministry of Finance has the reputation of being the most prestigious of the government departments. At a more specific level MOF has bureaus that deal with issues of international finance and international trade. MITI/METI, as its names suggest, has the role of promoting Japan's international trade while also developing industrial policy at home. In the latter respect it has the reputation for being interventionist and protectionist, an approach that has been buttressed by its close relations with business interests. MITI/METI is involved in international trade negotiations and in protecting and expanding markets for Japanese exports.

While MOFA, MOF, and MITI/METI are the main government departments involved in formulating Japanese foreign policy, other departments and agencies should also be mentioned. The expanding scope of foreign policy and the increasing interaction between the international and the domestic means that departments not normally associated with foreign policy matters are increasingly involved; examples include departments concerned with labor issues, education, agriculture, and telecommunications.[25] The expanding role of the Self Defense Forces has given the Japan Defense Agency a more prominent role in relation to security issues, but still not at the cabinet level. Finally, although the coordinating role of the Japanese prime minister is not necessarily a strong one, there is a small prime minister's office that assists in this task for both foreign policy and other policy areas.[26]

In assessing the impact of Japanese society on the country's foreign policy, there are clearly various elements to consider. These include pressure groups and social movements, the media, and public opinion.

In terms of the tripartite model used to characterize Japanese politics under the 1955 system, business interests had a significant influence on foreign policy as well as on other policy areas. Since the collapse of that system, business remains an important player but within a more complex situation. The most significant of the business organizations was the Federation of Economic Organizations (Keidanren), which represented big business and was closely linked to the LDP, even maintaining representatives in Japan's overseas embassies.[27] In 2002, the Keidanren merged with the Japan Federation of Employers' Associations, also an influential business group, to form the Japan Federation of Economic Organizations. Two other significant business organizations today are the Japan Committee for Economic Development and the Japan Chamber of Commerce.

Other economically based pressure groups that have influence on at least some aspects of foreign policy include agricultural organizations and labor unions. The most significant of the agricultural organizations is the Agricultural Cooperative Association (Nokyo), which has campaigned for agricultural protectionism. Since 1989 the major peak union body has been the Japanese Trade Union Council (Rengo). Previously there had been two main federations of unions, with the larger of the two, the General Council of Japanese Trade Unions (Sohyo), providing strong support for the Japan Socialist Party and its left pacifist ideology of foreign policy.

Pressure groups on the left of Japanese politics relate to various social movements concerned with the environment, human rights, and other issues that can have an international dimension. Peace movements have often been important in supporting left pacifist norms. Such movements might take the form of opposition to US bases or to the security alliance with the United States more generally, or they might focus on antinuclear goals.

Among Japan's media, there are five national newspapers with large readerships. The *Asahi Shimbun* and the *Mainichi Shimbun* are more to the left, whereas the *Yomiuri Shimbun,* the *Nihon Keizai Shimbun* (*Nikkei*), and the *Sankei Shimbun* are more to the right. These newspapers are also linked to television outlets and potentially have a significant influence. News management by government and other political organizations can limit this influence, as do some of the ways in which journalists practice their craft (through restrictive clubs, for example).

Public opinion as an influence on Japanese foreign policy covers the three broad approaches that were previously delineated. At the same time public opinion in Japan, as in other countries, is not necessarily well defined and is perhaps best characterized as a "mood." The way public opinion develops and expresses itself is subject to various influences, both international and domestic. It can be shaped by major international developments and the key relationships in which Japan is involved. At the same time the various dimensions of Japanese politics that have been outlined can both influence and be influenced by public opinion. There is not a direct transmission belt in either direction. Nevertheless the interaction between the various elements affecting Japanese foreign policy is having an impact on Japanese public opinion. The left pacifist position is still important but perhaps less so than was previously the case. The mainstream approach is being broadened to accommodate some emphases associated with the "Japan as a normal state" position. However, these changes do not go as far as the nationalist right would prefer.

Japan's Power

Whatever the foreign policies espoused by Japan either in relation to specific issues or at a more general level, its ability to achieve its objectives is determined by the power resources it has available. At one level evaluating Japan's power requires a comparison between its power resources and those available to other states involved in issues affecting Japan. This task will be undertaken at a general level in the next section, which provides an overview of Japan's policies in Asia Pacific, and also in the specific chapters on US-Japan and China-Japan relations. Here the focus is on assessing Japan's power in more absolute terms, with reference to military, economic, and qualitative dimensions. One issue here is that Japan, because of its recent history, does not necessarily meet the definition of a normal state. There has been less emphasis on military power than with most states, and a widely supported argument that Japan should see itself as a civilian power.

In assessing Japan's military power it is important to keep in mind the restraints deriving from the wide acceptance of antimilitarist norms in Japanese society. While the data suggest that Japan is a formidable military power, the antimilitarist norms limit what Japan can do with that power. This explains the observation, reported by J. A. A. Stockwin, that Japan has "punched below its weight" in international affairs (unlike the United Kingdom, which is sometimes characterized as "punching above its weight").[28] On the basis of international comparisons of defense spending, Japan ranked fifth in 2003 (after the United States, Russia, China, and France).[29] The defense budget in 2005 amounted to US$44.7 billion.[30] The proportion of GDP spent on defense has been about 1 percent throughout this period. However, Japan does not count spending on pensions for retired military personnel as part of this figure, and it also contributes large sums to support US forces stationed at Japanese bases (42,700 people in 2005). The Self-Defense Forces numbered some 239,900 in 2005, with about 148,200 in the Ground Self-Defense Force, about 44,400 in the Maritime Self-Defense Force, and up to 45,600 in the Air Self-Defense Force. Major items of equipment included about 980 main battle tanks, about 90 attack helicopters, 16 submarines, 44 destroyers, 9 frigates, and 300 combat aircraft.[31] These forces lacked combat experience, although (as previously discussed) there had been some peacekeeping deployments under restricted conditions from 1992.

Nuclear issues have been an increasing concern for Japan. With both the USSR (and subsequently Russia) and China nuclear-armed, Japan has relied on the US nuclear umbrella for protection against nuclear threats. Since the early 1990s this issue has attracted increased attention because of the possibility of North Korea acquiring nuclear weapons. While Japan's advanced technology would enable it to acquire nuclear weapons if it so chose, the strength of pacifist ideology deriving particularly from the experiences of Hiroshima and Nagasaki makes this a difficult option. Nevertheless, there have been voices on the right of Japanese politics calling for Japan to exercise the nuclear option. In the context of the North Korean nuclear weapons crisis, Ishiba Shigeru, the head of the Japan Defense Agency, said that Japan could launch a preemptive strike against North Korea. Although he subsequently retracted this statement, the fact that he said it in the first place is a measure of the shift in opinion in Japan.[32] Concerns arising from a perceived North Korean nuclear threat have also strengthened support for Japan to develop theater missile defense in collaboration with the United States. In August 2003 the Japan Defense Agency said it planned to have an operational TMD by 2007.[33]

These developments concerning TMD suggest that circumstances in Japan's immediate region are leading to some rethinking about the role of military power as part of Japan's overall strategy. For the most part, however, despite the fact that Japan does have quite large defense forces, it does not place a high priority on the role of military power as a vehicle for exerting influence. The concept of comprehensive security as put forward in a 1978 report from the National Institute for Research Advancement (NIRA) and the Nomura Research Institute, and then endorsed by a prime ministerial task force in 1980, has had some influence in succeeding years.[34] According to this concept Japan should see security in terms of political, economic, and military dimensions, and should develop a multifaceted strategy accordingly. The military aspect was just one part of security. In terms of this aspect Japan should focus on burden sharing and peacekeeping as the ways it could contribute most effectively to both the Western alliance and the international community more generally.

Despite its large military forces, it is in the economic realm that Japan has been best placed to exert influence. Key statistics indicate that Japan is among the world's leading economic powers. One can see how Japan uses its economic position to exert influence. In 2004 Japan's GDP was US$4.66 trillion, with a per capita income of US$36,598. This compared with figures for the United States of US$11.7 trillion for GDP and per capita income of US$40,047.[35] In terms of individual countries Japan was second only to the United States for GDP and accounted for about 10 or 11 percent of world product. Japan occupies a significant place in world trade, with exports of US$538.8 billion and imports of US$401.8 billion in 2004. In 2004 the major destinations for Japan's exports were the United States (22.7 percent), China (13.1 percent), South Korea (7.8 percent), Taiwan (7.4 percent), and Hong Kong (6.3 percent). For imports the major sources in 2004 were China

(20.7 percent), the United States (14.0 percent), South Korea (4.9 percent), Australia (4.3 percent), Indonesia (4.1 percent), Saudi Arabia (4.1 percent), and the United Arab Emirates (4.0 percent).[36] Japan also plays a leading role in foreign investment. For the period 1990–2003 the net outflow of foreign investment from Japan stood at US$325.2 billion. This put Japan third among the OECD (Organisation for Economic Cooperation and Development) countries (the United States was seventh); Japan contributed about one-third of the OECD's total net outflow.[37] Among OECD countries Japan is second only to the United States in terms of the total amount of foreign aid it provides.[38] Although Japan has experienced economic difficulties from the 1990s, with negative growth rates, this situation has not affected Japan's position as one of the world's leading economic powers.

A significant question is how Japan uses its economic strength to exert influence. This issue can be considered both at the level of Japan's bilateral relations and in the context of multilateral relationships, including global economic institutions. Many countries wish to foster trade with Japan as a means of developing their own economies. This in turn gives Japan bargaining power in relation to those countries, particularly when there is competition over acting as supplier for particular commodities. This bargaining power is generally confined to the economic relationship as such but can affect the relationship's overall dynamics. The same situation applies when one considers Japan's role as a major source of foreign investment. Japan's ability to invest is not necessarily used as a bargaining tool in the general relationship, but can affect how Japan and the recipient country interact. On the issue of foreign aid, Japan at one level has been intent on protecting the interests of Japanese companies providing relevant services. At another level there has been an assumption that foreign aid promotes economic development and will in turn lead to political stability, which is in Japan's economic and political interests.

As a major economic player Japan has also been involved in the key international economic institutions. This began with Japanese entry to the World Bank and the International Monetary Fund in 1952. In 1955 it was admitted to the General Agreement on Tariffs and Trade (GATT), and then to the World Trade Organization in 1995. In 1964 Japan joined the OECD. It was a founding member of the G7 in 1975. In the World Bank and the IMF there has been a lag between Japan's financial contribution and its voting power. The most recent allocation of voting rights (2005) gave Japan 7.86 percent in the World Bank (also known as the International Bank for Reconstruction and Development, or IBRD) and 6.13 percent in the IMF (compared with the United States at 16.39 percent and 17.08 percent respectively). Japan has been disadvantaged by not being a founding member of these organizations. Nevertheless Japan has attempted to provide some economic leadership on issues relating to the Asian region. Although the Asian Development Bank (ADB) derived from a US initiative, Japan has played a leading role in it since its establishment in 1966; the president of the ADB has always come from Japan. Japan saw the ADB as complementing the role of the World Bank in Asia. Japan was also a key country in the foundation of APEC as a GATT-compatible regional economic grouping in 1989. In 1997 Japan proposed an Asian Monetary Fund (AMF) as a means of responding to the Asian economic crisis, which emerged in that year. The United States, however, saw the AMF as undermining the position of the IMF and the Japanese initiative was stillborn. In the G7/G8 Japan has pursued a course of quiet diplomacy. It contributed significantly to the plan for relieving the Latin American debt crisis in 1988–1989.[39] In the G7/G8 context Japan has seen itself as contributing an East Asian voice. It was critical of the plan to admit Russia while not doing likewise for China. Within the WTO Japan has attempted to provide regional leadership, although there can be differences among East Asian states on various issues; on some issues, Japan is more aligned with the United States and the European Union. Japan has a protectionist attitude toward agriculture and an interventionist industry policy, while also subscribing to the goals of liberalizing trade on a more general level.

The qualitative dimension of power covers such issues as the contribution made by the Japanese political system and leadership to Japan's influence in the world. The concept of soft power as developed by Joseph Nye in relation to the United States is also applicable to other countries.[40] In the Japanese case it involves asking whether Japan has influence because other countries might see it as a model in some respects or be attracted by Japanese culture. On the issue of the political system and leadership, it could be argued that these factors have been crucial in the "economic miracle" that has underpinned Japan's recent and current role in the world. The close relationship between the state and industry was very important in securing Japan's economic growth. The Yoshida Doctrine derived from the leadership of the prime minister of the same name and depended on the willingness of the United States to underwrite Japanese security. The tripartite model and its aftermath have also been characterized as "immobilist." This system was successful in facilitating Japanese development, but Japanese leaders at times found it difficult to bring about significant change even when there were strong arguments for doing so (for example, in the context of Japan's more recent sluggish economic performance).

In the regional context Japan has provided a model for other countries in East Asia to follow, without that influence necessarily being acknowledgcd explicitly. (One might speculate, however, about that influence declining in the light of Japan's more recent economic problems.) The interventionist role of the state in encouraging economic development has been important in a number of countries, including both Taiwan and South Korea. It has also been important in a number of Southeast Asian countries, as well as post-Maoist China. Japan has been active in promoting its own culture and particularly the teaching of Japanese language through bodies such as the Japan Foundation. Japan is relatively generous in the support it gives to teaching and research concerning Japan in other countries. The main focus for its cultural diplomacy is East Asia, the United States, and Australasia, although some attention is also given to Europe.[41] This is not to say that Japan's soft power through cultural influence is anywhere near comparable to that exerted by the United States. In addition, there is strong resistance to Japanese cultural influence in countries such as China and South Korea because of wartime and colonial experiences.

■ An Overview of Japan's Policies in Asia Pacific

Having examined some of the key factors influencing Japan's policies in Asia Pacific, this chapter turns next to the policies themselves. The aim is to provide an overview of the direction taken by Japanese policies in the region in the post–Cold War period, with particular reference to political-strategic and economic aspects. The emphasis is on the regionwide dimension. Subsequent chapters deal in particular with US-Japan and China-Japan relations. Japanese policies are also considered in the chapters on Korea, Southeast Asia, and Russia and Australia. The major questions concern the nature of Japan's objectives and the means used to advance them. As previously discussed, Japan has a number of power assets available. However, there are constraints on Japan's ability to use its military power. It has more scope in terms of its economic power and soft power. Japan has generally adopted a low profile approach in attempting to realize its objectives. This does not mean that Japan is not prepared to exercise leadership, but its means of doing so emphasize quiet diplomacy.[42] While the relationship with the United States remains central to Japanese policies in the region, Japan also pursues its own policies with the states of the region and has been increasingly involved in the development of multilateral approaches.

Political-Strategic Dimensions

In terms of the political-strategic dimension, Japan's objectives in Asia Pacific focus on the maintenance of a secure environment where its independence can be assured and its economy protected.[43] In the past it has been concerned that communist powers such as China and the USSR should not become dominant. It still has concerns about China in that respect. Conflicts such as those relating to Korea and Taiwan should be contained so that they do not threaten the stability of the region and Japan's position in it. Japan also regards stability in Southeast Asia as an important objective in the Asia Pacific region. Although Japan is less important than Northeast Asia, it has significant economic links with Southeast Asia. Conflicts in Southeast Asia can have a destabilizing effect on Asia Pacific more generally.

Although Japan has substantial military forces, its ability to use those forces in the context of its overall diplomacy is constrained by Article 9 of the constitution. In pursuing its political-strategic objectives in Asia Pacific, Japan relies mainly on diplomatic means. Diplomacy strengthens Japan's role as the major economic power of the region. At a broad political-strategic level Japan's approach is also underpinned by the security relationship with the United States. Although there can be differences of emphasis, in most cases the objectives Japan has in Asia Pacific complement those of the United States. Where a military component is required in the pursuit of objectives shared by the two countries, it is the military forces of the United States that will be most relevant, with Japan playing a supporting diplomatic role. Even a minor Japanese military role in these circumstances would be contentious.

Although these issues will be taken up in more detail in later chapters it is relevant at this point to outline the general direction of Japan's political-strategic policies in relation to both Northeast Asia and Southeast Asia. In Northeast Asia Japan's major concern is China. Japan is opposed to Chinese domination of the region, while at the same time seeking a cooperative relationship with China. The alignment with the United States provides the major backing for the policy Japan pursues in this respect. Japan also generally supports the status quo in relation to the Taiwan issue. Although Japan has substantial economic links with Taiwan, it has diplomatic relations with China and opposes any Taiwanese declaration of independence. While mostly siding with the United States on issues concerning China, Japan also tends to be more cautious on the whole.

Issues concerning Korea are also very prominent in Japan's political-strategic policies in Northeast Asia. There are tensions with both Koreas deriving from the period when the peninsula was under Japanese colonial rule (1910–1945). Nevertheless Japan generally aligns with South Korea and supports US policy concerning the Korean conflict (although with differences of emphasis from time to time, the George W. Bush period being a good example). Japan sees the acquisition of nuclear weapons by North

Korea as a threatening development, and supports multilateral attempts to deal with this issue.

In the case of Japanese policy toward Russia, there is a history of antagonism going back to Tsarist times that is perhaps best signified in the Russo-Japanese war of 1904–1905. During the Cold War Japan saw the USSR as a major threat in Northeast Asia. A particular point of contention was the Soviet occupation of four small islands north of Hokkaido from 1945. Japan wants the return of these islands, which it terms the Northern Territories. In the post–Cold War era post–Soviet Russia is not a major threat to Japan but the territorial issue remains. Any general improvement in relations has been hostage to this issue, although the Japanese do not feel a close affinity to Russia.

In Southeast Asia historical memories relating to World War II in particular have been obstacles to Japan pursuing a more active diplomacy, although not to the same extent as with China and Korea. Japan's political and economic interests have focused for some decades on the original ASEAN countries (Indonesia, Malaysia, the Philippines, Singapore, Thailand). It has not taken a prominent role in relation to major issues concerning these countries but has used quiet diplomacy to strengthen its links. More recently Japan has played a role in relation to the countries of Indochina and Burma (which became members of ASEAN between 1995 and 1999). Japan contributed peacekeeping forces in Cambodia in 1992–1993. With both the Indochinese countries and Burma, Japan has argued that measures to strengthen their economies will bring stability and create conditions where there is more hope of democratic institutions developing. This policy has been controversial given that Western countries have been critical of governments in the region that have violated human rights, Burma being the most notable example. However, Japan's approach to this issue is in accord with the ASEAN strategy of engagement.

An interesting development in the post–Cold War era concerns how Japan has broadened its approach to political-strategic issues in Asia Pacific to include more scope for multilateralism. This does not mean that Japan is reducing its emphasis on either its US relationship or its various bilateral relationships in Northeast and Southeast Asia. The multilateral context, however, does provide another dimension for Japan to pursue its political-strategic objectives. The relationship with ASEAN as a group goes back at least as far as 1976 when Japan became a dialogue partner. Japan was involved in the establishment of APEC in 1989, and has supported the greater political role for the organization that has developed since the institution of summit meetings for heads of government in 1993. Japan also played a leading role in the establishment of the ASEAN Regional Forum for discussing Asia Pacific security issues in 1994. A Japanese proposal in 1991 was an important development in the events leading up to the formation of this group. Japan has also supported initiatives for dealing multilaterally with Korean issues, although nothing has been established at a formal level. Following the Asian economic crisis of 1997, Japan has taken part in the ASEAN Plus Three, which has provided a focus for dealing with both political and economic issues within an East Asian framework. It has played a leading role in the development of the East Asian Summit that was established in 2005.

Economic Dimensions

While Japan failed in its attempt to establish a Greater East Asia Co-prosperity Sphere in the early 1940s, it clearly occupies a leading role in Asia Pacific economic affairs today. The United States is also important as an economic power in the region, and China is an emerging economic power. Here the aim is to indicate the extent of Japanese economic involvement, and then to discuss the ways in which Japan pursues its economic objectives. As compared with security issues, Japan is much more prepared to act independently of the United States in the economic realm. Because of its economic strength Japan has considerable bargaining power with the United States; at the same time the United States is even stronger economically and can sometimes compel Japan to modify its policies.

Japan's economic involvement in Asia Pacific can be assessed in terms of trade, investment, and aid. (See Table 4.1.)

There is a triangular pattern of trade involving Japan, East Asia, and the United States. Japan exports technologically advanced goods to East Asian countries. These countries in turn export some manufactured goods to Japan but mainly to the United States. Japan has a large trade surplus in relation to the East Asian countries. These countries have a surplus in relation to the United States. Japan also has a surplus in relation to the United States (see Table 4.1).[44]

In the late 1990s about 40 percent of Japanese investment was going to the United States, about 20 percent to East Asia, and about 20 percent to the European Union.[45] In the case of the United States, Japanese investment was a way of circumventing restrictions designed to reduce Japanese imports. In East Asia Japanese investment was related to a strategy for exporting the Japanese development model. Increasingly the Japanese economy became more focused on high-level technology, with industries using lower-level technology and reliant on cheaper labor located elsewhere in the region. This process of exporting industries originally based in Japan

Table 4.1   Japanese Trade, Total Exports and Imports, 2004 (percentages)

	Exports	Imports
United States	22.5	13.7
China	13.1	20.7
Hong Kong	6.3	0.4
Taiwan	7.4	3.7
South Korea	7.8	4.8
Singapore	3.2	1.4
Thailand	3.6	3.1
Malaysia	2.2	3.1
Indonesia	1.6	4.1
Philippines	1.7	1.8
Australia	2.1	4.3
East Asia	46.9	43.1
ASEAN	12.9	14.8
ASEAN-4	9.1	12.1
Asian NIEs	24.7	10.3

Source: Japan External Trade Organization, Economic Research Department, "Japanese Trade in 2004," Appendix 1, Foreign Trade by Country and Region, www.jetro.go.jp/en/stats/statistics, accessed 16 September 2005.

Notes: ASEAN-4: Thailand, Malaysia, Indonesia, Philippines.

Asian NIEs (newly industrializing economies): Hong Kong, Taiwan, South Korea, Singapore.

involved a hierarchy with the newly industrializing economies (NIEs) (South Korea, Taiwan, Hong Kong, Singapore) at one level, followed by the ASEAN-4 (Indonesia, Malaysia, the Philippines, Thailand) at the next level, and then China at the bottom level. Labor is cheapest and the level of technology lowest at the bottom level. This pattern has been described as a "regional production alliance."[46] Another term used is "flying geese" formation where Japan is always the leading goose in terms of economic development and the other levels in the hierarchy follow behind. (See Table 4.2.)

Japanese foreign aid is directed primarily toward East Asia. It complements the pattern of Japanese trade and investment in the region and supports Japanese political and economic objectives. Japan sees its aid as facilitating economic development and leading to political stability. Much of the aid pays Japanese companies with the aim of providing a stimulus for the Japanese economy (see Table 4.3).

This material indicates that Japan's economic involvement in Asia Pacific, and in East Asia in particular, is quite extensive. Japan's objectives have been to maintain and develop that involvement with a view to sustaining its own economic well-being. These objectives are pursued at one

**Table 4.2   Japanese Foreign Investment, Major Destinations, 2004
(US$ millions)**

Netherlands	8,058
United States	4,677
China	4,567
Cayman Islands	3,947
Australia	1,845
United Kingdom	1,789
Panama	1,282
Thailand	1,184
Asian NIEs	2,678
ASEAN-4	1,938
ASEAN-5	2,652
East Asia	9,291

Source: Japan External Trade Organization, *Current Japanese Economy and Trade Statistics,* "Japan's Outward FDI by Country/Region," www.jetro.go.jp/en/stats/statistics, accessed 16 September 2005.
Notes: ASEAN-4: Thailand, Malaysia, Indonesia, Philippines.
ASEAN-5: ASEAN 4 plus Singapore.
Asian NIEs (newly industrializing economies): Hong Kong, Taiwan, South Korea, Singapore.

level through the activities of Japanese companies and Japanese-based transnational corporations. At another level the Japanese government is heavily involved in such matters as negotiating trade agreements and creating the conditions for encouraging foreign investment. The role of MITI (now METI) has been very significant in formulating Japan's international trade strategy.

Table 4.3   Japanese Foreign Aid, Top Ten Recipients, 2003 (US$ millions)

China	1,297
Indonesia	891
Philippines	810
India	768
Thailand	651
Vietnam	452
Pakistan	284
Bangladesh	262
Sri Lanka	249
Malaysia	187
Total official aid	8,880

Source: Organisation for Economic Cooperation and Development, "Japan's Aid at a Glance," www.oecd.org/dataoecd/42/5/1860382.gif, accessed 16 September 2005.

Multilateralism has been an important aspect of Japanese involvement in economic issues in Asia Pacific. As mentioned earlier, the Asian Development Bank was an early example of Japan's commitment to supporting economic development in the region through multilateral assistance. Japan's links with ASEAN provided support for the furthering of Japanese economic goals in relation to Southeast Asia. From 1989 APEC has been important to Japan for encouraging trade liberalization that will benefit the Japanese economy. While some aspects of the Japanese development model have been criticized as causes of the Asian economic crisis of 1997 (for example "crony capitalism" arising from too cozy a relationship between the state and private enterprises), Japan also contributed significantly to attempts to ease the crisis. It was a leading contributor to the rescue packages mounted under the auspices of the IMF and also proposed a regionally focused Asian Monetary Fund. The latter would have been more sensitive to political conditions in the affected countries in Asia than the IMF, which was under the influence of neoliberalism. The fact that the AMF proposal was abandoned because of US pressure was indicative of the relative bargaining power of the United States and Japan at the time. China's opposition, motivated by a desire to protect its own currency as well as concerns about Japan's leading role, was also a factor.[47] The emergence of ASEAN Plus Three and the proposed East Asian Community, with Japan playing a prominent role, could be seen as an attempt by all of the countries involved to strengthen their ability to deal with regional problems.

While the political-strategic and economic aspects of Japanese involvement in Asia Pacific can be seen as complementary, there are also important differences between the two. Since the time of the enunciation of the Yoshida Doctrine in the 1950s, Japan has given primacy to the economic dimension. It has worked in conjunction with the United States in this sphere but has also pursued its own independent policies. In the security sphere Japan has maintained a lower profile, one subordinate to the United States. Increasingly it has become more independent in relation to security matters but the US relationship remains a primary focus. A significant issue here is that Japan is constrained from using its military power to support its objectives in the way that other states do. In the economic realm the military dimension is less significant and Japan's status as a civilian power carries more weight.

▪ Notes

1. Hook et al., *Japan's International Relations,* p. 27.
2. Stockwin, *Dictionary of the Modern Politics of Japan,* p. xv.

3. Ibid., p. xix.

4. Shinohara, "Japan as a World Economic Power," p. 18.

5. Ibid.

6. Drifte, *Japan's Foreign Policy,* p. 34.

7. Ibid., p. 35.

8. Stockwin, *Dictionary of the Modern Politics of Japan,* p. 246.

9. Shintaro Ishihara, *The Japan That Can Say No.*

10. See Green, *Japan's Reluctant Realism,* chapter 1; Klien, *Rethinking Japan's Identity and International Role,* chapter 4.

11. Akaha, "Japan's Comprehensive Security Policy," p. 329.

12. Malik, *The Gulf War,* pp. 81, 84, 86.

13. Ibid., pp. 82–83.

14. Gordon, "Japan," p. 60; Hook et al., *Japan's International Relations,* p. 324.

15. Ibid., pp. 325–326.

16. Ibid., p. 326.

17. *Strategic Survey 2002–2003,* p. 256.

18. *East Asian Strategic Review 2002,* p. 326.

19. *Strategic Survey 2002–2003,* pp. 256–257.

20. For more detailed but still concise treatments, see Green, *Japan's Reluctant Realism,* chapter 2; Hook et al., *Japan's International Relations,* pp. 40–65. A useful text on Japanese politics is Stockwin, *Governing Japan.*

21. Green, *Japan's Reluctant Realism,* pp. 41–44.

22. Hook et al., *Japan's International Relations,* p. 42.

23. See Stockwin, *Governing Japan,* chapter 7.

24. Stockwin, *Dictionary of the Modern Politics of Japan,* p. 166.

25. Hook et al., *Japan's International Relations,* p. 48.

26. Ibid., p. 49.

27. Stockwin, *Dictionary of the Modern Politics of Japan,* p. 95.

28. Ibid., p. 96.

29. Based on 2003 figures as reported in Table 38, "International Comparisons of Defence Expenditure and Military Manpower, 2001–2003," in International Institute for Strategic Studies, *The Military Balance 2003–2004,* pp. 353–358.

30. *The Military Balance 2005–2006,* p. 279.

31. Ibid., pp. 279–282.

32. *Strategic Survey 2003–2004,* p. 272.

33. "Japan's Push for Missile Defence."

34. Akaha, "Japan's Comprehensive Security Policy," pp. 324–325. See also Tetsuya, "Comprehensive Security and the Evolution of the Japanese Security Posture"; Tow, *Asia-Pacific Strategic Relations,* pp. 47–48; Chapman et al., *Japan's Quest for Comprehensive Security.*

35. *The Military Balance 2005–2006,* pp. 20, 279.

36. The figures for exports and imports are from the US Central Intelligence Agency, *The World Factbook,* "Japan," www.odci.gov/cia/publications/factbook/print/ja.html (accessed 15 September 2005).

37. Organisation for Economic Cooperation and Development, "OECD Statistical Profile of Japan—2005," http://stats.oecd.org/wbos/viewhtml.aspx?QueryName=14&QueryType=View&Lang=en (accessed 15 September 2005).

38. See Organisation for Economic Cooperation and Development, "Aid from DAC Members—Statistics," www.oecd.org/statisticsdata/0,2643,en_2649_34485_1_119656_1_1_1,00.html (accessed, 15 September 2005).

39. Green, *Japan's Reluctant Realism,* pp. 234–236.

40. Nye, *Soft Power.*

41. On Japanese cultural diplomacy, see Drifte, *Japan's Foreign Policy in the 1990s,* pp. 145–151, 158–160.

42. On Japanese leadership in the region, see Rix, "Japan and the Region."

43. A comprehensive recent study of Japan's security policy is Hughes, *Japan's Security Agenda.*

44. See Hook et al., *Japan's International Relations,* pp. 196–198.

45. See ibid., table 2, pp. 450–457.

46. Hatch and Yamamura, *Asia in Japan's Embrace.*

47. Green, *Japan's Reluctant Realism,* p. 248.

The Japanese-US Relationship | 5

This chapter is the first of three chapters that examine major power relationships in Asia Pacific: Japan-US, China-US, China-Japan. These relationships are the most significant dimension of the international architecture of Asia Pacific, and particularly so in Northeast Asia. Each chapter provides an overview of developments in the postwar context before presenting a more detailed assessment of the key strategic and economic issues in the particular relationship. We begin with the Japan-US relationship, which has been central to US engagement in Asia Pacific throughout the entire post-1945 period.

Certain general differences between Japan and the United States are worth noting as part of the context in which the relationship has developed. Geographically the United States is a large, continental country, sharing borders only with Canada and Mexico. Japan, on the other hand, is a small, island country. It has no land borders but is in a turbulent part of the world and close to major powers such as China and Russia (although Russia is less significant than was the USSR). The United States is predominantly an immigrant and multicultural society. Blacks and Hispanics are the most significant minorities. As an independent state the United States has a history of over two hundred years; including the colonial era there is a history of about four hundred years. Japan is a much more homogeneous society, but with a history going back to the first millennium. The United States is a more individualistic and mobile society. Japan is more hierarchical and ordered. The United States has been the major influence on Japan since 1945 but clearly there is plenty of scope for tensions between the two. Japan is protective toward its social arrangements and more limited in its geopolitical outlook. The United States believes that its open, democratic society should be a model for others to follow. Although it has a particular interest in certain areas of the world (Northeast Asia is one), its geopolitical outlook is global in scope. Japan-US tensions often derive from an attempt on Japan's part to protect its own society and to play a more limited international role than the United States would like. Despite their differences of emphasis, both Japan and the United States see themselves as upholding liberal democracy and economic capitalism. Japan has supported the international role of the United States, although not always to the extent that the United States would like.

▧ The Postwar Context

As a consequence of US occupation immediately after World War II, Japan came to assume an important role in the strategy of containment, serving as the linchpin for US efforts to counter the communist powers (the USSR and, after 1949, China) in Northeast Asia. When the occupation ended in 1951, this role was formalized with the concurrent signing of a Mutual Security Treaty between Japan and the United States. The security and political relationship was further consolidated with the signing of a new Treaty for Mutual Cooperation and Security in 1960.

Essentially, Japan's role was to play host to US forces deployed as part of the US defense strategy in the Asia Pacific region. In this respect, Japan played a significant role in both the Korean and Vietnam Wars. Article 9[1] in the US-designed constitution of 1947 had a constraining effect on Japan's military role. Ostensibly, this article proscribed the development of armed forces by Japan, but it was subsequently interpreted to allow for the development of their Self-Defense Forces. Under the Yoshida Doctrine, Japan was content to rely on the US security guarantee while concentrating on its own economic development.

By the 1970s and 1980s, however, Japan's situation had changed considerably; the country had become a major economic power in its own right. During the 1980s, the United States emerged as the world's major debtor country, Japan being responsible for the financing of much of this debt. The increasing deficit of the US government became a major political issue. US-Japan trade relations were characterized by the large surplus in Japan's favor. Many in the United States argued that the inferior US position in the trade relationship was exacerbated by restrictions on access to Japan's domestic market.

In these circumstances, the US-Japan security relationship was increasingly scrutinized. The cry arose in the United States that Japan was having a free ride and had exploited the situation to its own benefit and to the detriment of the United States. Paul Kennedy popularized the concept of "imperial overstretch," whereby great powers were undermined by the economic costs of their need to maintain large military forces. Many people voiced their support of increased Japanese defense spending and defense burden sharing. In the early 1980s, under Prime Minister Suzuki Zenko, Japan did modify its approach to defense: 1 percent of GNP was no longer the absolute limit for defense spending and Japan would defend its sea lanes to a distance of one thousand nautical miles. In absolute terms, only the defense spending of the United States and the USSR exceeded that of Japan.[2]

During the 1980s, technology transfer issues caused some tensions in Japan-US relations; the Toshiba episode of 1987 is a good example. The Toshiba Corporation illegally sold US-imported equipment to the USSR, which in turn made it easier for Soviet submarines to escape detection by the United States. The United States therefore had to improve its own technology if its submarine detection capability were to remain effective. This meant that the overall cost of deterrence increased. The members of Congress who smashed a Toshiba radio-cassette player with a sledgehammer outside the Capitol symbolized US outrage over the incident.

A more crucial issue for the security relationship was the FSX episode of the late 1980s. The issue arose originally in 1986, when Japan's Defense Agency put forward a proposal for Japan to construct its own fighter aircraft to be known as the FSX. Japan hoped that building the FSX would help the country develop an internationally competitive aircraft industry, even though fighter aircraft could be purchased more cheaply from the United States. The United States subsequently pressured Japan to make the project a joint one, on the grounds that it would lead to the development of a more effective fighter. An agreement providing for joint development was concluded in November 1988.

In the meantime, the issue became mired in US domestic politics. The US State and Defense departments had actively pushed for joint development. The Commerce Department, however, was concerned that the project would give Japan access to US technology, which in turn would bring economic benefits to Japan. If Japan were serious about reducing its trade surplus with the United States, the Commerce Department reasoned, it should simply buy the US F-16 aircraft. The issue was taken up in Congress and the Bush administration was forced to negotiate a revised agreement whereby the United States would perform about 40 percent of the work involved in the production of the FSX. The Senate narrowly approved the agreement in May 1989.[3]

The relationship of defense to technology was examined in a 1987 Pentagon report on the semiconductor industry. The report pointed out that Japan dominated the semiconductor industry and that because the nature of much modern weaponry was high-tech, this had implications for US defense. The report recommended that the United States reduce its dependence on Japan in the semiconductor industry and, by implication, in all other defense-related areas of advanced technology where Japan played the leading role.[4]

The question of defense burden sharing, especially the cost of maintaining US forces in Japan, has been of continuing importance in the US-Japan security relationship. Congressional critics have charged that Japan, with its healthy economy and trade surplus with the United States, should be responsible for the cost of US forces stationed there. In 1989, at a time when Japan was paying 40 percent of the costs of US forces in Japan, Congress passed legislation requiring the administration to negotiate for full payment. The outcome was that Japan agreed to pay all yen-based expenses by 1995, or about one-half of the full cost.[5]

▨ Post–Cold War Strategic Issues

With the end of the Cold War, economic differences became more prominent in Japan-US relations. Nevertheless, the broader strategic context of the relationship also required reassessment. In the aftermath of the Cold War, would Japan continue to play an important role in the US approach to Asia Pacific security?

US Secretary of Defense Richard Cheney took up this question during a visit to Tokyo in February 1990. Cheney announced that although there would be a 10 percent reduction in US military personnel in the Pacific, a "major portion" of the US presence would remain. Without such presence, according to Cheney, "a vacuum would quickly develop. . . . There almost surely would be a series of destabilizing regional arms races [and] an increase in regional tension." With potential instability in Burma, Cambodia, China, North Korea, and Vietnam, noted Cheney, "it's an open question as to how those changes will affect regional stability." China and India would "continue to emerge as regional powers. We don't know what the regional effects will be. . . . Given these potential dangers to regional security, it should be clear that the United States could not ever think of a withdrawal from Asia."[6] Selig Harrison and Clyde Prestowitz reported that privately US officials also argued that the US presence was important in constraining eventual Japanese military domination of the region.[7] US Marine commander in Japan, Major General Henry Stackpole III, echoed this sentiment in March 1990 when he said that US forces in Japan provided "a cap in the bottle" to prevent a revival of Japanese military power.[8]

A broader political basis for the Japan-US security relationship was proposed by Richard Solomon, US assistant secretary of state for East

Asian and Pacific Affairs, in a speech in Tokyo on 10 April 1990. This was an elaboration of President George H. W. Bush's previous offer to Prime Minister Kaifu Toshiki to develop a "global partnership" with Japan.[9] Solomon said that "the US-Japan partnership . . . [i]s of paramount importance to the future of international economic, security, and political relations in Asia—and, indeed, in the world at large. . . . A restructured and reinvigorated US-Japan relationship—along with a united, integrated Europe—will be one of the pillars of the international architecture of the 21st century."[10]

The Gulf Conflict, 1990–1991

Despite the views advanced by spokespeople for the Bush administration, the achievement of a US-Japan global partnership was not necessarily straightforward. Sentiment associated with Article 9 of the Japanese constitution acted as a powerful restraint in the security sphere. This was well illustrated when Japan, despite US urging, found it difficult to assume a more active role during the Gulf conflict of 1990–1991. In 1987 political opposition had prevented the Nakasone government from sending minesweepers to the Persian Gulf to assist Western efforts to keep sea lanes open during the Iran-Iraq War. In the end, Japan provided financial aid only, setting a precedent for its actions during the Gulf conflict.

The United States wanted Japan to become directly involved in the crisis through the provision of personnel and equipment, as well as financial assistance to both the multinational forces and the countries affected by the crisis.[11] In October 1990, the Kaifu government was defeated in the Diet when it proposed sending Japanese military personnel in a noncombat role to assist the operations of the US-led coalition in the Gulf. Again, Japanese involvement took a financial form; US$13 billion was provided to underwrite the costs of the operation (roughly one-quarter of the total cost). Two Japanese relief planes were sent carrying food and medical supplies to multinational forces.[12] In the aftermath of the war, Japan sent six ships, including four minesweepers, to join minesweeping operations in the Persian Gulf.[13] In spite of these efforts, Japan was criticized in the United States for the tardiness of its contribution and its unwillingness to assume the military burden expected of a major power.

Beyond the Gulf Conflict

The frictions experienced over the Gulf conflict could also occur within the Asia Pacific region. Without the perception of a Soviet threat as a unifying factor in Asia Pacific, there was more scope for differences to arise.

Japan was generally more pragmatic than the United States on issues involving China, North Korea, and Vietnam. However, aid to Russia was more difficult for Japan than for the United States because the issue of the Northern Territories remained unsettled.

Both US and Japanese leaders continued to use the language of cooperation in their rhetoric. In the Tokyo Declaration, issued by George H. W. Bush and Miyazawa Kiichi in January 1992, the two leaders spoke of the "US-Japan Alliance" as "the political foundation on which the two countries cooperate in assuming their respective roles and responsibilities for securing world peace and stability in their Global Partnership."[14] Similarly, in an address to the Diet on 22 January 1993, Miyazawa proposed that Japan and the United States should work together in "coordinated leadership under a shared vision."[15] He argued that "the US military presence in the Asia-Pacific region will be more important than ever for stability . . . and close Tokyo-Washington ties will be essential as Japan pursues a greater role in the region."[16]

Although the Clinton administration placed an even stronger emphasis on economic issues in Japan-US relations, security issues continued to play a role. In February 1993, Secretary of State Warren Christopher said that trade issues should "not overshadow the many areas where we work together on global, bilateral, and regional issues."[17] On the Japanese side, the instability resulting from domestic political realignment—during the coalition governments of Hosokawa Morihiro (August 1993–April 1994) and Hata Tsutomu (April–June 1994); in a coalition of the Liberal Democratic Party and the Social Democratic Party of Japan under Murayama Tomiichi (June 1994–January 1996); and in the Hashimoto Ryutaro government (January 1996–July 1998)—affected the process of redefining the security relationship.

Concerns about North Korea, among other factors, led to discussions between Japan and the United States about the development of a TMD system.[18] A problem with the proposal was that both sides feared it might become "the son of FSX"; it also might violate Japanese policy about avoiding involvement in collective defense.[19] In a visit to Tokyo on 2 November 1993, US Secretary of Defense Les Aspin stressed that technological collaboration would not be required in the development of a TMD directed against North Korea.[20]

During 1995, largely on the initiative of US Assistant Secretary of Defense Joseph Nye, a Japan-US declaration was prepared reaffirming the security ties between the two countries. The declaration was to have been signed at the time of Clinton's visit to Osaka in November, for the meeting of the Asia-Pacific Economic Cooperation forum. When Clinton had to cancel his visit because of the budgetary impasse with Congress, the signing of the declaration was postponed.

When Clinton did visit Japan in April 1996, the joint security declaration was finally issued. The commitment by both countries to "bilateral policy coordination, including studies on bilateral cooperation in dealing with situations that may emerge in the areas surrounding Japan" was widely taken to mean that Japan could become more involved in regional security issues such as those in Korea, Taiwan, and the South China Sea, particularly by providing increased logistical support to the United States.[21]

Following the issuing of the Joint Declaration on Security, the US-Japan Security Consultative Committee recommended revised US-Japan Defense Guidelines in September 1997.[22] The Diet passed legislation in 1999 to enable the development of cooperation under these guidelines. The emphasis was on functional cooperation to enhance regional security rather than focusing on the defense of Japan as such. This reinforced the perception of Japan's neighbors that the Japanese defense role in the region was expanding.

Issues concerning Okinawa were a cause of tension in US-Japan relations in the mid- and late 1990s. US forces in Japan are particularly concentrated in Okinawa, with some 25 percent of all US facilities being located there; such facilities occupy almost 20 percent of the island of Okinawa and 10.7 percent of the prefecture.[23] Okinawans resent the massive physical, environmental, and social impact of the bases, while also being aware of the economic benefits they bring. This resentment came to a head in September 1995 when three US servicemen raped a twelve-year-old Okinawan schoolgirl. Okinawans vented their anger in massive demonstrations. In September 1996, Okinawa passed a referendum opposing the US military presence.[24] Governor Ota Masahide, an anti-bases campaigner, attempted to block renewal of the leases of US bases due to expire in 1997. Prime Minister Hashimoto overrode this action in the interests of maintaining the relationship with the United States. Authorities in other parts of Japan would not have accepted the transfer of US bases from Okinawa. Ota himself failed to win reelection as governor of Okinawa in 1998.

2001 and Beyond

Since 2001 issues arising from the war on terror initiated by the United States after the terrorist attacks of September 11 have dominated Japan-US strategic relations. January 2001 marked the inauguration of George W. Bush as US president and in April of that year Koizumi Junichiro took office as prime minister in Japan. Prior to winning the US presidency, the

Republicans had indicated that Japan would be given priority in US relations in Northeast Asia. Richard Armitage, deputy secretary of state in the new administration, had led a Republican-dominated group on US-Japan relations whose recommendations were released in October 2000. The Armitage Report, officially titled "The United States and Japan: Advancing Toward a Mature Partnership," argued that the relationship between the United States and Britain should become a model for the Japan-US alliance. The authors of the report urged the two countries to develop "a common perception and approach" to their relationship. They favored an expanded Japanese security role, neoliberal economic reforms in Japan, and increased intelligence and diplomatic cooperation.[25]

September 11 resulted in increased security cooperation between the United States and Japan. Following passage of the Antiterrorism Measures Special Law of 2001, five Japanese vessels were dispatched to the Indian Ocean to act in a refueling and support role to coalition naval forces directly involved in Operation Enduring Freedom against the Taliban regime in Afghanistan.[26] In December 2002 Japan sent its first Aegis destroyer to the Indian Ocean.[27] Koizumi gave strong diplomatic support to the United States in its war to topple Saddam Hussein in Iraq in March–April 2003. In July 2003 Koizumi announced that Japan would send one thousand members of the Self Defense Forces to Iraq to undertake reconstruction tasks.[28]

North Korea was another issue that assumed greater significance in Japan-US relations in the aftermath of September 11. Although George W. Bush had named North Korea as part of the axis of evil in his State of the Union address in January 2002, Japan had maintained hopes of improving relations with the regime of Kim Jong Il. In September 2002 Koizumi visited Pyongyang and signed a declaration with Kim Jong Il aimed at facilitating normalization and promoting peace- and confidence-building measures in Northeast Asia.[29] However, these efforts were stymied from late 2002 when North Korea threatened to develop nuclear weapons in response to the Bush administration's more hawkish policy toward the communist state. A key issue was the failure to maintain the schedule for building light water nuclear reactors in North Korea. North Korea's development of long-range missiles and the possible acquisition of nuclear weapons were particularly threatening for Japan. Japan was committed to a peaceful resolution of the crisis, and supported multilateral talks convened by China. At the same time this situation strengthened calls for Japan to be more proactive in its own defense. (Korean developments are discussed further in Chapter 9.)

The North Korean situation was a major factor in the renewed interest Japan showed in 2003 in collaborating with the United States in the development of theater missile defense. Previously Japan's approach to TMD had been cautious, with some concern that any initiatives should not violate constitutional restraints. Concern about a perceived North Korean threat led Japanese leaders to consider how they might respond. Ishiba Shigeru, director general of the Japan Defense Agency, went so far as to suggest that Japan should have the ability to launch a preemptive attack against North Korean missile facilities.[30] In August 2003 the Japanese government announced that it would have a missile shield in place by 2007. Japan's TMD would involve extensive collaboration with the United States, including collaboration in testing programs. Japan also reacted very strongly to the testing of Taepodong 2 missiles by North Korea in the Sea of Japan in July 2006; there was an acceleration of plans to upgrade missile defenses in conjunction with the US.

■ Post–Cold War Economic Issues

Alongside the strategic issues, economic issues have also played a key role in the relationship between the United States and Japan. While in the initial period of Japanese recovery in the late 1940s and 1950s the United States had believed that Japan would play the role of a second tier economy, by the 1970s Japan was clearly a major economic power. Rather than being economically dependent on the United States, the two countries competed in some respects. The expanding Japanese economy created resentment in the United States that Japan was not sharing the burden sufficiently in areas such as defense. In general US resentment toward Japan is greatest when the Japanese economy is most buoyant and when the trade balance is most strongly in Japan's favor. It should be noted, however, that strong demand in one economy can serve as a stimulus for the other economy.[31]

During the Cold War two important indicators of tensions in US-Japan economic relations were the "Nixon shocks" of 1971 and the Plaza Accords of 1985. Both these developments were designed to force the appreciation of the yen and thus increase the cost of Japanese imports into the United States. One of the Nixon shocks (the other being the announcement that Nixon would visit China) was the decision to suspend the convertibility of the US dollar into gold and to impose a 10 percent surcharge on imports into the United States. The Plaza Accords also brought about a lowering of the value of the US dollar in relation to the yen. One of the consequences was increased Japanese investment in the United States as a means of ensuring continued returns to Japanese companies.

During the post–Cold War period the United States, under the George H. W. Bush administration and the first Clinton administration, made particular attempts to make the Japanese market more open. The Structural Impediments Initiative (SII) took place from September 1989 to June 1990 and the US-Japan Framework Talks on Bilateral Trade from July 1993 to June 1995. Part of the impetus for these talks was the argument of revisionist scholars that Japanese society and the economy were structured in such a way as to minimize outside competition. While the United States subscribed to neoliberal norms of free competition (at least in theory), economic policy in Japan was motivated above all by a desire to support the existing social order. This might, for example, involve limiting large-scale retail outlets in order to ensure a continued role for small shopkeepers. Rural industries were protected to uphold rural society, and so on. Among the leading revisionists were James Fallows, Chalmers Johnson, Clyde Prestowitz, and Karel van Wolferen.[32] At a political level the "Japan bashers" favored more drastic action in support of US economic interests and an end to Japan's perceived free ride in defense.

In Japan some critics responded to Japan bashing by making extreme and even racist statements attributing US economic problems to an underlying malaise in US society. Professor Aida Yuji of Kyoto University, for example, suggested that "Iberian and African cultural traits seem to impede industrialization"; the United States, "with its vast human and technological resources . . . could become [simply] a premier agrarian power— a giant version of Denmark, for example—and the breadbasket of the world."[33] In January 1992 Yoshio Sakurauchi, speaker of the House of Representatives in the Diet, spoke of the United States as "Japan's subcontractor" and described many US workers as "lazy and illiterate."[34] Prime Minister Miyazawa also caused a stir with his comment that the United States had lost its "work ethic."[35]

The Structural Impediments Initiative of 1989–1990 was an attempt to deal more comprehensively with the issues that had been raised with the Semiconductor Trade Agreement of 1986. The United States believed that there was scope for reducing, if not eliminating, restrictive trade practices affecting a number of products in Japan. This would make it easier for foreign firms to compete with Japanese firms. Under the agreement concluded in June 1990 Japan committed itself to action in six SII-related areas: the reform of savings and investment patterns, land policy, the distribution system, restrictive business practices, *keiretsu* relationships (i.e., groupings of companies), and pricing. The United States undertook to reduce the federal deficit.[36]

With the inauguration of the Clinton administration the Japanese concern was that there would be an attempt by the United States to move toward managed trade. This might mean setting limits on Japanese access to the US market that would be related to the access the United States had to the Japanese market. The Japanese preference was for a macroeconomic approach that would focus on Japan's demand for imports and a reduction in the US fiscal deficit.[37] When Clinton met Prime Minister Miyazawa on 16 April 1993, he presented demands for sectoral quotas for US exports to Japan and supported a revaluation of the yen.[38] Clinton and Miyazawa announced the basis for the US-Japan Framework Talks on Bilateral Trade in July 1993. The United States would accept "objective criteria" rather than numerical targets as the basis for assessing market access. Japan promised to reduce its trade surplus, and the United States its budget deficit. Negotiations would cover motor vehicles, insurance, government procurement of high technology products such as computers and satellites, and the reform of regulations affecting imports and direct investment.[39] By October 1994 agreements had been concluded on government procurement, insurance, window glass, and the criteria for determining the extent to which Japan was opening its markets. While numerical targets were avoided, the United States could claim that objective criteria were being used. In procurement, for example, the criteria involved "annual evaluation of progress in the value and share of procurement of foreign products and services."[40] Agreement on cars and car parts proved more elusive, with the United States threatening sanctions under Section 301 of its 1988 trade law. By June 1995 the matter had been resolved when the five major Japanese car manufacturers announced that the production of their vehicles in the United States would increase from 2.1 million units in 1995 to 2.65 million units in 1998. US officials estimated that as a consequence the purchase of parts in the United States would increase by US$6.75 billion over the same period. US$6 billion would be spent on foreign car parts in Japan by 1998.[41]

Clinton's results-oriented approach to trade did not prove very effective. Japan remained strong enough to resist American pressure.[42] The year 1995 was also when the WTO was established, with both the United States and Japan among its members. The WTO was henceforth one arena where Japanese-US economic differences could be aired. Japan was forced to make some concessions in relation to the barriers it imposed on rice imports, for example.[43] Japan and the United States were also members of APEC. Although APEC was ostensibly committed to promoting trade liberalization, East Asian members (including Japan) resisted this approach in relation to agriculture.

Since at least 1997 the atmospherics in Japanese-US economic relations have changed because of the focus on Japan's sluggish economic performance. The Japanese example of a close relationship between government and business was a factor in other East Asian economies (particularly Thailand, South Korea, and Indonesia) experiencing a financial crisis in 1997. The United States successfully resisted Japan's proposal for an Asian

Monetary Fund, with less stringent conditions than those offered through the IMF, to assist affected economies. While Japan has been able to offer some assistance, its ability to do so has been affected by its own straitened economic circumstances. The United States has generally urged Japan to commence restructuring along neoliberal lines, but this has not proved politically possible to any significant extent. In these circumstances, however, there has generally been far less pressure on Japan over matters such as trade surpluses and market access. Nevertheless irritants remain. Under the George W. Bush administration US Trade Representative Robert Zoellick urged Japan to reduce agricultural protection. In March 2003 there was controversy when the United States imposed 30 percent tariffs on Japanese steel imports for three years; this was subsequently modified to allow exemption for 250,000 tonnes.[44]

Having reviewed the major strategic and economic issues in Japanese-US relations in the post–Cold War era, it is useful in conclusion to examine explanations for the underlying dynamics of the relationship.[45] Realists focus on the disparity in power between the United States and Japan. While Japan is a major power in its own right, the United States is much more powerful. Hence the United States is in a stronger position to achieve its objectives in relation to Japan than vice versa. These circumstances go back to Japan's defeat in 1945, the subsequent US occupation, and the establishment of the San Francisco system in 1951. The Yoshida Doctrine indicated Japan's acceptance of its subordinate position while also attempting to advance its own goals of economic reconstruction and expansion. However, the realist explanation is only relevant at a very broad level; its assumptions have to be accepted by the key actors if it is to have a determining effect. There are many dimensions of the Japanese-US relationship that have other explanations. While the realist approach has been particularly important in the context of the security relationship, one could argue that this dimension is becoming less central. Military power as a feature of international politics does not carry the weight that it previously did. As other features become more important there needs to be a broader view of the underlying factors that are at work.

In the case of Japanese-US relations the concept of complex interdependence provides a useful approach for analyzing the range of issues involved. Security and high politics more generally are not ignored, but there is a strong emphasis on low politics and particularly economic issues. Complex interdependence takes account of the complexities of domestic politics as a major influence on policymaking. The range and type of domestic actors involved can vary depending on the issue. In determining policy on any issue, governments are influenced by domestic considerations as well as by external pressures. US power is a factor influencing Japanese governments but they also need to take account of the role of domestic groups, whether the issue is US bases in Okinawa or US pressure to reduce the protection for Japanese agricultural produce. US governments are also influenced by domestic factors in the United States, particularly in relation to economic issues. On any given issue in Japanese-US relations the outcome is likely to be influenced by different kinds of domestic pressures and by international considerations. Domestic pressures are likely to be particularly relevant with economic issues, but can also be relevant with some security issues. Divisions within either or both societies can be a major complication with some issues. The United States will not necessarily get its own way simply because it is more powerful in gross terms.

Notes

1. "Aspiring sincerely to an international peace based on justice and order, the Japanese people forever renounce war as a sovereign right of the nation and the threat or use of force as a means of settling international disputes.

"In order to accomplish the aim of the preceding paragraph, land, sea and air forces, as well as other war potential, will never be maintained. The right of belligerency of the state will not be recognized."

2. Mochizuki, "To Change or to Contain," p. 348.

3. Holland, *Japan Challenges America*, p. 117.

4. Destler and Nacht, "US Policy Toward Japan," p. 295.

5. Mochizuki, "To Change or to Contain," p. 350; Brock, "The Theory and Practice of Japan-Bashing," p. 39.

6. Based on Harrison and Prestowitz, "Pacific Agenda: Defense or Economics?" p. 68.

7. Ibid.

8. Ibid., p. 62.

9. Polomka, "Towards a 'Pacific House,'" p. 177.

10. Richard Solomon, "US and Japan: An Evolving Partnership," *Current Policy* (US Department of State), no. 1268, p. 2.

11. Purrington and A.K., "Tokyo's Policy Responses During the Gulf Crisis," pp. 308–309.

12. Ibid., p. 309.

13. Purrington, "Tokyo's Policy Responses During the Gulf War and the Impact of the 'Iraqi Shock' on Japan," p. 171.

14. "Tokyo Declaration Issued by Bush, Miyazawa," *Japan Times,* 10 January 1992, p. 33.

15. "Miyazawa Vows Reform, 'Shared Vision' with US," *Japan Times* (Weekly International Edition), 1–7 February 1993, p. 6.

16. Ibid.

17. "Still on Honeymoon: Japanese Visit to Washington Smoother than Feared," *Far Eastern Economic Review,* 25 February 1993, p. 13.

18. Susumu Awanohara, "My Shield or Yours?" *Far Eastern Economic Review,* 14 October 1993, p. 22.

19. Ibid.; Ako Washio, "Diplomatic Efforts Continue to End Pyongyang Standoff," *Japan Times* (Weekly International Edition), 15–21 November 1993, p. 3.

20. *Keesing's Record of World Events,* vol. 39 (1993), p. 39738.

21. *The Military Balance 1996/97,* p. 170.

22. Tow, *Asia-Pacific Strategic Relations,* p. 53. The guidelines are summarized in table 3.1, pp. 55–58.

23. See Hook et al., *Japan's International Relations,* p. 143.

24. Sebastian Moffett, "Back to the Barracks," *Far Eastern Economic Review,* 19 September 1996, pp. 16–17.

25. "The United States and Japan."

26. Okamoto, "Japan and the United States," p. 59.

27. Miller, "The Glacier Moves," p. 139.

28. *The Military Balance 2003–2004,* p. 146.

29. Stockwin, *Dictionary of the Modern Politics of Japan,* pp. 143–144.

30. "Japan's Push for Missile Defence."

31. Grimes, "Economic Performance."

32. See Fallows, *Looking at the Sun;* Johnson, *MITI and the Japanese Miracle;* Prestowitz, *Trading Places;* Van Wolferen, *The Enigma of Japanese Power.*

33. Quoted in Johnson, "History Restarted," p. 52.

34. T.R. Reid, "Tokyo Official Calls US 'Subcontractor' to Japan Economy," *International Herald Tribune,* 21 January 1992, p. 1.

35. Johnson, "History Restarted," p. 59.

36. Marshall, "The US and Japan," p. 334.

37. Michiyo Nakamoto and Charles Leadbeater, "Japan Ready to Come Out Fighting," *Financial Times,* 8 February 1993, p. 3.

38. Robert Delfs, "A New Ball Game," *Far Eastern Economic Review,* 3 June 1993, p. 49; Maya Maruko, "Clinton Remark Causes Yen to Rise," *Japan Times* (Weekly International Edition), 26 April–2 May 1993, p. 5.

39. Steven Brull, "Price of Victory: Trouble Seen in US-Japan Trade," *International Herald Tribune,* 12 July 1993, pp. 1, 16.

40. Ako Washio and and Maya Maruko, "Despite Breakthrough, Trade 'Deal' Remains Ambiguous," *Japan Times* (Weekly International Edition), 10–16 October 1994, p. 3.

41. Nigel Holloway, "Collision Averted," *Far Eastern Economic Review,* 13 July 1995, p. 76.

42. Zeiler, "Business Is War in US-Japanese Economic Relations, 1977–2001," p. 239.

43. Stockwin, *Dictionary of the Modern Politics of Japan,* p. 249.

44. *Strategic Survey 2002–2003,* p. 258.

45. A useful reference focusing on interpretations of Japanese-American relations is Vogel, ed., *US-Japan Relations in a Changing World,* especially the chapters by Michael J. Green (realism), Keith A. Nitta (constructivism), and Leonard J. Schoppa (domestic politics).

The Sino-US Relationship 6

S ino-US relations have passed through a number of phases since 1945. This chapter summarizes those phases and then examines the post–Cold War era in more detail, with particular reference to the impact of Tiananmen Square in 1989, to strategic and economic issues, and to human rights.

■ The Postwar Context

Sino-US relations were antagonistic for more than two decades following the establishment of the People's Republic of China in 1949. Initially, the United States saw China as part of a single communist bloc led by the USSR. The US policy of containment therefore applied just as much to China as to other parts of the bloc. The Korean War reinforced US hostility toward China, particularly after Chinese "volunteers" entered the conflict on the side of North Korea. At the same time, the US relationship with the nationalist government on Taiwan (the Republic of China, or ROC) was strengthened, leading to the signing of a mutual security treaty in 1954.

The US view of China as the major threat to security in the Asia Pacific region was reciprocated by China's view of the United States as the major threat to China's security. The development of the Sino-Soviet conflict complicated this situation but, certainly in the 1950s, the United States was preeminent in China's perception of external threats. Reinforcing the perception were such developments as the strengthening security relationship between the United States and the nationalist government on Taiwan (including US support for that government's claim to be the legitimate government for the whole of China), the Taiwan Strait crises of 1955 and 1958, and the establishment of the Southeast Asia Treaty Organization (SEATO) in 1954. The Chinese viewed SEATO—which was complemented by US defense treaties with Australia and New Zealand (ANZUS), Japan, and the ROC—as a manifestation of US "encirclement" of China. Apart from its extensive naval forces in the region, US forces were stationed in countries such as Japan, South Korea, and the Philippines.

By the 1960s, the United States had become aware of the intensity of the Sino-Soviet conflict. US hostility toward China remained strong, however, and it was one of the factors leading to US intervention in Vietnam, where communist success was seen as assisting Chinese expansionist designs. For its part, China was hostile to any shift by the United States toward a "two Chinas" policy (which was contemplated, for example, by the Kennedy administration). In addition, the onset of the Vietnam War meant that again there was a major military conflict on China's borders. The escalation of that war coincided with an intensification of the Sino-Soviet conflict. China thus felt threatened by both superpowers, a feeling that was heightened by the xenophobia of the Cultural Revolution.

By the late 1960s, the situation was beginning to change again. The Nixon administration sought improved relations with China as part of its strategy for stabilizing international politics and, more particularly, as a means for facilitating a settlement in Vietnam. China was influenced by a desire to avoid simultaneous conflicts with both the United States and the USSR. Although the more radical elements preferred to maintain China's opposition to "imperialism" and "social imperialism," the dominant view was that it was better to come to terms with one of China's foes.

The rapprochement between China and the United States was formalized with the signing of the Shanghai Communiqué in February 1972.[1] This development coincided with a period of détente in Soviet-US relations. Thus, China and the USSR remained in conflict with each other but were simultaneously trying to improve relations with the United States. This meant that the United States could use its relationship with one of the communist powers as a means of putting pressure on the other. When Soviet-US relations deteriorated in the late 1970s, there was talk in the Carter administration of "playing the China card." A de facto Sino-US alliance could provide a means of containing the USSR.

In 1978 the Carter administration and the PRC agreed to full diplomatic normalization, an agreement that required the severing of official US diplomatic relations with the ROC on Taiwan. However, the Taiwan Relations Act of 1979 allowed the United States to continue an unofficial relationship with Taiwan and signaled US interest in a peaceful resolution of the Taiwan issue. US arms sales to Taiwan continued to be a problem for Sino-US relations. A resolution of the issue was attempted in the Sino-US joint communiqué of 17 August 1982, in which the United States stated its intention "to reduce gradually its sales of arms to Taiwan."[2]

An indication of the changing Sino-US relationship was the large-scale arms sales by the United States to China during the 1980s. In 1979 China and the United States had reached an agreement to establish a joint missile-monitoring station in Xinjiang. The United States also assisted China in the peaceful development of nuclear energy under the 1985 nuclear cooperation agreement.[3] US Secretary of Defense Caspar Weinberger formalized the Sino-US military relationship in September 1983 as a "three pillars" approach involving senior visits, exchanges, and technological cooperation.[4] By 1986, US military sales to China under FMS (foreign military sales) agreements exceeded US$37 million; commercial sales were nearly US$20 million.[5]

Despite these developments, by this stage there was less talk of Sino-US strategic cooperation. In March 1983 US Secretary of State George Shultz had stated that Japan was the most important US ally in Asia and that China, though important, was a regional power.[6] This attitude was reinforced by the improved Soviet-US relationship that developed during the Gorbachev period. A cooperative security relationship with China was important to the United States, but not in terms of a global strategy.

Even before the end of the Cold War, then, changes in Soviet-US relations had made China less strategically significant to the United States. The relationship remained important in terms of security because of China's regional role and the influence it could exert in areas such as the Middle East. At the same time, improvements in PRC-Taiwan relations augmented the US perception that China was mostly playing a constructive role in international affairs. The improved relations between Taiwan and the PRC were prompted by Beijing's switch to "peaceful reunification" in 1979 and its subsequent adoption of the goal of "one country, two systems" in 1983 (which was also the basis for the 1984 agreement to transfer Hong Kong from British to Chinese sovereignty in 1997).

▇ The Impact of Tiananmen Square

All aspects of the Sino-US relationship were jeopardized by the massacre at Tiananmen Square on 4 June 1989. Let us look first at the US response to the massacre before turning to the Chinese response.

The US Response

Tiananmen Square events led to a much stronger emphasis on human rights considerations in US relations with China. These considerations were articulated most clearly through Congress. President George H. W. Bush attempted to maintain the substance of the US relationship with China but was forced to make modifications.

In the immediate aftermath of Tiananmen Square, George H. W. Bush announced that US military sales and visits by military personnel to China would be suspended. At the same time, he said, "I don't want to see a total break in this relationship and I will not encourage a total break."[7] Subsequently, it was announced that high-level exchanges would be suspended and that the United States and its allies would oppose loans to China by international financial institutions.[8] Bush suggested that the United States could exert some influence to ameliorate the human rights situation in China by maintaining the existing relationship. The US relationship with China was also important in terms of regional security if conflicts in countries such as Afghanistan and Cambodia were to be resolved, and it provided the United States with a means of pressuring North Korea.

George H. W. Bush had been the US representative in China in 1974–1975, which influenced the formulation of policy toward China during his administration. Because maintaining the relationship with China was important to Bush, even in the aftermath of the massacre, National Security Adviser Brent Scowcroft and Deputy Secretary of State Lawrence Eagleburger were sent on a secret mission to Beijing on 1–2 July 1989 and on another mission in December 1989.[9] Although it is questionable whether any significant changes resulted from these missions, their purpose was to secure some modification in China's domestic policies and to maintain the momentum of Sino-US relations.

What was seen by some as Bush's weak response to the Beijing massacre provoked widespread criticism in Congress. On 22 June 1989 Senate Majority Leader George Mitchell, referring to the execution of dissidents in China, said: "I am saddened by the president's refusal to give outlet to the feelings of the American people about these executions, which now have reached the point which can only be described as organized murder."[10] Similarly, after the second Scowcroft-Eagleburger mission, Mitchell said Bush had "kowtowed to the Chinese government." Arguing that the administration had adopted a "business as usual" approach, Mitchell continued: "There are times when what America stands for and believes in is more important than economic or geopolitical considerations. This is one of those times."[11] Stephen Solarz, the Democratic chairman of the House Foreign Affairs Subcommittee on Asian and Pacific Affairs, took the view that Bush "has demonstrated that he is far more concerned about the sensibilities of the Chinese leadership than the aspirations of those in China who hope to bring a greater measure of democracy to their homeland."[12]

The Chinese Response

In his study of Chinese elite perceptions of the United States, David Shambaugh distinguishes between Marxist and non-Marxist perspectives on US foreign policy. The Marxists, following Lenin, see the "motive force" of US foreign policy as "monopoly capitalists who seek ever-higher profits and ever-expanding areas of control abroad."[13] The non-Marxists, by contrast, see "a more variegated, ad hoc US foreign policy" deriving from "a multiplicity of interests that are defined in the context of this or that specific region, country, or domestic interest group."[14] These different perspectives paralleled political divisions within the Chinese leadership that were exacerbated by the crisis of mid-1989. Conservative leaders saw Sino-US relations from a Marxist ideological perspective; moderate leaders saw the relationship in more pragmatic terms.[15] Whereas the former group advocated responding in kind to Western sanctions after Tiananmen, the latter group counseled patience and a conciliatory stance. Deng Xiaoping's position was ambiguous. At times Deng blamed the United States for the troubles China experienced; in the long term, however, he worked toward achieving accommodation.[16]

Even before the crisis of mid-1989, Chinese leaders had warned the United States against interfering in China's domestic affairs. When Bush visited Beijing in February 1989, he was told by Zhao Ziyang, the reformist general secretary of the Chinese Communist Party, that "the fact that there are some people in American society who support people dissatisfied with the Chinese government will not contribute to the stability of China's political system and the process of reform, nor will it be conducive to relations with the USA."[17] US support for dissidents, such as astrophysicist Fang Lizhi, was likely to undermine the position of reformists within the Chinese leadership.[18]

In the aftermath of the Beijing massacre, the official Chinese response was to declare: "What is happening in China is China's internal affair. . . . [The] Chinese government is completely capable of quelling the current rebellion in Beijing."[19] The imposition of sanctions by the United States was angrily rejected. This sentiment was clearly expressed in a statement by the Foreign Affairs Committee of the National People's Congress on 19 July 1989:

> We hereby express our utmost indignation at such acts by the US Congress of grossly interfering in China's internal affairs. . . . [The Beijing disturbances] were a planned, organized and premeditated political turmoil started by a tiny number of people in collusion with some hostile forces

abroad through taking advantages [*sic*] of student demonstrations. The turmoil later escalated into a counter-revolutionary rebellion in Beijing.[20]

The Marxist ideological perspective was evident in an article entitled "Anti-China Clamour Cannot Intimidate Chinese People" by the *People's Daily* commentator.[21] The actions of the US Congress derived from "anti-communist class instincts." The quelling of the "counter-revolutionary rebellion" was "a justifiable and legitimate measure that any sovereign country in the world would take when faced with a similar situation." The advocates of sanctions in the US Congress were responsible for "persistent, flagrant interference in China's internal affairs, such as on the question of Taiwan, the 'Tibetan question' and the so-called 'human rights question.' . . . [Only] a China practising bourgeois liberalization and taking a capitalist road will please them."

It is interesting to observe that the commentary distinguishes between the advocates of sanctions in Congress and the Bush administration:

We have noted the Bush administration's opinion that the United States should make a discreet response to events in China and that it is in accord with US national interests to keep good relations with China. . . . We hope that the US government and the majority of American Congressmen will not do things which damage bilateral relations out of consideration for maintaining the fundamental interests of the Chinese and American people and the overall situation in Sino-US relations.

Speaking in New York on 2 October 1989, Foreign Minister Qian Qichen of China rejected US interference in "China's internal affairs" but advocated reconciliation on the basis of the Five Principles of Peaceful Coexistence.[22] The first two principles were perhaps most important to the improvement of Sino-US relations: "It is essential to recognize and respect differences, and seek and enlarge common ground" and "The domestic politics of a country should not be taken as a precondition for the restoration and development of bilateral relations."

Deng Xiaoping made his views clear when he spoke to Richard Nixon in Beijing on 31 October 1989.[23] On the one hand, he said, "Frankly speaking, the US was involved too deeply in the turmoil and counter-revolutionary rebellion which occurred in Beijing not long ago. China was the real victim and it is unjust to reprove China for it." On the other hand, the influence of the non-Marxist perspective can be seen in Deng's argument that "national interest" should be taken as the "highest criterion" in the conduct of a country's affairs. In Deng's view, "We can never forget state sovereignty and national honour, nor can we do away with national self-respect."

Stability was crucial to China: "Without a political situation marked by stability and unity, and without a stable social order, we can accomplish nothing in a country with such a huge population and poor foundation."

China protested against amendments on sanctions adopted by Congress in mid-November 1989; China also objected to US measures making it easier for Chinese students to stay in the United States.[24] The December 1989 visit to Beijing by National Security Adviser Scowcroft and Deputy Secretary of State Eagleburger benefited those elements favoring a return to normality in Sino-US relations and undermined the more conservative elements. As Deng said on this occasion, "Despite certain disputes and differences, ultimately Sino-US relations must be improved. It is necessary for world peace."[25]

■ Post–Cold War Strategic Issues

In the post–Cold War era Sino-US relations have focused on important strategic and economic issues. Nevertheless human rights have also played a role. In this overview of Sino-US relations during the post–Cold War era we will focus on strategic, economic, and human rights issues in turn.[26] In each case we examine the domestic politics involved in each country, before turning to the broad developments and specific issues that have arisen. At a general level we also consider where the relationship appears to be heading in the early twenty-first century.

Strategic issues are just one aspect of the Sino-US relationship that is affected by domestic politics. For both China and the United States we need to be aware of the relevant general attitudes and how the political process has a bearing on Sino-US relations. From the US perspective there are certain underlying attitudes toward China that derive both from the long history of US involvement in that country and then, more recently, from the experience of China under communist rule. During the nineteenth and early twentieth centuries China became a favorite US "charity," with many US missionaries active there. There were also hopes that US interests would benefit from economic engagement with China. At the time of World War II the United States hoped that China would take over from Japan as the major power of East Asia, while also remaining US-aligned. These various hopes were disappointed when China became a communist state in 1949. The United States viewed China as part of the totalitarian communist threat. The US image of China was clearly negative, and this stance was reinforced when compared to its previous hopes. With Sino-US rapprochement in 1972, attitudes became more mixed. As an authoritarian system China remained alien. At the same time there was scope for a more positive view because the United States stood to gain both strategically and economically by strengthening its relationship with China. These attitudes, deriving from the most recent phase in Sino-US relations, have continued to be important during the post–Cold War era. China is still viewed as essentially an authoritarian system, but there can still be strategic and economic benefits for the United States in the relationship. Nevertheless there are also those who continue to see China as at least a potential foe and who are therefore more wary about the relationship. Some people in the United States also emphasize the negative effects of the economic relationship with China on particular sectors of the US economy.

On the Chinese side, nationalism has been the most important underlying attitude affecting the relationship with the United States. As with the US attitude, the Chinese attitude has important historical roots. The Chinese see the United States as one of the imperialist powers that took advantage of China during the nineteenth and early twentieth centuries. Although the United States followed the open-door principle, this simply meant that all outside powers should have access to China on the same footing. With the emergence of China as a communist state, the United States continued to be seen as the leading imperialist and capitalist state. The US role in supporting Taiwan reinforced this view. By 1972, however, China's conflict with the USSR led to a change of attitude: the United States as the leading imperialist power could assist China in its struggle with Soviet "social imperialism." With the emphasis on economic modernization in post-Mao China after 1976, the link with the United States was seen as beneficial in terms of trade, investment, and access to technology. In David Shambaugh's words, the United States became the "beautiful imperialist."[27]

While these underlying attitudes help shape all aspects of Sino-US relations in broad terms, it is also necessary to examine the political processes involved. These can vary to some extent, depending on the aspect of the relationship. In the case of strategic issues there tends to be a more restricted set of players as compared with either economic or human rights issues. This generalization applies to both the United States and China. In the case of the United States there are various departments and agencies within the executive branch that deal with security issues concerning China. These include the Department of State, the Department of Defense, and the Central Intelligence Agency. The National Security Council plays the key role in coordinating policy, with the president also being involved with major issues. Congress can have an influence on US security policy toward China through committee hearings and its general power over legislation and finance. However, it is the executive branch that takes the lead. Lobbying relating to security issues can take place by groups promoting particular views, for example on Taiwan. Other groups with particular views on human rights or political issues might lobby for US security policy toward China to take a certain direction. Such lobbying might be directed toward both the executive branch and Congress.

In the case of China, the political process is less open but it has become more pluralistic. China remains an authoritarian political system but the role of the leader, while remaining important, is less dominating than it was in the days of Mao or Deng. David Lampton argues that six organizational levers are the "key to political supremacy and foreign policy control": the positions of general secretary, chairman of the Central Military Commission, and the presidency are most important overall, with the Foreign Affairs Small Group, the Foreign Propaganda Small Group, and the Taiwan Affairs Leading Small Group having a specific role in foreign policy as coordinating groups.[28] Foreign policy matters, including Chinese security relations with the United States, are thus dealt with primarily at the central level of the Chinese party state. However, different institutions within the political system can attempt to influence the direction of Chinese policy. These institutions include the People's Liberation Army.[29] The key leaders and bodies are also influenced by popular attitudes, particularly as manifested in Chinese nationalism.

During the post–Cold War era the strategic relationship between China and the United States has been problematic in many respects. A common interest in restraining the USSR made the two powers effectively strategic partners during the 1970s and 1980s. With the collapse of the USSR the situation appeared different. The United States was now the global power without any rivals on a world level. China was a major power within the East Asian region and intent on asserting its position there. The position of the United States was that no one power should dominate East Asia. This meant that the United States would attempt to restrain China if it believed China was acting to become the regional hegemon. At the same time it was often helpful to the United States to have China's cooperation in dealing with regional problems. For its part, China sought acknowledgment of its major role in the region, while also aiming to have a significant influence in dealing with the important issues. With these different perspectives there was scope for both conflict and cooperation between China and the United States. Conflict would arise if the United States regarded China as essentially a rival to be blocked or contained, or if China viewed the United States as an implacable enemy. Cooperation was more likely when each power saw the other as having a legitimate role in the region, with common interests in dealing with many issues. On the US side the tension between the two perspectives is expressed in the competing notions of China as either a "strategic partner" or a "strategic competitor." Under the Clinton administration the emphasis was mostly on the former. Under the George W. Bush administration the emphasis was initially on the latter, although that subsequently changed. Books such as Richard Bernstein and Ross H. Munro, *The Coming Conflict with China* (1997), and Bill Gertz, *The China Threat: How the People's Republic Targets America* (2000) portrayed China as a rival to the United States.[30] From the Chinese side strong nationalist sentiment is likely to lead to an anti-US perspective. Economic modernizers, on the other hand, can see the benefits to China of a strong relationship with the United States and thus focus on cooperation.

Within the context of these broad strategic perspectives, the Taiwan issue has been a particular touchstone. This will be discussed in detail in Chapter 8; however, Taiwan is indicative of how China and the US approach their relationship. For China, Taiwan is a nationalist issue. Reunification of the motherland is a fundamental aspiration and essential if China's dignity is to be restored. China sees US support for Taiwan, despite official recognition of the People's Republic, as an affront and an obstacle to the development of cooperation on other issues. The United States is committed to a peaceful resolution of the Taiwan issue. Use of force by China would confirm the view of those who see China as a rival, if not foe. Resort to arms would clearly make the relationship conflictual rather than cooperative.

Specific developments during the 1990s gave some insight into the strategic perspectives underlying the Sino-US relationship. At the beginning of the decade a major issue was the Iraqi occupation of Kuwait in August 1990.[31] China followed the United States in supporting the UN Security Council resolution demanding that Iraq withdraw (Resolution 660). However, China was far more hesitant about agreeing to UN authorization of the use of force to end the Iraqi occupation. When a resolution to this effect was put to a vote on 29 November 1990 (Resolution 678), China abstained. China was concerned about the United States using this situation to assume a more dominant position in international politics. China also wanted to restrict the possibility that UN-authorized force might be used in situations contrary to Chinese interests in the future. When the Gulf conflict became the Gulf War in January–February 1991, China was able to witness the prowess of the United States in waging "high tech" war. This had a major impact on the direction of China's military modernization.[32] It showed how such a war could be fought, while also stimulating thinking about countermeasures.

In terms of the Taiwan issue the most serious Sino-US clash during the 1990s was the missile crisis of 1995–1996.[33] While the broader context of the crisis is discussed in more detail in Chapter 8, from a strategic perspective the crisis posed two important issues. One was the extent to which China could compel Taiwan to behave in certain ways. The other was how far the United States was prepared to go in defending Taiwan. The context of the crisis was the way Taiwan was making various moves to assert its independent status, including moves by President Lee Teng-hui to travel to the United States. Such travel was a problem for Sino-US relations because China would take the granting of a US visa to President Lee as signifying official recognition of his position. Facing strong pressure from Congress, the Clinton administration issued a visa to Lee Teng-hui, enabling him to travel to Cornell University, his alma mater, to give a speech in June 1995. Of even more concern to China was the holding of presidential elections in Taiwan in March 1996, and fears that the proindependence Democratic Progressive Party would make gains. China put Taiwan under various forms of military pressure to indicate that it would take strong action if there were any moves toward independence. In July 1995 China conducted missile tests and military exercises in the Taiwan Strait as part of this strategy. In March 1996, at the time of the presidential election, China held a second set of tests and exercises, even closer to Taiwan.[34] In response the United States deployed two carrier battle groups to the vicinity of Taiwan but without going into the Taiwan Strait itself. One group was led by the USS *Independence,* and the other by the USS *Nimitz,* with thirteen ships overall and more than 150 aircraft.[35] While this crisis was overcome subsequently through diplomatic means, it clearly showed the potential that existed for the Taiwan situation to escalate into war. The United States made clear its opposition to the use of military means by China, while at the same time attempting to restrain Taiwan and signaling to China its interest in improving political relations.

The issues raised for China at the time of the Gulf conflict in 1990–1991 arose again in the Kosovo crisis. The Kosovo crisis developed in 1998–1999 because of Serb attempts to bring about an "ethnic cleansing" of the majority Albanian population. Kosovo was a Serb-ruled region in what remained of the Federal Republic of Yugoslavia after the earlier fragmentation of that country. At one level China opposed US and NATO intervention in Kosovo because such action was seen as a manifestation of US hegemonism. However, China was also concerned about any precedent that might be set in relation to situations of concern to China such as Tibet and Taiwan. Russia also took the view that Kosovo was a domestic matter for Yugoslavia, led by Slobodan Milosevic. Because both China and Russia had vetoes on the UN Security Council, action under the auspices of the UN to restrain Milosevic proved impossible. The United States turned to

NATO to provide legitimacy for intervention in Kosovo. The bombing campaign against Yugoslav targets, which began on 25 March 1999, took place under NATO auspices.

In the context of the Kosovo war a specific crisis in Sino-US relations arose after the accidental bombing of the Chinese embassy in Belgrade on 7 May 1999 by US warplanes. This bombing not only destroyed the embassy, but also killed three Chinese nationals. Although the bombing was explained as the result of inadequacies in the US targeting process, many Chinese believed the accident was a deliberate ploy to humiliate China. This feeling was compounded by a perception that President Clinton and US officials did not show sufficient remorse in their apologies. For example, when Clinton first made a statement on the matter in the course of a visit to Oklahoma on 8 May, he was dressed in casual clothes. Widespread demonstrations erupted in China. In Chengdu the house of the US consul-general was burned, and there were fears about the security of the embassy in Beijing itself. There was a widespread US belief that China was using the demonstrations to express its opposition not only to US policy in the Balkans, but to what was viewed by them as US hegemonism more generally.

A new phase in the Sino-US strategic relationship emerged with the inauguration of George W. Bush as US president in January 2001. During the presidential election campaign of 2000 the Republicans had indicated that they saw China in more adversarial terms than had been the case with the Clinton administration. Condoleezza Rice, who became Bush's national security adviser, had described China as a "strategic competitor."[36] Paul Wolfowitz, the new deputy secretary of defense, had said that China was "the major strategic competitor and potential threat to the United States and its allies in the first half of the next century."[37] The new administration had also signaled that its policies in Northeast Asia would give priority to US allies, and particularly Japan.

With China also adopting an assertive approach, the situation was ripe for tensions over specific issues to develop into a more serious crisis. This occurred in April 2001 when a US EP3 surveillance aircraft hit a Chinese F-8 fighter jet off the coast of southern China. The jet crashed and its pilot was killed. The US plane was forced to land on Hainan where its crew was detained by Chinese authorities. Delicate negotiations were required to recover the US aircraft and to repatriate the crew to the United States.[38] While tensions had been high during this crisis, both sides realized in the end that they needed to restrain their rhetoric if they were to prevent such episodes from spiraling out of control.

Nevertheless, another tension developed soon after when Bush declared on 25 April 2001 that the United States would do "whatever it takes" to defend Taiwan.[39] This clearly indicated a stronger US commitment to the defense of Taiwan, much to the chagrin of China. However, the United States also had to take care that Taiwan did not exploit this situation to move toward asserting independence. Despite official attempts to explain that there had been no significant change in the US position, the impression remained that there had been a shift in the policy of "strategic ambiguity."

It was against the background of these tensions in Sino-US relations that the attacks of September 11 occurred. The relationship between the two powers was affected in various ways.[40] With Bush's declaration of the war on terrorism, China indicated its general support. This was most clearly given when Bush met Jiang Zemin at the annual APEC heads of government meeting in Shanghai in October 2001. China and its leaders were clearly shocked by the attacks mounted by Al-Qaida in New York and Washington. At the same time China saw this situation as providing opportunities for improving relations with the United States. China supported the war against the Taliban in Afghanistan, and exerted pressure on Pakistan to cooperate with the United States. It also accepted the deployment of Japanese vessels to the Indian Ocean in support of the war in Afghanistan, despite Chinese sensitivities about any expansion of Japan's military role. China hoped to win US support in its campaign against Muslim separatists in Xinjiang, who were now characterized as "terrorists." The United States was reluctant to support China over Xinjiang, and the differences over Tibet and Taiwan remained.

Despite expressions of support for the United States in the war on terrorism, China remained concerned that the United States would exploit the situation to advance its hegemonist designs. The United States was now much more strongly engaged in areas to the west and southwest of China. Apart from the war in Afghanistan, the United States also had forces deployed in the Central Asian states of Kyrgyzstan and Uzbekistan, and strengthened its relationships with both Pakistan and India. While avoiding confrontation with the United States, China has an interest in balancing behavior that would restrain US power.[41] China prefers a multipolar to a unipolar world and has encouraged developments supporting that objective.

This perspective was relevant when the issue of going to war against Iraq arose in late 2002 and early 2003. China believed that existing international arrangements to constrain Iraq were effective and should continue. It believed the United States was too intent on using its military power to achieve domination of the Gulf region. Within the UN Security Council China opposed any attempts to authorize the use of military force against Iraq. Rather than taking the lead in opposing the United States over this issue, China was content to support the position taken by France, Germany, and Russia. China would either have voted against or abstained from voting on the resolution proposed by the United States in March 2003.[42] With the United States withdrawing this resolution, China did not have to make the choice. This outcome prevented any further damage to Sino-US relations, but China regretted the bypassing of the Security Council. Despite the difficult postwar circumstances in Iraq, China believed the situation continued to reflect US hegemonist goals.

In Northeast Asia developments relating to North Korea highlighted the importance of Sino-US cooperation. These developments are discussed more fully in Chapter 9, but also need to be considered in terms of their relevance to Sino-US relations. The George W. Bush administration had a critical view of the Geneva Accords of 1994 that had brought an end to an earlier nuclear crisis on the Korean peninsula. Under the accords North Korea was to acquire state-of-the-art light-water nuclear reactors in return for giving up its own ambitions to acquire nuclear weapons. These would be mainly funded by Japan and South Korea. The United States would provide oil to North Korea in the period before the reactors were completed. Progress in implementing the accords had been slow even before Bush came to office. The Republican administration believed that North Korea was being given too much without there being any guarantee that North Korea would not renege on its commitment. North Korea reacted by reactivating its plutonium-based nuclear plants and signaling its intention to acquire nuclear weapons. North Korea was prepared to negotiate with the United States on a bilateral basis, whereas the United States wanted a multilateral approach. China was in a stronger position than any other power to put pressure on North Korea, but could by no means compel Kim Jong Il to behave as it might wish. China did not wish any major conflict to erupt on the Korean peninsula, and generally favored compromise to resolve the issue. The United States needed Chinese cooperation in facilitating diplomacy and to assist in putting pressure on North Korea. China was skeptical about the US maximalist goal of achieving a verifiable nuclear disarmament of North Korea.

At one level US concerns about North Korea related to the more general issue of WMD. North Korea had been characterized as a "rogue state" and in Bush's State of the Union address in January 2002 it had been named as part of the "axis of evil" because of its policy on WMD. US counterproliferation policy under Bush indicated a willingness to use nuclear weapons against states such as North Korea in certain circumstances. The Bush administration also put a strong emphasis on the development of missile defense as a means of countering threats from states such as North Korea (accentuated by North Korean missile tests in July 2006). Missile defense could be based on the continental United States or it could be more localized in nature, centering on Japan for example. In the latter case it was known as theater missile defense. While the Bush administration stated that these various developments were not directed against China, they would have the effect of weakening China's nuclear defenses. Since China's nuclear forces were at a simple level compared with those of the United States, any strategy directed against North Korea could also be used against China. Missile defense could also be directed against China. In addition China had a concern that theater missile defense would be deployed in relation to Taiwan.

Issues concerning the proliferation of WMD have been an important aspect of Sino-US relations throughout the post–Cold War period.[43] The United States has been concerned that China has been involved in exporting WMD and associated materials and technologies to Pakistan in particular. Allegations arose that Pakistan in turn became a conduit for assisting other nuclear aspirants. While China adhered to many of the relevant agreements, it did not subscribe to all of them. China signed the Nuclear Nonproliferation Treaty in 1992 and the Comprehensive Nuclear Test Ban Treaty in 1996. It observed the Missile Technology Control Regime (MTCR), established in 1987, but without being a member.[44] Even where China was a signatory to a relevant agreement there was scope for differences of interpretation. China's priorities were often different from those of the United States. For example, China opposed US moves to develop missile defense, and argued that this issue should be addressed in international regimes attempting to control the spread of WMD. China has argued that F-16 fighter aircraft, as supplied to Taiwan by the United States, can deliver WMD just as easily as Chinese missiles.[45]

China's approach to WMD issues is ambivalent in some respects. On the one hand, China is part of the "nuclear club" and has an interest in restricting nuclear and other WMD proliferation. On the other hand, it also engages in balancing behavior in relation to the United States. It has therefore been prepared to provide some assistance to states pursuing policies that might run counter to US interests. In the case of Pakistan, China has had a long-standing interest in supporting that state as a means of restricting India. The United States has preferred a more balanced approach. Pakistan became important to the United States in the context of the war on terrorism, and specifically in relation to Afghanistan, but not to the extent of supporting Pakistan's nuclear role. In early 2004 fears about Pakistan's role in assisting nuclear proliferation were confirmed when the head of its nuclear weapons program, Abdul Qadeer Khan, confessed that he had made relevant knowledge and technology available to North Korea, Iran, and Libya.[46] While critics of China might argue that Chinese assistance to Pakistan thus facilitated a wider nuclear proliferation, it might also be noted that the United States had trained Pakistani rocket scientists, as well as some 1,300 Indian nuclear scientists.[47]

In 2002–2003 US concerns about WMD proliferation to Iran were reflected in sanctions imposed on a number of Chinese organizations relating to exports of technologies that could be used in making biological and chemical weapons.[48] Generally, however, China has acceded to US wishes that it limit its nuclear cooperation with Iran. China is unlikely to support the imposition of sanctions on Iran to limit its nuclear program, but generally avoids taking a lead on the issue, preferring to leave that role to Russia.[49]

◼ Post–Cold War Economic Issues

While the issue of a "rising China" is normally seen as primarily a strategic matter, the economic dimension of China's position in the world is clearly fundamental. At one level the United States has contributed to China's advance by becoming a major trade partner and source of investment and technology. China has benefited from the economic relationship, but so too has the United States at an aggregate level. Despite the way China's economic growth contributes to its power base in international politics, the focus in discussions of Sino-US economic relations tends to be on their underlying politics. In our examination of economic issues in the post–Cold War US-China relationship we first assess the relevant aspects of domestic politics, before providing an overview of the major developments and some important specific issues such as technology transfer.

In both China and the United States there are important political forces either favoring or critical of expanding Sino-US economic ties. In the United States the groups most favorable to the economic relationship are those businesses involved in exporting to the Chinese market. This includes exporters of advanced technology such as aircraft and telecommunications. Importers of Chinese goods such as textiles, footwear, and toys also have a clear interest in an expanding economic relationship. US farmers anticipated making gains in areas such as grains, oilseeds, pork, beef, poultry, cotton, and fruits following China's accession to the WTO.[50] There is also an argument, not necessarily associated with any one interest group but expressed by people with an interest in the broader strategic relationship, that strengthening Sino-US economic links contributes to China's enmeshment in the global economy. This in turn means that China develops a stronger interest in the modalities of interdependence, not just in the economic sphere but in other spheres as well. Insofar as China is reliant on its economic relationship with the United States, the leverage the United States has in relation to a range of issues affecting China is enhanced.

Among the US groups that are critical of expanding Sino-US economic ties are those that see their own economic interests as being adversely affected. Manufacturers and unions in industries producing textiles, footwear, and toys have felt the heat of Chinese competition most intensely and have reacted politically. These groups generally favor protectionist measures such as tariffs or quotas to reduce Chinese imports. They sometimes make common cause with groups that are critical of China because of its human rights record, or because they fear China as a strategic competitor or even foe. Pro-Taiwan groups also lobby in favor of restricting the expansion of Sino-US economic ties.

In China the groups most favorable to the development of economic relations with the United States are those that stand to benefit or see China benefiting as a whole. Broadly speaking these are the people who have been at the fore of China's economic modernization. They could be part of China's expanding private sector, or from coastal provinces that have benefited disproportionately from China's economic growth. Within the political leadership they are the economic modernizers and reformers. They favor a China that is more open to the world and see many benefits in promoting economic interdependence.

Groups and people within China that stand to lose from expanding economic ties with the United States take a critical stance. These include people involved in state-owned enterprises and from inland provinces that have not benefited from China's economic opening. More conservative political leaders are fearful that China's authoritarian political system is being undermined by the move toward a capitalist economy. Economic ties with the United States contribute to this process. Such leaders also tend to be more attached to traditional communist ideology, at least in its Chinese formulation. Both reformers and conservatives can have a strong nationalist orientation, but whereas the former see economic ties with the United States as strengthening China, the latter fear that such ties will have a negative impact in the long term.

The stances adopted by these different groups in both the United States and China need to be seen in the context of the tremendous growth in Sino-US economic relations. Table 6.1 indicates the growth in Sino-US trade between 1999 and 2004.

US exports to China focus on advanced technology products such as computers and aircraft. China exports low-cost consumer items, particularly clothing, footwear, and toys, with electrical appliances also becoming important. While foreign investment in China comes predominantly from

Table 6.1   Sino-US Trade, 1999–2004 (US$ millions)

	1999	2000	2001	2002	2003	2004
US imports from China	81,785	100,062	102,280	125,167	152,379	196,698
US exports to China	13,117	16,253	19,234	22,052	28,418	34,721

Source: International Trade Administration, US Department of Commerce, "TradeStats Express—National Trade Data," http://tse.export.gov/NTDChart.aspx?UniqueURL=hoc pebzyj42il5rn1msd5l55-2005-10-7-5-32-12, accessed 7 October 2005.

Asian sources, the United States also plays a very important role. In 2004 the United States ranked fifth as a source of foreign investment in China after Hong Kong, the British Virgin Islands, South Korea, and Japan.[51] The US share of total contracted investment in 2004 was 7.93 percent, amounting to US$12.17 billion; utilized investment in 2004 was US$3.94 billion.[52] Much of the investment occurs in manufacturing, taking advantage of the low labor costs in China. Many plants are being relocated from Japan and Taiwan as part of this process.

Important political issues have arisen in the context of the expanding Sino-US economic relationship. A major focus has been the growing trade balance in China's favor. In the United States this situation has been used by groups critical of China as a weapon in support of a more protectionist policy. At various times, such groups have linked up with human rights groups wanting to use trade to pressure China. Opposition to this approach has come not just from groups that benefit from trade with China but from those who favor a liberal international trade regime. The debate between the different groups in the United States can be seen in the early to mid-1990s in reference to the issue of extending China Most Favored Nation (MFN) status in trade. Subsequently similar issues arose in the context of obtaining US agreement to China's accession to the WTO. After reviewing these phases in the development of the US-China trade relationship, we will give some attention to the specific issue of technology transfer; some comment on the most recent phase in the economic relationship is also warranted.

Most Favored Nation was a term used to denote states that had normal trading relations with the United States. It did not indicate special privileges. Any state with MFN would not be treated in a discriminatory way as compared with other states in its trading relationship with the United States. In 1974 the Jackson-Vanik amendment to the Trade Act stipulated that MFN status would only apply to nonmarket economies if they did not block emigration (Soviet Jews being the particular concern at this time).[53]

In China's case MFN status was achieved in 1980, and its annual renewal did not become contentious until the time of the Tiananmen Square episode in 1989.[54] Thereafter, a coalition of human rights activists and China critics of various backgrounds (economic and otherwise) attempted to block MFN renewal or to impose conditions. Both President George H. W. Bush and then President Bill Clinton found that they needed to maintain China's MFN status. Any move to the contrary would seriously have undermined the US-China relationship.

In the period of George H. W. Bush's presidency after Tiananmen, China critics attempted to attach conditions to the renewal of China's MFN status, rather than blocking renewal altogether. Bush resisted these moves on the grounds that they would jeopardize any influence the United States had in China (on human rights and other issues). Bush also believed these moves would adversely affect the burgeoning free market sector in China and the interests of those in the United States who benefited from Chinese imports or sold products to China.[55]

Despite these arguments, lobbying on the issue came primarily from US interests that would suffer from a revocation of China's MFN status— wheat exporters and retail interests (importers of Chinese toys and textiles) in particular.[56] Although China maintained its MFN status, Bush nevertheless needed to show that he would take an active role in pressuring China on various issues. Indicative of this role was Bush's letter to Democratic senator Max Baucus in July 1991, in which he outlined steps to ensure better access to China for US exports.[57] Similarly, the Dalai Lama's visit to Washington, DC, in April 1991 demonstrated that Bush was active in pursuing human rights issues in China.[58] Nevertheless, in 1992 Bush was forced to veto two bills linking the renewal of China's MFN status to improvements in China's human rights policies and better access to its markets.[59]

During Clinton's presidential candidacy, his position on MFN had been close to that of Bush's congressional critics. On coming to office, however, Clinton soon realized the problems the MFN issue created for US relations with China. His initial approach was to support MFN renewal on the basis of China meeting certain conditions. Although the administration favored consensus with Congress on this issue, it argued that determining conditions on the basis of presidential policy rather than through legislation would be more flexible. It was expected that these conditions would relate to progress on human rights, trade issues, and the proliferation of missiles, but the 1993 renewal confined itself solely to human rights.[60]

By 1994, the Clinton administration had concluded that linking MFN to human rights was an ineffective way to achieve change and jeopardized the ability of the United States to work with China on other areas of common interest. On 26 May 1994 Clinton announced that China's MFN status would be extended; trade would not be used to pressure China on human rights issues. In Clinton's words, his decision "offers us the best opportunity to lay the basis for long-term sustainable progress in human rights and for the advancement of our other interests with China."[61]

China's position all along had been that it would not allow the MFN issue to be a pretext for interference in its internal affairs. As Jiang Zemin commented in 1993, MFN "should be the basis for normal economic relations and trade between the two countries and should not have become an issue."[62] China continued to advance its own position vigorously in 1994.[63] This might have partly been an attempt to disarm criticism from more conservative elements at home. It might have also been related to a perception that Clinton's own domestic position on this issue was weak.

In subsequent years the renewal of China's MFN status in the House of Representatives did not attract significant opposition. In 1998 the term MFN was replaced with the phrase "normal trade relations" to avoid any misunderstanding that preferential treatment was involved.[64] In the context of negotiating China's entry to the WTO, Clinton made a major effort in 2000 to secure "permanent normal trade relations" (PNTR) for China.[65] This aroused opposition from some groups that had been opposed to MFN, particularly labor unions. Human rights groups were reluctant to lose a form of leverage against China; environmentalists and critics of globalization also expressed their concerns. Amendments to provide means for monitoring China's human rights and labor practices and its economic behavior assisted in the passage of the legislation through Congress. In signing the bill into law on 10 October 2000, Clinton hailed the achievement of PNTR for China as one of the major achievements of his administration.[66]

China had initiated discussions about entry to the General Agreement on Tariffs and Trade, the precursor to the WTO, in 1986. Members of GATT, and then the WTO from 1995, needed to conclude bilateral agreements with China to ensure harmonization in their approach to China's entry. The United States was very significant in this process because of its role as both the world's leading economic power and as one of China's major trading partners. The task of reaching agreement with China raised similar issues to those that had arisen with the MFN controversy, although there also tended to be a stronger emphasis on the economic dimension as such. For the United States a major issue was improving its access to the Chinese market. This involved such issues as reducing direct state involvement in the economy, for example in state monopolies and in subsidies for state-owned enterprises.[67] The development of a transparent and independent legal system within which commercial enterprises could operate was also important. The United States wanted China to take action to uphold intellectual copyright, with the illegal copying of music being a particular problem. Whereas China preferred to be treated as a developing country for the purposes of WTO accession (given that this would entail a number of concessions), the United States generally argued for China to be viewed as developed.

After many years of negotiations, momentum for achieving agreement developed in late 1998 and early 1999. The major actors in the Clinton administration were in favor of an agreement as a way of strengthening the US-China relationship.[68] Within China the groups most involved in export-oriented economic development were most favorable; state-dominated sectors of the economy were more critical. Premier Zhu Rongji, a leading modernizer, visited Washington in April 1999 prepared to make concessions and to conclude an agreement. Having reached this point, however, Clinton decided that the time was not quite opportune. He anticipated problems with Congress and was not convinced that the lobbying of the business community would be sufficient to overcome opposition. This made the situation difficult for Zhu Rongji, given that he had had to overcome considerable opposition himself in China. Agreement was finally reached in Beijing in November 1999, with the United States represented by a delegation led by US Trade Representative Charlene Barshefsky.[69] This agreement prepared the way for Clinton's efforts to secure PNTR status for China. Having secured agreement with the United States, China finally entered the WTO on 11 December 2001.[70]

One specific focus of controversy in Sino-US economic relations has been technology transfer. A significant part of US exports to China relate to the role of the United States as the world's leading manufacturer of high-tech products. Concerns arise, however, when US exports can have military applications. One allegation has been that China has encouraged weapons proliferation, with access to US technology sometimes assisting in this process. Another allegation has been that China has improved its own military arsenal on the basis of some technology acquired from the United States, ostensibly for civilian purposes. Critics have suggested that some US companies have been too lax in making relevant technology available to China, and that the US government should also have more stringent controls. These criticisms culminated in the appointment of a Select House Committee in June 1998 to consider the issue of technology transfer to China. The Cox Report of January 1999 was very critical of the Clinton administration. The report alleged that Loral Space and Communications had close links to the Democrats in the 1996 elections. This company, which was involved in launching satellites using Chinese rockets, provided information to China that resulted in more accurate missiles.[71] The Cox Committee also made allegations about Chinese espionage, including at the Los Alamos laboratories. Although many elements of the Cox Report were clearly partisan, it did result in a more stringent approach toward US exports that might assist China's missile and space programs.

Since 2001 the issues that were important in Sino-US relations during the 1990s have continued but in a more acute form. The strength of the Chinese economy has grown apace, and the volume of Sino-US trade has expanded exponentially; the trade imbalance in China's favor has become considerably worse. While US consumers have benefited from the competitive prices of Chinese imports, manufacturers and unions in affected industries (such as textiles and furniture) have complained that China's cheap labor gives it an unfair advantage. There have also been concerns that China has derived advantages from a deliberately undervalued currency (the yuan). In response to criticisms coming from the United States, China has emphasized its adherence to WTO rules and has at times imposed restraints on exports of some products such as textiles.[72] Announcements of major purchases from the United States (such as aircraft) can be used as a means of deflecting criticism.[73]

On the currency issue, China announced in July 2005 that it would link the yuan to a basket of currencies rather than to the US dollar alone. However, because of the limited impact of that measure there was pressure on China to go further; some members of Congress favored the imposition of retaliatory tariffs on Chinese imports.[74] Congress also became involved in mid-2005 when CNOOC (China National Offshore Oil Corporation) put in a US$18.5 billion takeover bid for Unocal, a major US oil firm.[75] Seventy percent of CNOOC is owned by the Chinese government. This was part of China's strategy for improving access to the resources it needed for its growing economy. In the end CNOOC withdrew its bid. Those members of Congress threatening to take action saw the takeover as detrimental to US security. Quite apart from the Unocal issue, concerns about the security implications of China's growing economic strength had led Congress to establish the US-China Economic and Security Review Commission in October 2000. The mandate of the commission was to report on the security implications of the US-China economic relationship.[76]

■ Human Rights Issues

Human rights issues have been an important focus in post–Cold War Sino-US relations. However, as revealed by the response to Tiananmen Square at the beginning of this period, pragmatic concerns focusing on strategic and economic issues ultimately prevailed. In the context of economic issues, this situation is revealed most clearly in the treatment of MFN status during the Clinton administration. We will begin by examining the domestic politics involved in human rights issues in both the United States and China. Then we will turn to the approach adopted by the two countries toward human rights at both a general level and in relation to specific issues.

The US approach to human rights issues in Sino-US relations is shaped by its underlying liberal democratic tradition. Whatever the reality of US foreign policy, there is an expectation that US governments will use their influence to achieve moral objectives. Various groups in the US attempt to hold governments to account in this respect. Some groups have a particular interest in human rights as such, while others focus on China's human rights record as a means of advancing their own interests. Labor unions, for example, highlight the way in which weak labor rights in China are detrimental not just for human rights, but for the interests of union members in the United States. Groups focusing on human rights in China usually engage in extensive lobbying, particularly in relation to Congress. Administrations usually prefer a more balanced approach, arguing in favor of engagement rather than sanctions as a means of improving conditions in China.

On the Chinese side there is usually resistance to US attempts to influence the human rights situation in China. China sees human rights as a domestic matter that should not be subject to external influence. Nevertheless human rights issues now feature prominently on the international agenda, and China defends its record in the relevant forums such as the UN Commission on Human Rights (replaced by the UN Human Rights Council in 2006).[77] A particular strategy that China uses in relation to the United States is to criticize the US record on human rights, particularly in relation to social and economic rights, and the position of minorities such as African Americans. Because the United States places some emphasis on human rights, China is forced to give some attention to these issues to avoid suffering adverse consequences in its strategic and economic relationships with the United States.

As far as the competing approaches to human rights are concerned, the US emphasis is on civil and political rights. It highlights the way authoritarian government in China prevents people from expressing their views on a range of issues. While the focus at one level is on the rights of individuals, the United States is also concerned about political repression in regions such as Tibet and Xinjiang, and the limits on political expression in Hong Kong since the reversion of the territory to China in 1997. A good statement of the range of US concerns is the report on China (including separate sections on Tibet and Hong Kong) issued each year by the Department of State as part of its series of Country Reports on Human Rights Practices.[78] A particular concern with the issue of freedom of religious expression is reflected in the report on China published by the department as part of its annual International Religious Freedom Report.[79]

For its part China argues that the US approach is overly influenced by Western individualism. The Chinese view emphasizes priorities arising from the need to make basic provision for a population of about 1.3 billion. Hence the emphasis is on social and economic rights: the right to work, to have shelter, to be nourished. These rights are regarded as more important than the rights of individuals and groups to freedom of political expression. From the Chinese perspective political expression needs to be restrained if it could jeopardize the social and economic rights of the vast majority. The needs of the whole take precedence over the political expression of the minority. A similar perspective influences China's approach to the issues of Tibet, Xinjiang, and Hong Kong: China has a right to uphold its territorial integrity against minorities who might wish to loosen the relationship or even break away.

Given the politics and perspectives involved, it is instructive to review some of the significant human rights developments affecting Sino-US relations during the period of the Bill Clinton and George W. Bush administrations. During the Clinton administration human rights issues were most prominent at the time of the debates in Congress about renewing MFN status. However, as we have seen, this opportunity for highlighting the issues was mainly prominent during Clinton's first administration and came to an end with the achievement of "permanent normal trade relations" with China in 2000. This is not to say that US concerns about a range of human rights situations in China came to an end. Rather these concerns were pursued in more ad hoc ways; for example, at the time of high-level US visits to China it became common for some dissidents to be released.[80]

The reversion of Hong Kong to China in 1997 occurred during the second Clinton administration. Congress had passed the United States–Hong Kong Policy Act in 1992 with a view to protecting US interests in Hong Kong, and to monitoring human rights in the territory after reversion. The United States has substantial economic interests in Hong Kong, particularly relating to the territory's role as a transshipment center. While China saw the act as unwarranted interference in its domestic affairs, US monitoring of human rights in Hong Kong did not become a major issue. In many respects Tibet was a more prominent issue on the Sino-US human rights agenda. For many in the United States, the Tibetans appeared as a persecuted minority, with religious persecution heightening this perception. The international role of the Dalai Lama, including his visits to the United

States, contributed to the understanding of this issue as one involving free-dom of religious expression. Even though the Dalai Lama supported auton-omy rather than independence for Tibet, China saw the movement he led as a threat to Chinese territorial integrity. Success for the Tibetans would en-courage separatists in Xinjiang, and would also provide moral comfort for the cause of Taiwanese independence. For this reason China strongly resis-ted US efforts to achieve some concessions on the Tibetan issue.

Under the George W. Bush administration pressure on China over human rights issues has eased in some respects because of the impact of September 11. Initially the Bush administration had indicated that it would take a stronger stance on human rights issues than had the Clinton admin-istration. In the first part of 2001 the United States sponsored a resolution at the UN Human Rights Commission that was critical of China's human rights record, and Bush himself received the Dalai Lama on an official visit in Washington.[81] Chinese cooperation in the war on terrorism appeared to be rewarded when the United States condemned the East Turkestan Is-lamic Movement (ETIM) in Xinjiang as a terrorist organization in August 2002, and then did not sponsor a resolution critical of China at the UNHRC in April 2003.[82] Condemnation of the ETIM did not, however, mean that the United States had abandoned support for the rights of the Uighurs in Xinjiang. Whatever the specific developments, the rhetoric of US policy remains critical of the human rights situation in China. While making some concessions from time to time, China continues to be defen-sive about its human rights record.

*   *   *

In the early twenty-first century relations between China and the United States were dominated by strategic and economic issues. While September 11, 2001, certainly affected US relations with China, in the long term the question was how the United States would adjust to China's growing power in the region. Would a policy of strategic cooperation prevail or would difficulties arise that could lead to serious conflict? The major cloud on the horizon in the latter respect was Taiwan. While China and the United States might be able to manage this situation on their own, Taiwan was also an independent factor. Any serious push for official independence by Taiwan would be unacceptable to China. If China took military action to counter Taiwan this could lead to Sino-US war. At a rational level this would be contrary to China's interests in expanding its economic ties with the outside world. However, rationality does not necessarily prevail when nationalist emotions take over. Apart from this uncertain strategic situation there will continue to be very important economic issues between China and the United States. China will wish to maintain its access to the US market, while the United States will encourage the further opening of China to the globalized economy. Human rights issues will be a continuing theme in the relationship, although not as significant as the strategic and economic issues. The cultural divergence between China and the United States has been an important theme in the relationship. While China's opening to the outside world might be expected to reduce this divergence, this is not necessarily the case. There are countless examples of xenophobic responses when there is increased interaction with other cultures. The social changes resulting from China's economic transformation might also lead to political instability. This might be a wild card not just for Sino-US relations, but for the future of China itself.

■ Notes

1. The development of Sino-US relations from 1972 until the early 1990s is covered in detail in Harding, *A Fragile Relationship,* and Mann, *About Face.* See also Garrison, *Making China Policy;* Foot, *The Practice of Power.*
2. "US-China Joint Communique, August 17, 1982," *Department of State Bulletin,* vol. 82, no. 2067 (October 1982), p. 20.
3. See Tan, "US-China Nuclear Cooperation Agreement."
4. Woon, "Chinese Arms Sales and US-China Military Relations," p. 602.
5. McLaurin and Moon, *The United States and the Defense of the Pacific,* p. 165.
6. Ross, "National Security, Human Rights, and Domestic Politics," p. 282.
7. *Congressional Quarterly Weekly Report,* 10 June 1989, pp. 1411, 1426.
8. Richard L. Williams, "US Response to Changes in China," *Current Policy,* no. 1195, p. 2.
9. Lawrence S. Eagleburger, "US Actions Toward China," *Current Policy,* no. 1247, pp. 3–4.
10. "A Policy Confrontation on China?" *Congressional Quarterly Weekly Report,* 24 June 1989, p. 1564.
11. "Bush Bid to Fix Beijing Ties Strains Those with Hill," *Congressional Quarterly Weekly Report,* 24 June 1989, pp. 3434–3435.
12. Ibid., p. 3435.
13. Shambaugh, *Beautiful Imperialist,* pp. 226–227.
14. Ibid., p. 235. See also Wang and Lin, "Chinese Perceptions in the Post–Cold War Era," which suggests that elite views of the United States can be seen from "ideological," "geopolitical," and "global interdependence" perspectives.
15. Harding, "China's American Dilemma," pp. 14–15.
16. See Yahuda, "Sino-American Relations," pp. 188–189.
17. *Keesing's Record of World Events,* vol. 35 (1989), p. 36455.
18. Robert Delfs, "Regrets Only," *Far Eastern Economic Review,* 9 March 1989, p. 11.
19. "US Interference Protested," *Beijing Review,* 12–25 June 1989, p. 7.

20. "US Congress' Bill Refuted," *Beijing Review,* 31 July–6 August 1989, p. 6.

21. "Anti-China Clamour Cannot Intimidate Chinese People," *Beijing Review,* 17–23 July 1989, pp. 14–15.

22. Qian Qichen, "Current International Situation and Sino-US Relations," *Beijing Review,* 9–15 October 1989, pp. 7–9.

23. "US Must Take Steps to Patch Up Sino-US Rift," *Beijing Review,* 13–19 November 1989, pp. 5–6.

24. "China Protests US Congress Bill," *Beijing Review,* 27 November–3 December 1989, p. 7; "US Bill on Student Visas Censured," *Beijing Review,* 4–10 December 1989, p. 7.

25. Robert Delfs and Susumu Awanohara, "Angling for Influence," *Far Eastern Economic Review,* 21 December 1989, p. 10.

26. Two detailed studies of Sino-US relations in the 1989–2000 period are Lampton, *Same Bed, Different Dreams,* and Suettinger, *Beyond Tiananmen.*

27. Shambaugh, *Beautiful Imperialist.*

28. Lampton, *Same Bed, Different Dreams,* p. 292.

29. See Shambaugh, *Modernizing China's Military,* especially chapter 2.

30. Bernstein and Munro, *The Coming Conflict with China;* Gertz, *The China Threat.*

31. See Suettinger, *Beyond Tiananmen,* pp. 111–117, for a more detailed discussion of the Gulf War as an issue in Sino-US relations.

32. See Shambaugh, *Modernizing China's Military,* pp. 69–74.

33. See Suettinger, *Beyond Tiananmen,* Chapter 6; Lampton, *Same Bed, Different Dreams,* pp. 46–55.

34. Lampton, *Same Bed, Different Dreams,* pp. 52–53.

35. Suettinger, *Beyond Tiananmen,* p. 255.

36. Rice, "Campaign 2000."

37. Quoted in Talbott, "US-China Relations in a Changing World," p. 7.

38. See Susan V. Lawrence, with David Murphy, Murray Hiebert, and Nayan Chanda, "How to Start a Cold War," *Far Eastern Economic Review,* 12 April 2001, pp. 14–18; Bruce Gilley and David Murphy, "Power Play in Hainan," *Far Eastern Economic Review,* 19 April 2001, pp. 16–20.

39. www.cnn.com/2001/ALLPOLITICS/04/25/bush.taiwan.03/ (accessed 6 August 2004).

40. See Friedberg, "11 September and the Future of Sino-American Relations"; Roy, "China and the War on Terrorism"; Malik, "Dragon on Terrorism."

41. See Deng, "Hegemon on the Offensive"; Roy, "China's Reaction to American Predominance," pp. 57–78.

42. Ward, "China and America," pp. 46–47.

43. See, for example, Lampton, *Same Bed, Different Dreams,* pp. 83–97; Kan, *China and Proliferation of Weapons of Mass Destruction and Missiles;* Malik, "The Proliferation Axis."

44. Lampton, *Same Bed, Different Dreams,* p. 83.

45. Ibid., p. 89.

46. Ahmed Rashid, "The Bomb Traders," *Far Eastern Economic Review,* 12 February 2004, pp. 14–16.

47. Lampton, *Same Bed, Different Dreams,* pp. 89–90.

48. Ward, "China and America: Trouble Ahead?" pp. 47–48.

49. Bernard Gwertzman, "Q & A: China Hoping to Avoid Confrontation over Iran's Nuclear Program," *New York Times,* 26 January 2006.

50. See statement of Patricia R. Sheikh, deputy administrator, International Trade Policy, Foreign Agricultural Service, US Department of Agriculture, before the US-China Commission, Washington, DC, 18 January 2002. http://japan.usembassy.gov/e/p/tp-ec0390.html (accessed 6 August 2004).

51. US-China Business Council, "Foreign Investment in China," www.uschina.org/statistics/2005foreigninvestment.html (accessed 7 October 2005).

52. US-China Business Council, "FDI in China (Total and US) 1979–2004," www.uschina.org/statistics/fdi_cumulative.html (accessed 7 October 2005).

53. Noland, "US-China Economic Relations," pp. 122–123.

54. Ibid., p. 122.

55. The arguments of the Bush administration are well presented in the statement by Richard Solomon, assistant secretary of state for East Asian and Pacific affairs, to the Subcommittee on East Asian and Pacific Affairs of the Senate Foreign Relations Committee, 6 June 1990. See Richard H. Solomon, "China and MFN: Engagement, not Isolation, Is Catalyst for Change," *Current Policy,* no. 1282.

56. Ross, "National Security, Human Rights, and Domestic Politics," pp. 305–306.

57. Ross, "US Policy Toward China," p. 354.

58. "Bush Meets with Dalai Lama; Visit Highlights China Policy," *Congressional Quarterly Weekly Report,* 20 April 1991, p. 1002.

59. "Issue: MFN Status for China," *Congressional Quarterly Weekly Report,* 31 October 1992, p. 3459.

60. Shirley A. Kan, "Clinton's China Syndrome," *Far Eastern Economic Review,* 1 July 1993, p. 23.

61. Susumu Awanohara, "Full Circle," *Far Eastern Economic Review,* 9 June 1994, p. 15.

62. "Jiang on Sino-US Relations," *Beijing Review,* 31 May–6 June 1993, p. 4.

63. See Tony Walker, "China Goes on Offensive over MFN," *Financial Times,* 17 March 1994, p. 7; Patrick E. Tyler, "Ready to Revert to Cold War, China Says," *International Herald Tribune,* 21 March 1994, pp. 1, 4; "A Mixed Approach by Beijing to US," *International Herald Tribune,* 7 April 1994, p. 6.

64. Suettinger, *Beyond Tiananmen,* p. 392.

65. See ibid., pp. 392–398.

66. Ibid., pp. 397–398.

67. Noland, "US-China Economic Relations," pp. 135–336.

68. Suettinger, *Beyond Tiananmen,* pp. 359–360.

69. For details of the negotiations in April and November 1999, see ibid., pp. 363–369, 386–388.

70. For an excellent overview of the issues involved in the Chinese entry to the WTO, see Lardy, *Integrating China into the Global Economy.*

71. See Suettinger, *Beyond Tiananmen,* p. 95. The report may be viewed at www.house.gov/coxreport/ (accessed 18 February 2006).

72. Pollack, "The United States and Asia in 2004," p. 6.

73. Pollack, "The United States and Asia in 2003," p. 7.

74. "Snow: US Wants Flexible China Currency," *Guardian Unlimited,* 6 October 2005, www.guardian.co.uk/uslatest/story/0,1282,-5326527,00.html (ac-

cessed 10 October 2005). On the prospects and implications of a US-China trade war, see Hughes, "A Trade War with China?"

75. Ben White, "Chinese Drop Bid to Buy US Oil Firm," *Washington Post,* 3 August 2005, www.washingtonpost.com/wp-dyn/content/article/2005/08/02/AR2005080200404.html (accessed 10 October 2005).

76. See the website for the US-China Economic and Security Review Commission, www.uscc.gov/ (accessed 10 October 2005).

77. On the international context of the human rights issue in China, see Foot, *Rights Beyond Borders.*

78. For the 2004 report, see www.state.gov/g/drl/rls/hrrpt/2004/41640.htm (accessed 7 October 2005).

79. For the 2004 report, see www.state.gov/g/drl/rls/irf/2004/35396.htm (accessed 7 October 2005).

80. Lampton, *Same Bed, Different Dreams,* p. 141.

81. Foot, "Bush, China and Human Rights," pp. 176–177.

82. Ibid., pp. 179, 181.

The Sino-Japanese Relationship | 7

In addition to the Japanese-US and the Sino-US relationships, the Sino-Japanese relationship has been essential to the dynamics of international politics in post–Cold War Asia Pacific. Whereas the United States theoretically has the option of reducing its presence or even withdrawing from the region, China and Japan are inextricably part of its future. To understand the development of the Sino-Japanese relationship in the post–Cold War era, it is helpful to consider how it developed in the past, particularly in the post-1945 period.

■ The Postwar Context

From China's perspective, Japan's international role in the post-1945 period was closely related to the US-Japan Mutual Security Treaty of 1951. This meant that insofar as there was an antagonistic relationship between China and the United States, there was also hostility between China and Japan. Conversely, when the Sino-US relationship improved, so did the relationship between China and Japan. When antagonism prevailed, it tended to be reinforced by the historical memories China had of Japan. In recent years, these memories concerned imperialist depredations, beginning with the loss of Taiwan in 1895. Japan's occupation of Manchuria in 1931 and its launching of war against China in 1937 were very fresh in Chinese minds. During the 1950s and 1960s, antagonism prevailed in Sino-US relations, and this was likewise the case in Sino-Japanese relations.

Japan's view of China was greatly influenced by the cultural similarities of the two peoples and the nature of their long-term historical relationship. Hidenori Ijiri sums up the situation: "The Japanese have an inferiority

complex due to their cultural debt to China and the sense of original sin
stemming from their past aggression against China, while having a superi-
ority complex based upon their assistance to China's modernization and
contempt for China's backwardness."[1]

In the post-1945 period, Japan's relationship with the United States
had a major bearing on its relationship with China. In the 1951 peace
treaty, Japan concluded peace with the Republic of China on Taiwan rather
than with the People's Republic of China. It followed the US lead in not
extending diplomatic recognition to the PRC and it supported the US policy of containing China. At the same time, Japan developed trade relations
with China under the guise of "the separation of politics from economics."
By 1965 Japan had succeeded the USSR as China's most important trading partner,[2] but Japan still maintained strong links with Taiwan.

Sino-Japanese diplomatic normalization came in the aftermath of the
Sino-US rapprochement proclaimed in the Shanghai Communiqué of February 1972. The Sino-Japanese communiqué of September 1972, which
prepared the way for full diplomatic relations, stated: "Neither power
should seek hegemony in the Asia Pacific region and each is opposed to the
efforts by any other country or group of countries to seek such hegemony."[3]
The Chinese believed that the first part of this statement placed limits on
Japan's role in the region and that the second part was directed against the
USSR.

The signing in 1978 of a long-term trade agreement and the Treaty of
Peace and Friendship further consolidated the Sino-Japanese relationship.
By this stage, Soviet-US relations had deteriorated again after a period of
détente earlier in the decade. Since the Sino-Soviet conflict continued as
before, this meant that there was a convergence in Chinese and US perceptions of the USSR, which had implications for Sino-Japanese relations.
China now looked favorably on Japanese rearmament; a stronger Japan
could make a positive contribution to a China-US-Japan alignment arrayed
against Soviet hegemonism.

Following the long-term trade agreement, there was considerable
growth in Sino-Japanese trade. The total trade between the two countries
rose from US$5 billion in 1978 to US$19.3 billion in 1988.[4] It has been argued that Japan was motivated not so much by economic factors as by a
"long-term political interest in a stable China."[5] Japan's problems in dealing
with China were clearly shown in 1982, when China unilaterally canceled
Japanese contracts worth 300 billion yen for the construction of the Baoshan
steelworks near Shanghai.[6] Despite China's claims that the location of the
works was faulty, it appeared that the real reason for China's action was the
effect on revenue of its inability to produce and export crude oil to the level

provided for under the long-term trade agreement.[7] This episode understandably contributed to Japanese caution about investing in China.

During the 1980s, there were further changes in the strategic situation, particularly with the development of Soviet-US détente during the Gorbachev era. One effect of the détente was that China became less strategically significant to the United States, a factor that encouraged Sino-Soviet rapprochement. Economic tensions between Japan and the United States led to questions about the future of the US-Japan security relationship. Increasingly, Japan was seen as a more independent element in Asia Pacific. Given that Japan was a potential future rival, China was less encouraging about Japanese rearmament and preferred to see Japan have a more limited defense role.

A number of episodes during the 1980s illustrated the importance of cultural and political sensitivities in the Sino-Japanese relationship.[8] In 1982 and 1986, there were Chinese protests against watered-down accounts in Japanese textbooks of Japanese actions in China during the Sino-Japanese war of 1937–1945. In August 1985, China took strong exception to an official visit paid by Prime Minister Nakasone Yasuhiro of Japan to the Yasukuni Shrine in Tokyo. This shrine honored Japan's war dead, including those who had been convicted as war criminals. China was also sensitive to Japan's development of closer relations with Taiwan, albeit on an unofficial level. This sensitivity was illustrated in China's reaction in February 1987 to a decision by the Osaka High Court, which said that ownership of a student hostel (known as Kokaryo) in Kyoto could be retained by Taiwan rather than switching to the PRC as a consequence of diplomatic normalization.

By 1989, then, Japan and China were clearly more involved with each other at both political and economic levels, but the relationship remained sensitive. Economically, Japan was much more significant to China than China was to Japan. In 1990 China accounted for 3.1 percent of Japan's exports and 5.3 percent of its imports. Japan's share of China's total trade in 1990 was 15.1 percent.[9] In that year, there was a trade surplus in China's favor of nearly US$6 billion; textiles, energy (coal and oil), and food were China's main exports, and machinery, manufactured goods, and chemical products its main imports.[10] Although Japan's direct foreign investment in China was limited, it was an important source of foreign aid. In 1988 Japan provided 36.3 percent of China's foreign aid, excluding multilateral sources.[11] Japan's interest in the long-term political stability of China was still a major consideration. Japan's private investors were wary about the investment climate in China, but the Japanese government wanted to support developments that would encourage greater stability.

The economic ties between China and Japan have been appropriately described as "the ties that bind."[12] That is, whatever the political tensions and cultural sensitivities in the relationship, both China and Japan have had a strong incentive to promote their mutual economic interests. By the early 1990s, Japan was China's most important trading partner, accounting for about one-fifth of its foreign trade; by comparison, China accounted for 4–5 percent of Japan's foreign trade.[13] For the most part, trade balances have been in Japan's favor, although the balance has changed more recently. China supplies foodstuffs, textiles, and energy sources to Japan and takes consumer goods, finished steel products, and fertilizers in return. Japan has been generous in providing official development assistance and loans to facilitate China's modernization, but private long-term investment (including technology transfer) has lagged.[14] On the basis of interviews, Allen Whiting reports a Chinese perception that Japan is "determined to hold China back,"[15] but Japanese investment behavior is linked more closely to an assessment of risks.

Post-1989 developments in the Sino-Japanese security relationship must be analyzed in the context of the economic relationship. China and Japan might see each other as potential political rivals, but economic realities encourage some modification in behavior that might otherwise lead to conflict. Although there have been some tensions in the relationship, in general China and Japan have not been involved in any major conflict in the post–Cold War period. Even Tiananmen Square resulted in only a minor setback to Sino-Japanese cooperation. China and Japan are concerned about how they relate to each other in the evolving strategic situation in post–Cold War Asia Pacific, but some issues have impinged on the broader relationship. These include not just the Beijing massacre, but also the Gulf crisis, the questions of Hong Kong and Taiwan, the Senkakus issue (known as the Diaoyu to the Chinese), and the war guilt issue. These issues will be considered in turn before presenting an assessment of the relationship as it appeared in the early twenty-first century.

■ Tiananmen Square

During the first part of 1989, the issues in Sino-Japanese relations were reflected in the official visits made by the two countries' leaders. Foreign Minister Qian Qichen represented China at Emperor Hirohito's funeral in February 1989. China failed to send a more senior representative because of its anger at a statement by Prime Minister Takeshita Noboru that Hirohito held no responsibility for Japanese atrocities in China during World

War II.[16] Premier Li Peng visited Japan in April 1989. According to Li, the bases of Sino-Japanese relations were the joint statement of 1972, the Treaty of Peace and Friendship of 1978, and the four principles of "peace and friendship, equality and mutual benefit, mutual trust, and long-term stability."[17] Prime Minister Takeshita said Japan would uphold the "one-China" principle and not develop official relations with Taiwan.[18]

As with China's relations with other countries, its relations with Japan were interrupted by the massacre at Tiananmen Square in June 1989. Japan was cautious in responding to this event. On the one hand, Japan did not want to be out of line with its Western allies, who were generally more forthright in condemning China's actions. On the other hand, there were special factors affecting Japan's relationship with China, including the legacy of Japan's past aggression against China, particularly in the 1930s and 1940s, that led Japan to be less critical of the event.

Although initially reluctant to follow the Western countries in applying sanctions on China, Japan did announce on 20 June 1989 that it would suspend a five-year aid program amounting to US$5.5 billion in soft loans that had been due to commence the following April.[19] At the same time, Japan remained reluctant to isolate China. While Foreign Minister Mitsuzuka Hiroshi criticized China for actions "not compatible with the basic values of our country," he also said that it was "China's internal affair."[20] When the G7 leaders met in Paris in mid-July 1989, Uno and Mitsuzuka lobbied in favor of a conciliatory approach and against the imposition of joint sanctions.[21] Nevertheless, Japan supported the G7 declaration, which said: "We look to the Chinese authorities to create conditions which will avoid their isolation and provide for a return to cooperation based upon the resumption of movement toward political and economic reform and openness."[22]

Japan was reluctant to ease its sanctions against China without modification in US policy. Prime Minister Kaifu Toshiki emphasized the need for a joint approach when he visited Washington, DC, in September 1989.[23] At the same time, Japan maintained contact with China through various business and unofficial political delegations.[24] Japan viewed the visit by US National Security Adviser Brent Scowcroft to Beijing in December 1989 as an indication that the United States was modifying its approach to China.[25] Nevertheless, while the United States continued its sanctions policy, it remained difficult for Japan to resume its aid program to China. In July 1990, at the G7 summit in Houston, Kaifu finally gained Bush's tacit approval for resuming Japan's proposed soft loans to China for 1990–1995. According to Kaifu, the loans would "encourage the process of reform and open-door policy" in China.[26]

In August 1991 Kaifu became the first leader from a major Western country to visit China following Tiananmen Square. The visit was indicative of the changing emphases in Sino-Japanese relations. Whereas in the past economic issues had been a priority in the relationship, the focus of this visit was on broader international issues in which Japan and China were both involved.[27] These issues included China's agreement to sign the Nuclear Nonproliferation Treaty, announced at the time of Kaifu's visit, as well as cooperation in relation to Cambodia and Korea. By acting as a bridge between China and the West, particularly in the regional context, Japan was attempting to develop a more significant international role for itself.

The Gulf Conflict

Even before Kaifu's visit to China, the Persian Gulf crisis of 1990–1991 had had some effect on Sino-Japanese relations. There was some concern in China that the Japanese debate about sending its troops to assist in peacekeeping operations might presage a more ambitious Japanese military role. Commentary in the Chinese press suggested that the proposed UN Peace Cooperation Bill allowing the dispatch of Japanese forces on such missions would cause "severe and emotional repulsion" from the Chinese people, who "worry that there will be a repetition of history."[28] Official reactions were more restrained.[29] Although the bill was not passed at the time of the Gulf crisis, a similar peacekeeping operations bill was passed in June 1992. Chinese concerns about the bill were similar to those expressed in 1990.[30]

Hong Kong, Taiwan, and Senkakus/Diaoyu

Hong Kong

The Hong Kong and Taiwan issues have also had a bearing on the development of Sino-Japanese relations. Japan's interest in these two newly industrializing economies has been primarily economic. In 2004, Hong Kong ranked fourth as a destination for Japanese investment in Asia and fifth in the world as a market for Japanese exports.[31] Hong Kong is important to Japan not only for the economic access it provides to China but also as a regional and global economic center in its own right.[32]

For these reasons, the Japanese government was active in lobbying the Chinese and British governments and the Hong Kong authorities about issues relating to Hong Kong. Japan's main concern was to preserve Hong Kong as an economic center; questions relating to the political system were regarded as secondary. When Chinese foreign minister Qian Qichen visited Japan in June 1991, Prime Minister Kaifu told him, "It is important for Hong Kong to maintain its economic freedom and vitality for the development of China's reform and Open Door policy, as well as for Sino-Japanese and Sino-British relations."[33] Since the reversion of Hong Kong to China under the "one country, two systems" formula in 1997, Japan has continued to focus on economic issues in its relations with Hong Kong. It has kept a low profile in relation to issues concerning democracy in Hong Kong and the role of the Chinese government in the "special administrative region."

Taiwan

Japan's links to Taiwan date to the period between 1895 and 1945, when the island was a Japanese colony. For many years Taiwan was actually of greater economic significance to Japan than was China. In 1990, for example, total bilateral trade between Japan and Taiwan was US$23.9 billion, exceeding Japan's trade with China by US$5.7 billion.[34] In 2004 Taiwan was Japan's seventh most important source of imports, and fourth most important destination for exports.[35]

Despite these economic links with Taiwan, since 1972 Japan has assiduously avoided having official relations with it. Although there was Taiwanese resentment, Japan did not want to anger China, which was far more important to Japan politically and strategically.[36] For its part, China wanted Japan to continue to adhere to the "one China" policy as agreed to in 1972. China believed that Japan's economic and political links with Taiwan tended to undermine its commitment to the policy.

When China undertook missile tests in the Taiwan Strait in March 1996 in an attempt to pressure Taiwan, Japan adopted a cautious line, expressing understanding for the US position but also noting, "China is a very important neighbour for us."[37] Nevertheless the Joint Security Declaration signed by President Clinton and Prime Minister Hashimoto in April 1996 caused tensions in Sino-Japanese relations. China saw the commitment in the declaration "to promote bilateral policy coordination, including studies on bilateral cooperation in dealing with situations that may emerge in the areas surrounding Japan"[38] as implying that Japan could become directly involved in the Taiwan issue. Similarly, with Japanese involvement in the development of theater missile defense, one of China's concerns is that this could encourage Japanese involvement in any crisis over Taiwan. Essentially Japan supports the status quo in relation to Taiwan, but is also strongly influenced by

US policy on the issue. Should there be a crisis over Taiwan leading to direct US involvement, Japan might attempt to maintain its cautious approach but would come under very heavy pressure from the United States to provide at least indirect support.

The Senkaku/Diaoyu Islands

The Sino-Japanese dispute over the sovereignty of the Senkaku or Diaoyu islands in the East China Sea flared in late 1990. In October, the Kaifu government, in response to strong protests from both China and Taiwan, announced that it was withdrawing recognition of a lighthouse built on the islands by a Japanese rightist group. The Chinese press saw this "brazen invasion" of Chinese territory as evidence of Japan's "expansionist mentality" and the "resurgence of the ghost of Japanese militarism."[39] As was the case in the Gulf crisis, however, the official Chinese reaction was more cautious. On 27 October Vice Foreign Minister Qi Huaiyuan declared China's "indisputable sovereignty" over the islands to the Japanese ambassador and also pointed out that in 1972 the two countries had agreed to "shelve the dispute." He proposed that China and Japan should discuss "shelving the sovereignty, jointly developing the resources in the waters around the Diaoyu Islands, and opening the local fishing resources to the outside world."[40]

The dispute over the Senkakus/Diaoyu flared again in July 1996, when Japanese rightists once more erected a lighthouse and other structures on the islands. Activists from Hong Kong and Taiwan vehemently protested Japanese actions. Japan was less than forthright in dealing with its own rightists, possibly because of Prime Minister Hashimoto Ryutaro's identification with a more nationalistic position. The Japanese government had in fact declared an exclusive economic zone (EEZ) of 200 miles (370 kilometers) around the Senkakus that took effect in July 1996.[41] The United States was equivocal when it came under Japanese pressure to state that the US-Japan security treaty covered the Senkakus, although eventually this was agreed to be the case.[42] In September 1997 China and Japan agreed to shelve the sovereignty issue and to establish a "joint management zone" covering the area previously declared an EEZ by Japan.[43]

Incidents involving Chinese and Japanese activists continued over subsequent years. In 2003 and early 2004 Chinese activists made four attempts to land on the islands. After a landing in March 2004 seven Chinese activists were arrested by Japanese police and subsequently returned to China. This led to demonstrations in Beijing, with Chinese protesters outraged that Japan should presume the islands to be Japanese territory.[44] Whatever the position taken by the activists, underlying the differences at an official level is the knowledge that the East China Sea is a potentially rich oil and gas area.[45]

▩ War Guilt

During the post–Cold war era the war guilt issue has continued as an important undercurrent in Sino-Japanese relations. China has used the issue as a means of restraining Japan from assuming a more prominent international role, particularly in terms of security issues. How the issue has featured in Sino-Japanese relations has been evident on a number of occasions. China would like Japan to issue a formal apology for Japan's behavior during the Sino-Japanese war of 1937–1945. For the most part Japanese leaders have been willing to express regret but not to the extent of a formal apology.

Following the enthronement of Emperor Akihito in November 1990, China had been keen to host an official visit by the new emperor as part of the process of restoring China's place in the international community. The problem for Japan, and right-wing nationalists in particular, was that such a visit might pressure the emperor to apologize for Japan's wartime behavior in China. In August 1992, however, Prime Minister Miyazawa said that the visit would take place to commemorate the twentieth anniversary of Sino-Japanese diplomatic normalization. In Beijing, on 23 October, Akihito spoke of his "deep sadness" about "an unfortunate period in which my country inflicted great sufferings on the people of China," but he did not give a formal apology.[46]

The issue of war guilt also featured in Japan's relations with China during the period of coalition governments, which was inaugurated under Hosokawa Morihiro in August 1993. Hosokawa stated on 10 August that Japan had fought "a war of aggression" and that he "would like to sincerely express [his] feelings for all war victims and their surviving families in the neighbouring nations of Asia as well as all the world."[47] During a visit to China in March 1994, he spoke in similar terms: "We deeply deplore [the suffering caused by Japan in the past] and we will, on the basis of the study of history, make continuing efforts to establish friendly ties with China."[48]

On 7 May 1994, Nagana Shigeto was forced to resign as justice minister in the Hata government after he claimed that the 1937 Nanjing massacre was a "hoax" and had "never really happened." He denied that Japan was the aggressor in World War II, saying, "We really believed in the Greater East Asian Co-prosperity Sphere."[49] Hata Tsutomu reiterated his "deep remorse and convictions over the Japanese military's aggressive behavior and colonial rule [in Asia]. . . . Looking ahead to the 50th anniversary of the end of the war next year, we must express to future generations [our remorse]."[50]

The war guilt issue was prominent in 1995 but was not resolved in Sino-Japanese relations. Prime Minister Murayama Tomiichi visited the Marco Polo Bridge in Nanjing (where hostilities in the Sino-Japanese war had commenced in 1937) during his visit to China in May 1995,[51] but efforts to pass a war apology resolution in the Diet proved less than satisfactory. The resolution as approved by the lower house on 9 June qualified "a sense of deep remorse" by referring to "many instances of colonial rule and aggression . . . in the modern history of the world."[52] Within the coalition government, the Socialists and the smaller Sakigake supported an apology, which much of the Liberal Democratic Party opposed. Murayama used the word "apology" when he spoke on 15 August, the anniversary of Japan's surrender in World War II.[53] Hashimoto Ryutaro, Murayama's successor, was unlikely to use such language given his links to the right. His visit to the Yasukuni war shrine on 29 July 1996 caused some controversy.[54]

When President Jiang Zemin visited Japan in November 1998, Prime Minister Obuchi Keizo spoke of his "deep remorse" for "the serious distress and damage that Japan caused to the Chinese people through its aggression against China," but avoided the term "heartfelt apology" that Jiang had sought. While this term had been used a short time before in a Japanese attempt to improve relations with South Korea, South Korea had also said that this statement would resolve the war guilt issue in its case. China was unwilling to give that guarantee.[55]

Visits to the Yasukuni shrine by Japanese ministers have continued to be an irritant in Sino-Japanese relations. Koizumi Junichiro, prime minister from April 2001, has visited the shrine annually. While Koizumi has said that the purpose of his visits is to pray for peace, Chinese leaders have made clear that he must cease these visits if he is to visit China.[56]

Chinese sensitivity over the treatment of Sino-Japanese relations in Japanese school textbooks has continued. In August 2004 the board of education in Tokyo approved a textbook undertaken by the Japanese Society for History Textbook Reform. Among other things the 1937 "rape of Nanking" became the Nanking "incident" in which a "large number of Chinese" died rather than the 300,000 in Chinese estimates.[57]

■ The Relationship in the Early Twenty-First Century

While the various specific issues as previously discussed have continued to feature in Sino-Japanese relations in the early twenty-first century, it is also helpful to focus on the main features of the overall relationship during this time.[58] This can be done from the perspectives of both Japan and China.

From Japan's perspective an important concern is that China might emerge as the hegemonic power of East Asia. It wants to guard against this possibility but without directly confronting China. This means that Japan has to be careful in any expansion of its security role, including the development of relationships with other powers in the region. The strengthening and modernization of the Japan-US security relationship is also relevant to restraining China, but again there is a problem if China interprets such changes as directed against it. Another concern for Japan is that the United States might accord higher priority to US-China relations than to US-Japan relations (the phenomenon of "Japan passing"). At the time of the presidential election campaign in the United States in 2000, this is what the Republicans accused the Clinton administration of having done. The Japanese view is that Japan should have a special role in US policy in the region because of the US-Japan security alliance. There is also an assumption in Japan that a strategy of economic engagement will encourage China to play a cooperative role. China is more dependent economically on Japan than vice versa. In 2004 China took 13.1 percent of Japan's exports (second only to the United States as a destination) and provided 20.7 percent of Japan's imports (the most important source).[59] For China in 2004, Japan took 12.4 percent of its exports (third after the United States and Hong Kong), and provided 16.8 percent of its imports (the most important source). China is an important destination for Japanese investment, ranking third in 2004 with US$4.6 billion.[60] China is also the single most important recipient of Japanese aid, receiving US$1.3 billion in 2003.[61]

A problem with this strategy is that closer economic relations do not necessarily lead to political harmony. Rationally, states should not act to damage themselves economically, but clearly irrational factors sometimes intrude into international politics. If a conflict arose over Taiwan, for example, this could be due to pressures relating to Chinese nationalism and possibly sentiment in favor of independence on Taiwan. This could occur despite the fact that the parties involved have a strong economic stake in continued peaceful relations. The same applies to relations between China and Japan. The economic benefits that both parties derive from Japan's engagement strategy could be overridden in some circumstances, such as a conflict over Taiwan. Because of this possibility Japan also follows a hedging strategy involving the maintenance and strengthening of its own defense posture, and a strong focus on the security relationship with the United States.

From China's perspective it aims to be the leading power in East Asia. Clearly Japan as the region's major economic power and as a country with a significant defense force, linked to the United States through a mutual security treaty, constitutes a potential obstacle in the way of China realizing its ambition. In the long term China has the potential to surpass Japan as an economic power. However, even in those circumstances, Japan would still have one of the world's major economies. China, as previously indicated, derives significant economic benefits from its links with Japan. Assuming China remains on its trajectory toward becoming a leading economic power, the issue is how to ensure that Japan does not challenge China's political position. On specific security matters China is certainly antagonistic to any Japanese defense role relating to Taiwan. China's attitude toward the US-Japan security relationship is ambivalent. On the one hand that relationship could be seen as strengthening the forces that wish to restrain China. On the other hand the US-Japan relationship could be seen as restraining Japan. It prevents the development of Japanese militarism that is so much opposed by China. Insofar as US-China relations are positive this could have benefits for China in terms of advancing Chinese objectives in relation to Japan. More generally China attempts to gain support within the region for its view that Japan should only play a low-profile political role. One way it does this is through the war guilt issue: Japan's past transgressions, it is argued, mean that it should be restrained in what it does in the contemporary world. China seeks support from other regional countries, such as South Korea, for the position it advances on the war guilt issue and on Japan's international role more generally. It also pitches this argument to appeal to the strong pacifist sentiment in Japan itself.

Tensions between Japan and China were highlighted in 2005 when there were moves to expand both the size of the UN Security Council and the number of permanent members. Japan was one of the leading contenders for permanent membership. However, China strongly opposed this proposal, ostensibly on the grounds that Japan was not morally fit for such a position: Japan's contrition for its role in the Pacific war was insufficient. In strategic terms, of course, giving other Asian countries such as Japan and India permanent membership on the Security Council would have detracted from China's role as the sole Asian permanent member. The controversy provoked anti-Japanese rioting in China in April 2005, which was slow to subside. In fact it was alleged that the Chinese government was behind these disturbances since they provided a vehicle for making its anti-Japanese point. China's opposition to Japan was one of the factors that ended the moves to reform the Security Council.

▨ Notes

1. Ijiri, "Sino-Japanese Controversy Since the 1972 Diplomatic Normalization," p. 639.

2. Johnson, "Japanese-Chinese Relations, 1952–1982," p. 110.

3. Quoted in Iriye, "Chinese-Japanese Relations, 1945–90," p. 628.

4. Arnold, "Political and Economic Influences in Japan's Relations with China Since 1978," p. 419.

5. Arnold, "Japan and China," p. 103.

6. Arnold, "Political and Economic Influences in Japan's Relations with China Since 1978," p. 426.

7. Ibid., p. 428.

8. See Ijiri, "Sino-Japanese Controversy Since the 1972 Diplomatic Normalization"; Whiting, *China Eyes Japan*, chapters 3, 8.

9. Delfs and do Rosario, "China," p. 38.

10. Ibid., p. 39.

11. Ibid., p. 40.

12. *Far Eastern Economic Review*, 24 April 1986, as quoted in Delfs and do Rosario, "China," p. 38.

13. Whiting, *China Eyes Japan*, pp. 40–41.

14. Ibid., pp. 42–44. For more detail, see ibid., chapter 6; Newby, *Sino-Japanese Relations*, chapter 2.

15. Whiting, *China Eyes Japan*, p. 127.

16. *Keesing's Record of World Events*, vol. 36 (1990), p. 37341.

17. "Li Peng Scores Tokyo Touchdown," *Beijing Review*, 24–30 April 1989, p. 6.

18. Ibid.

19. "Japan to Suspend $5.5bn Aid to Peking," *Financial Times*, 21 June 1989, p. 26.

20. Stefan Wagstyl and Robert Thomson, "Japan Caught Between Awe and Contempt for China," *Financial Times*, 22 June 1989, p. 4.

21. Kesavan, "Japan and the Tiananmen Square Incident," p. 674.

22. Quoted, ibid.

23. Ibid., p. 675.

24. See Zhao, *Japanese Policymaking*, chapter 8.

25. Robert Thomson, "Japan Looks at Ties with China," *Financial Times*, 12 December 1989, p. 4.

26. "Japan's China Aid Plan Gets Bush's Tacit Support," *Japan Times*, 9 July 1990, p. 14.

27. Tai Ming Cheung and Louise do Rosario, "Seal of Approval," *Far Eastern Economic Review*, 22 August 1991, p. 10.

28. Quoted in "Quarterly Chronicle and Documentation (October–December 1990)," *China Quarterly*, no. 125 (March 1991), p. 209.

29. Whiting, "China and Japan," pp. 46–47.

30. *Keesing's Record of World Events*, vol. 38 (1992), pp. 38962–38963.

31. Japan External Trade Organization (JETRO), "Current Japanese Economy and Trade Statistics," www.jetro.go.jp/en/stats/statistics (accessed 21 September 2005).

32. Segal, *The Fate of Hong Kong*, p. 166; Goldstein and Rowley, "Hong Kong," p. 67.

33. Quoted in Segal, *The Fate of Hong Kong*, p. 167.

34. Baum and do Rosario, "Taiwan," p. 54.

35. Japan External Trade Organization, "Current Japanese Economy and Trade Statistics," www.jetro.go.jp/en/stats/statistics (accessed 21 September 2005).

36. See Masahiko Ishizuka, "Wrong End of the Telescope," *Far Eastern Economic Review,* 23 May 1991, p. 26.

37. Nigel Holloway, "Strait Talking," *Far Eastern Economic Review,* 21 March 1996, p. 16. On this issue, see further Drifte, *Japan's Security Relations with China Since 1989,* pp. 64–70.

38. "Japan-US Joint Declaration on Security: Alliance for the 21st Century," Appendix 6.1 in Hook et al., *Japan's International Relations,* p. 478.

39. Quoted in "Quarterly Chronicle and Documentation (October–December 1990)," *China Quarterly,* no. 125 (March 1991), p. 209. See also Tai Ming Cheung and Charles Smith, "Rocks of Contention," *Far Eastern Economic Review,* 1 November 1990, pp. 19–20.

40. Quotations from Whiting, "China and Japan," p. 48.

41. Drifte, *Japan's Security Relations with China Since 1989,* p. 51.

42. Green, *Japan's Reluctant Realism,* p. 87.

43. Ibid.

44. Roy, "The Sources and Limits of Sino-Japanese Tensions," p. 199.

45. Norimitsu Onishi and Howard W. French, "Japan's Rivalry with China Is Stirring a Crowded Sea," *New York Times,* 11 September 2005.

46. *Keesing's Record of World Events,* vol. 38 (1992), p. 39141. See also Lincoln Kaye, "Saving Faces," *Far Eastern Economic Review,* 5 November 1992, pp. 13–14.

47. Jonathan Friedland, "Blood Money," *Far Eastern Economic Review,* 26 August 1993, p. 21.

48. "China, Japan Vow Long-Term Friendship," *Beijing Review,* 28 March–3 April 1994, p. 4.

49. Charles Smith, "Foot in the Mouth," *Far Eastern Economic Review,* 19 May 1994, p. 30.

50. "Justice Chief Resigns After Denying Nanjing Massacre," *Japan Times* (Weekly International Edition), 16–22 May 1994, p. 5.

51. Lincoln Kaye, "Politics of Penitence," *Far Eastern Economic Review,* 6 July 1995, p. 23.

52. Charles Smith, "Sort of Sorry," *Far Eastern Economic Review,* 22 June 1995, p. 21.

53. *Strategic Survey 1995–1996,* p. 186.

54. Matt Forney et al., "Mute Point," *Far Eastern Economic Review,* 15 August 1996, p. 21.

55. Green, *Japan's Reluctant Realism,* pp. 96–98.

56. Roy, "The Sources and Limits of Sino-Japanese Tensions," p. 202.

57. Ibid.

58. More detailed assessments include Hook et al., *Japan's International Relations,* pp. 164–173; Tow, *Asia-Pacific Strategic Relations,* pp. 67–73; Green, *Japan's Reluctant Realism,* chapter 3; Drysdale and Zhang, ed., *Japan and China;* Australian Department of Foreign Affairs and Trade, East Asia Analytical Unit, *Asia's Global Powers;* Söderberg, ed., *Chinese-Japanese Relations in the Twenty-first Century;* Drifte, *Japan's Security Relations with China Since 1989.*

59. Japan External Trade Organization (JETRO), Economic Research Department, "Japanese Trade in 2004," appendix 1, Foreign Trade by Country and Region, www.jetro.go.jp/en/stats/statistics (accessed 16 September 2005).

60. Japan External Trade Organization (JETRO), *Current Japanese Economy and Trade Statistics,* "Japan's Outward FDI by Country/Region," www.jetro.go.jp/en/stats/statistics (accessed 16 September 2005).

61. Organisation for Economic Cooperation and Development, "Japan—Aid at a Glance Chart," www.oecd.org/dataoecd/42/5/1860382.gif (accessed 16 September 2005).

Part 2
Conflicts in Northeast Asia

Taiwan | 8

Having discussed the roles and interrelationships of the three major powers in Asia Pacific in Part 1, in this section we turn to a more detailed examination of two of the major conflicts of the region: Taiwan and Korea. Both conflicts are relevant to all three powers and also feature in the interrelationships of those powers. Taiwan, of course, is particularly important to China, and is a key issue in Sino-US relations. Although it is the United States that maintains a military commitment in South Korea, the Korean issue is equally important to all three powers. It features in the triangular relationship among those powers, while also involving other relationships such as those between each of the three powers and the two Koreas, not to mention the involvement of Russia.

In examining the Taiwan issue we need to establish why a conflict arose over this island, and what the course of that conflict has been. Then we will review more recent developments and assess the prospects for resolving the conflict.[1] The Taiwan conflict arose essentially as an unresolved issue at the time of the Chinese civil war in the late 1940s. With the onset of the Korean War in 1950 the United States intervened to prevent Chinese communist forces (representing the People's Republic of China) from crossing the Taiwan Strait and winning control of the province. Under the protection of the United States, Taiwan became effectively an independent state, all the while proclaiming that as the Republic of China it was the government of the whole of China. A significant change from the late 1980s was the gradual democratization of Taiwan. This reinforced sentiment on the island in favor of an independent Taiwan, while at the same time claims to represent the whole of China were abandoned. Throughout the course of the Taiwan conflict, the key factors have been the political situation on Taiwan itself (and the policies pursued as a consequence), the policies of the PRC, and the policies of the United States. In examining the various phases in the conflict we will focus on these three dimensions and how they have interacted in light of changing circumstances.

The first section of the chapter will examine the historical context, with reference to the 1949–1979 period, the 1980s, and the period of democratization on Taiwan from the late 1980s (corresponding roughly with the post–Cold War era). In the second section the focus is the post-2000 era, beginning with the election of Chen Shui-bian (the candidate of the proindependence Democratic Progressive Party) as president of Taiwan in March 2000. In the third section we examine the prospects for resolving the conflict, assessing the most significant factors and their likely impact in relation to different scenarios.

■ The Historical Context

Before 1949–1950, Taiwan's history had gone through various phases. Taiwan became an outlying province of the Chinese empire in the late seventeenth century. After the Sino-Japanese war of 1894–1895 China ceded sovereignty over the island to Japan. Taiwan remained a Japanese colony until Japan's defeat in 1945. At the Cairo Conference in 1943 the Allied powers had promised that sovereignty over Taiwan would revert to China upon Japan's defeat. From 1945 Taiwan became once again a province of China. In the meantime the conflict between nationalists and communists in China reached a peak in the civil war of the late 1940s. From their bases in northern China the communists gradually expanded their area of control to the whole of the mainland, with the People's Republic of China being proclaimed on 1 October 1949. The nationalist government that had previously been in control was known as the Republic of China. Led by Chiang Kai-shek, the nationalist government fled to Taiwan in late 1949. The Nationalists (Kuomintang or Guomindang) were not necessarily welcomed by the native Taiwanese, many of whom had taken part in an abortive uprising against mainland rule in February 1947. From the PRC's perspective Taiwan remained the last issue to settle to make the victory over the nationalists complete; the PRC confidently expected that its forces would accomplish this goal during 1950.

1949–1979

As with most developments affecting the Taiwan conflict, the frustration of PRC expectations was the outcome of the interaction between the situation in Taiwan, the position of the PRC, and the involvement of the United States. US intervention in the Taiwan conflict in 1950 arose in the context of the outbreak of the Korean War. The United States had not set out deliberately to intervene in the Chinese civil war; however, with the onset of the Korean War in June 1950, President Truman ordered the Seventh Fleet to the Taiwan Strait to prevent communist forces from attacking the nationalists on Taiwan. The US administration viewed the Korean War in Cold War terms. North Korea was part of the communist bloc and had attacked South Korea, an anticommunist state. Action in relation to Taiwan was part of a regional and global strategy to prevent any further communist expansion.

With the United States intervening, it was impossible for the PRC to gain control over Taiwan. The nationalist government was in effect protected by the United States. Even though the nationalist government ruled only Taiwan, it claimed to be the government of the whole of China. From the nationalist perspective the Chinese mainland was in rebellion, with the PRC leadership viewed as "communist bandits." The ROC's view of China was in fact broader than that of the PRC; most notably, the ROC maintained a claim to Mongolia as part of China. In the PRC's view Taiwan was rightfully part of China; this had been recognized by Roosevelt, Churchill, and Chiang Kai-shek in the 1943 Cairo Declaration. The PRC continued to proclaim its goal of bringing about Taiwan's "liberation," implying that force would be used if necessary.

By deploying its forces in the Taiwan Strait the United States had effectively intervened in the Chinese civil war. Some US leaders, such as General Douglas MacArthur (commander of UN forces in the Korean War), wanted to use nationalist forces in the context of widening the Korean War to include China, but the Truman administration opposed this. Although many Republicans were critical of the Truman administration on this issue, the Eisenhower administration also declined to "unleash" Chiang Kai-shek when it took office in 1953. However, Eisenhower said the Seventh Fleet would not prevent the nationalists from taking action on the mainland. He also moved to formalize the defense relationship with the ROC, with a mutual defense treaty being concluded in December 1954. When a crisis developed in 1955 over the communist shelling of the offshore islands of Quemoy and Matsu, however, the United States acted to prevent the situation from escalating into full-scale war. In effect the United States was upholding the status quo in the Taiwan Strait. It did not want to see a wider war resulting from the Taiwan conflict.

Taiwan was one of the major issues in the Sino-US conflict in the 1950s and 1960s. The PRC believed that the United States was using Taiwan as part of a strategy for encircling and thereby weakening China. The

United States believed that China had aggressive intentions in the region, and that the PRC's policy toward Taiwan was part of its expansionist design. The defense link with Taiwan was part of the US system of alliances in Asia Pacific that had the containment of China as a primary objective. While the United States deployed a formidable military power in the region, it did not wish to see the confrontation with China result in war.

By recognizing the ROC the United States upheld the principle of "one China." This recognition continued in the 1960s, although there were signs at this stage that the United States would have supported a shift to a "two Chinas" approach. Such an approach would have been opposed by both the PRC and the ROC. A complicating factor for the United States was the onset of the Vietnam War, with the United States often portraying the Chinese communists as the force behind the Vietnamese communists. Despite the opposition of both the PRC and ROC, any shift toward a two Chinas policy on the part of the United States would have been seen as a compromise with the PRC. Given the circumstances of the Vietnam War, this would have been difficult in terms of US domestic politics. Despite these undercurrents, there were no significant changes in the Taiwan issue during the 1960s.

Major changes occurred during the 1970s and were the result of the Sino-US rapprochement of 1972. Under the terms of the Shanghai Communiqué of February 1972, the United States put its position as follows: "The United States acknowledges that all Chinese on either side of the Taiwan Strait maintain there is but one China and that Taiwan is a part of China."[2] The United States did not oppose that position but wished to see the issue resolved peacefully. Essentially the United States extended diplomatic recognition to the PRC, with both governments opening "liaison offices" in their respective capitals. In 1978 there was an agreement on establishing full diplomatic relations, to take effect from the beginning of 1979. This meant that formal diplomatic relations between the United States and the ROC ended. It was now the United States and Taiwan that had informal liaison offices in each other's capitals. Another consequence of the 1978 agreement was that the mutual defense treaty between the United States and the ROC ended. Defense links continued but on a different basis. Congress passed the Taiwan Relations Act in 1979 to provide a framework for the new relationship between the United States and Taiwan. Among other things this provided for the continuation of extensive commercial links, with defense support to continue to maintain Taiwan's ability to defend itself.

The 1980s

With the formalization of US-PRC relations, and the consequent changes in Taiwan's position, the Taiwan issue appeared in a different light from what had prevailed previously. The PRC did not abandon its goal of integrating Taiwan with the mainland. However, whereas previously the emphasis had been on liberation, from 1979 onward the PRC said its aim was to bring about "peaceful reunification." In 1984 the PRC reached agreement with Britain about the transfer of Hong Kong to Chinese sovereignty in 1997. This transfer was to be on the basis of "one country, two systems," indicating that Hong Kong would remain a separate political and economic entity even after it became part of the "one China." The PRC saw this formula as relevant to Taiwan, suggesting also that Taiwan could retain its own armed forces. While the emphasis now was on peaceful reunification, Deng Xiaoping indicated in 1985 that force could be used against Taiwan in certain circumstances.[3] Five situations were relevant in this respect: if Taiwan leaned toward Moscow rather than Washington; if Taiwan developed nuclear weapons; if Taiwan claimed to be an independent state; if there was a loss of internal control in Taiwan as a result of the succession process; and if Taiwan continued to reject reunification talks for "a long period of time."

While the PRC appeared more confident during the 1980s about its ability to achieve its objectives in relation to Taiwan, Taiwan itself felt more threatened. It resisted overtures from the PRC, maintaining its policy of "three noes": no contact, no compromise, no negotiation. In practice there was some flexibility in Taiwan's position. In 1987 the ban on people from Taiwan traveling to the mainland was lifted, and from 1988 indirect trade and investment were permitted. Political change was occurring in Taiwan. Following Chiang Kai-shek's death in 1975, he was succeeded as president by his son, Chiang Ching-kuo. More significant was the emergence of Lee Teng-hui as president in 1988 after Chiang Ching-kuo's death. While all three presidents were from the Kuomintang, Lee Teng-hui was the first Taiwanese-born leader. It was under Lee that the moves toward democratization began, leading to significant changes in the Taiwan issue in future years.

In the context of Sino-US rapprochement, the United States generally maintained an accommodating position toward the PRC over the Taiwan issue in the 1980s. In the US presidential election campaign in 1980, Reagan had expressed a position more sympathetic to Taiwan but this did not last long once he was in office. The United States maintained its position in favor of a peaceful resolution of the issue and was the de facto guarantor for Taiwan's security. At the same time the statement agreed upon with the PRC on 17 August 1982 indicated that the United States "intends to reduce gradually its sales of arms to Taiwan."[4] Nevertheless, on 20 August 1982, Reagan issued his "Six Assurances" to Taiwan in which he said that no date had been set for ending arms sales, and that the US position on the

Taiwan issue had not changed. Taiwan would not be pressured to negotiate with the PRC.[5]

Post–Cold War: The Era of Democratization

From the 1990s the most significant development in the Taiwan issue has been the process of democratization occurring in Taiwan. This has given greater legitimacy to the government in Taiwan, while also reinforcing sentiment in favor of becoming an independent state. Democratization has also strengthened Taiwan's claims for international acceptance, particularly with public opinion in the United States. The PRC has felt threatened by moves to assert Taiwan's independence, again raising the possibility that force would be used to prevent such an eventuality.

Under Lee Teng-hui the focus was on strengthening the position of Taiwan, both domestically and internationally. He abandoned claims that the ROC was the government of the mainland as well as of Taiwan. In 1991 Lee declared an end to the "state of communist rebellion." Previously the ROC had said the reason it did not have effective as well as legal control of the mainland was that the area was in rebellion led by the Chinese communists. In terms of the new approach announced by Lee, the PRC was a "political entity which controls the mainland area," whereas the ROC was "a sovereign state on Taiwan." Under the Guidelines for National Unification announced in March 1991,[6] Lee envisaged a process involving three phases that would begin with people-to-people contacts, with government-to-government contacts, and with talks coming only later. Lee insisted that talks and negotiations should be on the basis of the PRC recognizing the ROC as a government. With his legitimacy further strengthened by his win in Taiwan's first fully democratic presidential election in 1996, Lee went further in July 1999 when he said that China and Taiwan had a "special state-to-state relationship."

At the international level Lee attempted to raise Taiwan's profile in various ways. Taiwan's "dollar diplomacy" won it recognition from about thirty small states, mainly in Africa, the South Pacific, Central America, and the Caribbean. However, most states continued to recognize the PRC. As a reflection of Taiwan's economic importance it had economic offices in about sixty countries. Although Taiwan campaigned for membership in the United Nations, the PRC's insistence on the "one China" principle blocked success. Generally Taiwan only had membership in international bodies if it was not recognized as a sovereign state. For example, in the Olympics and APEC Taiwan was involved as "Chinese Taipei"; Taiwan joined the World Trade Organization in 2002 as the "Customs Territory of Taiwan, Penghu, Kinmen and Matsu."

In response to the developments concerning Taiwan, the PRC essentially adhered to the position it had articulated during the 1980s. It refused to negotiate on a government-to-government basis, preferring to see the Taiwan issue as "unfinished business" from the civil war. The PRC's position was that negotiations should be on a party-to-party basis. This would maintain the fiction of the continuing civil war between the Chinese Communists and Nationalists (Kuomintang), although there was also a suggestion that parties other than the KMT could also be represented. "Peaceful reunification" remained the preferred approach, but China was not willing to renounce the use of armed force. In 1996, for example, Jiang Zemin stated: "We consistently stand for achieving reunification by peaceful means and through negotiations. But we will not undertake not to use armed force."[7] Renouncing the use of force in relation to Taiwan would be inconsistent with China's position that Taiwan is Chinese sovereign territory. Ahead of the presidential elections in Taiwan in March 1996, China carried out missile tests and naval exercises in the Taiwan Strait as a warning that it would not tolerate any moves toward independence.

With the very different approaches of China and Taiwan, contact between the two sides was mostly at an unofficial level. In this context there was agreement between the two sides to support "one China," but Taiwan said there was no agreement as to what this meant. For the PRC "one China" means the People's Republic of China; however, and this was the interpretation favored by Taiwan, "one China" could mean "one Chinese nation" but not necessarily "one Chinese state."

Despite the diverging approaches to the reunification issue, links between Taiwan and the mainland developed steadily during the 1990s. Although they could not travel directly from Taiwan to the mainland, there were an estimated 16 million visits by Taiwanese to the PRC between 1987 and 1999.[8] By the end of 1998 Taiwan had invested an estimated US$30 billion in China, amounting to 43 percent of the ROC's total overseas investment. At this point the PRC was Taiwan's third largest trading partner, with exports to China amounting to 20 percent of Taiwan's total exports.[9] As China and Taiwan became more connected at the people-to-people and economic levels, there was a suggestion that this would lead to greater political engagement, if not reunification. However, these developments did not appear to undermine Taiwanese sentiment in favor of either maintaining the status quo or asserting independence. Similarly the nationalism underlying China's position did not diminish.

The US position in relation to Taiwan might be characterized as one of "strategic ambiguity." The United States acted as a security guarantor for Taiwan but did not want to encourage any attempts by Taiwan to change the status quo. Any such attempts clearly had the potential to provoke China.

Similarly the United States wanted to signal to China that any attempt to change the status quo by force might lead to a US military response. Hence the United States responded to the Chinese military exercises in the Taiwan Strait in March 1996 by dispatching its own forces as a warning to China to desist. These forces were two aircraft carrier battle groups headed by the USS *Nimitz* and USS *Independence*.[10] The previous year, in 1995, Clinton had reluctantly allowed Lee Teng-hui entry to the United States for the award of an honorary degree from Cornell University, Lee's alma mater. China saw this visit as part of a strategy by Lee to gain greater official recognition and thereby enhance Taiwan's international status.

Despite the emphasis on strategic ambiguity in US policy, there appeared to be some shift toward Taiwan during the 1990s. With the end of the Cold War there was less need to cultivate China as a means of limiting the USSR. There were also concerns that Taiwan needed additional defense support if it were to counter China's growing armaments. This led to a liberal interpretation of the communiqué of 17 August 1982, allowing the United States to continue arming Taiwan because of the presumed dangers in the area. In 1992 President George H. W. Bush undertook to sell Taiwan 150 F-16 fighter aircraft. As mentioned previously, democratization in Taiwan led to greater support in the United States because Taiwan could be presented as a fellow democracy. With both the George H. W. Bush and Clinton administrations, however, the preference in the debate about whether to "contain" or "engage" China was generally in favor of the latter. While Taiwan could be useful in attempts to contain China, focusing on engagement meant that any pro-Taiwan sentiments had to be modified. Clinton made his position clear in his "three noes" statement of 1998: no independent Taiwan, no two Chinas or one Taiwan/one China, no membership for Taiwan as a state in international organizations.[11]

■ 2000 and Beyond

In March 2000 the Taiwan issue entered a new era with the election of Chen Shui-bian, the candidate of the proindependence Democratic Progressive Party (DPP), as Taiwan's president. Chen's victory with only 39 percent of the vote was due to a division in KMT support between two candidates, Lien Chan (vice president) and James Soong (previously Taiwan governor). Chen's success did not lead to a declaration of independence and, in fact, he committed himself at his inauguration in May 2000 to "five noes": no declaration of independence, no referendum on independence, no change in the ROC title, no reference to the "state-to-state" formula in the constitution, and no change in the Guidelines for National Unification.[12] Despite these commitments Chen's presidency was characterized by his attempts to enhance the sovereign status that he believed Taiwan already had. In August 2002 Chen referred to the Taiwan Strait as having "a country on each side,"[13] recalling Lee Teng-hui's special state-to-state relationship.

In 2003 there was debate in Taiwan about a proposal to hold a referendum on the issue of membership in the World Health Organization. There were concerns that this could be an attempt by Taiwan to strengthen its sovereignty status. At the time of the presidential elections in March 2004 a referendum was held with questions on the purchase of advanced anti-missile weapons and the establishment of a "peace and stability" framework for cross-Strait relations, but these only attracted 45 percent support.[14] In the election Chen won narrowly as the candidate for the pan-green coalition headed by the DPP. The pan-blue coalition of the KMT and the People First Party was headed by Lien Chan, with James Soong as vice presidential candidate.

In the aftermath of the election Chen signaled moves toward constitutional amendment, with a primary emphasis on "good governance" rather than sovereignty issues. Nevertheless Chinese observers also noted that Chen saw the aim of the referendum as making Taiwan a "normal, complete, and great democratic nation." Chen proclaimed that "Taiwan is an independent and sovereign state."[15] In January 2006, Chen said he planned to hold a referendum on a new version of Taiwan's constitution in 2007, with a view to enactment in 2008.[16] If this were to occur, it would be in the same year as the Beijing Olympics.

Despite the DPP's push toward recognition of Taiwan's independent status, economic links between Taiwan and the mainland continued to grow. For 2004 Hong Kong and China were taking 36.6 percent of Taiwan's exports (19.5 percent and 17.1 percent respectively), ahead of the United States with 16.2 percent; China was Taiwan's third most important source of imports (9.9 percent).[17] For the same year Taiwan was China's second most important source of imports (11.5 percent), after Japan (16.8 percent).[18] Mainland China was the major destination for Taiwanese investment, with US$40 billion invested there by the end of 2004, or over half Taiwan's foreign investment; unofficial estimates put the figure at US$100 billion.[19]

Direct transportation links have developed between Taiwan and the mainland in recent years. Direct shipping links with the mainland and the offshore islands of Kinmen and Matsu commenced in 2001. Air links have been slower to develop. China allowed Taiwanese airlines access to the mainland through Hong Kong during the Chinese New Year in 2003, and this was resumed in 2005. Taiwan reciprocated by allowing mainland air-craft to land on its soil for the first time ever during the Chinese New Year in 2005 (as with the Taiwanese flights, flying via Hong Kong).[20]

In October 2004 Chen proposed that China and Taiwan proceed on the basis of accepting ambiguity in the definition of one China as they had sup-posedly done in 1992.[21] This would enable the two sides to deal with prac-tical issues, while putting their fundamental differences to one side. China rejected this proposal, arguing that Chen's position in practice had been a proindependence one. Under Chen, as with Lee Teng-hui before him, de-mocratization had helped Taiwan to win greater international support. Tai-wan could argue that its policies had legitimacy because they had popular support as expressed through elections. A strong economy helps Taiwan's international diplomacy, but increasingly it was difficult to compete with China in this respect. International support as reflected in the number of countries recognizing Taiwan remained limited. Similarly, Taiwan's cam-paign to win a seat in the United Nations was unsuccessful. Taiwan relied most crucially on the United States for backing in the event that there was a showdown with Beijing. However, this also meant that Taiwan had to be careful not to be unduly provocative for fear this would undermine US sup-port. While Taiwan put some emphasis on developing a military force to deter a Chinese attack, without US backing this would be insufficient. At 2.4 percent of GDP (2003), Taiwan's defense spending was moderate by in-ternational standards.[22]

While China has been critical of the direction taken by Chen since 2000, its problem is how to restrain him. Clearly China as a major power is far stronger than Taiwan in economic and military terms. However, this does not translate into Taiwan conceding to China on this issue. Even with-out the tacit US backing that Taiwan has, it would be a difficult task for China to mount a military assault on Taiwan. China would be more likely to put Taiwan under military pressure by conducting exercises and deploy-ing forces in the Taiwan Strait. This could have great psychological, politi-cal, and economic consequences for Taiwan. China attempts to keep Taiwan under political pressure through various means. It tries to influence politics in Taiwan by pointing out the consequences of certain policies. While Tai-wan's economic involvement in China assists the Chinese economy, this in-volvement is even more crucial for Taiwan. Taiwanese business interests do not wish to see their investments in China jeopardized by risky policies.[23] Such interests are likely to lend their weight to promoting reconciliation be-tween China and Taiwan. Internationally China isolates Taiwan as much as possible, having diplomatic relations only with those states recognizing the PRC and blocking Taiwan's membership in the United Nations and other international organizations. Given the importance of US support for Taiwan, China gives particular attention to its own relationship with the United States. It tries to persuade the United States that there is more to be gained through strengthening the relationship with the PRC and supporting the "one China" principle, than from supporting Taiwan and particularly the policies of Chen and the DPP. If successful, this strategy would mean that the United States would act at least as a restraining influence on Taiwan.

Under the George W. Bush administration, in office from January 2001, the United States initially appeared very sympathetic to Taiwan's position. In April 2001 Bush famously said that the United States would do "whatever it took to help Taiwan defend herself."[24] This seemed to be a significant shift away from "strategic ambiguity." The Bush administration also announced plans for significant arms sales to Taiwan, including four Kidd-class destroyers and eight diesel-powered submarines.[25] The Bush administration allowed visits by Taiwan officials at a more official level than had previously been the case. These included "transit visits" by Chen Shui-bian and Annette Lu (vice president) to New York.[26] Against this pro-Taiwan disposition there was increasing appreciation of the advantages of maintaining a level of cooperation with the PRC and of restraining Taiwan. China was generally cooperative toward the United States in the war on terrorism. It was critical of the Iraq war but helped to restrain North Korea over the nuclear issue. There were concerns in the United States that Chen's policies could be too provocative and drag the United States into a war. At the time of Premier Wen Jiabao's visit to the United States in December 2003, President Bush expressed the opposition of the United States to "any unilateral decision, by either Taiwan or China, to change the status quo."[27] Secretary of State Colin Powell, on a visit to Beijing just before the 2004 US presidential elections, said: "Taiwan is not independent. It does not enjoy sovereignty as a nation."[28] Essentially it was in US interests to maintain the status quo on the Taiwan issue.

Prospects

In looking to the future the main issue is to assess the prospects for resolving the conflict. More pessimistically this issue also implies assessing the likelihood of war occurring. Various factors are relevant. The most significant are the political situation in Taiwan, the political situation in China, the position of the United States, and the impact of economic ties between China and Taiwan. Each of these factors will be examined in turn, before considering likely scenarios.

The political situation in Taiwan has been the most significant factor affecting the Taiwan issue in recent times. Democratization has enabled sentiment in favor of an independent Taiwan to assert itself. This sentiment has been most obvious in the rise of the DPP, and particularly with the election of Chen Shui-bian as president in 2000, and then his reelection in 2004. Although Chen foreswore any intention to declare independence when he was inaugurated in 2000, other steps he has taken have indicated a commitment to moving in that direction. The referendum held at the time of the 2004 presidential election did not attract sufficient support to be carried, but could be seen as a trial run for using the referendum device to give Taiwan's claim to independence some substance. The plan to hold a referendum in 2007 is construed as an attempt to improve Taiwan's governance, but reference to Taiwan as a "democratic nation" inevitably has connotations of independence. While Chen's policies have set the pace in Taiwan politics, there are also significant divisions in Taiwanese society. There is still strong support for a "one China" approach, although clearly not as defined by the PRC. Majority support in Taiwan for maintaining the status quo in cross-Strait relations (although not necessarily indefinitely) in the 1990s declined to a plurality by the early years of the new century; nevertheless this group was still more significant than those supporting independence (above 20 percent) or reunification.[29] Within Taiwan, opposition to Chen has centered on the pan-blue coalition led by the KMT; this grouping has generally controlled the legislature (the Legislative Yuan). Given the position of Chen and the DPP the independence issue is likely to remain at the center of Taiwanese politics, but any intensification of the conflict with China will also increase polarization within Taiwan.[30]

With Chen Shui-bian setting the pace on the Taiwan issue, China has been on the defensive in many respects. It has maintained its goal of achieving "one China" under the auspices of the PRC, ideally to take the form of "peaceful reunification," but China has not forsworn the use of force in some circumstances. The most relevant circumstances would be where there is an overt push by Taiwan to declare its independence. For China the issue remains the nationalist one of restoring its territorial integrity. However, it is not necessarily clear how China would react to a given situation. While nationalist assumptions might be universally held, there can be differences about how to proceed in particular circumstances. Sometimes statements can be made at a symbolic level without necessarily translating into action. The more conservative elements in Chinese politics put a stronger emphasis on nationalist rhetoric, and are more inclined to support at least some action on the issue. The Taiwan issue is also very central for the PLA in terms of its role in Chinese politics. The promodernization and generally dominant elements in Chinese politics share the nationalist goals but are more cautious about action if that is likely to disrupt their general political and economic objectives. Chinese leaders can support strong statements on the Taiwan issue as a means of enhancing their nationalist credentials; action does not always follow. The anti-secession law passed by the National People's Congress in March 2005 might be a case in point. It reinforced the message that action would be taken against Taiwan if there were any overt moves toward independence. It did not represent a change in policy, and its significance would only become clear if Taiwan did take a more proindependence course.

For the United States its key interest is having the Taiwan issue dealt with peacefully. It has strong strategic and economic reasons for having a cooperative relationship with China. At the same time it has strategic and economic reasons for supporting the status quo in relation to Taiwan. PRC control of Taiwan would have implications for the strategic situation in the western Pacific. While the United States could undoubtedly adjust to this new situation, many would see it as a setback. Economically the links with Taiwan are also important to the United States, although clearly they are on a smaller scale than the ties with China. Politically and morally, democratization in Taiwan has strengthened Taiwan's case for US support. Within US politics there is a range of views on the Taiwan issue. Taiwan is often able to marshal significant support within Congress. There is often more sympathy for Taiwan among Republicans than among Democrats, although it was a Republican president (Nixon) who established Sino-US rapprochement. Once in office most presidents recognize the advantages of strategic ambiguity as a means of maintaining the status quo, and this has been the trend under George W. Bush also. If ambiguity is lost and there is a clear tilt toward Taiwan, this could be interpreted by Taiwan leaders as a green light for moving toward independence. The consequence could be war between China and Taiwan, with the United States also becoming involved. If ambiguity is lost in the sense that the United States signals disengagement from the Taiwan issue, this could be seen by Beijing as allowing more decisive action against Taiwan. Again, the consequences could be detrimental to US interests and credibility. In recent times the United States has had to act to restrain moves in the direction of independence by Chen Shui-bian. At the same time it has had to indicate to the PRC that it should not react to this situation by resorting to the use of armed force. Hence the United States reacted unfavorably to the anti-secession law passed by China in March 2005.

In assessing the prospects for the Taiwan conflict, another issue is whether the increasing economic interdependence across the Taiwan Strait will lead to peace. As indicated previously, Taiwan has become very dependent economically on its ties with China. China is both Taiwan's most significant export partner (if we include Hong Kong) and the major destination for Taiwan's investment. This situation might be of particular interest to Taiwanese businesspeople, but it also benefits Taiwan's economy as a whole. China also benefits from the trade and investment relationship with Taiwan, but is less dependent on it than is Taiwan. This might suggest that China could use the economic relationship to extract concessions from Taiwan. There is some suggestion that China has used the argument about the economic benefits of the relationship as a means of trying to win over public opinion in Taiwan. This is not so much a strategy for achieving reunification as for maintaining the status quo and restraining proindependence sentiment. Beijing can expect Taiwanese businesspeople with mainland connections to put the case in favor of the status quo, if not a pro-PRC position. China can also restrict the activities of any pro-DPP groups that might wish to participate in the mainland economy. At this broad level then, economic interdependence does help to contain the Taiwan conflict. At the same time nationalist appeals on both sides of the Taiwan Strait can be very powerful. In the event of a crisis leaders do not necessarily act rationally and give priority to mutual economic interests. Economic interdependence strengthens the case for dealing with the Taiwan issue peacefully but should not be regarded as having a decisive influence.

Given the situation in relation to these various relevant factors, the most likely scenario is that the pressures for Taiwan to move in a proindependence direction will increase but that there will be countervailing action by both China and the United States. This will mean that an overt declaration of independence by Taiwan is unlikely, even though there could be moves by the DPP government to give more substance to the de facto independence that Taiwan already enjoys. In taking countervailing action China will continue its military buildup in the vicinity of the Taiwan Strait, while also issuing political statements, passing laws, and so on designed to restrain Taiwan. China will also attempt to exert influence on Taiwan, building on the majority sentiment that prefers minimal disruption. The United States is likely to react by emphasizing strategic ambiguity as its underlying approach to the Taiwan issue. This should bring a realization on Taiwan's part that the defense support provided by the United States does not amount to a blank check. If Taiwan goes too far it could find itself without US defense support. Strategic ambiguity is also important as a means for the United States to warn China that military action against Taiwan could elicit a US response. While Taiwan remains the most unpredictable factor in this scenario, the likelihood overall is that the status quo will be maintained and conflict avoided.

For war to occur over the Taiwan issue there would have to be adverse developments affecting one or more of the three main parties, in turn setting off a negative reaction in the other parties. The greatest danger is that the push toward greater independence by Taiwan will become too overt for China. China could then react by stepping up pressure, possibly involving a military dimension, although not necessarily taking the form of a direct attack (missile tests or a blockade might be more likely). Such a reaction would be more likely if more strongly nationalist elements were dominant in China. If there were an economic downturn in China, or if China suffered significant international reverses, this might be more likely. In the event of the conflict escalating along these lines the United States might attempt to act as a restraining influence. However, if China actually attacked Taiwan the United States would have to decide whether to respond in kind or else to determine that Taiwan's behavior had been so provocative that US support would not be warranted. In either case there could be great political division within the United States. If the United States acted to support Taiwan there would also be the danger of escalation to a broader Sino-US conflict. Given that both powers possess nuclear weapons the implications could be very serious indeed.

▨ Notes

1. Recent edited books on the Taiwan issue include Tucker, ed., *Dangerous Strait,* and Zagoria, ed., *Breaking the China-Taiwan Impasse.*
2. "Excerpt from the Shanghai Communiqué on the Taiwan Issue, February 27, 1972," appendix 3, in Zagoria, ed., *Breaking the China-Taiwan Impasse,* p. 224.
3. Huan, "Taiwan," p. 1068.
4. "US-PRC Joint Communiqué, August 17, 1982," appendix 6 in Zagoria, ed., *Breaking the China-Taiwan Impasse,* p. 238.
5. "Ronald Reagan's Six Assurances to Taiwan, August 20, 1982," appendix 7 in ibid., p. 239.
6. "Guidelines for National Unification, March 14, 1991," appendix 9, in ibid., pp. 243–244.
7. *Jiang Zemin and Li Peng on Taiwan Question,* p. 4.
8. "The One-China Principle and the Taiwan Issue" (China White Paper), February 2000, www.chinaembassy.org/eng/zt/twwt/White%20Papers/t36705.htm (accessed 10 October 2005).
9. Roy, "Tensions in the Taiwan Strait," p. 81.
10. Roy, *Taiwan,* p. 200.
11. Scalapino, "Cross-Strait Relations and the United States," p. 7.
12. "Excerpt from President Chen's Inaugural Speech: The Five No's, May 20, 2000," appendix 1Gu3, in Zagoria, ed., *Breaking the China-Taiwan Impasse,* p. 253.

13. Rigger, "Taiwan in 2002," p. 47.

14. Australia, Department of Foreign Affairs and Trade, "Taiwan—Country Information." www.dfat.gov.au/geo/taiwan/taiwan_brief.html (accessed 17 March 2005).

15. Peng, "The Taiwan Issue in the Context of New Sino-US Strategic Cooperation," p. 12.

16. Frank Ching, "Chen Shares Independence Dream Anew," *Japan Times,* 13 January 2006, http://taiwansecurity.org/News/2006/JT-130106.htm (accessed 18 February 2006).

17. Australian Department of Foreign Affairs and Trade, "Taiwan Fact Sheet," www.dfat.gov.au/geo/fs/taiw.pdf (accessed 10 October 2005).

18. Australian Department of Foreign Affairs and Trade, "China Fact Sheet," www.dfat.gov.au/geo/fs/chin.pdf (accessed 10 October 2005).

19. Australian Department of Foreign Affairs and Trade, "Country Brief: Taiwan—July 2005," www.dfat.gov.au/geo/taiwan/taiwan_brief.html (accessed 10 October 2005).

20. Australian Department of Foreign Affairs and Trade, "Country Brief: Taiwan—July 2005," www.dfat.gov.au/geo/taiwan/taiwan_brief.html (accessed 10 October 2005); Robert Marquand, "Air Links for China, Taiwan," *Christian Science Monitor,* 28 January 2005, http://csmonitor.com/2005/0128/p07s01-woap.html (accessed 10 October 2005).

21. Chan, "Taiwan in 2004," pp. 56–57.

22. *The Military Balance 2004–2005.*

23. Chan, "Taiwan in 2004," pp. 56–57.

24. Quoted in Wu, "Taiwan in 2001," p. 35.

25. Ibid.

26. Peng, "The Taiwan Issue in the Context of New Sino-US Strategic Cooperation," p. 18.

27. Quoted in Peterson, "Dangerous Games Across the Taiwan Strait," p. 24.

28. Chan, "Taiwan in 2004," p. 57.

29. Peterson, "Dangerous Games Across the Taiwan Strait," p. 30.

30. On the divisions within Taiwanese society, see Lijun, *China and Taiwan,* pp. 61–64.

Korea | 9

After Taiwan, Korea is another major flashpoint in Northeast Asia. This chapter asks how Korea came to assume that status, and what the issues have been. This involves providing some background on the long-term historical context, before turning to major developments in the 1945–1990 period and during the 1990s. Finally, particular attention is given to the situation that has emerged since 2001.

In reviewing Korea's history the main point to emerge is the strong sense of national unity. Korea's division since 1945 is an affront to national sentiment, and is the result of the involvement of external powers on the peninsula. The Korean War of 1950–1953 reinforced the division imposed in 1945. Two separate states developed on the peninsula, the communist Democratic People's Republic of Korea (DPRK) or North Korea, and the anticommunist Republic of Korea (ROK) or South Korea. While the ROK was predominantly an authoritarian system during its early decades, by the 1990s it was undergoing a process of democratization. The ROK was also much more economically developed than the DPRK. The DPRK was a Stalinist system focused on its leader Kim Il Sung, who died in 1994 and was succeeded by his son, Kim Jong Il. While the level of North Korea's economic development in the 1950s and 1960s had been comparable to that of South Korea, by the 1990s the DPRK was well behind and in fact experiencing economic decline. This added to the sense of vulnerability that North Korea felt as a result of the collapse of the communist world in the late 1980s and early 1990s. To increase its bargaining power North Korea began moves to acquire nuclear weapons, leading to the crisis of 1993–1994. Through the Agreed Framework of 1994 concessions were made to North Korea, and the DPRK in turn abandoned its plan to acquire nuclear weapons. However, after 2001 a similar situation to that of 1993–

1994 arose when the George W. Bush administration essentially abandoned the Agreed Framework, with North Korea then reverting to its earlier plan to acquire nuclear weapons.

In examining the main phases in the development of the Korean issue, one observes an interaction of various factors. At one level there are issues deriving primarily from within Korea itself, or from the two Korean states in more recent history. At another level, Korea has been very greatly affected by the way in which external powers have interacted with the peninsula. For a long time China was the most significant power in this respect, but from the latter part of the nineteenth century, Russia, Japan, and the United States also became significant. We can trace the evolution of these two dimensions, the internal and the external, in each of the major phases underlying the development of the Korean issue.

▇ The Historical Context

A major point about Korea's history, still very relevant today, is that the peninsula had a long history of political unity. It was first unified in 668 CE, and became known as Koryo from 935. Within the context of political unity, there was considerable stability; the Yi dynasty, for example, ruled from 1392 until 1910. Korea existed within the broader Chinese culture area, Confucianism being an important influence. The peninsula was under Chinese suzerainty from 1644; Korean rulers paid tribute to the Chinese emperor. Apart from this very significant influence, Korea was mostly isolated from the external world, living up to its title as the "Hermit Kingdom."

In the latter part of the nineteenth century China faced increasing competition from other powers for influence in Korea. Japan's victory over China in the Sino-Japanese war of 1894–1895 signaled that Japan was an emerging power in Northeast Asia; Korea and Manchuria were important arenas for expanding Japanese influence. In both situations Japan's major rival was Russia. This rivalry came to a head in the Russo-Japanese war of 1904–1905. Japan's success on this occasion cleared the way for Japanese ascendancy in Korea, with the peninsula becoming a Japanese protectorate from 1905 and then a colony from 1910. The United States was the other major influence in Korea in the late nineteenth and early twentieth centuries. As in China, the United States was not so much intent on political domination as on upholding the open-door principle, an approach that suited the economically strong. In the context of Russo-Japanese competition, the United States sometimes acted as a mediator. The Treaty of Portsmouth (New Hampshire), concluding the 1904–1905 war, involved President

Theodore Roosevelt using his good offices to facilitate negotiations. The United States also had a cultural influence in Korea, particularly through its missionaries. The fact that nearly a quarter of the South Korean population is Christian is largely a legacy of this influence.[1] Christian churches also exist in North Korea, although clearly they are much more restricted than in the south. Kim Il Sung himself grew up in a Christian family.

With Japanese domination the outcome of the major power rivalry played out in Korea at the end of the nineteenth century and the beginning of the twentieth century, Korea entered a phase of Japanese colonial rule that lasted from 1910 to 1945. Koreans experienced this rule as very oppressive and it still influences the relations of the two Korean states with Japan today. Korean resentment toward Japan was exacerbated by the proximity of the two countries; a parallel might be the relationship between Ireland and Britain. In comparative terms Japanese colonial rule in Korea was very intrusive. Between 1935 and 1945 an estimated 246,000 Japanese civil servants ruled 21 million Koreans. In 1937 in Vietnam France had 2,920 administrative personnel and 11,000 French troops ruling a population of 17 million; in the British colonies the numbers of British personnel in proportion to the local population were even smaller.[2] A particular cause of resentment, which still rankles, is how the Japanese military forced between 100,000 and 200,000 Korean women into sexual slavery as "comfort women" during World War II.[3] However, rather than being liberated as a result of Japan's defeat in 1945, Koreans found themselves experiencing further suffering through the division of their country.

■ 1945–1990

The division of Korea came about because of the situation that existed at the end of the Pacific War in August–September 1945. The Soviet Union had entered the war against Japan only on 8 August 1945. It moved rapidly into Manchuria, northern Korea, and the Kurile Islands (north of Japan). To forestall Soviet occupation of the whole of the Korean peninsula, the United States concluded an agreement in early August 1945 whereby Soviet forces would occupy the area north of the 38th parallel, with US forces occupying the area to the south of this line. This effectively divided Korea in half, running contrary to almost 1,300 years of Korean unity. Under this agreement US forces, commanded by General John R. Hodge, entered Seoul on 8 September 1945. In their occupation zones the USSR and the United States went about establishing political and social systems that would be favorable to their own preferred goals. Thus the USSR established a communist system, giving its support to Kim Il Sung as the leader of the Korean Workers' Party. In the south the United States favored more conservative elements, with the staunchly anticommunist (but not necessarily democratic) Syngman Rhee emerging as a strong figure. All Korean groups wanted the establishment of Korean unity, but under their own auspices. Without foreign occupation it is likely that some version of revolutionary nationalism would have become dominant in Korea (as happened in China and Vietnam).[4] Given the situation as it was, however, by 1948 two separate states had emerged on the peninsula: the DPRK in the north and the ROK in the south. In the course of 1948 and 1949 both Soviet and US forces withdrew from Korea.

The establishment of the DPRK and the ROK did not mean that the two states accepted the division of the country. Both official titles refer to "Korea," rather than to "North Korea" or "South Korea." Support for the revolutionary cause existed in a number of regions in the south. When North Korean forces launched an attack across the 38th parallel on 25 June 1950, this was interpreted by the United States as a classic case of interstate aggression. With the Soviet Union boycotting the Security Council at the time (in support of the claim by the People's Republic of China to the Chinese seat), the United States was able to have the Security Council declare the North Korean attack a threat to international peace and security. Action led by the United States to counter North Korea thus had UN authorization. The United States located the conflict in the context of the Cold War. From this perspective North Korea's action was a manifestation of "communist expansionism," with North Korea acting at the behest of the USSR. The civil war dimension was ignored. Based on the Cold War interpretation, the Korean War could be seen as an attempt to give substance to the doctrine of containment that President Truman had announced in March 1947.[5]

Under the command of General Douglas MacArthur, US forces landed at Inchon on Korea's west coast not far from Seoul on 15 September 1950. Despite North Korean forces having previously occupied all but the southeastern corner of the peninsula, the United States and its allies were soon able to gain the upper hand in the south and then began pushing into the north. With the fighting approaching the Yalu River, the border between China and North Korea, China became involved. China believed the war was a threat to its position in Manchuria. Hence Chinese "volunteers" entered the war from late October 1950. Allied forces were pushed south again, with the fighting becoming stalemated roughly along the 38th parallel. This situation continued for about two years. When an armistice was signed on 27 July 1953, the ceasefire line (the Demilitarized Zone or DMZ) ran very close to the 38th parallel. The armistice simply meant that the two sides agreed to cease fighting; a peace treaty was not concluded and never has been. Restoring the situation as it had been before the war was at the cost of about 750,000 military and 800,000 civilian lives; the military dead included nearly 300,000 North Koreans, 227,000 South Koreans, 200,000 Chinese, and 57,440 UN troops (over 33,000 from the United States).[6]

With the division of the peninsula confirmed by the outcome of the war, the two Korean states went their separate ways. Both the DPRK and the ROK remained committed to reunification but they now knew the cost of any attempt to impose a unilateral solution. The Korean conflict became a standoff, with two highly armed states facing each other across the DMZ. North Korea had the backing of the USSR and China. The United States gave support to South Korea, including the stationing of troops. Each Korean state pursued its own development, based on the underlying assumptions of its particular political system. South Korea was a strongly anti-communist and largely authoritarian state. North Korea developed as a communist and Stalinist state focused on its leader, Kim Il Sung.

In the case of South Korea the link to the United States was formalized in a mutual security treaty in 1954. South Korea thus became part of the US-centered alliance network in Asia Pacific. As part of the security arrangement the United States maintained forces in South Korea, close to the DMZ and astride the main invasion route to Seoul. United States and ROK forces came under a joint command, with the United States providing the commanding officer. The existence of a joint command was an indication of the significance the United States attributed to Korea as a front in the Cold War; at this level Korea was comparable to NATO where there was also a joint command. Another factor for the United States was that this arrangement meant greater control over South Korea; there was a concern that South Korea might resume the war against North Korea. South Korea had refused to sign the armistice in 1953, although it abided by its provisions.

While concerns remained about the possible resumption of armed conflict on the Korean peninsula, from the 1950s to the 1980s South Korea was ruled by a series of right wing, authoritarian governments. Syngman Rhee remained as South Korea's strong man during the 1950s. In April 1960 Rhee was deposed following a popular uprising in opposition to widespread vote rigging in the presidential election. An interim government was short-lived, with a military coup in May 1961 installing Park Chung Hee as president. President Park remained in office until his assassination in October 1979. It was under Park's rule that South Korea emerged as one of Asia's newly industrializing countries. This development was fostered by strong government involvement in the economy, the support of the United States (through military and other means), and the availability of a well-educated population. As with any NIC, such as Taiwan, the focus was on export-oriented industrialization.

Following Park's assassination, South Korea experienced a period of political turmoil, culminating in the declaration of martial law in May 1980, and the installation of yet another military leader, Chun Doo Hwan, as president. Among the popular reactions to these events, the most costly was the Kwangju uprising in southwest Korea, resulting in the deaths of hundreds of people. Chun remained president for one term of seven years. However, by this time South Korea was becoming a more complex society. Its development as an NIC had resulted in the emergence of a strong middle class, and growing demands for political representation. Continued authoritarian rule was likely to cause severe tensions and damage South Korean society. This prepared the way for moves toward democratization. The presidential election in 1987 was thus relatively free. Although Roh Tae Woo, identified with the former authoritarian system, was successful, this was mainly because the opposition vote was split between Kim Young Sam (leader in the parliamentary opposition) and Kim Dae Jung (leading figure in the nonparliamentary opposition).

Apart from continuing the process of democratization, President Roh was associated with moves to broaden South Korea's international orientation through Nordpolitik (Northern policy). South Korea's image as anticommunist bastion was modified with the opening of diplomatic relations with some Eastern European countries in the late 1980s, followed by the USSR in 1990 and China in 1992.

In the case of North Korea, its trajectory after the Korean War was completely different. North Korea's international alignment was with China and the USSR. Neither communist power stationed forces in North Korea. In 1961 the two powers signed mutual security treaties with the DPRK. North Korea was able to maintain its independent position in relation to the USSR and China, while at the same time using the Sino-Soviet conflict to play the two powers off against each other. Despite the intensity of the Sino-Soviet conflict, North Korea believed that its position within the communist world was a factor in its favor.

North Korea's domestic development followed a model known as "Juche" or "self reliance." This meant minimizing interaction with the outside world, and achieving economic development based on the country's own resources. Until the 1970s the level of economic development in North Korea was roughly comparable to that in South Korea. Both could be seen as predominantly agricultural Third World countries. However, with South Korea's export-led industrialization elevating it to the status of an NIC, North Korea began to lag behind. This was the beginning of the very great economic differences that exist today. Growing economic differences added to North Korea's sense of vulnerability.

While South Korea had a succession of political leaders (some serving long terms), North Korea had just one leader up until his death in 1994: Kim Il Sung. The political system promoted a cult of personality, focused on Kim Il Sung as the Great Leader and other such titles. North Korea was not just a one-party state under the Korean Workers' Party. Kim Il Sung was supreme within the party, controlling all the significant levers of power, including the large military forces.

Even with South Korea and North Korea taking such divergent paths they were still linked by certain issues. Chief among these was the question of the status of Korea as a whole, with both states remaining committed to reunification. Since the end of the Korean War in 1953 was based on an armistice rather than a peace treaty, the issue remained unresolved. Having refused to sign the armistice, South Korea held to its position that North Korea was an illegitimate entity, and that reunification should come about by force if necessary. The use of force, however, was unacceptable to the United States, the guarantor of South Korea's security. While there was undoubtedly a large element of rhetoric involved, in 1972 the two Koreas agreed that reunification should be by peaceful means.[7] Beginning in 1960, North Korea put forward proposals for confederation whereby the two Koreas would retain their separate domestic arrangements but would combine as an international entity. In 1980 it was proposed that the combined entity be known as the Democratic Confederal Republic of Koryo. This approach was also the basis of Kim Il Sung's Ten Point Program for the Great Unity of the Whole Nation for the Reunification of the Country.[8] In 1991 the two Koreas entered the UN as separate states. By this stage a particular concern for South Korea was that reunification would come about through North Korea's political and economic collapse.

The 1990s

During the 1990s South Korea continued on the course that had emerged in the late 1980s: democratization and the broadening of its international position. Apart from the North Korean issue, the major problem it confronted was the Asian financial crisis of 1997. North Korea saw a major change with the death of Kim Il Sung in July 1994 and the passing of the leadership to his son, Kim Jong Il. The most significant crisis affecting the peninsula occurred in 1993–1994 when North Korea indicated its intention to acquire nuclear weapons. In reviewing the 1990s, we will give attention in the first instance to the major domestic developments affecting the two Korean states before examining in more detail the 1993–1994 crisis. It is this situation that provides the essential background to understanding the crisis that has emerged again in the period since 2001.

In South Korea the two major presidencies during the 1990s were those of Kim Young Sam and Kim Dae Jung. Kim Young Sam was elected in December 1992 and served as president from February 1993 to February 1998. At the election Kim Young Sam had won 42 percent of the vote as compared to 38 percent for Kim Dae Jung, his major opponent. As president, Kim Young Sam instituted important financial reforms and took steps to combat corruption. One of the highlights of Kim Young Sam's administration was the trial of former presidents Chun Doo Hwan and Roh Tae Woo in relation to both financial corruption and their involvement in the Kwangju uprising. In August 1996 Chun was sentenced to death and Roh received a long prison term; Chun's death sentence was later commuted to life imprisonment and Roh's term was shortened.[9]

One of the major issues facing Kim Young Sam was the onset of the Asian financial crisis in 1997. South Korea's economic growth had been built on export-led industrialization, but by the mid-1990s the country was experiencing declining terms of trade. In 1996 external debt amounted to 22 percent of GDP.[10] International investors were unwilling to support this level of debt, and South Korea turned to the International Monetary Fund for assistance.[11]

It was in this context that Kim Dae Jung won the presidential elections in December 1997, securing 40.2 percent of the vote compared to 39.7 percent for Lee Hoi Chang from the ruling party.[12] Kim Dae Jung was reformist in orientation but was also South Korea's leading antiestablishment figure. He had a regional base in the Cholla region in the southwest of the country. His dissident credentials included nearly winning the 1971 elections (despite corrupt practices by the incumbent, President Park), and almost being executed after accusations that he led the Kwangju uprising in 1980.[13] In addition to his appeal to dissidents, Kim Dae Jung also won support from some conservative elements.[14] Because of the financial crisis the initial focus of Kim Dae Jung's administration was on implementing the economic restructuring required by the IMF. This meant that there was less emphasis than one might have expected on other aspects of reform. There was limited success in bringing about the reform of the *chaebol*, the economic conglomerates that had played a central role in South Korea's economic development.[15] Corruption scandals also weakened the administration in the late 1990s.[16] Apart from responding to the financial crisis,

Kim Dae Jung placed considerable emphasis on developing a policy of reconciliation with North Korea known as the "sunshine policy." To put this policy in context we need to review the significant developments affecting North Korea, and particularly the nuclear crisis of 1993–1994.

In the case of North Korea, Kim Il Sung's death on 8 July 1994 did not lead to any major change in the country's direction. Some observers suggested that under Kim Jong Il there was a strengthening in the role of the military and a corresponding decline in the influence of the Korean Workers' Party.[17] While Kim Jong Il received less adulation than had been the case with Kim Il Sung, the role of the leader remained central to the functioning of North Korea. North Korea's major problem was its economic decline. Whereas in its earlier decades the DPRK had been able to compete economically with the ROK, by the 1990s this era had long passed. The decline in per capita GDP for the period 1990–2002 was about 25 percent.[18] The most drastic effects of this situation were evident in the widespread food shortages. In the mid-1990s floods exacerbated the situation, and many people died as a consequence of famine. By the end of 1995 the estimated number of dead was 500,000 and this had grown to one million by the end of 1996; another one million had died by 1998.[19]

North Korea's declining economic situation was an important factor in the nuclear crisis of 1993–1994.[20] The decline of the economy made North Korea feel more vulnerable to the various international pressures it faced. Economic concerns thus overlapped with North Korean perceptions of security. Since the Korean War North Korea had seen the United States as the main threat to its existence. The 1953 armistice had been concluded between North Korea and the United States. North Korea had opposed South Korean proposals for reunification, but it was the United States that was the ultimate guarantor for South Korea. North Korean proposals for developing nuclear facilities, with the acquisition of nuclear weapons as a possible consequence, were designed to increase North Korea's bargaining power. By playing the nuclear card North Korea hoped to secure assistance toward developing its energy facilities. This would help to strengthen the North Korean economy, thus shoring up the political system and also enhancing North Korean security.

North Korea had been interested in developing nuclear energy since at least the 1970s. During the 1980s it sought assistance from the USSR in pursuit of this goal. The USSR indicated a willingness to assist if North Korea entered the nuclear nonproliferation regime; this would provide assurance that North Korea had no intention of developing nuclear weapons. On the basis of this understanding North Korea signed the Nuclear Nonproliferation Treaty in December 1985. In return the USSR undertook to provide North

Korea with four light-water nuclear power reactors.[21] In subsequent years arranging for inspections by the International Atomic Energy Agency (IAEA), as provided for by the Nuclear Nonproliferation Treaty, became a major issue. The secretive North Korean regime did not welcome this intrusion. Interest centered on North Korea's nuclear facilities at Yongbyon, near Pyongyang. There was concern that plutonium from these facilities was being stockpiled, thus providing the basis for North Korea to acquire nuclear weapons.

One reason for North Korea's ambiguous position in relation to nuclear weapons was its concern about the threat posed to its security by the United States. On 25 November 1991 North Korea said it would agree to international inspection of its nuclear facilities if the United States began the withdrawal of its nuclear weapons from South Korea.[22] Relations between the two Koreas appeared to improve with the signing of an Agreement on Reconciliation, Nonaggression and Exchanges and Cooperation between the south and the north in December 1991.[23] This was followed by the Joint Declaration of the Denuclearization of the Korean Peninsula in January 1992.[24] Under the declaration the two Korean states agreed not to "test, manufacture, produce, receive, possess, store, deploy or use nuclear weapons"; nuclear energy would be used "solely for peaceful purposes." Inspection of "objects selected by the other side and agreed upon between the two sides" would be according to procedures agreed upon by a South-North Joint Nuclear Control Commission.

Despite this seeming progress, North Korea's commitment to allow inspections under IAEA procedures remained an issue. On 12 March 1993 North Korea announced that it intended to withdraw from the Nuclear Nonproliferation Treaty. North Korea agreed to suspend its notice of withdrawal following talks between itself and the United States in New York in June 1993.[25] North Korea admitted IAEA inspectors between 3 and 10 August 1993, but did not permit inspection of the two sites in the Yongbyon nuclear complex where it was believed there was evidence of weapons-grade nuclear material being acquired.[26] Another crisis came at the end of October 1993, when North Korea refused to allow the IAEA to replace the batteries and film in the surveillance cameras at North Korea's declared nuclear sites.[27] During talks between the United States and North Korea on 3 December 1993, North Korea offered to open its five declared nuclear facilities to inspection. Because the proposal did not include the suspected Yongbyon facilities, the United States did not accept the offer.[28] In January 1994 it was reported that North Korea would allow IAEA inspection of seven nuclear facilities but would reject "challenge" inspections of suspected sites.[29] This proposal was unacceptable to both the

United States and the IAEA,[30] and the issue then moved to the UN Security Council, which had the power to impose sanctions on North Korea. In the face of Chinese opposition to sanctions, the Security Council, on 31 March 1994, simply issued an appeal to North Korea to allow IAEA inspections.[31] At this stage, Secretary of Defense William Perry warned that the United States was prepared to risk war rather than see North Korea develop "a substantial arsenal of nuclear weapons."[32]

Having reached the brink, the Clinton administration subsequently moved to consider more positive measures as a means of encouraging North Korea to comply with the nuclear nonproliferation regime. By the end of April 1994, it was reported that these measures might include diplomatic normalization between North Korea, the United States, and Japan, the cessation of joint ROK-US military exercises, and encouragement for Japan to pay war reparations to North Korea.[33] However, when the IAEA announced that North Korea had definitely broken nuclear safeguards, Clinton made it clear that economic sanctions would need to be considered. At the same time he said, "The door is still open for them to become part of the world's community and that's what we want."[34] Although North Korea proceeded to withdraw from the IAEA, the suggestion by Clinton that accommodation was still possible may have facilitated an attempt at mediation by former president Jimmy Carter during a visit to North Korea in late June.[35]

Carter won Kim Il Sung's agreement to a temporary freeze on North Korea's nuclear development and a continued role for IAEA inspectors. Carter gave his support to the acquisition of light-water reactors by North Korea and the reconvening of US-DPRK negotiations.[36] Carter's mediation prepared the way for the Nuclear Framework Agreement between North Korea and the United States that was announced on 17 October 1994.[37] The United States would be responsible for organizing an international consortium including South Korea and Japan to build two 1,000-megawatt light-water reactors for North Korea. Since the building of these reactors was expected to take until 2003, the United States would supply crude oil to North Korea for energy purposes as an interim measure. North Korea would cease building new graphite-type reactors and would suspend operation of its Yongbyon reactor. North Korea's reprocessing facility would also be closed, and the 8,000 spent nuclear fuel rods from Yongbyon would be available for IAEA inspection. The IAEA could inspect all nuclear facilities in North Korea, but not until one of the light-water reactors was completed (which was expected to take five years). North Korea and the United States would work toward reducing trade barriers and establishing liaison offices; intra-Korean dialogue would also be resumed.

In May 1995 the Korean Peninsula Energy Development Organization (KEDO) was established to provide the means for building the light-water reactors in North Korea. The primary members of KEDO were the United States, Japan, and South Korea. Funding for the new reactors was to come mainly from Japan (20 percent) and South Korea (70 percent).

The major weakness in the agreement was the provision that full IAEA inspection of North Korean nuclear facilities would not occur until at least one light-water reactor was operational. Republicans in the United States argued that North Korea had achieved a favorable result for itself through blackmail; there was no guarantee of good behavior in return. The test firing of a missile by North Korea in August 1998 did not assist its case. The Clinton administration commissioned the Perry Report to reassess US policy toward North Korea. Released in October 1999, this report argued for a continuation of the existing "carrot and stick" approach.[38] The Republican position was articulated in the North Korea Advisory Group (NKAG) Report, prepared for the House of Representatives International Relations Committee and issued in November 1999.[39] NKAG opposed the appeasement of North Korea, arguing that the focus should be on military deterrence. Political problems in the United States had the effect of delaying the implementation of the Agreed Framework, leading in turn to disenchantment on the part of North Korea and providing a pretext for that country to revert to the course that it had been following in the early 1990s. Although oil deliveries to North Korea continued until 2002, work on the promised light-water reactors remained at a very preliminary stage.

South Korea, particularly under Kim Dae Jung, was very much in favor of the approach toward North Korea that was embodied in the Agreed Framework. Conscious of North Korea's difficult economic situation, South Korea believed that failure to provide assistance could lead to North Korea's collapse. This would be catastrophic for the people of North Korea, but could also create great difficulties for South Korea. South Korea could be forced to provide massive aid to North Korea to relieve the situation there. Reunification might come about but under circumstances that would be much more difficult than those facing Germany after the unification of that country in 1990. East Germany had been the most economically advanced of the communist countries whereas North Korea was virtually a basket case. South Korea's preference was to assist North Korea to make a soft landing. Kim Dae Jung's sunshine policy sought to achieve reconciliation with North Korea, facilitating assistance to that beleaguered country and thereby reducing the risks to South Korea itself. In June 2000 the sunshine policy took a dramatic form when Kim Dae Jung visited Pyongyang for a summit meeting with Kim Jong Il. In 2003 it was revealed by a special prosecutor investigating the matter that the South Korean government had used "inducements" totaling US$500 million to obtain North Korean agreement to this meeting: about US$400 million from the Hyundai Group and about US$100 million directly from the government.[40]

2001 and Beyond

Since 2001 the most significant issue affecting Korea has been the onset of another crisis focused on North Korea's nuclear intentions. The issue arose because of a breakdown in the implementation of the Agreed Framework of 1994. The major factor was the unwillingness of the George W. Bush administration to proceed with an agreement that it believed had rewarded North Korea for intransigence. North Korea responded by reverting to its behavior of the early 1990s. The other relevant actors preferred to continue the strategy of engagement and were critical of the United States to varying degrees. This was most obvious in the case of South Korea, but also applied to China, Japan, and Russia. Here we will focus on explaining the position of the various actors as a means of understanding how the crisis developed.

The George W. Bush administration assumed office inherently skeptical of the Agreed Framework. This skepticism reflected the position taken in the North Korea Advisory Group Report in 1999. As a tyrannical regime, North Korea was not to be trusted. In January 2002 George W. Bush named North Korea as part of the so-called axis of evil in his State of the Union address. There was no dramatic break with North Korea but it was clear that the US position had hardened. The occasion for a major shift was the statement in Pyongyang by James Kelly, assistant secretary of state for East Asian and Pacific affairs, on 4 October 2002, that the United States had evidence of a uranium enrichment program in North Korea. This would enable North Korea to develop nuclear weapons. Subsequently, on 14 November 2002, oil shipments to North Korea under the Agreed Framework were suspended. Essentially the United States wanted to renegotiate the agreement with North Korea to ensure that there was no possibility of nuclear development leading to the acquisition of nuclear weapons. Neoconservatives wanted to go further to bring about regime change, using military pressure if necessary.

North Korea reacted to this situation by announcing on 12 December 2002 that it would lift the freeze on the development of its nuclear facilities at Yongbyon. It was already dissatisfied with the slow progress on building the promised light-water reactors, but the suspension of oil shipments was the immediate pretext for the action it took. From North Korea's perspective failure to implement the Agreed Framework was having an adverse effect on its energy requirements and therefore its economy. More importantly, North Korea saw US policy as a threat to its security. The action it took was designed to enhance its bargaining power in relation to both its economic and security goals. On 10 January 2003 North Korea announced that it was withdrawing from the Nuclear Nonproliferation Treaty. Whereas the United States wanted negotiations on the North Korean nuclear issue within a multilateral framework after verification that uranium enrichment was not occurring, North Korea's preference was for bilateral negotiations ahead of verification. Apart from obtaining assistance to meet its energy needs, North Korea sought reassurance on security matters through the conclusion of a bilateral treaty with the United States.

US policy on North Korea ran directly contrary to the sunshine policy espoused by South Korea under Kim Dae Jung. Kim Dae Jung's policy continued under his successor, Roh Moo Hyun, who was elected in December 2002 with 48.91 percent of the vote.[41] Roh's election, following the earlier election of Kim Dae Jung, indicated an important shift in political sentiment in South Korea. Contrary to the position of the South Korean conservatives, both Kim Dae Jung and Roh Moo Hyun represent a center-left or progressive position that is more critical of the United States. They do not advocate a severing of the relationship with the United States, but will not necessarily support the United States on every issue. Despite domestic criticism, South Korea under Roh Moo Hyun became the third most significant contributor of troops in Iraq. The progressives embody the nationalist suspicion of Japan, while also favoring improved relations with China. A poll of government legislators in April 2004 had 63 percent identifying China as South Korea's most important partner compared to 28 percent for the United States.[42] Given these attitudes it is no surprise that South Korea has been critical of the approach taken by the United States toward North Korea. At the same time the United States has sought to undermine the South Korean policy of reconciliation with the DPRK. Selig Harrison argues that the statement by James Kelly on 4 October 2002 was related to this goal (as well as to concerns about Japan pursuing reconciliation with North Korea).[43]

Apart from the United States, the major external powers that are affected by Korean developments are China, Japan, and Russia. With some differences of emphasis these powers have all sought a diplomatic solution to the North Korean nuclear crisis. Of all the powers, China is the one that has the closest diplomatic ties with North Korea and therefore is best able to exert leverage. China believes that the United States is too narrowly focused in dealing with North Korea. From the Chinese perspective political, military, and economic issues relating to North Korea are all related; the way to resolve them is to establish a comprehensive package that will be acceptable to all parties. Such a package would not only forestall the acquisition of nuclear weapons by North Korea, but address issues of economic and political reform. While it is China's judgment that the survival of the North Korean regime is the best outcome in current circumstances, it also wants to see the reform of that regime.[44] More broadly the way in which China approaches the North Korean situation is influenced by its aim of maintaining and developing its relationship with South Korea. China favors a phased approach to reunification, emphasizing stability and the maintenance of Chinese influence throughout the peninsula. Given that China has more influence with North Korea than does any of the other external powers, China has played a leading role in establishing a multilateral framework within which the United States and the DPRK can deal with their differences. Such a framework puts pressure on the United States to move toward reconciliation with North Korea as favored by the other parties.

Japan, too, has had an interest in improving its relations with North Korea. Given its proximity to North Korea there have been particular concerns about that state's development of nuclear weapons and missiles. There have also been issues dating back to the period of Japanese colonial rule in Korea (1910–1945). Japan achieved a settlement of those issues with South Korea in 1965, but the differences with North Korea remain unresolved. Efforts toward normalization between Japan and the DPRK were made in the early 1990s, and Japan then became the second most important financial contributor to KEDO under the Agreed Framework of 1994. Relations suffered a setback with North Korea's launch of a Taepodong missile in 1998. Another problem in Japanese-DPRK relations has been the fate of Japanese nationals abducted by North Korea in the 1970s and 1980s, probably for purposes of identity theft.[45] The popular resonance of this issue in Japan has sometimes made it difficult for Japanese governments to develop improved relations with North Korea. Nevertheless, in 2001–2002 Prime Minister Koizumi Junichiro moved to resume discussions with North Korea about improving the relationship with Japan. This culminated in a visit by Koizumi to Pyongyang on 17 September 2002. As indicated previously Kelly's statement a little over two weeks later has been interpreted as partly an attempt to preempt Japan on this issue. In the context of the crisis as it has subsequently unfolded, Japan has generally favored an approach that would involve a return to the principles of the Agreed Framework; that is, inducements to encourage good behavior rather than punitive measures that might escalate into military confrontation.

Before 1991 the USSR competed with China as a major external influence on North Korea. In the aftermath of the collapse of the USSR, Russia has exerted far less influence in North Korea and generally has less significance than the other three major powers in relation to the Korean issue. Nevertheless Russia retains a strong interest in Korean affairs and wishes to exert such influence as it can. While Russia has opposed the acquisition of nuclear weapons by North Korea, it has generally favored a conciliatory approach. In dealing with North Korea's economic and political problems, Russia's preference has been for the soft landing. In the post–Cold War era Russia has also sought to further develop its relations with South Korea. In general terms, then, Russia finds itself aligned with China in terms of its approach to North Korea, and strongly behind the sunshine policy initiated by Kim Dae Jung. Indicative of Russian attempts to influence North Korea was a summit meeting held in Moscow between Vladimir Putin and Kim Jong Il on 4 August 2001. In the resulting DPRK-Russia Moscow Declaration, Russia showed an understanding for North Korea's position on a number of issues.[46] Cooperation between Russia and North Korea in relation to both security and economic matters was evident when Kim Jong Il visited the Russian Far East in August 2002.[47] The similarity between the Russian and Chinese approaches to the North Korean issue was underlined when Putin and Jiang Zemin held a summit meeting in Beijing in December 2002.[48]

Given the deterioration in relations between the United States and North Korea in 2001–2002, how has the issue been dealt with subsequently? While North Korea responded to the collapse of the Agreed Framework by reviving plans for its own nuclear development (implying also the possibility of acquiring nuclear weapons), the United States said it would only assist North Korea if there were verification in advance that nuclear development was not occurring. Whereas North Korea wanted negotiations on a bilateral basis, the United States said it would only negotiate in a multilateral context. China took the lead in brokering differences between the United States and North Korea. Six-party talks commenced in August 2003 following three-party talks (North Korea, United States, China) in April 2003. While these were multilateral in form (involving the two Korean states, the United States, China, Japan, and Russia), there was scope within that framework for the United States and North Korea to negotiate bilaterally. The sticking point has been US insistence on "complete, verifiable, and irreversible disarmament" in advance. In general the other parties would be satisfied with an agreement along the lines of the Agreed Framework. North Korea has wanted a nonaggression guarantee from the United States, while also maintaining its right to develop nuclear energy for peaceful purposes. In October 2003 North Korea claimed that it had reprocessed 8,000 spent uranium fuel rods, sufficient to make six nuclear weapons, but this claim was not verified and was probably a bargaining ploy.[49]

In the context of the crisis that emerged in 2001–2002 there has been considerable debate about the best way to deal with North Korea.[50] Essentially the argument is about whether inducements or sanctions are the best way to gain a guarantee of good behavior by North Korea. Good behavior in this context means that North Korea would eschew nuclear development, including the possibility of obtaining nuclear weapons. Inducements would involve providing economic assistance to North Korea, including light-water nuclear reactors to help meet its energy requirements. The parties supporting this approach have generally been willing to allow North Korea to show that it has complied with its side of the bargain either after or concurrently with the provision of assistance (specifically the provision of light-water nuclear reactors). The main opposition to this approach has come from the George W. Bush administration. If there is no guarantee that North Korea is following a nonnuclear path, then sanctions should be adopted to achieve compliance. Sanctions could take an economic form in the first instance. However, sanctions could also have a military component; for example, there could be an attack on North Korea's nuclear facilities. The problem with this approach is that there could be military retaliation by North Korea, with the possibility of an attack across the 38th parallel. This would be very costly in terms of lives and completely undermine the delicate political balance in Northeast Asia. The challenge, therefore, is to achieve an agreement that will satisfy North Korea that its security and economic needs are being addressed, while also allowing the United States to claim that North Korea does not pose a nuclear risk. In more specific terms this becomes a matter of how much North Korea is prepared to guarantee in advance, as compared with what the United States is willing to accept.

These underlying issues were highlighted in September 2005 with the announcement of a joint statement among the various parties involved in the six-party talks.[51] North Korea declared its intention to abandon existing nuclear weapons and nuclear weapons facilities, and to resume membership of the Nuclear Nonproliferation Treaty, with provision also for international inspections. The United States stated that it had no nuclear weapons in South Korea and "no intention to attack or invade the DPRK with nuclear or conventional weapons." The United States and North Korea would respect each other's sovereignty and right to peaceful coexistence, while working toward normalized relations. The issue of providing a light-water reactor was left unresolved. The problem with the statement will be in its implementation.[52] North Korea has not said when its pledge to abandon nuclear weapons will take effect, and when inspections will resume. It presumably will argue for a light-water reactor to be provided in advance, whereas the United States would want North Korea's nonnuclear status verified ahead of any discussions on this matter. Having abandoned the military option as nonviable and in danger of being isolated from the other parties in the six-party talks, the United States came under strong pressure from China to support the statement. While a breathing space had been achieved, the challenge remained of implementing the principles in agreed phrases.

■ Notes

1. Macdonald, *The Koreans,* p. 102.
2. Cumings, *Korea's Place in the Sun,* p. 153.
3. Ibid., p. 179.
4. Cumings, "Decoupled from History," p. 21.
5. The leading revisionist interpretation of the Korean War, emphasizing the civil war dimension, is Cumings, *The Origins of the Korean War.*
6. Buzo, *The Making of Modern Korea,* p. 88.
7. "South-North Joint Communiqué of July 4, 1972," in Kihl, ed., *Korea and the World,* pp. 341–342.
8. "North Korean Proposals on Unification," in Hoare and Pares, *Conflict in Korea,* pp. 128–129.
9. See Oberdorfer, *The Two Koreas,* pp. 376–382.
10. Buzo, *The Making of Modern Korea,* p. 184.
11. For a succinct analysis of the crisis, focusing on causes and the subsequent response by South Korea and the IMF, see Smith and Eccles, "Lessons from Korea's Crisis." A useful analysis of the crisis and its aftermath in the context of developments in South Korean politics from 1997 to 2000 is Bridges, *Korea After the Crash.*
12. Buzo, *The Making of Modern Korea,* p. 183.
13. Cumings, *Korea's Place in the Sun,* p. 361.
14. See Buzo, *The Making of Modern Korea,* pp. 185–186.
15. Ibid., pp. 186–187.
16. Ibid., p. 187.
17. Ibid., pp. 174–175.
18. Noland, *Korea After Kim Jong-il,* p. 22.
19. Buzo, *The Making of Modern Korea,* p. 176.
20. A good overview of the 1993–1994 nuclear crisis is Oberdorfer, *The Two Koreas,* pp. 249–368. More detailed studies are Sigal, *Disarming Strangers,* and Wit et al., *Going Critical.*
21. Oberdorfer, *The Two Koreas,* p. 254.
22. *Keesing's Record of World Events,* vol. 37 (1991), p. 38576.
23. See appendix B in Kihl, ed., *Korea and the World,* pp. 343–346.

24. See appendix B in ibid., pp. 347–348.

25. *Keesing's Record of World Events,* vol. 39 (1993), p. 39509.

26. *Keesing's Record of World Events,* vol. 39 (1993), p. 39597.

27. See Nayan Chanda, "Bomb Cradle," *Far Eastern Economic Review,* 28 October 1993, p. 20.

28. *Keesing's Record of World Events,* vol. 39 (1993), p. 39776.

29. Nayan Chanda and Shim Jae Hoon, "Devil in the Details," *Far Eastern Economic Review,* 13 January 1994, p. 14.

30. See Nayan Chanda, "Bomb and Bombast," *Far Eastern Economic Review,* 10 February 1994, pp. 16–18.

31. Julia Preston, "U.N. Bows to China, Issues Mild Call to N. Korea to Permit Nuclear Checks," *Washington Post,* 1 April 1994, p. A27.

32. R. Jeffrey Smith, "Perry Sharply Warns North Korea," *Washington Post,* 31 March 1994, p. A1.

33. Nayan Chanda, "Forgive and Forget?" *Far Eastern Economic Review,* 12 May 1994, p. 15.

34. Nayan Chanda, "No Soft Options," *Far Eastern Economic Review,* 16 June 1994, p. 15.

35. Nayan Chanda, "Enough Is Enough," *Far Eastern Economic Review,* 23 June 1994, pp. 14–15.

36. Oberdorfer, *The Two Koreas,* p. 329.

37. Shim Jae Hoon, "Give and Take," *Far Eastern Economic Review,* 27 October 1994, p. 15.

38. www.state.gov/regions/eap/991012_northkorea_rpt.html (accessed 11 August 2005).

39. www.fas.org/nuke/guide/dprk/nkag-report.htm (accessed 11 August 2005).

40. Lee, "South Korea in 2003," p. 135.

41. Lee, "South Korea in 2002," p. 76.

42. Cha, "South Korea in 2004," p. 35.

43. Harrison, "Did North Korea Cheat?"

44. On Chinese objectives in Korea, see Shambaugh, "China and the Korean Peninsula."

45. International Crisis Group, "Japan and North Korea."

46. Ahn, "North Korea in 2001," p. 53.

47. Ahn, "North Korea in 2002," p. 56.

48. Shambaugh, "China and the Korean Peninsula," p. 54.

49. Park, "North Korea in 2003," p. 143; Park, "North Korea in 2004," pp. 14–15.

50. See, for example, O'Hanlon and Mochizuki, "Toward a Grand Bargain with North Korea"; O'Hanlon and Mochizuki, *Crisis on the Korean Peninsula;* "Can North Korea Be Engaged?"; Cha and Kang, *Nuclear North Korea; Meeting the North Korean Nuclear Challenge.* Critical perspectives on US policy include Harrison, *Korean Endgame;* McCormack, *Target North Korea.*

51. Joseph Kahn, "North Korea Says It Will Abandon Nuclear Efforts," *New York Times,* 19 September 2005.

52. Joseph Kahn and David E. Sanger, "US-Korean Deal on Arms Leaves Key Points Open," *New York Times,* 20 September 2005. On subsequent difficulties in implementation, see "A Frustrating Game of Carrots and Sticks," *The Economist,* 11–17 February 2006.

Part 3
Changing Dynamics in Southeast Asia

International Politics in Southeast Asia | 10

W e now shift our attention from Northeast Asia to Southeast Asia. Although Northeast Asia is the subregion of Asia Pacific that has the greatest significance for world politics because it is home to China and Japan, as well as directly involving the United States, Southeast Asia is also important. With nearly 600 million people Southeast Asia has a smaller population than either China or India, but this is still a significant proportion of the world's population. Indonesia has more Muslims than any other country on Earth.

This chapter provides an overview of international politics in Southeast Asia.[1] It begins with an attempt to define the underlying features of international politics in the region, and then examines both maritime and mainland Southeast Asia, its two subregions, in terms of those features. Maritime Southeast Asia encompasses Indonesia, Malaysia, Singapore, the Philippines, and East Timor. Mainland Southeast Asia covers Thailand, Vietnam, Cambodia, Laos, and Burma (Myanmar). Since Indonesia is the most important of the Southeast Asian states it is discussed more fully in Chapter 11 and only referred to briefly here. While there is considerable reference to the Association of Southeast Asian Nations (ASEAN) as the major manifestation of regionalism in Southeast Asia, it is discussed more explicitly in Chapter 13. In the final section of this chapter we consider the significance of "new" issues in the international politics of the region, taking as our examples unregulated people movements and HIV/AIDS.

In outlining the main features of international politics in Southeast Asia, a number of general points will be made. Examples will be suggested in the subsequent sections focusing on maritime and mainland Southeast Asia. The features we will focus on are the tension between state and society, state-to-state relations within Southeast Asia, and the involvement of the major powers (United States, China, Japan).

A key feature of Southeast Asian politics, whether the focus is domestic or international, is the tension that exists between the states of the region and the societies over which they preside. Many elements of society in Southeast Asia do not accept the states system as currently constituted. In a world of nation-states, the assumption is that each state derives its legitimacy from being the political expression of a "nation," that is, a group with common cultural characteristics such as language, religion, and shared history. While nation-states so defined rarely exist in practice, there is frequently a tendency for ethnic groups dissatisfied with their minority status to claim that they should secede and establish their own nation-state. Such a claim assumes a geographical concentration of the group in question. Separatist claims exist in a number of Southeast Asian states, while arguments for reconstituting states to give a greater voice to particular ethnic groups are even more common.

If fragmentation did occur it would mean that the total number of states in Southeast Asia would increase, thus adding another layer of complexity to the region. Movements to reorganize states to give a greater voice to ethnic groups or regions that believe themselves to be underrepresented would, if successful, usually lead to some form of decentralization or federalism. The total number of states in Southeast Asia would not increase, but the way in which the affected states function could alter. They could become weaker in some respects, although there is also the argument that their popular basis could be enhanced through reorganization. This would make such states more stable. Pressures for secession are frequently treated by the states concerned as matters of internal security. This can become a bigger preoccupation than external security. Support for separatist movements by external actors (whether governments or nongovernmental organizations) can be viewed as threatening. Sometimes external actors are concerned primarily with human rights abuses that might occur when states attempt to suppress separatist movements, rather than focusing on the separatist claims as such.

Another form of state-society tension occurs when there is an argument that an existing state should be reorganized to reflect different political principles from those that currently prevail. This is most commonly the case when there is pressure on an authoritarian government to move in the direction of democracy. In states with large numbers of Muslims, however, there have been movements wanting greater recognition of Islamic principles, and sometimes reorganization along Islamic lines. Where claims for reconstituting the state occur at the national level they might be viewed as security issues in some circumstances, but perhaps less so than when they occur in relation to separatist movements. If movements for democratization or Islamicization were successful, again the total number of states in Southeast Asia would not increase, but the way in which those states behaved externally as well as internally could. States encountering such movements are likely to view external involvement (whether through governments, international organizations, or nongovernmental organizations) with suspicion if not overt hostility.

While state-society tensions suggest an underlying fragility in Southeast Asian politics, with manifestations at both international and domestic levels, the dynamics of international politics in the region also have an important state-to-state dimension. We will consider initially the relationships among the Southeast Asian states, and then turn to the issue of involvement by the major powers. (See Table 10.1.)

There is no clear hierarchy among the Southeast Asian states. While Indonesia is the most significant state, it does not play the role of regional hegemon. Nor do states function in terms of well-defined blocs or groupings. Interaction occurs primarily on the basis of overlapping interests or concerns. One possible division is between the subregions of maritime Southeast Asia and mainland Southeast Asia. Another possible division is on the basis of level of economic development. Although its circumstances as a predominantly Chinese city-state are unusual, Singapore functions as

Table 10.1 Southeast Asia: Population, Gross Domestic Product, and Per Capita Gross Domestic Product

	Population 2005	GDP 2004 (US$ billions)	Per Capita GDP 2004 (US$)
Burma	49,362,000	69.0	1,483
Brunei	372,361	5.2	14,249
Cambodia	13,636,398	4.51	337
East Timor	1,040,880	0.328	357
Indonesia	241,973,879	251.0	1,055
Laos	6,217,141	3.12	515
Malaysia	23,953,136	117.0	5,000
Philippines	87,857,473	86.5	1,003
Singapore	4,425,720	105.0	24,176
Thailand	64,185,502	161.0	2,497
Vietnam	83,535,576	45.4	550

Source: International Institute for Strategic Studies, *The Military Balance 2005–2006* (London: Routledge, 2005); GDP and per capita GDP figures for East Timor are from Department of Foreign Affairs and Trade, Australia, "East Timor Fact Sheet," www.dfat.gov .au/geo/fs/timo.pdf, accessed 14 February 2006.

an international financial center and commercial entrepôt, and has the highest living standards in the region. Brunei is also unusual as a small, rich sultanate, deriving its wealth from oil. Thailand and Malaysia were adversely affected by the Asian financial crisis in 1997, but in general have experienced significant levels of economic growth. Indonesia's experience was similar in some respects but it has found it more difficult to overcome the effects of the Asian financial crisis. States that are clearly Third World in terms of economic development include Indonesia, the Philippines, Vietnam, Burma, Cambodia, Laos, and East Timor.

Within either maritime or mainland Southeast Asia there can be interaction based on sharing borders and dealing with problems relating to that subregion. There can be disputes involving the delineation of borders and even over particular territories. Shared borders can lead to issues concerning people movement (refugees, illegal immigration, criminal activity). There can be concerns about river development and the control of sea and seabed resources. States with similar levels of economic development might cooperate to improve the terms upon which they engage with their major partners. Alternatively they might regard states comparable to themselves in economic terms as competitors. Issues of cooperation, and the constraints that prevail, are considered further in the context of regionalism.

A third broad feature of the international politics of Southeast Asia concerns the involvement of the United States, China, and Japan. We need to consider how those states relate to the region, and how the Southeast Asian states in turn relate to them. The particular strategic and economic interests of each of the major powers affect the way they become involved in the region. As the world's global power, the United States wants to ensure that developments within Southeast Asia do not threaten its own primacy. This means ensuring that the involvement of other major powers complements rather than competes with the US role. The United States also has a concern that stability prevails within Southeast Asia, particularly in Indonesia, which is both Southeast Asia's most significant state and the world's most populous Muslim country. Since September 11, 2001, the United States has viewed Southeast Asia as one of the main fronts in the war on terrorism. Indonesia has been of particular interest in this respect, although there has been more specific US military involvement in the Philippines. Given its own liberal ideology, the United States also takes a particular interest in issues concerning democratization and human rights in Southeast Asia. Trade and investment issues have some bearing on US involvement in the region but are not an overriding consideration. Particular interest groups often have a bearing on bilateral US relationships with Southeast Asian countries, with economics and human rights concerns usually being foremost. (See Table 10.2.)

Table 10.2   Trade Between China, Japan, the United States, and Southeast Asia, 2002 (US$ millions)

	China's Exports	China's Imports	Japan's Exports	Japan's Imports	US Exports	US Imports
World total	325,711	295,440	416,632	337,149	693,000	1,202,000
Brunei	21	242	319	1,515	47	306
Burma	725	137	115	110	11	380
Cambodia	252	25	70	75	29	1,146
Indonesia	3,427	4,501	6,237	14,174	2,581	10,385
Laos	54	10	18	7	4	3
Malaysia	4,975	9,295	11,016	11,173	10,348	24,734
Philippines	2,042	3,217	8,457	6,498	7,270	11,431
Singapore	6,969	7,054	14,183	5,001	16,221	15,093
Thailand	2,959	5,599	13,217	10,507	4,860	15,683
Vietnam	2,150	1,115	2,135	2,529	580	2,585

Source: International Monetary Fund, *Direction of Trade Statistics Yearbook 2003* (Washington, DC, 2003).

In the case of China, strategic concerns are also very much to the fore. Southeast Asia is an important region in terms of China's goal of asserting its preeminence in East Asia as a whole. While it is particularly interested in those states adjoining China (i.e., mainland Southeast Asia), China's involvement extends throughout the region. It wants to influence the states of the region away from too close a relationship with the United States and Japan. There are border and broader territorial issues in China's relations with a number of states (most notably, in the dispute over the South China Sea). China also has an interest in protecting the position of ethnic Chinese (the overseas Chinese) in Southeast Asian countries, although it has to be sensitive to possible criticism that it is interfering in domestic affairs. Again, trade relationships are significant but not the fundamental factor in how China relates to Southeast Asia.

For Japan, economic considerations play a very important part in its relations with the Southeast Asian countries. Japan's economic involvement in Southeast Asian countries has been part of its strategy of exporting low-cost manufacturing jobs to cheap labor countries throughout East Asia. Some countries in Southeast Asia are also important to Japan as suppliers of raw materials (for example, oil from Indonesia and Brunei). To maintain its economic position in Southeast Asia political stability is important. Japan's political involvement in the region has stability as a major goal. Japan's foreign aid is based on the assumption that economic development contributes to political stability. Japan's diplomatic and more broadly political involvement has also been designed to contribute to stability in the region.

From the perspective of the Southeast Asian states there is at one level a desire to maximize regional control over regional affairs. At a more pragmatic level, however, Southeast Asian countries have usually been prepared to engage with the major powers if they see this as useful for their own objectives. This willingness to cooperate can vary according to the Southeast Asian country and the major power in question. Clearly there can also be conflicts and disputes between particular major powers and individual Southeast Asian states or groups of states. This point will be developed when we examine major power involvement in the subsequent sections of this chapter.

The various features of international politics in Southeast Asia can be elaborated through an examination of the situation in the two subregions: first, maritime Southeast Asia and, second, mainland Southeast Asia.

■ Maritime Southeast Asia

In discussing international politics in maritime Southeast Asia we begin by asking what justification there is for thinking in terms of such a subregion. All regions and subregions are constructs, based on emphasizing certain features allegedly held in common. In the case of maritime Southeast Asia the states covered are Indonesia, Malaysia, Singapore, Brunei, the Philippines, and East Timor. Apart from West Malaysia (the Malay Peninsula), these states all occupy a chain of islands to the southeast of the Asian land mass. Even West Malaysia, as a peninsula jutting into this area, could be regarded as effectively an island. As "island" states these countries all have a strong orientation to the sea and to influences that are borne by maritime means. Ethnically the greater proportion of people in maritime Southeast Asia is of Malay background, but with significant minorities who have migrated to the area. Ethnic Chinese are of most relevance in this respect, with Singapore being overwhelmingly a Chinese city-state. Among the Malays, Islam is the dominant religion, although the northern areas of the Philippines became Christianized during the colonial era and there are also many Christians in eastern Indonesia. The colonial powers involved in maritime Southeast Asia were the Netherlands (in the Netherlands East Indies, the precursor to Indonesia), Britain (in Malaysia's antecedent states and Singapore), Spain (in the Philippines up to the end of the nineteenth century), the United States (the Philippines from the end of the nineteenth century), and Portugal (in East Timor known as Portuguese Timor, but earlier in centers such as Malacca and the Moluccas or Maluku). Japan occupied this entire area from 1942 to 1945, and was a major factor in bringing colonial rule to an end. The colonial era had a major impact on the borders, the institutions, and the outlook of the contemporary states of maritime Southeast Asia.

Society-State Tensions

In examining international politics within maritime Southeast Asia, we can begin by focusing on society-state tensions that have international manifestations. Separatist conflicts are most evident in Indonesia, with strong movements for secession in both Aceh and West Papua. Indonesia's incorporation of East Timor came to an end following the 1999 referendum in that territory and subsequent international intervention. Aceh, West Papua, and East Timor are discussed more fully in Chapter 11. The conflicts in Aceh and West Papua continue to weaken Indonesia as a state. Other conflicts derive from tensions between different religious or ethnic groups (for example, in Maluku, Kalimantan, and Central Sulawesi) but usually do not involve claims for secession. Nevertheless these conflicts can weaken the authority of the Indonesian state. On a broader level, decentralization reforms were enacted in 1999 in response to pressures from resource-rich provinces for a greater share of the revenues from the wealth they produced. Formally speaking Indonesia has remained a unitary state but some powers have been devolved to the local level. These reforms could contribute to greater stability in Indonesia, but they do make the system of governance more complex. Again, these issues are examined in more detail in the next chapter.

Apart from the conflicts affecting Indonesia, the most serious separatist issue in maritime Southeast Asia is in the southern Philippines where Muslims are a significant proportion of the population. Although only 5 to 8 percent of the Philippines' total population of nearly 90 million is Muslim,[2] there is a higher concentration in the southern Philippines: some parts of Mindanao, Sulu, Palawan, Basilan, and Tawi-Tawi. In the decades following independence in 1946, Muslim consciousness in the southern Philippines increased as a result of Christian immigration into the area; by 1990 Muslims were less than 18 percent of Mindanao's population.[3] Muslim political aspirations focused on the Moro National Liberation Front (MNLF), set up under the leadership of Nur Misuari in 1969. In 1972 an uprising led by the Bangsa Moro Army commenced, with the aim of establishing a Muslim state in the southern Philippines. Under the Tripoli Agreement of 1976, political autonomy was promised to thirteen provinces and nine cities in the southern Philippines, but this was never implemented. Following the Jeddah Agreement of 1987, a plebiscite in thirteen provinces led to the Autonomous Region of Muslim Mindanao (ARMM) being proclaimed in four provinces only in 1990: Maguindanao, Lanao del Sur (both on Mindanao), Sulu, and Tawi Tawi. The MNLF accepted the ARMM in 1996, and the Bangsa Moro Army was absorbed into the Philippines' security forces.

A more militant and more Islamic manifestation of the Muslim movement in the southern Philippines is the Moro Islamic Liberation Front (MILF). The MILF split from the MNLF in 1978. It was led by Salamat Hashim, an Islamic scholar and also a Maguindanao (whereas Misuari was a Tausug). The MILF continued the armed struggle after the MNLF accepted the ARMM in 1996. Peace negotiations between the MILF and the Philippines government have occurred over a number of years, but without any final settlement being reached. Another group involved in the conflict in the southern Philippines is Abu Sayyaf, founded in 1991 and based on Basilan. Its leader, Abubakar Janjalani, was also an Islamic scholar, but was killed in 1998. Abu Sayyaf has achieved notoriety for its kidnappings and other attempts at extortion. It is more significant for its links to international terrorism through Al-Qaida than as a major representative of the Muslim movement in the southern Philippines.[4]

Apart from the claims of separatist movements, other general areas of society-state tensions in maritime Southeast Asia relate to pressures for democratization and for greater recognition of Islam. On the issue of democratization the greatest changes have been in Indonesia following the fall of Suharto in May 1998 (see Chapter 11). While these changes have enhanced Indonesia's legitimacy, they have also made government weaker in various respects. This in turn affects the way Indonesia relates to the rest of the world. An earlier and dramatic instance of democratization was the fall of Ferdinand Marcos and the assumption of the presidency by Cory Aquino in the Philippines in 1986 on a wave of "People Power."

In Malaysia and Singapore the political institutions are formally democratic but in terms of practice there are some authoritarian features. In Malaysia governments are controlled by the Malay-dominated coalition, the Barisan Nasional (National Front). The strong laws on internal security can restrict civil liberties, and the independence of the judiciary has been challenged at times. This situation is taken further in Singapore where the ability of opposition parties to challenge the ruling People's Action Party is heavily circumscribed, mainly through draconian legal provisions. In Brunei, which is run as a sultanate, there is not even a pretense of democracy. In East Timor, independent since May 2002, the political institutions have been established along democratic lines but clearly do not have deep roots. While there is one dominant party, Fretilin, opposition parties have not been restricted in their functioning. There are some tensions in East Timor, relating to issues such as unemployed youth and differences within the security forces. A breakdown in security in May 2006 led the East Timor government to invite foreign military intervention (mainly Australian). While noting the situation in relation to Indonesia, none of the other governments have been impeded in the way they relate to the world by challenges deriving from pressures for democratization.

Pressures for greater recognition of Islam arise in a number of contexts in maritime Southeast Asia. At one level such pressures are evident with some of the separatist issues in the region, most notably in Aceh and the southern Philippines. Part of the motivation for establishing Aceh as an independent state is a desire to have this region governed according to Islamic principles. Adherence to Islam is also a defining feature for the supporters of the separatist cause in the southern Philippines, although in practice the main emphasis has been on establishing autonomy in Muslim majority areas rather than proclaiming an independent state run along Islamist lines. As we have seen, both these separatist struggles have international implications. International involvement has occurred in the course of these struggles. As neighboring countries, Malaysia and Singapore have taken an interest in the Aceh situation. The United States pressured Indonesia to work with the Henri Dunant Centre, an NGO in Geneva, to achieve an agreement (short lived) with Gerakan Aceh Merdeka (Free Aceh Movement; GAM) in December 2002. In the case of the southern Philippines both Indonesia and Malaysia have taken an interest in the plight of Muslims there, and both Libya and Saudi Arabia have assisted in negotiating agreements in 1976 and 1987 respectively. If Muslim-based separatist movements in Aceh and the southern Philippines were to achieve their maximalist goals, this would lead to the emergence of new states in Southeast Asia, adding further to the complexity of international politics at both the regional level and beyond.

At a broader level, arguments about the role of Islam are an important dimension of politics in both Indonesia and Malaysia. In Indonesia there are mass organizations for Muslims: Nahdatul Ulama (NU) representing the traditionalists, and Muhammadiyah representing the modernists. Neither organization advocates a reorganization of Indonesia along Islamic lines. They provide a vehicle for Muslim views to be expressed, while also being liberal in their support for political tolerance. (See Chapter 11 for further discussion of this issue.) If Indonesia were to become an Islamic state, then clearly this would have major international consequences, but there is no credible scenario whereby this might occur.

In Malaysia the main support for an Islamic state has come from PAS (Parti Islam Se-Malaysia), a Malay-based party that stands in opposition to the dominant UMNO (United Malays National Organization). While UMNO, the major party in the ruling Barisan Nasional (National Front), has supported a privileged political position for the Malays within Malaysia, it has been opposed to the establishment of an Islamic state. This might appear to be recognition of the demographic realities of Malaysia where Malays are only a small majority of the population (Muslims, predominantly Malays, constitute 54 percent), with the Chinese (27 percent) and the Indians (9 percent) as the most significant minorities.[5] PAS's main strength has been in the northeastern states of West Malaysia (Kelantan, Terengganu), which are predominantly Malay. The ethnic homogeneity of these states has made it easier for PAS to implement Islamic measures when in government there. Paradoxically PAS has been able to cooperate with non-Malay opposition parties, most notably in the Barisan Alternatif (Alternative Front) of 1999. However, that cooperation focuses on opposition to the ruling coalition; over PAS's goal of an Islamic state there would be fundamental disagreement. In the unlikely event of PAS ever achieving a measure of power at the national level in Malaysia, it might attempt to entrench Islam within the polity in various symbolic ways, but it is difficult to see its goal of an Islamic state ever being realized. Nevertheless PAS does maintain pressure on UMNO to show its Malay credentials, including recognition of Islam in various ways. The attempts by Mahathir (prime minister, 1981–2003) to strengthen Malaysia's Islamic identity were in part a response to the challenge from PAS within the Malay community. At the international level the support given by Malaysia for Muslim countries and Muslim causes could be seen in some respects as the outcome of the domestic situation in Malaysia.

Since 2001 the US-led war on terrorism has highlighted issues concerning the role of Islam in Southeast Asia. Groups such as Abu Sayyaf in the southern Philippines and Jemaah Islamiah (JI) in Indonesia have come under greater scrutiny. Abu Sayyaf represents an extremist fringe of the movement seeking the secession of Muslim areas in the southern Philippines. While the mainstream organizations within that movement have engaged in violence as part of their struggle for self-determination, they have generally been more restrained in their methods as compared to Abu Sayyaf. In Indonesia JI does have some links with the modernist stream of Islam, but its methods and goals are disowned by virtually all Indonesian Muslims. JI's goal is the establishment of an Islamic state embracing all of the Muslim majority areas of maritime Southeast Asia: that is, Indonesia, Malaysia, and the southern Philippines. In Aceh the Indonesian government routinely portrayed GAM as "terrorist," but GAM claimed its use of violence was limited and was part of its strategy for achieving independence.

State-to-State Relations

Turning next to the state-to-state dimension of international politics, there are a number of points to note in relation to maritime Southeast Asia. The role of ASEAN as a vehicle for conducting state-to-state relations in Southeast Asia (maritime and mainland) will be discussed in a subsequent section. Indonesia's most important relations in the area will be noted, followed by a discussion of the relationships among Malaysia, Singapore, and Brunei, and state-to-state relations involving the Philippines and East Timor.

Indonesia's most significant relationships within maritime Southeast Asia are with Malaysia, the Philippines, and Singapore. Indonesia assumes that it has preeminence as the leader of the Malay world. Indonesian leaders have sometimes appeared annoyed by some of the strident postures adopted by Malaysia, particularly during the Mahathir prime ministership. Under Suharto, Indonesia was more pro-Western and some of Mahathir's anti-Western rhetoric would have jarred. With the fall of Suharto in 1998 and the retirement of Mahathir in 2004, some of the tensions in Indonesian-Malaysian relations have eased. Mahathir's successor, Abdullah Ahmad Badawi, appears much more restrained in his approach, and there is greater harmony in the outlooks of Indonesia and Malaysia. In the case of the Philippines, there have been some tensions with Indonesia because of the situation in the southern Philippines. Muslims in Indonesia have some sympathy for their co-religionists in the Philippines, but the issue has not been a major impediment in the bilateral relationship. Indonesia can be sensitive to the close relationship the Philippines has with the United States. Tensions between Indonesia and Singapore relate to the latter's role as essentially a Chinese city-state set in a Malay world. Indonesia would prefer Singapore to be more subdued in relation to its Malay neighbors, and regards some of Singapore's stances as unduly provocative. Insensitivity to Muslim views and an undue focus on the island state's vulnerability would be examples. For its part, Singapore believes it needs to adopt a high profile on some issues and to focus on relations outside maritime Southeast Asia, in order not to be overwhelmed.

Another set of state-to-state relations in Southeast Asia concerns the interactions involving Malaysia, Singapore, and Brunei. These relationships have their roots in the colonial era and have an important domestic dimension. During the colonial era the antecedent of Malaysia was a series of states that were either under British protection or directly ruled by Britain. Singapore was similarly under British rule while Brunei was a British protectorate. It was during the colonial period that large numbers of Chinese and (to a lesser extent) Indians entered the west coast of what is now West Malaysia and also Singapore. Ethnic relations were a major problem in achieving decolonization, mainly because the Malays wanted to ensure they retained a privileged position as the "sons of the soil" (*bumiputera*) and were not overwhelmed by the Chinese. For this reason the Malayan Union proposal of 1946, providing for equal citizenship rights, did not proceed and a Malayan Federation favorable to the Malays was established instead. When independence came in 1957, following several years of communist insurgency based on the support of elements of the Chinese community, it was on the basis of the existing federation but with Singapore excluded. The formation of Malaysia in 1963 was an attempt to bring independence to Singapore, and concurrently to achieve the decolonization of the British territories in north Borneo (Sarawak and Sabah), while not upsetting the racial balance in Malaya itself. The indigenous people of north Borneo were seen as the equivalent of Malays for the purposes of this exercise. Brunei was originally proposed for inclusion in Malaysia but withdrew following the pro-Indonesian Azahari revolt of December 1962. The Sultan of Brunei also feared for his oil wealth if his state were to be merged with Malaysia. Singapore's inclusion in Malaysia lasted only two years. Strong opposition by the Malay political elite to Singapore's campaign for a "Malaysian Malaysia" (implying equal rights for members of all ethnic groups) resulted in Singapore's separation in 1965 and its establishment as an independent state.

Given these circumstances there are many domestic elements in Malaysia-Singapore relations. Singapore, with its deliberately nonracial approach (even though a large proportion of the population is Chinese), stands as an alternative to the political model that has prevailed in Malaysia where the Malays have a privileged position. Singapore's economic success also constitutes a challenge for Malaysia, even though Malaysia has generally been one of the economic success stories of Southeast Asia. Singapore has given a high priority to maintaining strong external defenses, with generally 5–6 percent of GDP devoted to defense spending. Singapore's cheek-by-jowl existence with Malaysia is reflected in disputes over such issues as water supplies (provided to Singapore from the neighboring Malaysian state of Johor) and the operation of the railroad connecting the two states.[6]

In the case of Brunei, the circumstances of the 1962 revolt contributed to a perception of vulnerability in relation to its neighbors, both Malaysia and Indonesia. Since A. M. Azahari was the leader of the successful People's Party (Partai Ra'ayat) in the August 1962 elections, which had among its aims the establishment of a state of North Borneo (based on Brunei, but including also Sarawak and Sabah), this situation put an end to Brunei's brief experiment in democracy. Having relied on British forces to suppress the revolt, the sultan was reluctant to move toward independence. When Brunei did become independent in 1984, it was on the basis of defense links continuing with Britain. A battalion of Gurkhas has remained in Brunei. In the context of independence Brunei has put some emphasis on its ASEAN membership as a means of enhancing its security. It has also looked to Singapore as another small state with which it shares concerns about vulnerability; Singapore has an infantry battalion based in Brunei.[7]

The significance of the relationship between the Philippines and Indonesia has already been referred to. The Philippines has also given some attention to issues in its relationships with Malaysia and Singapore. As a Malay-dominated state Malaysia has taken some interest in the plight of fellow Muslims in the southern Philippines. The most significant dispute between the two countries has been over Sabah. A Malaysian state since 1963, Sabah had previously been known as British North Borneo. The Philippines' claim to Sabah is based on an interpretation of an agreement whereby the territory was leased to British commercial representatives by the Sultan of Sulu in 1878, with the British North Borneo Company and later the British government inheriting the terms of that agreement. According to the Philippines, Britain had no right to assign sovereignty over the territory to Malaysia. Since the dispute over the formation of Malaysia in the early 1960s, the Sabah issue has generally been quiescent but the Philippines has not given up its claim.[8] The Philippines has had some disputes with Singapore over human rights issues, particularly the treatment of Filipinos working in Singapore. One noted instance was in March 1995 when Flor Contemplacion, a Filipino maid working in Singapore, was hanged following her conviction for murdering a fellow maid and the four-year-old child she was caring for.[9]

As a newly independent state East Timor's most significant relationship within maritime Southeast Asia is clearly that with Indonesia. It has looked outside the region for relationships to help overcome its perceived vulnerability. Australia, Portugal, and the United Nations are particularly important in this respect. In maritime Southeast Asia the Philippines was a significant contributor to peacekeeping in East Timor, reflecting not just a concern with human rights but perhaps also a link with fellow Catholics. Singapore and Malaysia have also provided assistance to East Timor. Malaysia contributed most recently to the intervention force in East Timor in 2006. In the case of Singapore, although the economic circumstances of the two states are completely different (East Timor being the poorest country in Southeast Asia), there is some overlap in geopolitical outlooks between the two states. They are both small countries that have major concerns about their vulnerability to external forces.

The Major Powers

The involvement of the major powers in maritime Southeast Asia should be seen in the light of the overview presented at the beginning of this chapter. As previously indicated, Indonesia is the most important concern for all three powers. While China is more strongly focused on mainland Southeast Asia, it also has various interests at stake in maritime Southeast Asia. By comparison, the United States and Japan are probably more strongly focused on maritime Southeast Asia. Here we can briefly review the involvement of all three of the major powers.

In the case of the United States, the earlier discussion suggested particular concerns relating to Indonesia. While encouraging democratization, the United States also wishes to see stability within Indonesia. As Southeast Asia's largest state and as the world's most populous Muslim country, Indonesia can have a significant impact not just in its immediate region but also within the wider Islamic world. In relation to post-1998 Indonesia, the United States has sought to encourage economic recovery and development. Since September 11, 2001, there have been major concerns about extremist Islamic groups in Indonesia such as Jemaah Islamiah. At the same time, past human rights abuses by the Indonesian military, particularly in East Timor, have inhibited military cooperation and efforts to counter terrorism.

In the case of the Philippines, the United States has generally had close relations deriving from its past colonial role. At the same time Philippine nationalism has sometimes led to tensions, with the closure of the US bases at Clark Field in 1991 and Subic Bay in 1992 being the most notable example in recent times. The Philippines has cooperated closely with the United States in the war on terrorism. The United States sent forces to the southern Philippines to assist in the campaign against Abu Sayyaf, with its alleged links to Al-Qaida. The Philippines contributed a contingent to the occupation of Iraq in 2003–2004, but it was withdrawn in return for the release of a Filipino hostage in July 2004.

In Malaysia and Singapore the United States historically was less involved since this area had been under British colonial rule. During the prime ministership of Mahathir (1981–2003), relations with the United States were sometimes strained. Mahathir espoused anti-US rhetoric at times and was sensitive to US criticisms of Malaysia's human rights record (over the Anwar case, for example). Mahathir was also critical of the US approach in the war on terrorism and opposed US intervention in Iraq. Singapore, on the other hand, developed a close relationship with the United States. This was part of Singapore's strategy of using its relationship with extra-regional powers to protect its position within its own region. The most notable benefit for the United States was obtaining access to naval facilities in Singapore for its vessels operating in the region.

Japan has a strong economic stake in maritime Southeast Asia. In 2004 Japan's exports to Singapore, Thailand, Malaysia, the Philippines, and Indonesia accounted for 12.3 percent of total exports; imports from the same countries in 2004 were 13.5 percent of total imports (with Indonesia at 4.1 percent the most significant source).[10] Japanese investment in these five ASEAN countries in 2004 amounted to about 7.5 percent of Japan's total foreign investment.[11] Japan's policies in maritime Southeast Asia give a high priority to protecting its economic interests. Stability within the region is particularly important from this perspective. Japan sees its foreign aid as contributing to this goal. Among the top ten recipients of Japanese bilateral development assistance in 2003–2004 were Indonesia (second), the Philippines (third), Thailand (fourth), Vietnam (sixth), and Malaysia (ninth).[12] Japan has also offered to assist Indonesia with anti-piracy patrols. It contributed a peacekeeping contingent in East Timor to assist with reconstruction work there.

China, while focusing primarily on mainland Southeast Asia, also has interests in maritime Southeast Asia. Given China's goal of becoming the preeminent power in East Asia, it is imperative that it have a significant involvement in this subregion. From China's perspective it would like to see the states of the region supporting its goals or at least not opposing them. In general, however, the maritime Southeast Asian states have not been particularly pro-Chinese and have been critical on some issues. In some cases the position of the ethnic Chinese within the regional states has been an important factor affecting the policy of both those states and China. Indonesia and Malaysia have been perhaps most critical of China, with their policies sometimes reflecting concerns about their own Chinese population having excessive influence. Singapore, on the other hand, with its predominantly Chinese population, has had to ensure that it maintains a certain distance from China for fear that it might otherwise risk being seen as a Chinese fifth column.

The South China Sea is a particular issue where China interacts with most of the maritime Southeast Asian states and also Vietnam.[13] There are two main island groups in the South China Sea (known as the Eastern Sea by Vietnam). To the north are the Paracel Islands, some of which were seized by China from Vietnam in 1956 and the rest in 1974. To the south are the Spratly Islands, including some small islands but mostly consisting of reefs. China seized seven of these islands from Vietnam in 1988.[14] China and Vietnam have the most extensive claims in the South China Sea. China, supported by Taiwan, has a historic claim covering the entire area: it claims that historically this area was regarded as under Chinese suzerainty. Vietnam's claim derives from French involvement in the area, with France controlling both the Paracels and the Spratlys, and French sovereignty being recognized by China in the Gulf of Tonkin. In terms of specific disputes with China, Vietnam also claims a strong position under the 1982 United Nations Convention on the Law of the Sea (UNCLOS), based on principles relating to the 200 nautical miles exclusive economic zone (EEZ), the continental shelf, and equidistance between territories.[15] Among the countries of maritime Southeast Asia, the Philippines, Malaysia, Brunei, and Indonesia all have claims in the South China Sea, based on UNCLOS principles. These claims are much smaller than those of China and Vietnam. They overlap with the claims of China and Vietnam, and to some extent with each other. Indonesia's claim is to the Natuna area of the continental shelf where there are significant gas reserves.

Apart from Brunei and Indonesia all of the claimant states (including Taiwan in one instance) have occupied islands and reefs in the South China Sea to strengthen their claims. Hostilities have almost broken out on some occasions, most notably in the case of Mischief Reef in 1994–1995. This reef is 135 nautical miles west of Palawan in the southwest Philippines. The Philippines detained Chinese fishermen found there in late 1994, and China did likewise with Filipino fishermen in early 1995. China also built structures on the reef to bolster its claim. While the underlying issue was not resolved, China and the Philippines agreed that the matter should be dealt with by peaceful means in August 1995.[16]

China has generally resisted attempts to resolve the South China Sea issue on a multilateral basis. It has proposed joint development of resources, but this does not mean any weakening of China's claim to sovereignty.[17] From the perspective of the ASEAN countries, even though some of their own claims overlap, a common strategy in dealing with China could strengthen their position. China appears to have been willing to deal with the ASEAN countries jointly when there appears to be no other option. The United States and Japan, both of which have interests in the sea lanes and economic development of the South China Sea, have supported a multilateral approach. In August 2000 China stated that it was willing to negotiate a code of conduct for the South China Sea, and negotiations subsequently took place with ASEAN.[18] China's accession to ASEAN's Treaty of Amity and Cooperation in July 2003 suggested a commitment to dealing with the issue peacefully rather than compromising China's underlying objectives.[19] Essentially the situation has been one of conflict management, rather than achieving an overall settlement of the dispute.

▓ Mainland Southeast Asia

Mainland Southeast Asia covers the states of Thailand, Burma/Myanmar, Vietnam, Cambodia, and Laos. The three latter states collectively constitute Indochina, although this is not a political entity as such. Apart from Laos, all of the states of mainland Southeast Asia border the sea. The Mekong River is a major geographical feature for Thailand and the Indochinese states (and also borders Burma's extreme northeast). Whereas Islam is the strongest religion in maritime Southeast Asia, Buddhism is most significant in mainland Southeast Asia. There are Muslim and Christian minorities throughout the region. Ethnic Chinese minorities play a role in all these countries. The major colonial powers in mainland Southeast Asia were France in Indochina and Britain in Burma. Thailand (Siam) maintained its independence as a buffer zone between the British in Burma and Malaya and the French in Indochina. Before the colonial era China was a major influence in this region, and this has become significant again in recent times. India was also a major influence, with the Hindu influence at Angkor (located in modern Cambodia) being the most obvious example. The term "Indo-China" suggests the competing Indian and Chinese cultural and political influences. In the aftermath of decolonization, communist influence was strong in Indochina, with Vietnam, Cambodia, and Laos emerging as communist states by 1975 after decades of war involving France and then the United States. Thailand generally pursued a pro-Western course and was aligned with the United States. Burma espoused nonalignment, coming under military rule from 1962. In the 1950s and 1960s Cambodia was also a leading exponent of nonalignment in Southeast Asia.

Society-State Tensions

As in maritime Southeast Asia, society-state tensions have been strong in mainland Southeast Asia. The main issues have concerned the position of minorities (including Muslim minorities) and pressures for democratization. The minorities have generally worked for greater recognition within the existing states, including the reconstitution of those states in some instances, rather than for secession. The pressures for democratization have been most obvious in Burma, but have also played a role in other situations.

The opposition of the minorities in Burma to the existing state has been a major feature of the situation in that country since the time of independence in 1948. The preference of groups such as the Karen, the Kachin, the Chin, the Shan, the Wa, and the Mon has been for a federal state, where they would have a good measure of autonomy and be less subject to domination by the ethnic Burman majority (also known as Bamar or Bhamese). Many of these groups have been engaged in an insurgency since 1948 to advance their goals. They are generally concentrated in Burma's border regions. The Muslim minority, known as Rohingyas, is located in the western part of Burma adjoining Bangladesh. Since 1948 the Rohingyas have supported the claims of the various minorities for greater autonomy. Periodic repression has led to many members of this group fleeing to Bangladesh.

While the minorities issue is most serious in Burma, the various other states of mainland Southeast Asia also have disaffected minorities to deal with. Some of these groups have engaged in violence against their respective governments. One such group is the Muslim minority in southern Thailand. The Pattani United Liberation Organization (PULO), representing the most militant of the Thai Muslims, aims for secession from Thailand. The Cham minority in Cambodia is also Muslim but suffered cruelly under the Khmer Rouge. In Laos and Vietnam there are various hill peoples who have often had difficult relations with the governments in those countries. In Laos the Hmong have been a source of opposition to the government in Vietnam; many have gone into exile in countries such as the United States. In Vietnam there are many groups known collectively as Montagnards, including the Tay, Thai, Muong, Nung, Hmong, Dzao, Giarai and E-de. After 1975 one group mounting resistance to the communist regime was the United Front for the Struggle of the Oppressed Races (FULRO), but this had declined by the 1990s.[20]

On the issue of democratization the most publicized situation since the late 1980s has been Burma. With a military regime in place since 1962, pressures for change built up during the 1980s as a means for overcoming Burma's economic problems and endemic corruption. Elections in 1990 resulted in a sweeping victory for the National League for Democracy (NLD), led by Aung San Suu Kyi, the daughter of Burma's founding father (Aung San) who had been assassinated just prior to independence. The military regime (the State Law and Order Restoration Council or SLORC) refused to recognize the election results, and Aung San Suu Kyi was placed under house arrest. ASEAN attempted to engage SLORC over the issue, accepting Burma as a member in 1997, but with little result. Stronger pressure from both the United States and the European Union likewise failed to bring about change. SLORC (renamed State Peace and Development Council or SPDC from 1997) remained adamant about rejecting democratization if it were likely to undermine the position of the military in Burma.

Democratization has been an issue in all the other states of mainland Southeast Asia, but has not attracted the same attention as in the case of Burma. The military has long occupied a dominant position in Thailand,

and remains a major factor there. In 1932 a military coup led to the replacement of the absolute monarchy with a constitutional monarchy. From the 1970s there has been a gradual consolidation of constitutional government; since 1992 democratic elections have proceeded in an orderly way without military intervention. The monarch retains great symbolic authority.

In the Indochinese countries democracy is either very fragile or else largely absent. Both Vietnam and Laos remain as communist regimes, run according to centralist principles. Following the experience of the Khmer Rouge regime (1975–1979) and the Third Indochina War (1978–1991), Cambodia has become democratic in form. The rule of law is weak in Cambodia, however, and the state apparatus has been used by Prime Minister Hun Sen to weaken his opponents and ensure his own electoral victories. The situations in all the Indochinese countries have attracted international attention, particularly on human rights grounds.

State-to-State Relations

On the issue of state-to-state relations we can consider how the states of mainland Southeast Asia relate to each other, as well as to the other Southeast Asian states. Then we will examine the involvement of the major powers in mainland Southeast Asia. Among the states of mainland Southeast Asia we will begin with Thailand before turning to Burma, Vietnam, Cambodia, and Laos.

Thailand occupies a geographically central position within mainland Southeast Asia. Historically it has tried to play a leading role against Vietnam to the east and Burma to the west. Both Vietnam and Burma continue to be major preoccupations for Thailand. Against Vietnam, Thailand has competed for influence in relation to both Cambodia and Laos. During the US war in Vietnam (1960s to mid-1970s) and then the Cambodian conflict (1978–1991), Thailand worked with the United States to try to restrict the extension of Vietnamese (communist) influence in Indochina. The latter conflict also involved cooperation with China, which was most adamantly anti-Vietnamese. With the end of the Cambodian conflict, Thailand has sought to pursue the goal of turning Indochina from a "battlefield into a marketplace."[21] In political terms, however, Thailand has increased its influence in Cambodia in relation to the Hun Sen government, although less so in Laos. Vietnam remains as a rival, although clearly the relationship is on a better basis than it was during the Cambodian conflict and before.

Burma has been not so much a rival state as a source of problems affecting Thailand itself. Issues such as drug trafficking and trafficking in women originate in Burma but then cause damage in Thailand. Thailand is not necessarily passive in relation to these matters because, although the Thai government might attempt to exercise controls, elements within Thai society benefit from the opportunities to advance criminal activity that Burma provides. Another major issue for Thailand concerns the refugees from the minority peoples in Burma who cross the border to escape the persecution of the Rangoon government. Other refugees have fled from Burma to Thailand because of the repression of the prodemocracy movement led by Aung San Suu Kyi. The United Nations High Commissioner for Refugees (UNHCR) estimated there were 120,000 Burmese refugees in Thailand in 2003.[22] Thailand has supported "constructive engagement" with Burma as a means of putting pressure on the military regime. This has included support for Burma becoming a member of ASEAN, which occurred in 1997.

Thailand was one of the founding members of ASEAN in 1967 and, until Vietnam joined in 1995, was the only member from mainland Southeast Asia. At one level ASEAN was useful to Thailand as a means of winning support from the anticommunist Southeast Asian countries in the conflicts centered on Vietnam from the 1960s to the beginning of the 1990s: the US war in Vietnam, and then the Cambodian conflict. With the expansion of ASEAN from the mid-1990s to include Vietnam, Burma, Laos, and Cambodia (the "new ASEANs"), Thailand has seen benefits in terms of strengthening political stability and promoting economic development among its neighbors.

From Burma's perspective Thailand is the most important of the Southeast Asian countries. As indicated, Burma's various problems affect Thailand, which means that the two governments have numerous dealings with each other. It is helpful to Burma that Thailand supports "constructive engagement" rather than advocating stronger pressure on the military regime. Entry into ASEAN has strengthened Burma's international position, making it easier to deflect the criticism that comes from Western countries. Before 1998 Burma looked to Indonesia as a model of a system that ensured a continuing and prominent role for the military, but clearly this is no longer the case. Within ASEAN Malaysia has taken the lead in attempting to persuade Burma of the need for reform; Singapore has been more interested than most ASEAN countries in maintaining high-level political relations.

Among the states that together constitute Indochina, Vietnam is clearly the most significant. In relation to other states in mainland Southeast Asia, Vietnam's first priority is Cambodia and Laos. It wants to ensure that those countries do not create problems for Vietnam. Ideally this would mean pro-Vietnamese governments in both countries. If this is not possible then Vietnam would aim to ensure, at a minimum, that developments in Cambodia and Laos do not have adverse consequences for itself. Since the end of the Vietnam War in 1975 Laos has generally had a pro-Vietnamese stance. In Cambodia the Khmer Rouge regime was strongly anti-Vietnamese. This situation led to Vietnamese intervention in late 1978 and the installation of a pro-Vietnamese government. The central issue in the Cambodian conflict was Vietnam's attempts to maintain its position in Cambodia. This was opposed by the ASEAN countries led by Thailand, and particularly by China. The United States also opposed Vietnam, whereas the Soviet Union was supportive. Since the end of the Cambodian conflict, the Hun Sen government has not been overtly pro-Vietnamese, but has also not deliberately antagonized Vietnam.

Since Thailand has often competed for influence with Vietnam in relation to both Cambodia and Laos, Vietnam's relations with Thailand have frequently been testy. However, since the early 1990s there have been no major conflicts in the relationship. Thailand's support for Vietnam's entry into ASEAN has been helpful in that respect. Within ASEAN, Vietnam has been able to broaden its relationships to encompass the full range of Southeast Asian countries. This has helped to overcome the isolation it previously experienced. Vietnam has been conservative in upholding ASEAN's principle of noninterference in domestic affairs. In relation to Burma, for example, this has meant that Vietnam has not supported proposals to use ASEAN as a means for pressuring the military regime. Similarly Vietnam does not want ASEAN becoming involved in issues concerning human rights in Vietnam.

In terms of relations with other Southeast Asian states, Cambodia and Laos are mainly concerned with Vietnam and Thailand. As indicated, Laos has generally been pro-Vietnamese since 1975, but has also had to deal with a number of issues concerning Thailand. These issues include developments affecting the Mekong and the Lao refugees in Thailand.[23] In the case of Cambodia it has moved into a nonaligned position as between Vietnam and Thailand since the early 1990s. ASEAN is useful to both Laos and Cambodia in giving them a broader context in which to operate. By bringing in other Southeast Asian countries they are in a better position to avoid becoming points of contention between Thailand and Vietnam.

The Major Powers

The three major powers vary in their interests and strategies in mainland Southeast Asia. This area is of greatest concern to China, but both the United States and Japan also have significant interests. For China mainland

Southeast Asia is an area of great strategic concern. China borders Vietnam, Laos, and Burma, and is within a short distance of northern Thailand. From China's perspective mainland Southeast Asia is a peninsula that abuts its own southern flank. China does not wish to see mainland Southeast Asia become a source of threats to its own security. In the past it was concerned about the US war in Vietnam, Thailand's pro-US orientation, and Vietnam's pro-Soviet orientation after 1975. During the Cambodian conflict China's goal was to assert its preeminent position in Indochina at the expense of Vietnam and the Soviet Union. With the end of the Cambodian conflict China has generally been the most significant of the major powers in mainland Southeast Asia. Vietnam has not attempted to challenge that position, in spite of the differences over the South China Sea. Thailand has bent with the wind and now sees China as the most influential power in this region. China also has a very close relationship with the military regime in Burma, clearly ignoring the human rights situation in that country. ASEAN provides a means for the Southeast Asian countries (mainland and maritime) to coordinate their policies in relation to China, with the potential to provide a limited check on China in certain circumstances.

US involvement in mainland Southeast Asia is partly related to an attempt to balance Chinese influence in this region and Asia Pacific more generally. In addition the United States has substantive interests and concerns of its own in relation to the various countries of the region. US balancing behavior focuses on developing links with those countries that are most concerned about Chinese hegemony. Vietnam would be particularly important in this regard. The US relationship also provides options for Thailand in avoiding dependence on China. For much of the post-1945 period Thailand was closely aligned to the United States and the United States saw Thailand as central to its own strategy in Southeast Asia. Since the end of the Cambodian conflict in 1991, the United States has continued to give a high priority to Thailand, but Thailand itself has changed in wanting to ensure that it does not give offense to China. US economic interests focus mainly on Thailand, with two-way trade amounting to US$20 billion in 2002 and US investment there also totaling about US$20 billion.[24] Trade with Vietnam has developed but there are still impediments going back to the era of the Vietnam War. Negative sentiment in the US Congress has impeded the granting of "permanent normal trade relations" (PNTR) to Vietnam. Although a Bilateral Trade Agreement commenced in 2001, normal trade relations require congressional renewal annually.[25] In relation to Burma the United States has concerns about the close relationship that has developed between that country and China. However, the United States has been mainly concerned about the human rights record of the military regime, and particularly the repression of the prodemocracy movement led by Aung San Suu Kyi. This has led to the imposition of a wide range of economic sanctions on Burma by the United States; the Burma Freedom and Democracy Act of 2003 consolidated these measures.[26] The United States has also had concerns about human rights abuses in Cambodia, where the Hun Sen government has frequently been ruthless toward political opponents. At the same time the United States does not wish to see Cambodia return to the conflict and suffering that prevailed in that country during the 1970s and 1980s.

For Japan, mainland Southeast Asia is important for both economic and political reasons. Japan is a major trading partner for most of these countries, with Thailand being the most important to Japan (taking 3.6 percent of Japan's exports and providing 3.1 percent of Japan's imports in 2004).[27] Thailand has been an important destination for Japanese investment, as part of the strategy of relocating labor-intensive manufacturing; Japan invested US$1.2 billion in Thailand in 2004, making it the most important recipient of Japanese investment among all the Southeast Asian countries.[28] Vietnam also has attracted more Japanese investment in recent years for similar reasons. As part of its strategy of developing its international role, Japan has contributed to the economic development of the various countries in mainland Southeast Asia through its foreign aid program, with Thailand (fourth most important recipient of Japanese bilateral aid in 2003–2004) and Vietnam (sixth most important) ranked most highly. Underlying this approach is the assumption that economic development leads to political stability and democracy. It is this approach that has led Japan to provide aid to Burma. Japanese aid is also motivated by a belief that it gives Japan greater diplomatic influence.[29] At a diplomatic level Japan has been involved in facilitating the resolution of some conflicts, most notably in Cambodia after the end of the conflict there in 1991, and again at the time of the political crisis in that country in 1997.

▨ "New" International Issues

In examining international politics in the two subregions of maritime and mainland Southeast Asia, we have focused on state-society tensions, state-to-state relations, and the involvement of the major powers. In this final section we will focus on some issues relating to the "new international agenda."[30] The issues covered by this agenda are not necessarily completely distinct from what has previously been discussed, particularly in relation to state-society tensions. However, the term "new international agenda" does highlight the way an increasing number of new types of issues, often social in nature, have become important in international politics. These issues often transcend national boundaries. They might originate in particular states but then affect a large number of additional states. Whatever the reasons for these issues emerging, the states of the region, relevant states outside the region, and international organizations (regional and global) have to respond. In this discussion we will focus on unregulated people movements and HIV/AIDS as examples of new issues that now feature in the international politics of Southeast Asia. Other issues such as environmental problems, drug trafficking, trafficking in women and children, and the role of international crime could also be seen as part of the new international agenda but will not be discussed here. With the issues that have been selected for discussion the aim is to outline the nature of the problem, and to show how it is dealt with in the context of the international politics of the region.

Unregulated People Movements

Unregulated people movements (UPMs) cover a range of situations where people are either forced to move from one area or country to another, or where they do so voluntarily for various reasons.[31] The first type of situation is most likely to occur when there is political upheaval occurring, including war in the worst instance. Where people fleeing such situations cross international boundaries they become refugees; if they move from one area to another but remain within the one state they are known as "internally displaced people" (IDPs). Undocumented labor migration occurs where people move to another country to improve their economic and social well-being but without necessarily having the official permission of that country. People smuggling, involving the assistance of criminal organizations, can be part of this process. Here we will give attention first of all to refugees and IDPs, and then move on to undocumented labor migration and people smuggling.

The situations in Southeast Asia leading to refugees and IDPs generally reflect state-society tensions. These tensions can involve conflicts in particular regions of a country. A group might be in conflict with the central government and aim either to secede or to gain some measure of autonomy. There might be conflict between particular groups in a certain region or regions. Sometimes there can be conflict between an authoritarian government and movements aiming for democratization. In recent decades an important exodus of refugees was that of the Vietnamese boat people in the late 1970s and 1980s. Many of these people were ethnic Chinese fleeing from the communist government that ruled the whole of Vietnam from 1975. Many people also fled from the Khmer Rouge regime in Cambodia, and from the communist government in Laos after 1975. Whereas the Vietnamese refugees generally went to Hong Kong or to Western countries via countries such as Malaysia and Indonesia, Cambodian and Laotian refugees were most likely to go to Thailand, with many remaining there in refugee camps. In 1989 the first asylum countries, Western resettlement states, and the United Nations High Commissioner for Refugees agreed to a Comprehensive Plan of Action for Vietnamese refugees whereby resettlement or repatriation to Vietnam was to occur by 1996.[32]

From the 1990s the worsening situation in Burma has been a major source of refugees, with Thailand being the main destination. Some people have become refugees because of their support for the prodemocracy movement in Burma. Others are members of minority peoples such as the Karen who have fled because of the conflict in their home region. Conflicts affecting Indonesia have mostly led to an increase in IDPs rather than refugees. At the time of the East Timor crisis in 1999, those East Timorese who crossed into West Timor were classed as refugees. People forced to move because of the conflicts in Aceh, West Papua, Maluku, Kalimantan, and Sulawesi mostly remained within Indonesia and therefore are described as IDPs. Where people are refugees, international assistance through the UNHCR is likely to be available. With IDPs, states generally have to cope on their own.

Undocumented labor migration in Southeast Asia mostly involves people from states where there is abundant labor moving to situations where significant economic development is occurring. People from Indonesia, Burma, and the Philippines move to Singapore, Malaysia, Brunei, and Thailand.[33] Sending countries benefit significantly from remittances returned from these workers in other countries.[34] Alan Dupont cites figures indicating that that in 1999 there were 1.3 million undocumented foreign workers in Malaysia, 750,000–1 million in Thailand, 10,000 in Singapore, 1 million in Cambodia, and 500,000–1 million in Burma.[35] In global terms the Philippines is second only to Mexico as an exporter of labor, and Thailand is also important.[36] While the movement of labor in this way can boost the economies of the recipient countries and also assist the sending countries, social tensions can sometimes result. This is particularly the case if the immigrant group is significantly different from the people in the receiving country. Tensions can also occur if there is a downturn in the economy in the receiving country and there are moves to return illegal immigrants to their home countries.

One aspect of undocumented labor migration is people smuggling. People smugglers assist illegal immigrants wishing to move to countries where economic circumstances are better than in their home countries. Southeast Asia is largely a staging area in this respect, particularly for illegal immigrants from China. People smugglers use Thailand and Cambodia as transit countries for Chinese on their way to other destinations.[37] People smugglers assist Indonesians wishing to move to Malaysia, Singapore, and Saudi Arabia.[38] People smugglers have used Indonesia to move people from Middle Eastern countries to Australia.

HIV/AIDS

The spread of HIV/AIDS provides a second example of the new international agenda in Southeast Asia. Since the late 1980s this health issue has reached epidemic proportions in some countries of Southeast Asia.[39] The worst affected are Thailand, Burma, and Cambodia. The problem, however, has also spread to Vietnam, Malaysia, and Indonesia. Singapore, the Philippines, Laos, and Brunei appear to have been less affected. (See Table 10.3.)

There has been some variation in how HIV/AIDS has spread in the various Southeast Asian countries. The effectiveness of government responses has also varied. In Thailand the main factor has been the country's dominant sexual culture. The use of brothels is widespread among Thai men. HIV/AIDS spread from gay men to other men who engaged in both homosexual and heterosexual behavior. Female sex workers in brothels were infected, who in turn infected their clients. These men in turn infected their wives. Unsafe practices, particularly avoiding the use of condoms,

Table 10.3　HIV and AIDS Estimates for Southeast Asia, 2003

	Adults and Children (age 0–49 years) Living with HIV	AIDS Deaths (adults and children)
Burma	330,000	20,000
Brunei	<200	<200
Cambodia	170,000	15,000
Indonesia	110,000	2,400
Laos	1,700	<200
Malaysia	52,000	2,000
Philippines	9,000	<500
Singapore	4,100	<200
Thailand	570,000	58,000
Vietnam	220,000	9,000

Source: United Nations Programme on HIV/AIDS, www.unaids.org, accessed 23 December 2004.

prevailed in Thailand's sexual culture. This was a major factor in the spread of HIV/AIDS. Thailand has been the most effective of the Southeast Asian countries in developing strategies to counter the epidemic. The main focus has been on promoting safe sex practices, particularly the use of condoms. Nurses and other health professionals have worked closely with sex workers and men using brothels to spread the message.

HIV/AIDS has also been a serious issue in Burma, but for different reasons. In Burma the problem derives from widespread drug addiction. Needles are used for injecting heroin, and then constantly reused, thus infecting more and more people. Sexual intercourse then leads to other people being infected, even though these people might not be drug users. While needle exchange and safe sex practices might help to deal with the problem, the military regime has done little. With a packet of condoms costing more than the average monthly income in Burma, the country faces "a health and human disaster."[40]

Cambodia similarly has faced major problems with HIV/AIDS, while also being relatively ineffective in dealing with the situation. HIV/AIDS has spread mainly through sexual practices, with the prevalence of the sex trade being a contributing factor. Condoms are too expensive for most people. Preventing HIV/AIDS is a low priority for the government given the various problems Cambodia has faced in the aftermath of the 1978–1991 conflict. In Vietnam the problem has spread mainly through needle sharing, in the context of widespread drug addiction. Infected people then infect others through their sexual behavior. The state has played an active role in promoting preventive practices, although with less impact than in Thailand.[41]

In Malaysia and Indonesia the role of Islam has inhibited the discussion of the HIV/AIDS issue, but without making those countries immune from the problem. Conservative Muslims associate HIV/AIDS with immoral behavior, arguing that the best prevention is adherence to the moral code that they advocate, but since many people do not adhere to this code, HIV/AIDS has spread, particularly through unsafe sex practices. The situation in Thailand and Burma affects Malaysia because many Malaysian men use the sex services in southern Thailand.[42] Both Malaysia and Indonesia have been forced to recognize the existence of the problem, but the prevailing culture makes the development of an appropriate strategy more difficult.

In discussing responses to HIV/AIDS in Southeast Asia we have focused on the strategies of the various national governments. The international character of the problem is clear from how transmission occurs across national borders, through such means as the sex trade, drug trafficking, tourism, and the movement of people more generally. The willingness of governments to cooperate in dealing with these issues varies, just as governments vary in terms of developing policies for HIV/AIDS within their own borders. While cooperation can occur on a bilateral basis, there can also be multilateral opportunities, including the involvement of regional and global organizations. ASEAN has had a task force on AIDS,[43] but the United Nations has been the most significant international organization combating the epidemic. In 1986 the World Health Organization (WHO) founded the Global Program on AIDS (GPA), and this was followed in 1996 by the establishment of UNAIDS as a joint UN program.[44] UNAIDS acts as the main advocate for action relating to AIDS, while also having a coordinating role in relation to six agencies involved in HIV/AIDS issues: WHO, the United Nations Development Programme (UNDP), United Nations Educational, Scientific and Cultural Organization (UNESCO), the United Nations Children's Fund (UNICEF), the United Nations Population Fund, and the World Bank.[45] The Program Coordinating Board (PCB) of UNAIDS includes the cosponsoring agencies, representatives of donor and recipient countries, and representatives of NGOs, including People Living with HIV/AIDS (PLWHA).[46] International NGOs, such as PLWHA, play a significant role in highlighting the problem, assisting sufferers of HIV/AIDS, and contributing to prevention in particular settings.

* * *

This chapter has provided an overview of international politics in Southeast Asia, focusing on three dimensions: state-society tensions, state-to-state relations within Southeast Asia, and the involvement of the major powers. Moving beyond Southeast Asia as a whole, these dimensions were examined in relation to the subregions of maritime and mainland Southeast Asia. The picture that emerges is one of considerable complexity. While we often focus on the state system in Southeast Asia, we need to keep in mind that many of its states rest on weak foundations. With eleven Southeast Asian states there are many bilateral and multilateral relationships possible. The involvement of the major powers adds another layer of complexity. The broadening of the international agenda has the same consequence. The more issues that have an international dimension, the more complex international politics will be in terms of the range of actors and how they behave.

▪ Notes

1. Recent book length studies on the international politics of Southeast Asia include Weatherbee et al., *International Relations in Southeast Asia;* Beeson, ed.,

Contemporary Southeast Asia; Neher, *Southeast Asia in the New International Era;* Acharya, *The Quest for Identity.*

2. *The Military Balance 2005–2006,* p. 294.

3. Quimpo, "Options in the Pursuit of a Just, Comprehensive, and Stable Peace in the Southern Philippines," p. 274.

4. For Abu Sayyaf's early period, see Turner, "Terrorism and Secession in the Southern Philippines."

5. *The Military Balance 2005–2006,* p. 288.

6. Leifer, *Singapore's Foreign Policy,* pp. 19–20, 147–149.

7. Leifer, *Dictionary of the Modern Politics of South-East Asia,* p. 5.

8. For background on the Philippines' claim to Sabah, see "Philippines' Claim to Sabah"; Gordon, *The Dimensions of Conflict in Southeast Asia,* chapter 1.

9. Dupont, *East Asia Imperilled,* p. 164.

10. Japan External Trade Organization, Economic Research Department, "Japanese trade in 2004," appendices 8 and 9, www.jetro.go.jp/en/stats/statistics (accessed 18 February 2006).

11. Based on Japan External Trade Organization, "2005 JETRO White Paper on International Trade and Foreign Direct Investment," table III-4, p. 20, www.jetro.go.jp/en/stats/white_paper/2005.pdf; JETRO, "Japan's Outward FDI, Country and Region-wise," www.jetro.go.jp/en/stats/statistics (accessed 18 February 2006).

12. See data on Japan's foreign aid on the website for the Organisation for Economic Cooperation and Development, www.oecd.org/dataoecd/42/5/1860382 .gif (accessed 30 May 2006).

13. Useful works on this topic include Valencia, *China and the South China Sea Disputes;* Lo, *China's Policy Towards Territorial Disputes;* Lee Lai To, *China and the South China Sea Dialogues.*

14. Valencia, *China and the South China Sea Disputes,* p. 32.

15. Ibid., p. 31.

16. Ibid., pp. 44–48.

17. Ibid., p. 12.

18. Odgaard, "Deterrence and Cooperation in the South China Sea," p. 304.

19. Alan Boyd, "South China Sea: Pact Won't Calm Waters," *Asia Times,* 2 July 2003, www.atimes.com/atimes/China/EG02Ad03.html (accessed 22 December 2004).

20. Vaqsavakul, "Vietnam," pp. 374–376.

21. This was a phrase used by Thai Prime Minister General Chatichai Choonhawan in 1988. Quoted in Battersby, "Border Politics and the Broader Politics of Thailand's International Relations in the 1990s," p. 479.

22. United Nations High Commissioner for Refugees, "Protracted Refugee Situations," Annex I (10 June 2004), www.unhcr.ch/cgi-bin/texis/vtx/statistics/ opendoc.pdf?tbl=STATISTICS&id=40ed5b384 (accessed 11 October 2005).

23. Freeman, "Laos," p. 128.

24. "Fact Sheet on Free Trade and Thailand," www.whitehouse.gov/news/ releases/2003/10/20031020-27.html (accessed 23 December 2004).

25. United States, Department of State, Bureau of East Asian and Pacific Affairs, "Background Note: Vietnam," www.state.gov/r/pa/ei/bgn/4130.htm (accessed 23 December 2004).

26. United States, Department of State, Bureau of East Asian and Pacific Affairs, "Background Note: Burma," www.state.gov/r/pa/ei/bgn/35910.htm (accessed 23 December 2004).

27. Japan External Trade Organization, Economic Research Department, "Japanese Trade in 2004," Appendices 8 and 9, www.jetro.go.jp/en/stats/statistics/ (accessed 18 February 2006).

28. Japan External Trade Organization, "Japan's Outward FDI, Country and Region-wise," http://www.jetro.go.jp/en/stats/statistics (accessed 18 February 2006).

29. See Oishi and Furuoka, "Can Japanese Aid Be an Effective Tool of Influence?"

30. See Halliday, "International Relations."

31. A useful discussion of this topic is Dupont, *East Asia Imperilled,* part II.

32. Ibid., p. 142.

33. Ibid., p. 160.

34. Ibid.

35. Ibid., p. 162.

36. Ibid., p. 161.

37. Ibid., p. 156.

38. Ibid., p. 158.

39. A good introduction is ibid., chapter 11. A book length study is Beyrer, *War in the Blood.*

40. Ibid., p. 47.

41. Ibid., p. 102.

42. Ibid., p. 93.

43. Ibid., pp. 222–223.

44. Altman, "AIDS and Questions of Global Governance," pp. 198–199.

45. Ibid., p. 200.

46. Ibid.

Indonesia | 11

Indonesia is Southeast Asia's most significant state, whether one judges by population, area, or political weight. In discussing the international politics of Southeast Asia it is therefore appropriate to have one chapter devoted entirely to Indonesia. The aim of this chapter is to show how Indonesia's international significance is very much related to its domestic situation. This relates to the general point about how politics in Southeast Asia, whether domestic or international, is shaped by tensions between state and society. Many groups do not accept the existing state system. This situation means that states are weaker than they would otherwise be, and are often preoccupied with issues of domestic security. Domestic conflicts can spill over into the international arena, and states seek to prevent or minimize international interference. This situation complicates the state-to-state relations, including the involvement of the major powers, which one normally associates with international politics.

To understand Indonesia's situation in the context of international politics it is necessary to give some attention to understanding the dynamics of its domestic politics. The international situation of post-1998 Indonesia is affected most directly by the prevalence of weak government and by the possibility of fragmentation of various kinds. To place this situation into perspective this chapter begins with an overview of the historical context, covering the emergence of an independent Indonesia, the Sukarno era, and the Suharto era. It then moves to an analysis of developments in post-1998 Indonesia, with particular reference to the issue of regional conflicts. The final section examines the international implications of Indonesia's domestic situation.

Indonesia is an archipelago of about thirteen thousand islands with a land area of 735,164 square miles (1,904,569 square kilometers).[1] It extends from Aceh at the western end of Sumatra to the border with Papua New Guinea in the east, a distance of about 3,200 miles or 5,120 kilometers (greater than the west-east distance across the continental United States). The major islands are Sumatra, Java, Kalimantan or Borneo (the northern part consists of Brunei and the Malaysian states of Sarawak and Sabah), Sulawesi or the Celebes, and the western half of New Guinea. Other island groups are Maluku (the Moluccas) and Nusa Tenggara, stretching from Bali to West Timor. Indonesia's population in 2005 was 241,973,879. Muslims made up 87 percent of the population, with Christians the most significant minority. Significant ethnic groups within the population were Javanese with 45 percent, Sundanese with 14 percent, and Madurese with 8 percent; the Chinese minority was 3 percent. GDP in 2004 was US$251 billion, with per capita income estimated at US$1,055.[2]

■ The Historical Context

Preindependence

As a political entity Indonesia is heir to the territory previously ruled as the Netherlands East Indies. Nationalists used the term "Indonesia," from the Greek "Indos Nesos" or Indian islands, because it was non-Dutch.[3] There were significant precolonial polities, but none covered the whole territory of modern Indonesia. The most important of these were Srivajaya and Majapahit. Srivijaya, based in southern Sumatra, was a Buddhist coastal empire that lasted from the seventh to the thirteenth centuries, holding sway not only over Sumatra but over the Malay Peninsula as well. More powerful still was Majapahit, based in eastern Java, and lasting from the thirteenth to the sixteenth centuries. Its domain extended from Java to include Sumatra and the Malay Peninsula, Madura, Kalimantan, Sulawesi, Maluku, Bali, and Nusa Tenggara.[4] While not coextensive with modern Indonesia, Majapahit did cover a considerable proportion.

Islam became an important influence in the Indonesian archipelago from the thirteenth century, spread initially through the activities of Arab and Indian traders.[5] Evidence of the earlier Indian cultural influence remained, with predominantly Hindu Bali being the most obvious example. *Abangan* or nominal Muslims reflect the interaction between Islam and earlier animist beliefs. *Santri* Muslims are more devout in their adherence to the faith. Malacca on the Malay Peninsula played an important role in the spread of Islam. In the archipelago itself in the sixteenth and seventeenth centuries Aceh in the west was significant as a center of power, whereas the sultanate of Ternate (in Maluku) played a major role in the east. The Mataram empire was significant in Java.[6]

European powers began to exert influence in this region at about the same time as Islam was spreading. Concerned particularly with developing trade, Portugal was first on the scene. Malacca fell to the Portuguese in 1511. In the long term the Dutch were more significant and the British also played a role, particularly in relation to the Malay Peninsula. Malacca became Dutch in 1641, but the main areas of Dutch interest were Java and Sumatra. The activities of the Dutch (United) East India Company (Vereenigde Ooste-Indische Compagnie or VOC) were centered in Batavia (modern Jakarta). Direct Dutch rule superseded that of the VOC from 1799, although as a consequence of the Napoleonic Wars Britain was the ruling power between 1811 and 1816. The focus on economic exploitation under the Dutch was well highlighted by the role of the *cultuurstelsel* (cultivation system) from the 1830s to the 1860s. Through the imposition of land taxes peasants were obliged to set aside a significant proportion of their land for the production of export crops.[7] Subsequently there was more emphasis on the role of private capital as a vehicle for economic exploitation.[8]

Beyond the areas that were of most direct economic interest, Dutch involvement was often superficial. Many outlying areas such as Aceh, Bali, inland Kalimantan, Sulawesi, and eastern Nusa Tenggara only came under direct Dutch rule in the first decade of the twentieth century.[9] The Dutch thought of the Netherlands East Indies not as an integrated whole but as a series of subcolonies.[10] The outer islands were important as a source of recruits for the Royal Netherlands Indies Army (Koninklijk Nederlands-Indisch Leger or KNIL), a factor contributing to division among the peoples of the archipelago.[11] Ambonese Christians were one group that was particularly associated with Dutch rule.

A new emphasis in Dutch rule emerged in the early decades of the twentieth century. Known as the "Ethical Policy," this change of direction grew out of humanitarian criticisms of previous Dutch policy.[12] The Ethical Policy gave more attention to the welfare of the indigenous people, particularly through the development of education. The increasing numbers of educated Indonesians in turn prepared the way for the emergence of a nationalist movement.

Nationalist organizations were initially elite-oriented and small. Budi Otomo (High or Noble Endeavor) was formed in 1908, and the Indisches Partij (Indies Party) in 1912. Sarekat Islam (Islamic Association), also formed in 1912, was more mass-oriented, reflecting resentments toward both the Dutch and the local Chinese. A Marxist group within Sarekat Islam founded the Indonesian Communist Party (PKI) in 1920, finally breaking with the parent organization in 1923. In 1927 the Indonesian Nationalist Party (PNI) was established. Under the leadership of Sukarno it became the most significant nationalist organization of all. Dutch policy toward emerging Indonesian nationalism was repressive. Before World War II, Indonesian nationalism did not represent a major challenge to Dutch rule.[13]

This situation was transformed with the Japanese occupation of the archipelago from 1942 to 1945. While exploiting the local people in various ways, the Japanese also encouraged Indonesian organizations they believed could help underpin Japanese rule. The Japanese established a volunteer army known as Peta (Pembela Tanah Air or Protectors of the Fatherland), with numbers of 37,000 in Java, 1,600 in Bali and 20,000 in Sumatra by the end of the war.[14] Peta became the core of the revolutionary forces in the subsequent struggle against the Dutch. As defeat loomed for Japan, plans to grant Indonesia independence were accelerated. Japan surrendered on 15 August 1945. In the ensuing vacuum in the archipelago Sukarno and Hatta proclaimed Indonesian independence on 17 August 1945.

The Allies did not recognize this declaration; the Netherlands was intent on reestablishing its rule. While Australian forces had been involved in some campaigns against the Japanese in the outer islands in the last months of the war, it was British (largely Indian) forces that played the key role in the initial period after the Japanese surrender. Dutch forces returned soon after. Conflict between the Dutch and the Indonesian Republic continued for about four years. The Dutch were strongest in the cities whereas the nationalist forces generally prevailed in the countryside. Areas such as Java and Sumatra were more strongly Republican than were the outer islands. As the basis for a settlement the Dutch preferred a federal system, reflecting their view of the archipelago as a series of subcolonies (and now states). Such an outcome would also facilitate a continued Dutch influence. An agreement along these lines was achieved in November 1949. The new state was constituted as a federal Republic of the United States of Indonesia (RUSI). West New Guinea did not come under this agreement and remained under Dutch rule.

The Early Independence Period

In the early period of independence weak government and the possibility of fragmentation plagued Indonesia. Up to 1957 Indonesia was essentially a parliamentary system, with the political parties playing a key role. *Santri* Muslims largely supported the Masyumi (Consultative Council of Muslims) from which the traditionalist NU split in 1952. The major parties for the *abangan* Muslims and non-Muslims were the PNI (Sukarno's party) and the PKI.[15] Fears about the republic breaking up led to the abandonment of the federal model on 15 August 1950. In April 1950 a Republic of the South Moluccas (Maluku) had been proclaimed on Ambon. The collapse of the RUSI was followed by an army rebellion in South Sulawesi that was quickly suppressed.[16] Nevertheless there was continuing resentment within the outer islands toward Javanese domination. This resentment culminated in the outer islands rebellion of 1957–1958, when army leaders in Sumatra, Sulawesi, and Nusa Tenggara attempted to loosen Jakarta's control. Another sign of discontent with Indonesia's direction was the Darul Islam (Nation of Islam) revolt from 1950 to the early 1960s. Focused on West Java, North Sumatra, and South Sulawesi, this revolt received support from Muslims who wanted Indonesia to become an openly Islamic state, rather than following the principles of the Pancasila as proclaimed in 1945. Among other things, the Pancasila involved mutual respect for the various religions practiced in Indonesia.

Weak government and the threat of fragmentation encouraged moves toward a more authoritarian system in Indonesia. By 1959 "Guided Democracy" had been formalized, with President Sukarno playing the leading role. With the Army and the PKI competing for influence over Sukarno, politics took an increasingly radical direction. In 1957 the Indonesian government had expropriated Dutch property. Economic conditions remained at Third World levels, with policy often focused on grand gestures rather than substantive matters. Foreign policy was used as a vehicle for promoting unity. In the late 1950s and early 1960s there was a major campaign to recover West New Guinea from the Netherlands. Under pressure from the United States, the Netherlands agreed in 1962 to transfer West New Guinea to Indonesia after a short period of United Nations administration. The other major campaign was in opposition to Malaysia, a federation of Malaya, Singapore, and the Borneo states of Sabah and Sarawak, which took effect in September 1963. Indonesia claimed that Malaysia was a scheme to perpetuate British influence in the area, and launched Konfrontasi (Confrontation) to undermine the federation. While Singapore did withdraw in August 1965, this was for reasons relating to Malaysia itself rather than the result of Indonesian pressure. In the international sphere more generally Sukarno proclaimed Indonesia as the leader of the New Emerging Forces (NEFOs) in opposition to the Old Established Forces (OLDEFOs) represented by the United States and other Western powers. In East Asia the NEFOs manifested themselves in the Jakarta-Phnom Penh-Hanoi-Beijing-Pyongyang axis opposed to Western domination.

Increasing competition between the PKI and the Army for influence over Sukarno provided the context for the dramatic political changes that occurred in 1965–1966. The outcome was the fall of Sukarno and the emergence of General Suharto as the new Indonesian leader. The PKI was eliminated as a political force, while the Army became dominant. Largely because of the self-interest of key players in the Suharto regime, the events of September–October 1965 were long wrapped in mystery. The attempted leftist coup of 30 September 1965 led by Colonel Untung and some other middle-ranking officers appears to have been designed to forestall action by Army leaders against Sukarno and the PKI. While some generals were killed, the suppression of the coup by the Army provided a favorable context for ending PKI influence and sidelining Sukarno. Continuing into 1966, the campaign against the PKI and its supporters resulted in "one of the bloodiest massacres in modern history,"[17] with probably half a million killed.[18] On 11 March 1966 Sukarno effectively transferred power to Suharto, with the latter authorized to restore order. It was not until March 1967 that Sukarno officially lost his powers.

The New Order

The political system that emerged from these events in 1965–1966 and lasted until 1998 was known as the New Order. The Indonesian Armed Forces (ABRI) were the key political institution. ABRI's dual function or *dwifungsi* provided for both domestic and external defense, but upholding the political order was its most important role. Golkar, originally established by the Army in 1964 to counter PKI influence, played a major role in generating support for the New Order. Although officially not a political party, Golkar ran candidates in elections from 1971. Government officials used their influence to ensure that Golkar always won by wide margins. From 1973 the government only allowed two parties. Islamic opinion was channeled into the United Development Party (PPP). Nationalist and Christian groups were supposed to coalesce in the Democratic Party of Indonesia (PDI).[19]

Contrary to Indonesia's parlous economic state in the latter part of the Sukarno era, the New Order placed a strong emphasis on economic development. From the 1960s to the early 1990s growth rates averaged 4 percent per annum; real per capita income grew from US$190 in the mid-1960s to US$610 in the early 1990s.[20] During this period the distribution of income remained relatively fixed in percentage terms. This meant that, considering Indonesia as a whole, both the absolute numbers and the percentage of people living in poverty declined; Hill cites figures indicating a decline in the number of people living in poverty from 54.2 million in 1976 (40.1 percent of the population) to 25.5 million in 1993 (13.5 percent of the population).[21] With Indonesia's generally pro-Western orientation and greater political stability, foreign investment increased. National wealth grew significantly during the 1970s because of the higher oil prices. Overconfidence in the management of Pertamina, the state-owned oil company, led to excessive borrowing. The Pertamina scandal of 1975–1976 arose when the company was unable to pay its debts and the government had to come to its rescue.[22] While Indonesian living standards rose, there was also greater scope for corruption, with Suharto and his family being the leading beneficiaries; Suharto amassed an alleged US$15–35 billion during the period of his rule.[23]

The authoritarian rule that prevailed under the New Order meant that regional tensions were less obvious than had previously been the case. In 1969 an "act of free choice" confirmed Indonesia rule in West New Guinea (known as Irian Jaya). However, the consultation involved only hand-picked village leaders. The emergence of the Organisasi Papua Merdeka (OPM or Free Papua Movement) reflected widespread proindependence sentiment. Concerns about an independent East Timor providing a model for disaffected provinces in East Indonesia were a factor in the Indonesian occupation of East Timor in December 1975. The question of Portuguese Timor's political future had arisen because of political changes occurring in Portugal in 1974–1975. The Jakarta government regarded Fretilin, the major political movement in East Timor, as too radical. Nevertheless the Indonesian occupation and incorporation of East Timor had horrendous consequences for the people of that territory.[24]

During the 1990s the New Order was subject to increasing strains. Economic change had resulted in a growing middle class, many of whom were frustrated by the limited opportunities for political expression provided by the Suharto regime. A pro-democracy movement emerged, centered on the role of Megawati Sukarnoputri. Megawati, the daughter of Sukarno, was elected as chair of the PDI in 1993. Fearing that Megawati would become a beacon for opposition to Suharto, the government acted to manipulate the political process within PDI to prevent Megawati continuing in her leadership role in 1996. Megawati's refusal to accept this situation strengthened sentiment in favor of democratic change in Indonesia.

Another source of opposition to the New Order came from supporters of Islam. While the government-authorized PPP was heavily circumscribed in what it could do, there was more scope within the Islamic social organizations. Traditionalist Muslims, often liberal in political outlook, were represented in the 30-million-strong Nahdlatul Ulama (NU), led by Abdurrahman Wahid (known as Gus Dur). NU linked rural Javanese and urban activists, with Wahid a strong advocate for pluralism and tolerance.[25] Modernist

Muslims were represented in Muhammadiyah, another mass organization with a membership approaching 30 million. As compared with NU, the modernists were more strongly urban based, more conservative, and less tolerant of other groups. Their leading figure during the 1990s was Amien Rais. Suharto attempted to win support from more politically conservative Muslims with the formation of ICMI (Indonesian Association of Muslim Intellectuals). This development attracted criticism from within the military and from the NU. Between 1996 and 1998 the PPP became important as a voice of opposition to Suharto, with many Megawati supporters backing the Muslim party as a tactical move.[26]

Given that military support was crucial to the functioning of the New Order, increased factional maneuvering during the 1990s was very relevant to the future of the regime.[27] The intensified maneuvering was related to the perception that the succession to Suharto would soon take place. Broadly speaking there were two main factions. The green faction favored an Islamic direction for Indonesia. The red and white faction (after the colors of the Indonesian flag) favored a more secular, nationalist approach. Within each faction there was further competition among subgroups and individuals. Generally the red and white faction was ascendant, with General Wiranto, the commander of ABRI from March 1998 being particularly important. Closely allied to Wiranto was Lieutenant-General Susilo Bambang Yudhoyono (SBY) who moved from his command in South Sumatra to take charge of ABRI's Social and Political Affairs office from 1997. An important rival was Lieutenant-General Prabowo Subianto, Suharto's son-in-law and commander of the army's Strategic Reserve (Kostrad).

The question of the presidential succession was brought to a head by the onset of the economic crisis during 1997. The Indonesian situation was one of the most serious within the broader Asian economic crisis. Although impressive rates of economic growth had been achieved during the Suharto era, many areas of activity were overcapitalized or nonproductive. Corruption was widespread, with Suharto and his family being the leading offenders. The banking system was poorly regulated. Foreign investment could be easily withdrawn. With the contagion of events elsewhere, the house of cards in Indonesia soon crashed, and the rupiah rapidly lost value. The social consequences were devastating, particularly for those least able to bear the burden. Food and other necessities became much more expensive. The legislative elections in May 1997 indicated the high level of unrest. Nevertheless Suharto persisted in his course. He attempted to modify some of the conditions proposed by the International Monetary Fund in a rescue package for Indonesia, mainly to avoid some of the political costs involved and to protect his own position. In March 1998 the People's Consultative Assembly elected Suharto to another five-year term as president. This term was to be short lived. Increasing unrest was manifested most obviously in student protests in Jakarta. The riots of 13–15 May in Jakarta have been described as "the worst urban riots in Indonesian history," with over a thousand people killed, widespread looting and burning, and many rapes.[28] Under pressure from a wide range of leaders and groups, Suharto initially sought to appoint a new reform government, but then announced his resignation on 21 May. B. J. Habibie, previously vice president, became the interim president.[29]

Post-1998 Indonesia

The collapse of the New Order meant that there was much freer rein for the various political forces within Indonesia to vie for influence. The contending forces were most evident in the context of elections instituted as part of the process of democratization that provided the basis for legitimacy in post-Suharto Indonesia. National elections were held in 1999 and 2004, with the former being the first free elections in Indonesia since 1955. The 1999 elections set the stage for the emergence of Abdurrahman Wahid as president, with Megawati Sukarnoputri as vice president. In July 2001 Wahid fell from power and was succeeded by Megawati who served as president until 2004 when two-stage direct presidential elections were held. The 2004 elections resulted in Susilo Bambang Yudhoyono becoming the fourth holder of the office since Suharto's fall. In reviewing the various political phases in post-1998 Indonesia, the focus will be on assessing the underlying political forces at play, the key political issues, and how governments have attempted to deal with them. Given Indonesia's fragile unity, many of the issues focus on the question of what is needed to maintain and strengthen that unity. While regional conflicts are dealt with in more detail in the following section, issues of institution building and economic performance are also relevant to strengthening the state. However, dealing with these issues effectively has been difficult because of the range of forces involved in the political process. Post-1998 Indonesia has had a series of weak governments. The challenge is to develop more effective government while also upholding democratic principles.

   B. J. Habibie's presidency was important in laying the foundations for democratization in Indonesia. His background was that of a technocrat and some of his attitudes were seen as eccentric. Golkar provided his main basis for support. The military, led by General Wiranto, remained powerful and tended to be critical of Habibie. This was most evident in relation to East Timor (discussed in the next section) where Habibie announced a referendum on autonomy without even consulting Wiranto. Military opposition to this referendum was a key factor in the mayhem visited on East Timor in September 1999 following the East Timorese decision in favor of independence.

During Habibie's presidency much political activity focused on elections for the House of Representatives (DPR) that were held in June 1999. Some forty-eight parties contested the election, with five being of particular importance. Apart from Golkar, there were the PDI-P (Indonesian Democratic Party of Struggle) that was led by Megawati and represented secular-nationalist forces, and three parties drawing on Muslim support. Wahid's PKB (National Awakening Party) represented the liberal political views to be found within the NU, while Amien Rais drew on Muhammadiyah for PAN (National Mandate Party). PAN's program was secular in orientation. The United Development Party also continued as a Muslim party.[30] In the 1999 elections the PDI-P took 33.8 percent of the vote, Golkar 22.5 percent, the PKB 12.6 percent, the PPP 10.7 percent, and PAN 7.1 percent (i.e., 30.4 percent for the three main Muslim parties).

The DPR elections prepared the way for choosing the president. DPR members were the main body within the larger MPR (People's Consultative Assembly) charged with selecting a president (other members came from provincial bodies and functional organizations). When the MPR met in October 1999 Wahid commanded majority support and was elected president. Although the PKB had only won 12.6 percent of the vote in the DPR elections, Wahid worked harder at coalition building than Megawati, who did not actively canvass support.

Despite this success at coalition building Wahid proved ineffective as president and was removed from office in July 2001. At one level the problems Wahid encountered were related to his very success in putting together a coalition. While that coalition might have produced the votes he needed to win office, this did not necessarily mean that it would work well as the basis for a government. All five major parties (i.e., PDI-P, Golkar, PKB, PAN, PPP) were represented in Wahid's government, as was the military. To accommodate the various interests there were some thirty-five ministries. Amien Rais from PAN became chair of the DPR, while Akbar Tanjung from Golkar held the chair of the MPR.[31] Because of the range of parties and competing perspectives in the government, it was difficult to develop strong policy. There were major issues in dealing with the aftermath of the East Timor crisis and the regional conflicts in Aceh, West Papua, Maluku, and Kalimantan (discussed in the next section). Corruption might not have been on the same scale as during the Suharto years but weak government made it difficult to deal with. While Wahid was not personally corrupt, some associates took advantage of their relationship with him to advance private economic interests.[32] Progress in tackling underlying economic issues remained limited.

One area where Wahid did have some success, at least in the short term, was in reducing the political role of the military. As head of the armed forces General Wiranto saw himself as being a more effective leader than Wahid. In February 2000 Wahid was able to remove Wiranto as coordinating minister for politics and security. This is not to say that the TNI[33] (as the Indonesian National Army had been known since early 1999) did not retain significant political influence. However, Wahid cultivated military leaders whom he thought were more sympathetic to his presidency, showing some preference for the navy and air force over the army.

In response to criticisms that his government was ineffective, Wahid appointed a second cabinet in August 2000. It was intended to remain representative while also reducing the influence of the parties that were critical of him (i.e., PDI-P, Golkar, PAN, PPP). Megawati had previously been promised a position as executive of cabinet affairs but this did not proceed.[34] Having reduced his political support through this reorganization, the new government did not become any more effective in dealing with the issues facing Indonesia. Wahid came under mounting criticism, with moves to impeach him in the MPR. Despite Wahid's threats to proclaim a state of emergency, the MPR convened in special session in July 2001 to end his presidency and elect his successor. Megawati became the new president, with Hamzah Haz from the PPP as vice president.

As the leader of the PDI-P, Indonesia's largest political party, Megawati did not owe favors to other political parties in the way that Wahid did. In some respects her new government was one of "experts," particularly in relation to economic affairs.[35] One of the leading figures was Susilo Bambang Yudhoyono, the coordinating minister for political and security affairs. Links with the Suharto regime were evident in the appointment of Bambang Kesowo as cabinet secretary; Kesowo had previously been vice cabinet secretary from 1993 to 1998. Although the position of defense minister remained as a civilian appointment, Megawati was generally favorable to a continuing strong role for the military in Indonesian politics.[36] While clearly Megawati had a much stronger political base from which to undertake the role of president than did Wahid, her effectiveness was vitiated by her political style. She was inclined to stand aloof from everyday politics, with the consequence that underlying problems were not dealt with. There was a sense of drift in Indonesian politics.

Among the issues confronting Megawati's government, those concerning regional conflicts are discussed subsequently. Other issues included economic and institutional reform, corruption, and the legal system.[37]

These issues were closely related. The major economic challenge was to improve growth rates and ensure that there was an equitable distribution of the country's wealth. Widespread corruption benefited members of the Indonesian elite but was a deterrent to foreign investment. Judicial corruption appeared endemic, again largely to the benefit of the powerful. This undermined confidence in Indonesia's ability to provide a transparent legal framework within which to do business. A major example of the way members of the elite attempted to ignore the legal system was the case of Akbar Tanjung, speaker of the DPR and leader of Golkar. Although found guilty of corruption in September 2002, Tanjung refused to resign while the appeal was taking place.[38] Similarly, high-level members of the Indonesian military (including General Wiranto) evaded conviction for human rights abuses in East Timor.

Initially Megawati's government moved to meet targets that had been set in agreements with the International Monetary Fund. At the beginning of 2002, for example, fuel subsidies were cut by one fifth.[39] At the end of 2003, however, Indonesia terminated its relationship with the IMF, hoping to renegotiate its debt on a bilateral basis.[40] Problems in the Indonesian banking system were generally dealt with at public expense rather than holding individuals accountable. There was a lack of political will to pursue people who were guilty of corruption. An anticorruption commission was established at the end of 2002 as evidence of continued public concern,[41] but enforcement remained an issue. Reforming the legal system would assist in achieving accountability but, again, little was done. While members of the elite benefited from the loopholes in the system they had no incentive for changing it, and popular pressures were not strong enough to overcome this situation.[42] In a similar vein the military retained their power under Megawati, who was generally sympathetic to the position they espoused.

The issue of the role of Islamic extremists within Indonesia came to the fore during Megawati's presidency. The Al-Qaida attacks in the United States on 11 September 2001 occurred soon after Megawati became president. Despite some criticism within Indonesia, she indicated general support for the United States in the war on terrorism. Indonesia's own vulnerability became more obvious with the Bali bombings of 12 October 2002, in which about two hundred people, mostly Western (and particularly Australian) tourists were killed. A further serious bombing occurred at the Marriott Hotel in Jakarta on 5 August 2003. In this case five Indonesians were killed. A further eleven Indonesians were killed in a bombing outside the Australian embassy in Jakarta on 9 September 2004, and over twenty people (mainly Indonesians) were killed in a second wave of Bali bombings on 1 October 2005. These incidents raised the question of whether radical Islam was a significant political force in Indonesia. Groups advocating violence are on the fringes of the modernist stream of Islam. Laskar Jihad became involved in the conflict between Christians and Muslims in Maluku. The bombings in Bali and Java have been linked to Jemaah Islamiah (JI), which aspires to a pan-Islamic state in maritime Southeast Asia. Repressive measures against groups such as JI arouse the ire of modernist Muslims more generally. While some Muslims support the goals, if not the methods, of groups such as JI, Indonesian Islam is generally tolerant in nature. The major Muslim parties (PKB, PAN, PPP) support a secular state in Indonesia. The number of people supporting, let alone undertaking, acts of violence is very small. Megawati's government adopted some antiterrorist measures, but avoided a draconian approach that might alienate significant elements of the population.

Megawati's weaknesses as president encouraged an active presidential election campaign in 2004. This was the first time that the Indonesian people chose their president directly. There was provision for a two-round process: if no candidate won an absolute majority in the first round there would be a second round election between the two candidates winning the most votes in the first round. This is what happened in 2004. While Megawati stood as the candidate for PDI-P, the major challenger was Susilo Bambang Yudhoyono. The other significant candidates were General Wiranto (Golkar), Amien Ras (PAN), and Hamzah Haz (PPP). Yudhoyono, a former general and security minister under both Wahid and Megawati, was backed by the newly formed Democratic Party and disaffected elements in a number of other parties. Yudhoyono (33 percent), Megawati (26 percent), and Wiranto (23 percent) were the top three candidates.[43] In the runoff between Yudhoyono and Megawati on 20 September, Yudhoyono was successful with 60.6 percent of the vote as compared to Megawati's 39.4 percent.[44]

Yudhoyono faced a challenging task in dealing with Indonesia's various problems. Institutional relationships and the political situation were in flux. As the first directly elected president Yudhoyono had more authority than his post-1998 predecessors. At the same time he shared political responsibility with the Indonesian parliament. Within the House of Representatives his own Democratic Party held only 55 seats (10 percent). A People's Coalition of sympathetic parties held 233 of the 550 seats; PDI-P and Golkar, which backed Megawati, held 109 and 129 seats respectively.[45] Yudhoyono's instinct seemed to be to maximize national unity in dealing with issues. This sometimes made his appointments and policies appear cautious. His cabinet retained five of Megawati's ministers (although not members of her party) and included several Golkar members.[46] The major issues facing the new president were the same as those that had faced Megawati: economic and institutional reform, including dealing with corruption and the inadequate legal system, and upholding national unity, including regional pressures and conflicts, and the position of Islam within the polity.[47] While Yudhoyono was committed to dealing with the issues, the need for a high level of political agreement made decisive change more difficult.

An unexpected issue facing Yudhoyono in the early part of his presidency was the Asian tsunami on 26 December 2004. Caused by a seabed earthquake off the western coast of Aceh, the effects were felt not just in that province but also in Thailand, India, Sri Lanka, and parts of East Africa. However, Aceh, with about 130,000 confirmed deaths, was the region most severely affected. Assistance came mainly from governments and nongovernmental organizations in the United States, Western Europe, Japan, and Australia, with the United Nations playing a coordinating role. This situation had implications for Indonesia's relations with these various governments and organizations, as well as for issues within Indonesia itself. Among Muslim groups and the more nationalistically minded there were concerns about increasing Western influence. Aceh itself, as discussed in the next section, was also the setting for Indonesia's most serious separatist conflict. Indonesia had attempted to quarantine Aceh from foreign influence but the involvement of foreign governments, the United Nations, and international NGOs in assisting with recovery operations in the aftermath of the tsunami meant that the conflict was likely to receive greater international attention than had previously been the case.

■ Regional Conflicts

A major concern for all governments in post-1998 Indonesia has been to maintain the unity of the state. While the possibility of fragmentation has been an issue throughout the period of Indonesian independence, the era of democratization has led to new challenges.[48] Not only has there been more scope for different groups to vie for influence at the central level, there have also been greater opportunities for regionally based movements and regional conflicts of various kinds to emerge. This section provides an overview of the different types of conflict, and of how post-1998 Indonesian governments have responded. In the next section there is a discussion of the international implications of these conflicts and of other issues affecting Indonesia in the post-Suharto era.

Three types of regional conflict can be identified in recent Indonesian history. One type of conflict is separatist in nature, with regionally based movements aiming to secede from Indonesia and constitute their regions as independent states. The main examples are East Timor, Aceh, and West Papua.[49] Indonesian governments have generally been strongly opposed to separatist claims. East Timor was a special case because it had been a Portuguese territory and its incorporation into Indonesia never received wide international recognition. The emergence of East Timor as an independent state cannot be seen as setting a precedent for Aceh and West Papua. For the latter two situations Indonesian governments have been prepared to consider some measure of autonomy, but have also employed military repression to counter separatist movements. A second type of conflict has been described as "horizontal."[50] This refers to regionally focused conflicts that do not normally involve claims for secession. In a number of parts of Indonesia there are conflicts between groups along ethnic, communal, or religious lines. Examples include Maluku, Central Sulawesi, and West and Central Kalimantan. Indonesian governments have generally adopted strategies aimed at achieving reconciliation in these situations, although political will has sometimes been lacking. Political actors outside the affected regions can sometimes use these situations to advance their own objectives. A third type of conflict has involved resource-rich provinces such as Riau (central Sumatra) and East Kalimantan claiming greater autonomy from the central government as a means of boosting their revenues (West Papua and Aceh are also resource rich). The post-1998 decentralization reforms are in part a response to this situation, as discussed below.

In relation to the three types of conflicts, how has the situation developed since 1998, both at the regional level and in terms of the responses of Indonesian governments? Here we will consider the separatist conflicts in the first instance (East Timor, Aceh, West Papua), followed by the horizontal conflicts (particularly Maluku), and then the claims of the resource-rich provinces for greater autonomy.

Separatist Conflicts

East Timor. Each of the separatist struggles has a different background. What they have in common is a refusal to accept incorporation into the Indonesian state as currently constituted. The common feature in Indonesian responses has been the combination of political and military measures to deal with each set of circumstances. Following the Dili massacre in November 1991, there was some liberalization of Indonesian rule in East Timor. There was more scope for political and cultural expression, and discussions did occur between pro- and anti-Indonesian groups. Discussions between Indonesia and Portugal under United Nations auspices remained intermittent. From the Indonesian perspective there was no suggestion that the incorporation of the territory into Indonesia would be reversed. Even autonomy within Indonesia seemed a distant hope.

As previously indicated, East Timor was in a different situation as compared to the other two territories because Indonesian claims were not widely recognized internationally. With the fall of Suharto there was more scope for the East Timorese to advance their political claims more vigorously. Habibie determined to deal with the situation once and for all when he said in January 1999 that the East Timorese would be given the opportunity to vote on a proposal that the territory should have autonomous status within Indonesia. Rejection of the proposal would be regarded as a vote for independence and this would then be put into effect. Habibie's announcement prepared the way for progress in the talks between Indonesia and Portugal. In May 1999 the two sides agreed that the forthcoming vote would be regarded as an act of self-determination that they would both respect. While the ballot would be conducted under UN auspices, Indonesia would remain responsible for security during the period leading up to the vote. This arrangement provided opportunities for the TNI to stymie the campaign of proindependence forces and to create havoc should the vote go in favor of independence. Wiranto and the TNI more generally were distinctly unhappy about Habibie's plan, which had involved no prior consultation with them. The TNI saw itself as upholding Indonesia's territorial integrity and did not wish to see East Timor setting a precedent for other territories to follow.

The TNI organized and supported pro-Indonesian militias in the period leading up to the vote on 30 August 1999. When 78.5 percent of those voting opted for independence (by rejecting the proposal for autonomy), the TNI embarked on its fallback strategy of creating mayhem in East Timor. With the destruction of property and thousands of killings, many East Timorese fled to the hills or across the border into West Timor. Apart from the goal of warning other regions to desist from separatist claims, the TNI probably hoped that the situation it had created would prevent the implementation of independence: Indonesia might remain as the only power capable of restoring order.

If this was the thinking within the TNI it proved to be wishful thinking. Indonesian behavior brought widespread international condemnation. Public opinion in neighboring Australia was particularly outraged, and it was the Australian government that took the lead in proposing international intervention to deal with the situation in East Timor. However, it was mainly US pressure that persuaded Indonesia to accept international intervention, first through INTERFET (International Force East Timor) from mid-September 1999, and later through UNTAET (United Nations Transitional Administration in East Timor). Indonesian control of East Timor effectively ended in September 1999 and, after a short period of United Nations administration, the territory became independent in May 2002. An international force that entered East Timor in May–June 2006 following a breakdown in order involved troops from Australia, New Zealand, Malaysia, and Portugal; Indonesia did not participate.

Aceh. Aceh differs from East Timor in having been part of Indonesia from the time of independence. The Dutch did not subdue Aceh until the early twentieth century. At the time of the Indonesian revolution it constituted itself as an autonomous Islamic state.[51] Aceh became one of the main centers in the struggle against the Dutch. The failure of successive Indonesian governments to give sufficient recognition to Aceh's distinctive features fueled separatist sentiment in the province. In addition there was a belief that the central government was exploiting Aceh's rich resources (particularly oil, gas, timber) to the advantage of the rest of Indonesia but with little benefit to Aceh itself. By 1999 Aceh provided about 11 percent of Indonesia's national revenue.[52]

The major separatist organization in Aceh is GAM (Gerakan Aceh Merdeka or Free Aceh Movement), established in 1976. Its leader is Hasan di Tiro, who has lived in exile in Sweden since 1979. GAM had limited support within Aceh before the late 1980s when there was a small-scale uprising. While this was soon suppressed, new opportunities arose in the context of Indonesia's post-1998 democratization. There was more scope for political movements such as GAM to organize, and military repression became more difficult.

Before becoming president in October 1999, Abdurrahman Wahid had supported proposals for a referendum in Aceh comparable to that undertaken in East Timor. Initially he continued to espouse this position when he became president, but soon changed tack. Apart from Aceh's continuing economic importance, Wahid faced strong opposition from the armed forces. There was also the Indonesian nationalist sentiment expressed, for example, by Amien Rais who said that the loss of Aceh "would be tantamount to the end of Indonesia as a nation."[53] For these reasons Wahid adopted a policy of making some concessions to the Acehnese position, while insisting that Aceh remain part of Indonesia. In November 2000 it was announced that legislation for "special autonomy" would be introduced into the DPR.[54] While there was some shift of responsibility for security to the police, armed operations in one form or another continued in Aceh.[55] Given the weak government in Jakarta, the restraints on the TNI following its own policy in Aceh were limited.

With Megawati's accession to the presidency in July 2001, the position of the armed forces became even stronger. Nevertheless Megawati apologized to the Acehnese for the human rights abuses that had occurred while also signing the legislation to give special autonomy to Aceh (August 2001).[56] Provisions of this legislation included increasing Aceh's share of oil and gas revenues from 5 percent to 70 percent, and allowing the introduction of elements of sharia (Islamic) law.[57]

The special autonomy law, taking effect from January 2002, proved insufficient to stem the conflict. GAM did not abandon its campaign for independence, and Indonesian military operations continued. On 9 December 2002 GAM and the Indonesian government concluded an agreement in Geneva under the auspices of the Henri Dunant Centre.[58] The agreement provided for a cessation of hostilities and a framework for resolving the conflict. The agreement soon unraveled, with Megawati declaring a military emergency in May 2003. With Jakarta ruling the province, "special autonomy" meant nothing; the extra revenue intended for Aceh went into funding military operations there.[59] With Yudhoyono's election to the presidency in October 2004, and then the tsunami in December 2004, there were moves to reopen negotiations between GAM and the Indonesian government. These culminated in an agreement in August 2005 whereby GAM accepted "special autonomy," and Indonesia undertook to end its military campaign.[60]

West Papua. West Papua is the other region where there is strong local support for separating from Indonesia. As with Aceh, governments in Jakarta have regarded West Papua as an integral part of Indonesia. The resurgence of Papuan nationalism in the post-1998 era has been met with a combination of political and military measures. The circumstances of West Papua's entry into the Indonesian republic have given the territory a special place in Indonesia's sense of identity. As Netherlands New Guinea the territory had remained under Dutch control after Indonesia became independent in 1949. Indonesia claimed that all territories of the former Netherlands East Indies should become part of Indonesia. Although the Netherlands saw West Papua having a future as an independent state, in 1962 it succumbed to pressure from the United States and agreed to transfer the territory to Indonesia after a short period of United Nations administration. As part of the transfer agreement an "act of free choice" was held in 1969, but this only involved consultation with a small number of leaders chosen by Indonesia. Most politically aware Papuans preferred independence and believed there should be genuine self-determination. It was argued that Papuans were ethnically and culturally distinct from Indonesians. The OPM was the main organization resisting Indonesian rule. However, the OPM was limited in its ability to mobilize popular support and mount an armed struggle. Indonesia repressed any attempts to express support for an independent West Papua, and any signs of armed resistance were countered with military force. Indonesian governments encouraged transmigration with the consequence that by the year 2000 an estimated 30 percent of the population of about 2 million was non-Papuan.[61] While there was public sympathy for the OPM in neighboring Papua New Guinea, governments in that country gave priority to maintaining a harmonious relationship with Indonesia.

The process of democratization after 1998 enabled the expression of Papuan nationalism to become more open. This was particularly marked after Wahid was chosen as president in October 1999. A poignant moment was the raising of the Morning Star flag, the symbol of Papuan nationalism, alongside the Indonesian flag on 1 December 1999. This was the anniversary of West Papuan independence being declared in 1961. While Wahid was prepared to accept such symbolism and to acknowledge Papuan grievances he remained opposed to independence. The Papuan Presidium Council, formed in 2000 as a movement to represent a range of Papuan groups, advanced the claim for independence most vigorously.[62] Its leader was Theys Eluay, previously known as pro-Indonesian but now identifying himself with Papuan aspirations. Supporting the presidium was a militia known as Satgas Papua (the Papuan Task Force).[63]

Wahid's political solution for the Papuan problem was to advance proposals to give the province special autonomy. The provincial legislature attempted to strengthen these proposals with such provisions as local control over the deployment of Indonesian security forces and stronger procedures for dealing with human rights issues.[64] Some of the Papuan suggestions were incorporated in the version of the law that passed the DPR in October 2001 and took effect in January 2002, but not the restrictions on the Indonesian security forces. A high proportion of the revenues derived from the exploitation of natural resources would be retained in the province, a Papua People's Council would protect the rights of the indigenous people, and the province would be officially known as Papua.[65] These concessions did not satisfy many Papuan nationalists, including Theys Eluay.

Under Megawati military repression of Papuan nationalism became more overt. There have been some incidents suggesting an inability to control some elements within the TNI. In November 2001 Theys Eluay was murdered, allegedly by Kopassus (Special Forces).[66] The ambush of a convoy outside the Freeport mine on 31 August 2002, leading to the deaths of two Americans and an Indonesian, has also involved allegations of military involvement (although there are also suggestions of involvement by a rogue OPM faction). There is some evidence that the military have attempted to exploit tensions between Papuans and non-Papuans in an attempt to portray the conflict as one deriving from ethnicity rather than the demand for independence.[67] In 2002 there were allegations that fighters from the militant Muslim group Laskar Jihad had moved to West Papua, and that the army was sponsoring militias to counter the proindependence movement.[68]

Another significant development under Megawati was the division of Papua into three provinces, to be known as West Irian Jaya, Central Irian Jaya, and Irian Jaya (coincidentally leading to the dropping of Papua as the official name). This occurred by presidential instruction in January 2003. Possible motives included an attempt to divide the independence movement, to weaken Golkar in the province, and to provide more scope for political patronage.[69] Although not as bloody a conflict as in Aceh, West Papua remained a significant source of concern for Indonesia. Indonesian attempts to overcome the demands of Papuan nationalism were not particularly effective, nor was the independence movement strong enough to overcome Indonesian opposition.

Horizontal Conflicts

Among the horizontal conflicts, we will give particular attention to the situation in Maluku, although reference will also be made to conflicts in Central Sulawesi and West and Central Kalimantan. For the most part these conflicts do not involve claims for independence, but focus on differences between religious or ethnic groups. If the Indonesian government is unable to resolve or at least manage these conflicts then its legitimacy is seriously undermined. The viability of Indonesia can be seriously threatened from within. (Although not geographically confined in the way the other horizontal conflicts are, violence directed against Chinese Indonesians also needs to be considered.)

Maluku. Maluku (the Moluccas) was a major center for the Dutch during the colonial period. Ambonese were prominent in the colonial administration and army. Christians formed a majority of the population. Attachment to the Dutch led to a revolt in 1950; a Republic of the South Moluccas was proclaimed but quickly suppressed, with many people going into exile in the Netherlands. Under the New Order there was considerable transmigration, with consequent changes in the balance between Muslims and Christians. Whereas the balance had been about even in 1971, by 1990 Muslims were 57 percent of the population.[70] Muslims had the upper hand in the provincial bureaucracy. This situation led to tensions between the two communities. Democratization worsened the situation by making the tensions more overt. Fighting began in Ambon in January 1999 and remained intense over the next two years. Estimates of deaths were between 5,000 and 10,000, and about 700,000 people became refugees (out of a population of 2.1 million).[71]

The involvement of the security forces at times exacerbated the conflict, with different elements siding with one group or another. The conflict also intensified when 6,000 armed members of Laskar Jihad arrived from Java after May 2000 to assist the Muslims.[72] Although separatist sentiment was not the underlying motive for Christians in the conflict, a proindependence organization known as FKM (Front Kedaulatan Maluku or Maluku Sovereignty Front) was established later in 2000.[73]

Conflict was even more intense in North Maluku. Fighting erupted in August 1999 after plans for a new administrative district in northern Halmahera were announced.[74] This district had been Protestant but was now dominated by Muslim migrants. The wider context was the establishment of North Maluku as a separate province in September 1999.[75] The fact that the new province was strongly Muslim highlighted Christian-Muslim tensions in the region.

The involvement of the Jakarta government in dealing with the Maluku crisis often appeared minimal. East Timor was a more serious issue confronting the government, and democratization meant the focus was often elsewhere. Megawati in her role as vice president had responsibility for Maluku but did little. In June 2000 the Indonesian government declared the two Maluku provinces to be in a "civil emergency."[76] After Megawati became president there was more stability in government, and the security forces appeared more effective in performing their role. There were some attempts to achieve reconciliation between the two communities,[77] and the Malino pact in February 2002 brought some measure of peace.[78] Laskar Jihad disbanded in October 2002;[79] nevertheless the potential for violence still remained. A ceremony staged by proindependence supporters on 25 April 2004 led to shootings and widespread destruction in Ambon, with 38 killed (two-thirds Muslim) and 10,000 people forced to flee from their homes.[80]

Central Sulawesi. In the case of Central Sulawesi tensions and subsequent violence relate to changes in the population balance, with Muslim migrants entering a predominantly Christian area. Christians believed their previously dominant position was under threat. Violence centered on the Poso district; as of early 2002 there had been up to 1,000 deaths and 80,000 people displaced out of a population of 300,000.[81] Peace talks between the two sides resulted in the Malino Declaration in December 2001. The involvement of outside groups such as Laskar Jihad, who had previously entered the conflict, was rejected.[82] Some violence continued, however, such as the attacks on Christian villagers in October 2003, resulting in 13 dead. It was suggested that the extremist Islamist group, Jemaah Islamiah, was behind these attacks.[83]

West and Central Kalimantan. In West and Central Kalimantan, conflict centered on differences between ethnic groups. The indigenous Dayaks, who were mainly Christian and animist, had generally been marginalized since Indonesian independence.[84] This experience of marginalization was exacerbated during the New Order with an influx of people from the island of Madura as part of the transmigration program. The Dayaks felt both economically and politically excluded, and their resentments were directed against the Madurese. Attacks by Dayaks against the Madurese began in West Kalimantan in 1996–1997 (that is, before Suharto's fall), with another wave coming in 1999. Malays joined the Dayaks in these attacks, with estimates of up to 3,000 deaths, and thousands of Madurese fleeing to Pontianak, the provincial capital.[85] In February 2001 violence spread to Central Kalimantan, with 2,000 deaths in the first fortnight and most Madurese (80,000–90,000) forced to flee the province for Madura and East Java.[86] The Jakarta government proved largely ineffective in dealing with the violence. When it subsided it was mainly because the Dayaks had been successful in expelling the Madurese.[87]

The Chinese minority. Another important aspect of ethnic conflict is that focused on the Chinese minority. Violence directed against Chinese Indonesians is not confined to one geographical region. As indicated earlier, the Chinese proportion of the Indonesian population is about 3 percent,[88] mainly concentrated in urban areas. The perception of Indonesian Chinese is that they are an economically privileged group; in some circumstances they have been viewed as a "fifth column" for China. With the collapse of the New Order, there was large-scale anti-Chinese violence in May 1998 in a number of cities, including Medan, Jakarta, Solo, and Surabaya.[89] This violence continued through 1998 and into 1999. Resentment alone is insufficient to explain the violence that occurred. The political context, involving interaction between local leaders and a "crowd," was very important in the chain of events leading to anti-Chinese rioting in particular places. Perceptions extended beyond the economic situation to include religious fears and issues of power.[90]

Resource-Rich Provinces

In addition to the separatist and horizontal conflicts, Indonesia has faced pressures deriving from the claims of resource-rich provinces for greater autonomy. In the case of Riau (central Sumatra), the province is an important producer of oil, natural gas, and timber, as well as having industrial zones on the islands of Batam and Bintan, adjacent to Singapore. Riau's oil accounts for 14 percent of Indonesia's GDP.[91] This wealth exists alongside widespread poverty, leading to claims that Riau should have greater control over its own resources. Generally this has meant support for greater autonomy, although there is also some support for independence. East Kalimantan is an example of another resource-rich province claiming greater autonomy. This province is Indonesia's richest, with per capita GRP (gross regional product) about sixteen times that of East Nusa Tenggara, Indonesia's poorest province. When oil is removed from the calculation the per capita GRP for East Kalimantan remains more than double the national average.[92] Clearly greater provincial control over oil revenues would boost East Kalimantan's economic position considerably.

Apart from the claims of the resource-rich provinces, the shift toward greater decentralization in post-1998 Indonesia has also been a response to the argument that the country's diversity needs to be reflected in its political arrangements. Indonesia's federal system at independence was soon rejected on the grounds of its association with the Dutch and the country's perceived need to foster unity over diversity. In the post-1998 era, however, there has been a reaction to the excessive centralization associated with the Suharto regime. The most significant changes occurred under the Habibie government. Law 22/1999 on regional governance devolved considerable powers to the district level. Provinces had a role in coordinating districts and representing the central government. By focusing on districts rather than provinces the risks of Indonesia fragmenting as a result of decentralization were reduced.[93] Law 25/1999 on financial relations between central and regional governments set up a general allocation fund involving at least 25 percent of central government revenues, with 10 percent of these funds going to the provinces and 90 percent to districts.[94] The central government would take 85 percent of the revenue from oil, 70 percent from gas, and 20 percent from mining and forestry, with the rest going to provinces and districts, and particularly the latter.[95] A major concern with these arrangements, of course, was that they would exacerbate regional in-equalities to the benefit of the resource rich but to the detriment of the re-source poor.[96]

The decentralization reforms have resulted in the formation of a num-ber of new provinces: Banten (from West Java), Gorontalo (from North Sulawesi), Bangka-Belitung (from South Sumatra), and North Maluku (from Maluku).[97] Rather than deriving from general principles about the desirability of devolution, these developments have generally been a re-sponse to specific local pressures.[98] As we have seen, that was also the case with the schemes for special autonomy in Aceh and Papua.

International Implications

At this point we are ready to examine the international implications of In-donesia's domestic situation in the post-1998 era. The major points con-cern Indonesia's weak government and the various regional conflicts. Weak government makes it difficult for Indonesia to participate in schemes of international cooperation that might benefit itself, the region, and the world beyond. Adverse consequences can flow from a lack of such coop-eration. Indonesia might also need the assistance of external actors to deal with some of its problems. Regional conflicts can affect both neighboring and more distant countries. An extreme scenario involves the fragmenta-tion or disintegration of Indonesia, which again would affect both neigh-bors and Asia Pacific more generally. We will consider issues relating to weak government before turning to the international implications of re-gional conflict in Indonesia.

The international impact of weak government in Indonesia can be seen in relation to issues such as terrorism, piracy, unregulated people move-ments, and forest fires. International involvement in relation to Indonesia's economic situation is also partly related to weak government within Indonesia.

Since the September 11 attacks in the United States focused world at-tention on the issue of international terrorism, Indonesia has been the scene of a number of bombings, with the worst being those occurring in Bali on 12 October 2002. As previously discussed, these bombings are linked to the role of extremist Islamic groups in Indonesia, the most prominent being Jemaah Islamiah. Foreign governments have become involved in as-sisting Indonesia to counter terrorist groups. With the large number of Aus-tralians killed in the Bali bombings and then the attack outside the Aus-tralian embassy in September 2004, the Australian government has been prominent in providing assistance, largely by making specialist personnel available. The United States has also been involved, not just because US citizens were among those killed in Bali, but because Southeast Asia is an important center in the wider war on terrorism. However, whatever the wishes of the Bush administration, there have been some constraints on US involvement because of congressional concerns about various human rights issues in Indonesia.

The prevalence of piracy in Indonesian waters is another issue that can be related to weak government. Indonesia is one of the major centers for piracy in the contemporary world. In 2002, for example, there were 103 reported incidents of piracy in Indonesian waters out of a worldwide total of 370 attacks.[99] This situation derives from the fact that pirates can operate with relative impunity in many parts of the vast Indonesian archipelago. Indeed there are allegations that elements of the Indonesian military are directly involved in piracy or else benefit from the proceeds of piracy.[100] There is also a link with terrorism with the suggestion that terrorist groups might attempt to mount an attack on shipping in the Malacca and Singapore Straits.[101] Both Japan and the United States have been active in promoting low-level, anti-piracy measures with relevant Southeast Asian states, including Indonesia. However, nationalist considerations have placed limits on this cooperation. A proposal by Indonesia for a trilateral approach involving Malaysia, Singapore, and itself led to the first Malacca Straits Coordinated Patrols (MALSINDO) in July 2004.[102]

Weak government in Indonesia means that there is a limited ability to deal with unregulated people movements. Indonesia is a transit country for many people attempting to move from the "poor world" to the "rich world." In some cases such people come from countries experiencing war and political turmoil (for example, Iraq and Afghanistan), with a view to seeking asylum in one of the Western countries. In other cases people are simply seeking better living conditions than would be available in their countries of origin. If they do not meet the requirements for immigration to the country they have in mind, they might become illegal immigrants. People smuggling has become an important means for facilitating unregulated people movement from the poor world into the rich world. In the Indonesian case, Australia has been a favored destination for illegal immigrants, with most claiming to be asylum seekers. Often aided by people smugglers, they have usually traveled by boat from Java with the aim of reaching Australian territory such as Christmas Island or Ashmore Reef, to the northwest of the Australian mainland. For large sums of money, people smugglers arrange the boats that take the illegal immigrants on this hazardous journey. From the Australian perspective the most effective way of preventing the entry of "boat people" would be to clamp down on people smugglers in Indonesia itself. However, the inadequacies of the police, the weak legal system, and the lack of political will in Indonesia make this difficult. While not abandoning the preferred preventive approach, the Australian government has resorted to other means such as naval patrols, the excision of nonmainland territories from the area where it allows claims for asylum, the dispatch of asylum seekers to Pacific Island countries pending resolution of their claim for refugee status, and the use of detention centers in Australia itself.[103]

Forest fires are another example of the ways weak government in Indonesia has international implications. Widespread and often illegal burning of forests to clear land for commercial plantations and other purposes, particularly in Sumatra and Kalimantan, created an extensive smoke haze for some months over a number of years in the late 1990s. The haze affected not just Indonesia but also neighboring Malaysia and Singapore. Corruption at various levels of government and the weak legal system encouraged this situation. Indonesia came under pressure from Malaysia and Singapore to clamp down on illegal forest fires. In December 1997 the ASEAN environment ministers agreed to a Regional Haze Action Plan. Indonesia was to adopt stronger measures to prevent the haze problem from arising, within the context of greater ASEAN cooperation in combating forest fires.[104]

Indonesia's economic situation is partly the consequence of weak government, and again has significant international implications. Since 1998, when GDP fell by 13 percent, the economic growth rate in Indonesia has only been half the average achieved under the New Order. Per capita income did not return to the pre-crisis level until 2004. Poverty levels also took several years to return to those prevailing before the crisis. In 2004 the official unemployment rate was over 9 percent, with another 30 percent underemployed.[105] Democratization has impeded attempts to simplify bureaucracy and establish processes that might encourage foreign investment; spending on infrastructure is also much lower than under the New Order. Democratization was also an impediment to the neoliberal reforms that the International Monetary Fund wanted Indonesia to implement. Nevertheless, if Indonesia had a stronger economy, it would benefit not only its own citizens, but also have a flow-on effect for neighboring countries.

The various types of regional conflicts affecting Indonesia have very serious international implications. Separatist conflicts, if successful, could lead to the creation of new states. Horizontal conflicts and claims for greater regional autonomy contribute to the perception of Indonesia as a weak state. While complete disintegration is an unlikely scenario, a trend toward some degree of fragmentation is a distinct possibility. Here we can consider the international implications of Indonesia's regional conflicts at a general level, while also giving particular attention to the separatist conflicts.

Indonesia's horizontal and separatist conflicts attract international attention for various reasons. The violence associated with these conflicts has caused much human suffering. There is often a concern among the international community, whether through governments or nongovernmental organizations, about whether international involvement might assist in resolving these conflicts. In the case of the separatist conflicts there can be concerns about whether the people in the particular territories had the opportunity to exercise the right to self-determination. Are those territories part of Indonesia on the basis of consent freely given? Where conflicts become particularly violent, people can flee in search of a safe haven. If an international border is crossed such people become refugees. Internally displaced people (IDPs) have similarly fled but have not crossed international borders. In the context of the regional conflicts affecting Indonesia, people fleeing from East Timor to West Timor were classed as refugees (because of East Timor's international status); small numbers of Papuans have also become refugees in Papua New Guinea. People uprooted because of the conflicts in Maluku and Aceh have generally had the status of IDPs. With refugees, international involvement can occur through the United Nations High Commissioner for Refugees. The UNHCR might establish refugee camps and assist in the assessment of refugees for acceptance by third countries.

With the separatist conflicts, the countries most affected are those in the vicinity of the disputed territory. Although they are separated from Sumatra by the Straits of Malacca, the conflict in Aceh has serious implications for Singapore and Malaysia. Some Acehnese opposition groups have based themselves in Malaysia, and refugees could also move there if there were major deterioration in the situation in Aceh. Singapore might be a less likely destination for refugees, but its ability to function as a city-state and economic entrepôt could be adversely affected. Because of the view that there should not be interference in the domestic affairs of member states, ASEAN has not been involved in the Aceh issue.

The West Papua situation has had major implications for Papua New Guinea. There is a natural sympathy among Papua New Guineans for their fellow Melanesians west of the border. At the same time Papua New Guinea governments have wished to remain on good terms with Indonesia and have therefore not given support to the West Papuan cause. Australian pressure has been a significant factor in reinforcing the position taken by Papua New Guinea. Any tensions between Papua New Guinea and Indonesia over West

Papua could lead to Australian involvement. Australia is the former colonial power and major aid donor in Papua New Guinea, while also giving a high priority to its relationship with Papua New Guinea. While Papua New Guinea has been very cautious in its approach to the issue, other Pacific Island states have openly supported the Papuan Nationalists. Vanuatu and Nauru have been most active in this respect, and the issue has been raised at meetings of the Pacific Islands Forum, most notably in 2000. In this context Australia has again been active in modifying resolutions to avoid offending Indonesia.

East Timor, and particularly the 1999 crisis, showed most clearly how a separatist issue affecting Indonesia could have international implications. However, this situation was different from the other conflicts we have referred to because the incorporation of East Timor into Indonesia had never been widely recognized. Beginning in 1983, the United Nations hosted talks between Indonesia and Portugal with a view to resolving the issue, but no progress was made. With Habibie's proposal in January 1999 for a referendum on special autonomy for East Timor (with rejection being taken as a vote for independence), the way was cleared for agreement between Indonesia and Portugal. Portugal's position had always been that self-determination meant the East Timorese had to vote on their future, rather than the matter being resolved on the basis of agreement between the Indonesian and Portuguese governments. Agreement was reached under UN auspices in May 1999. The UN, through the United Nations Mission in East Timor (UNAMET), then assumed the role of organizing the referendum held on 31 August 1999.

With the breakdown of order following the vote in favor of independence, UNAMET did not have the capacity or mandate to deal with the situation. The ASEAN countries were not in a position to pressure Indonesia over the issue, nor would that have been consistent with ASEAN practice in dealing with such matters. Australia was the neighboring country that was most affected by the situation in East Timor. There was a perception that Indonesia could no longer control the situation and was, in fact, exacerbating matters by refusing to accept the will of the East Timorese people as expressed in the referendum. Public opinion in Australia was strongly in favor of international intervention on moral grounds. However, Australia on its own could not mount such an intervention. The United States became involved in putting pressure on Indonesia, largely through threatening to suspend various forms of economic support, with the result that the Jakarta government did give its consent to a UN-authorized intervention. The fact that the annual summit of APEC heads of government was held in Auckland in mid-September 1999 greatly facilitated the diplomacy preceding the intervention. Although Australia provided the major contribution to the intervention force, a range of other countries (mainly from Asia and Europe) were also involved, with the United States providing logistical and communications support. Subsequently the UN became the administering body in East Timor, with an independent state being proclaimed in May 2002.

The transition to independence in East Timor shows how external actors can become involved in a separatist conflict affecting Indonesia. In the cases of Aceh and West Papua the struggles for independence are likely to be much more difficult. In relation to Aceh it is difficult to know whether the agreement in favor of special autonomy in August 2005 will last. If independence should become a real option for either Aceh or West Papua there could be some parallels with the international involvement that occurred in East Timor, but there are also likely to be distinctive features relating to the circumstances of these two regions. Some form of UN involvement would be a possibility, but the Islamic orientation of Aceh and the Melanesian orientation of West Papua would also be relevant.

In assessing the international implications of Indonesia's domestic situation, a major concern has been the impact of fragmentation or even disintegration.[106] Clearly there is a range of possibilities here. At one level fragmentation would not necessarily extend much beyond the weak government that currently exists in Indonesia. It implies a further weakening of the authority of the central government and a shift in power toward the various regions. Indonesia might remain as a polity in a formal sense but there would be a considerable devolution of power to centers beyond Jakarta. The international implications of this situation would be along the lines that have previously been suggested in relation to the impact of weak government. Indonesian governments would be in a more difficult position to deliver in terms of agreements that might have been concluded with other powers. Those powers would also need to seek the cooperation of the regional centers, making the whole task of establishing international regimes involving Indonesia much more complex.

A more drastic scenario involves the disintegration of Indonesia. This would imply not just the separation of Aceh and West Papua, but the acceleration of the process of devolution to the point where many regions function effectively as independent states. De facto independence might be followed by de jure independence. Such a process might be accompanied by violence, particularly given the commitment of the armed forces to maintaining Indonesian unity. There could also be violence within regions as particular groups vie for supremacy. On the other hand many regions could move in this direction gradually and without major attempts to block the process. External powers and international organizations, particularly the UN, could become involved if disintegration were accompanied by considerable violence; there would be strong public pressure to intervene to stem a major bloodletting. Intervention in these circumstances would be in the context of a transition to a post-Indonesian future. If Indonesia were replaced by a series of independent states, the problem of obtaining cooperation to establish international regimes involving the archipelago would be comparable to that with the fragmentation under weak government scenario. There could also be tensions and conflicts among the successor states, again with the potential for international involvement in some circumstances. Such states might, of course, function with some degree of harmony within an expanded ASEAN. It is important to keep in mind that the disintegration scenario is far less likely than the scenario of weak government, with perhaps some element of fragmentation. Indonesia could also become stronger at the central level, with devolution providing effective means for implementing the goal of diversity within unity.

This discussion has focused on the international implications of Indonesia's domestic situation. This approach highlights the most significant aspects of Indonesia's interaction with the international environment in recent times. At the same time it is important to keep in mind that Indonesia has also interacted with the rest of the world according to more conventional understandings of international politics. As a state it has pursued its national interests in relation to its immediate region, particularly through ASEAN, and in East Asia more generally. Apart from ASEAN, Indonesia has been involved in APEC and the ASEAN Regional Forum as the major Asia Pacific regional groupings. It has been concerned about developments in the Islamic world, adopting a critical stance toward US intervention in Iraq in particular.

Outside Southeast Asia, Indonesia's relationship with Australia has been slow to recover from the 1999 East Timor intervention, although there have been some cooperative efforts on issues such as counterterrorism and people smuggling. The election of Yudhoyono and the provision of substantial Australian aid to assist rebuilding after the tsunami in late 2004 facilitated improved relations; a setback occurred in early 2006 when Australian immigration authorities accepted a group of asylum seekers from West Papua. Most importantly Indonesia has very significant relationships with Japan and the United States. Japan is Indonesia's single most important economic partner, and has also taken a low-key interest in assisting Indonesia in dealing with some "new" security issues such as piracy. The United States is interested in Indonesia as Southeast Asia's most important country, as the world's most populous Muslim country, and as an arena in the war on terrorism. For Indonesia the United States plays a crucial role in assisting Indonesia's economy, particularly through the influence exerted in the major international economic institutions. The relationship with China is important not just because of Beijing's interest in the position of the ethnic Chinese, but also because of China's emerging role in East Asia, including its arguably dominant position in mainland Southeast Asia.

*   *   *

This chapter has attempted to show how Indonesia's international significance is related to the country's domestic situation. Beginning with an overview of key features of the historical context, we saw how Indonesia's domestic situation evolved through the colonial, Sukarno, and Suharto eras. Indonesia's diversity makes the achievement of effective government difficult. Since 1998 democratization has exacerbated this situation: the forces encouraging diversity are more able to express themselves and have influence. Diversity is seen most clearly in the range of regional conflicts, both separatist and horizontal, but there is also a range of forces contending for influence at the central level. Indonesia's international significance derives from the impact of both weak government and the regional conflicts. The former dimension makes it more difficult for Indonesia to deal with foreign governments and to participate in the development of various kinds of international regimes. The regional conflicts at a minimum contribute to weak government. Where separation is a possibility, neighboring countries can become involved, and there can be international concerns relating to issues such as human rights, refugees, and the impact on regional stability. While the domestic situation in most Southeast Asian states has significant international implications, it is in Indonesia that the impact is greatest.

▣ Notes

1. *SBS World Guide*, p. 354.
2. Figures on population, GDP, and per capita income are from *The Military Balance 2005–2006*, p. 276.
3. Smith, "Indonesia," p. 80.
4. Acharya, *The Quest for Identity*, p. 19; Kingsbury, *South-East Asia*, p. 355.
5. See Ricklefs, *A History of Modern Indonesia Since c.1200*, chapter 1.
6. Kingsbury, *South-East Asia*, pp. 357–358.
7. See Ricklefs, *A History of Modern Indonesia Since c.1200*, pp. 156–161.
8. Kingsbury, *South-East Asia*, p. 360.
9. Ibid., p. 360. See further Ricklefs, *A History of Modern Indonesia Since c.1200*, chapter 13.
10. Kingsbury, *South-East Asia*, p. 362.

11. Kingsbury, *The Politics of Indonesia,* p. 27.

12. Ricklefs, *A History of Modern Indonesia Since c.1200,* pp. 193–194.

13. Details in this paragraph are from McDougall, *Studies in International Relations,* p. 59.

14. Ricklefs, *A History of Modern Indonesia Since c.1200,* p. 255.

15. Smith, "Indonesia," p. 103; Kingsbury, *The Politics of Indonesia,* p. 41. See further Feith, *The Decline of Constitutional Democracy in Indonesia.*

16. Kingsbury, *The Politics of Indonesia,* p. 39.

17. Legge, *Sukarno,* p. 399.

18. This is the view of the scholarly consensus presented in Ricklefs, *A History of Modern Indonesia Since c.1200,* p. 347. Legge's earlier work puts the figure at 200,000 to 250,000 (Legge, *Sukarno,* p. 398).

19. Kingsbury, *South-East Asia,* pp. 371–372.

20. Hill, *The Indonesian Economy,* pp. 5, 6.

21. Ibid., p. 198.

22. Ibid.

23. This is the figure given in Transparency International's Global Corruption Report. See "Suharto Tops Corruption Rankings," BBC News, 25 March 2004. http://news.bbc.co.uk/2/hi/business/3567745.stm (accessed 13 January 2005).

24. Ben Kiernan estimates a minimum population loss in East Timor in the period 1975–1980 of 116,000 in relation to a minimum population estimate for 1975 of 643,000. Taking other population estimates into account, he suggests a low order of magnitude for the 1975–1980 toll of 116,000 to 174,000, with a median estimate of 145,000. Kiernan, "The Demography of Genocide in Southeast Asia," p. 593.

25. Hefner, "Islam and Nation in the Post-Suharto Era," p. 46.

26. Kingsbury, *The Politics of Indonesia,* pp. 229–230.

27. See, for example, ibid., pp. 219–227; Shiraishi, "The Indonesian Military in Politics."

28. Ricklefs, *A History of Modern Indonesia Since c.1200,* p. 406.

29. For an analysis of the causes of the Indonesian economic crisis, emphasizing the political inadequacies of the Suharto regime, see Hill, *The Indonesian Economy,* pp. 272–285. See also Hill, *The Indonesian Economy in Crisis.*

30. See Ricklefs, *A History of Modern Indonesia Since c.1200,* p. 415.

31. Kingsbury, *The Politics of Indonesia,* p. 255.

32. Ibid., pp. 268–269.

33. Tentara Negara Indonesia or Indonesian National Army.

34. Kingsbury, *The Politics of Indonesia,* p. 262.

35. See Malley, "Indonesia in 2001," pp. 126–127.

36. Malley, "Indonesia in 2002," p. 141.

37. For an appraisal of various issues facing Megawati in the early part of her presidency, see Soesastro et al., ed., *Governance in Indonesia.*

38. Malley, "Indonesia in 2002," p. 144.

39. Ibid., p. 142.

40. Kipp, "Indonesia in 2003," p. 66.

41. Malley, "Indonesia in 2002," p. 144.

42. See further John McBeth, "The Betrayal of Indonesia," *Far Eastern Economic Review,* 26 June 2003, pp. 14–18.

43. John McBeth, "The Real Race Begins," *Far Eastern Economic Review,* 15 July 2004, p. 16.

44. Australia, Department of Foreign Affairs and Trade, "Indonesia Country Brief—December 2004," www.dfat.gov.au/geo/indonesia/indonesia_brief.html #2004_elec (accessed 13 January 2005).

45. "Time to Deliver: A Survey of Indonesia," *The Economist,* 11–17 December 2004, pp. 13–14.

46. "Hail to the Chief," *The Economist,* 23–29 October 2004.

47. On issues of economic reform, see John McBeth, "A Plan in Place," *Far Eastern Economic Review,* 4 November 2004, p. 20; Hal Hill, "Yudhoyono's Six Challenges to Get Indonesia Growing," *Far Eastern Economic Review* 168, no. 1 (December 2004), pp. 55–58.

48. On the issue of fragmentation in Indonesia, see Cribb, "Not the Next Yugoslavia"; Aspinall and Berger, "The Break-up of Indonesia?"; Emmerson, "Will Indonesia Survive?"; Huxley, *Disintegrating Indonesia?*

49. West Papua is the term used by Papuan nationalists for the Indonesian-ruled territory of western New Guinea. In the 1950s the territory was generally known as West New Guinea or West Irian by the Indonesians. Under Indonesian rule it became known as Irian Jaya. In response to pressure from Papuan nationalists, President Wahid agreed to rename the territory Papua. Papua became the official term with the passage of the special autonomy law in October 2001 but then was dropped with Megawati's presidential instruction of January 2003.

50. Huxley, *Disintegrating Indonesia?* p. 55.

51. Ibid., p. 35.

52. Sukma, "Aceh in Post-Suharto Indonesia," p. 150.

53. Quoted in Huxley, *Disintegrating Indonesia?* p. 37.

54. Ibid., p. 38.

55. Reid, "War, Peace and the Burden of History in Aceh," p. 310.

56. Huxley, *Disintegrating Indonesia?* p. 39.

57. Ibid., pp. 39–40.

58. See International Crisis Group, "Aceh: A Fragile Peace."

59. International Crisis Group, "Aceh: How Not to Win Hearts and Minds," p. 2.

60. See "Memorandum of Understanding between the Government of the Republic of Indonesia and the Free Aceh Movement," 15 August 2005, www.thejakarta post.com/RI_GAM_MOU.pdf (accessed 11 October 2005). There is a comprehensive analysis in International Crisis Group, "Aceh: A New Chance for Peace."

61. See International Crisis Group, "Indonesia: Ending Repression in Irian Jaya," p. 6.

62. See ibid., pp. 12–15.

63. See ibid., p. 12.

64. Huxley, *Disintegrating Indonesia?* p. 44.

65. Ibid., p. 45.

66. Bertrand, *Nationalism and Ethnic Conflict in Indonesia,* p. 159.

67. See International Crisis Group, "Indonesia: Ending Repression in Irian Jaya," p. 8, referring to violence in the highlands town of Wamena on 6 October 2000 (i.e., during Wahid's presidency).

68. Malley, "Indonesia in 2002," pp. 140–141. See further, International Crisis Group, "Indonesia: Resources and Conflict in Papua," pp. 9–11.

69. International Crisis Group, "Dividing Papua," p. 7.

70. Huxley, *Disintegrating Indonesia?* p. 57.

71. International Crisis Group, "Indonesia: The Search for Peace in Maluku," p. i.

72. Huxley, *Disintegrating Indonesia?* p. 58.

73. Ibid., p. 56.

74. Ibid., pp. 58–59.

75. International Crisis Group, "Indonesia: The Search for Peace in Maluku," p. 2.

76. Ibid., p. 3.

77. Ibid., pp. 22–23.

78. Bertrand, *Nationalism and Ethnic Conflict in Indonesia,* p. 133.

79. Ibid.

80. International Crisis Group, "Indonesia: The Search for Peace in Maluku," p. 1.

81. Huxley, *Disintegrating Indonesia?* p. 61.

82. Ibid., p. 62.

83. International Crisis Group, "Indonesia Backgrounder: Jihad in Central Sulawesi."

84. See Bertrand, *Nationalism and Ethnic Conflict in Indonesia,* pp. 47–58.

85. Huxley, *Disintegrating Indonesia?* p. 63.

86. Ibid.

87. Ibid., p. 64. On the violence in Central Kalimantan, see further International Crisis Group, "Communal Violence in Indonesia."

88. Writing in the early 1980s, Charles Coppel claimed the proportion was 2.5 percent at most. See Coppel, *Indonesian Chinese in Crisis,* p. 1.

89. Purdey, "Anti-Chinese Violence and Transitions in Indonesia: June 1998–October 1999," p. 15.

90. Ibid., p. 32.

91. Huxley, *Disintegrating Indonesia?* pp. 47–48.

92. Hill, *The Indonesian Economy,* p. 230. For further background on East Kalimantan, see Pangestu, "East Kalimantan."

93. Turner and Podger et al., *Decentralisation in Indonesia,* pp. 23–27.

94. Bertrand, *Nationalism and Ethnic Conflict in Indonesia,* p. 202.

95. Ibid.

96. Turner and Podger et al., *Decentralisation in Indonesia,* p. 143.

97. Sakai, "Resisting the Mainland," p. 189.

98. Turner and Podger et al., *Decentralisation in Indonesia,* p. 17.

99. Figures from International Maritime Bureau Piracy Reporting Centre (IMB-PRC) as reported by P. Mukundan, "Scourge of Piracy in Southeast Asia," p. 10.

100. Chalk, *Grey-Area Phenomena in Southeast Asia,* p. 35.

101. Richardson, *A Time Bomb for Global Trade,* pp. 38–39.

102. "Piracy and Maritime Terror in Southeast Asia."

103. For critical perspectives on Australian involvement in this issue, see Mares, *Borderline;* Brennan, *Tampering with Asylum.*

104. Dauvergne, "The Political Economy of Indonesia's 1997 Forest Fires."

105. Figures in this paragraph are from "Time to Deliver."

106. Dibb, "Indonesia"; Cribb, "Not the Next Yugoslavia."

Part 4

Other Key Regional Actors

Russia and Australia | 12

The previous sections of this book have focused on Northeast Asia and Southeast Asia as the key subregions in Asia Pacific. In Northeast Asia the emphasis was on the roles of the United States, China, and Japan, and their interrelationships, as well as the Taiwan and Korean issues. In Southeast Asia we saw some of the ways the underlying international dynamics differed from those in Northeast Asia, giving particular attention to Indonesia. In Part 4 the focus is on some other significant actors within Asia Pacific, Russia and Australia in this chapter, and then international organizations in the following chapter.

On maps of Asia Pacific, using Mercator's projection, Russia and Australia appear to dominate the region. This projection exaggerates the size of countries the farther they are from the equator. Both Russia and Australia occupy extensive territories, but are not quite as dominant as the maps suggest. The two countries have extensive interests in Asia Pacific but are also on its edge in some respects. In this chapter we will provide some basic data about Russia and Australia before proceeding to a discussion of the ways they have been involved in Asia Pacific. In both cases there will be an initial overview of the historical context of that involvement, and then a more detailed examination of the post–Cold War era. The way Russia and Australia have pursued their political-strategic and economic interests is a major theme. At the end of the chapter the main points in the analysis will be highlighted through a comparison of Russian and Australian involvement in the region.

As a starting point it is useful to have some basic data on Russia and Australia (see Table 12.1). In the case of Russia it is also helpful to have some specific data on the Russian Far East (RFE) since Russian involvement focuses on the position of that region. The RFE occupies a vast area

Table 12.1   Russia and Australia, Basic Data

	Russia	Australia
Size of territory	17,075,200 square kilometers	7,686,850 square kilometers
Population, 2005	143,420,309	20,090,437
Gross domestic product, 2004	US$1.4 trillion	US$598 billion
Per capita GDP, 2004	US$9,779	US$30,059
Size of military force, 2005	1,037,000	52,872
Defense spending as a percentage of GDP, 2005	2.78	1.9

Sources: The Military Balance 2005–2006 (London: Routlege, 2005); *CIA World Fact-book,* www.cia.gov/cia/publications/factbook/index.html, accessed 10 February 2006.

amounting to 6.216 million square kilometers, about 36 percent of the Russian Federation. The region is about two-thirds the size of the United States (9.629 million square kilometers).[1] The RFE is ten or eleven hours' flying time from Moscow. The population is about 7.5 million.[2] About 81 percent of people are ethnic Russians but there are also other Slavic groups (such as Ukrainians), Koreans, and various indigenous groups (the largest being the Yakuts).

In the case of Russia as a whole the population is about 80 percent ethnic Russian. Australia's population is mixed in terms of ethnic background but the dominant culture is British-derived. Indigenous people are 2–3 percent of the population in Australia; since 1945 the British-Irish mix has been diversified with an influx of immigrants from continental Europe and in recent decades from various Asian countries. Australia's democratic institutions developed from its origins as a series of British colonies that federated in 1901. Although Russia has a long history going back to Tsarist and Soviet times, the Russian Federation as such only came into existence in 1991 with the collapse of the Soviet Union. Significant moves toward democratization were made under Boris Yeltsin (president, 1991–1999) but these have been arrested to some extent under his successor, Vladimir Putin.

■ Russia

Historical Context

To understand Russia's more recent involvement in Asia Pacific, it is helpful to have some appreciation of how that involvement developed historically. This can be done in relation to both the Tsarist and Soviet periods.

Russian involvement in the Far Eastern region began from about the early seventeenth century.[3] The activities of the tribal peoples had focused on the major river valleys: the Lena, the Kolyma, and the Amur. Reindeer herding was common in the more northerly parts, whereas hunting, fishing, and some agriculture occurred in the more temperate areas.[4] When Russians entered the region they came initially as explorers and fur gatherers. The imposition of Russian authority led to conflicts with local tribes, such as the Yakut rebellion of 1642. Another problem for Russian expansion was that China controlled the Amur region (the site subsequently for Khabarovsk and Vladivostok). With the Manchurian based Q'ing ruling China from the early seventeenth century, they were determined to oppose Russian expansion. Russia recognized Chinese control of the Amur region in the Treaty of Nerchinsk in 1689.[5] At this point Russian involvement focused on the more northerly parts of what is now the RFE; from there Russian expansion extended to reach Alaska during the eighteenth century.

During the nineteenth century there was a renewed and ultimately successful push by Russia to win control of the Amur region.[6] This came to a head in the 1850s when Nikolai Nikolaevich Muraviev was governor-general in the RFE. Under the treaties of Aigun (1858) and Beijing (1860) China ceded control of the Amur region to Russia. Vladivostok was established in 1860. An important development linking the region to European Russia was the building of the Trans-Siberian Railroad between 1892 and 1905.

The Amur region became an important base for Russia in its quest for further expansion in Northeast Asia. With China weak, there were opportunities for Russia to make further gains at China's expense. Russia's main rival in this quest was Japan, which was also intent on expansion at this time. Manchuria and Korea were the two areas where this rivalry was most evident. The contest came to a head in the Russo-Japanese war of 1904–1905, which resulted in Russia's defeat. As a consequence Korea came under Japanese control, first as a protectorate (from 1905) and then as a colony (from 1910). Japan also became stronger in Manchuria, although Russia maintained some influence. Russia's territorial losses included the southern part of Sakhalin.

The next major shock to Russia's position in Northeast Asia occurred in the aftermath of World War I and the Russian Revolution in 1917. The RFE was one of the regions where civil war occurred between Bolsheviks, Whites, and local forces. Foreign forces were involved, mainly from the United States and Japan. Ostensibly these forces were protecting their own nationals but they also had an impact on the local political situation. For a short period a White regime held power with Japanese support. In 1920 the

Bolshevik government established a separate Far Eastern Republic; this was absorbed into the Russian Federation in 1922, and subsequently into the Soviet Union.[7]

During the Soviet period, Russia's objectives in relation to its position in Northeast Asia remained broadly similar to what they had been during the Tsarist period. Domestic political and broader geopolitical circumstances, however, varied in many, but not all, respects. With Stalin's rise to power after Lenin's death in 1924, he saw the economic development of the RFE as contributing to the objective of strengthening Soviet power. The purges and the Great Terror in the 1930s saw many opponents being sent to prison camps in the RFE under the Gulag system. Russia continued to exert influence in China and played a leading role in the establishment of Mongolia as a separate state in 1924. Rivalry with Japan also continued and there were major clashes along the border between the RFE and Japanese-controlled Manchuria in 1939. However, a treaty of neutrality between Japan and the USSR in 1941 meant that the RFE was not a major Soviet concern during World War II. In August 1945, however, the USSR did enter the war against Japan, with Soviet forces occupying Manchuria, northern Korea, and the Kuriles.

During the Cold War the main significance of the RFE for the USSR was in relation to Soviet policy toward China, Japan, and the United States. While economic development of the region remained limited, the RFE was one of the major centers for Soviet military forces. Vladivostok was an important naval base and land forces were concentrated along the border with China. A major issue for the USSR in the early Cold War period was the Korean War (1950–1953). The initiative came from Kim Il Sung as leader of North Korea, but the conflict had very direct implications for the USSR given the adversarial relationship with the United States. However, unlike China, the USSR opted to remain out of the conflict.

The Korean War was one of the developments that contributed to friction between the USSR and China. Although many Western commentators assumed that there was a close alignment between China and the USSR, there were many tensions. In relation to Korea, China believed that the USSR had not responded vigorously enough to a conflict that directly affected China. The USSR was suspicious of the peasant-based revolution in China. From a geopolitical perspective the emergence of a strong China could also pose a challenge to the USSR. The USSR was opposed to China's development as a nuclear power. During the 1960s and in subsequent decades conflict between the two communist giants became quite open. Ideologically the USSR attacked the "debased" communism it saw in China; for China the Soviet communists were "revisionists" who had compromised with capitalism. The conflict had racial overtones with the USSR concerned about the "Chinese hordes" on the borders of the RFE. For the Chinese the USSR represented another and, indeed, worse version of imperialism. During the 1970s and 1980s a major manifestation of the Sino-Soviet conflict in Asia Pacific was the Third Indochina War. Following Vietnam's intervention in Cambodia in 1978, the main backing for Vietnam came from the USSR; China supported the anti-Vietnamese resistance led by the deposed Khmer Rouge. With Gorbachev's emergence as Soviet leader in 1985, the possibilities for Sino-Soviet reconciliation improved and a rapprochement was achieved in 1989.

In the case of Japan, the geopolitical rivalries dated from the late nineteenth century. These continued during the Cold War, with some variations. Japan's alliance with the United States added another dimension to the tensions between Japan and the USSR. In addition there was the specific issue of the Northern Territories (the Japanese term) or the southern Kuriles (the Soviet term). While accepting the Soviet occupation of the Kuriles chain, Japan argued that the southernmost islands of Etorofu, Kunashiri, Shikotan, and the Habomais were integral parts of Japan itself. When diplomatic relations were resumed between Japan and the USSR in 1956, the USSR said that Shikotan and the Habomais would be returned to Japan in the context of a peace treaty, but a treaty has never been concluded.

While the Cold War contest between the United States and the USSR centered on Europe, the Asia Pacific dimension was also relevant. The Korean War was a major manifestation of the Cold War in Northeast Asia. The United States was linked to Japan, South Korea, and Taiwan (Republic of China) through mutual security treaties. US rapprochement with China from 1972 could be seen as an attempt to "play the China card" as a means of pressuring the USSR. One should also note that the RFE and Alaska at the closest point are only a few miles apart, with the United States and USSR thus sharing a maritime boundary. More generally the situation in Asia Pacific, and Northeast Asia more specifically, highlighted the global dimension of the Cold War. This region, including the position of the RFE, was a very important part of the contest.

Post–Cold War

In examining the involvement of Russia in Asia Pacific in the post–Cold War era we can take 1991 as the starting point. This was when the USSR collapsed, with the Russian Federation becoming the major successor state. Although the RFE remained within the Russian Federation, the geopolitical circumstances affecting Russian involvement in Asia Pacific became more complex with the emergence of various successor states in Soviet Central Asia: Kazakhstan, Kyrgyzstan, Tajikistan, Turkmenistan, and Uzbekistan. This dimension will be considered subsequently as an aspect of Russia's political-strategic involvement in Asia Pacific. The other aspect to consider is Russia's economic involvement. The general argument in both instances is that Asia Pacific has remained just as important to Russia as in previous eras, but that Russia's reduced circumstances have made it less significant as an influence. Russia's involvement has also been affected by events in other countries in the region. Initially, however, it is helpful to have an overview of the political developments affecting the RFE.

Under Yeltsin's presidency (1991–1999) democratization in Russia was accompanied by decentralization. Under Putin there have been moves toward recentralization. These developments have affected the RFE along with the other regions of Russia. The Russian Federation consists of eighty-nine "subjects" or subnational units of varying kinds, with ten of these being in the RFE. Under Yeltsin these subjects elected their own governors and legislatures. Yeltsin also appointed presidential representatives to work with the governors, but the power of these representatives was limited in practice. In 2000 Putin went further by dividing Russia into seven super-districts, one of which was the RFE, and appointing new presidential representatives known as governors-general.[8] This was all part of a general trend to shift more power toward Moscow. The central government assumed more control over local police forces and tax revenues; governors and legislatures could be dismissed. Evgenii Nazdratenko, the controversial and authoritarian governor of Primorye (based on Vladivostok), resigned his office in February 2001 after coming under pressure from Putin.[9]

During the Soviet period the RFE was important as a military center. In post-Soviet Russia the position of the military in the RFE, as well as in other parts of Russia, has declined.[10] The Far Eastern Military District, one of six military districts, has its headquarters in Khabarovsk. There are 76,000 military personnel within this district; equipment includes 3,000 tanks and 345 combat aircraft. The Pacific Fleet, based mainly in Vladivostok, has fifteen submarines, including four nuclear-armed.[11] There are major problems with morale, training, and corruption within the military. The Pacific Fleet is a major environmental hazard, with over one hundred nuclear submarines not properly decommissioned.[12] The United States has been providing funding through the Nunn-Lugar Program to facilitate the safe dismantling of these submarines, and to avoid the theft of nuclear materials.[13]

While the RFE is distant from Moscow and there are many local issues, the overwhelmingly Russian character of the population means that pressure for greater autonomy or even independence is limited. Most people identify with Russia as a state. Concerns about local issues are expressed through the existing political institutions. Decentralization allows local people more influence over local issues. With recentralization occurring, Moscow has more influence. This means that Russia's broader political-strategic and economic objectives have a greater influence on Russian policies than pressures emanating from the RFE as such.

Political-strategic objectives. In the straitened circumstances of the post-1991 era, the political-strategic objectives that Russia has pursued in Asia Pacific have emanated primarily from Moscow. Influences from the RFE, however, have been important on some issues. Although Russia is primarily centered on Europe it has continued to aspire to major power status not just in relation to that continent but in relation to all its adjoining regions, and indeed beyond. In Asia Pacific, Russia's concerns have focused on Northeast Asia, particularly relations with China and Japan. Developments on the Korean peninsula have also been important. Russian involvement in Central Asia, too, has a bearing on its broader objectives in Asia Pacific. Russia's relationship with the United States is relevant to a number of these situations. Russia's ability to pursue its objectives is constrained by its declining power base. Although estimates can vary, one writer claims that by 2004 Russia's GDP was only just above that of the Netherlands and a little more than a third that of China.[14]

One of Russia's major strategic concerns in Northeast Asia is the relationship with China. While China was clearly shocked by the collapse of the Soviet system, both Russia and China have generally had a cooperative relationship in the period since 1991. At times they have found themselves making common cause in an attempt to place some limits on the hegemonic role of the United States; the situation in the UN Security Council ahead of the commencement of the Iraq war in March 2003 is a good example. Russia has also become a major supplier of arms to China. This suggests that Russia does not see China as a strategic threat, although the economic benefits for Russia's defense industries are probably the major motivation.

On the issue of the long-running border dispute between China and Russia significant progress has been made. In 1992 the two governments agreed on demarcation of the eastern part of the border, and in 2001 the Russo-Chinese Treaty of Neighborliness, Friendship, and Cooperation recognized the legitimacy of the current borders.[15] Putin and Hu Jintao signed a final Russo-Chinese border agreement during the former's visit to Beijing in October 2004. The three islands that had remained under dispute were to be divided on a 50/50 basis between the two countries: Bolshoi Island in the Argun River, Tarabarov (Yinlong to the Chinese), and Bolshoi Ussuriiskii (Heixiazi) in the Amur River near Khabarovsk.[16] Some of these developments aroused hostility in the RFE where there is more suspicion and resentment of the Chinese than in Moscow. At the time of the 1992 agreement, when the issue of the disputed islands was postponed, Evgenii Nazdratenko, governor of Primorye, had declared any cession of land to China to be "a sale of the motherland."[17] Resentment in the RFE is also fueled by the obvious economic growth occurring in China and suspicions of illegal Chinese immigration. Chauvinistic Russian politicians such as Nazdratenko sometimes exploit these attitudes.

In the case of Russo-Japanese relations one would have expected some improvement with the ending of the Cold War. The perception of a Soviet threat was no longer relevant. At the same time some tensions have remained, particularly over the Northern Territories/Southern Kuriles issue. Although the Cold War context is no longer relevant, Russia generally takes the view that Japan is too closely aligned with the United States. In the event of both a reduced US role and deterioration in Sino-Japanese relations, one option for Japan would be to strengthen its relationship with Russia.

On the specific issue of the Northern Territories/Southern Kuriles, the Russian government in December 1991 affirmed its adherence to the 1956 declaration concerning the return of the Habomai islands and Shikotan in the context of a peace treaty with Japan;[18] however, there has been no commitment about returning the islands of Etorofu and Kunashiri. Russian governments have to be sensitive to nationalist sentiment in Russia, particularly in the RFE where there is suspicion of Japan. During a visit by Yeltsin to Tokyo in October 1993 he committed the Russian government to negotiations on the territorial dispute but no agreement was achieved.[19] By the time Putin visited Japan in November 2005 the situation had changed little.[20] Rather than allowing the whole relationship to become hostage to the territorial dispute, the Japanese government has preferred to pursue a strategy of engagement with Russia. The assumption here is that Russia will be more accommodating if it perceives "goodwill" on Japan's part. Japan also has an interest in being involved in the development of the resources of the RFE and Siberia. For these reasons Japan has been a major donor to Russia, generally coming third behind the United States and Germany (although it is first in the RFE).[21]

As far as the Korean peninsula is concerned, the USSR maintained its alignment with North Korea throughout the Cold War, frequently competing for influence with China. By the late 1980s a new situation had emerged with South Korea's Nordpolitik and Gorbachev's reformist leadership in the

USSR. The prospect of economic gains was an important motivation for the USSR in improving the relationship with South Korea, and diplomatic relations between the two countries were established in September 1990. The focus on improving relations with South Korea continued under Yeltsin after 1991. When Yeltsin visited Seoul in November 1992 he and President Roh Tae Woo signed a Treaty on Basic Relations to provide a basic framework for the bilateral relationship.[22] While Russian hopes of economic gains from the relationship with South Korea might not have lived up to expectations, there was clearly more to be gained from that relationship than the one it had with North Korea.

Russia hoped to maintain influence in relation to North Korea on a state-to-state basis. The 1961 friendship treaty remained in force until 1996 when the two countries were unable to conclude a revised treaty. A new friendship treaty was concluded in 2000, with Russia maintaining some influence but not automatically being committed to the defense of North Korea in the event of an attack upon that country. In practice Russian influence over North Korea was far less than it had been during the Soviet period. At the time of the North Korean nuclear crisis in 1994 the issue was resolved primarily on the basis of negotiations between the United States and North Korea, with Russia not being directly involved. When there was a further nuclear crisis after 2001, Russia became one of the states involved in the six-party talks. Russia's position was very close to that of China: opposed to North Korea acquiring nuclear weapons but preferring inducements rather than sanctions to achieve that goal. However, it was China that had the major influence in relation to this issue and Russia was really only a minor player.

The concerns about Chinese immigration in the RFE do not exist to the same extent with Korean immigrants. Each year 15,000 to 20,000 North Korean guest workers provide labor for the timber industry in the RFE, and North Korean farm workers also contribute to agriculture in Amur, Sakhalin, and Primorye.[23] Some North Korean workers are provided for free as a means of reducing North Korea's debt to Russia.[24]

Although Central Asia is not normally defined as part of Asia Pacific, Russian involvement in this region has a bearing on Russian relations with both the United States and China.[25] The five states of Central Asia (Kazakhstan, Kyrgyzstan, Tajikistan, Turkmenistan, and Uzbekistan) were part of the USSR before 1991. With the dissolution of the USSR, China has become more involved in Central Asia as a means of limiting support from fellow Turkic peoples for disaffected Muslim peoples in Xinjiang (mainly Uighurs). Although the United States had mainly respected Central Asia as part of Russia's "near abroad," the situation changed after September 11,

2001. The United States found it useful to establish military links with the various Central Asian states as part of the war on terrorism, which initially focused on Afghanistan. Uzbekistan became the main US ally in the region,[26] and a military presence was established at Manas airport in Kyrgyzstan; cooperation with Kazakhstan, Tajikistan, and Turkmenistan was also secured.[27] Russia acquiesced in this situation as part of its policy of cooperating with the United States in the war on terrorism.

Russia attempted to maintain influence in Central Asia through its leading role in various regional groupings. In the Shanghai Cooperation Organization (SCO), Russia shares leadership with China. The SCO was formed in June 2001 as a successor to the Shanghai Five, which dated from 1996. Apart from Russia and China, the Shanghai Five consisted of Kazakhstan, Kyrgyzstan, and Tajikistan; Uzbekistan joined these five states to form the SCO.[28] Russia dominates the Eurasian Economic Community (EEC), an economic grouping formed in October 2000, with Belarus, Kazakhstan, Kyrgyzstan, and Tajikistan as the other members.[29] Russia sees another grouping known as GUUAM (Georgia-Ukraine-Uzbekistan-Azerbaijan-Moldova) as too closely linked to the United States. This grouping was formed in October 1997 with Georgia, Ukraine, Azerbaijan, and Moldova as members; Uzbekistan joined in April 1999.[30] In October 2003 Russia opened a military base at Kant airport in Kyrgyzstan, with plans also to expand its military presence in Tajikistan.[31] These developments were seen as attempts to counter US influence in the region. The United States suffered a setback in its relations with Uzbekistan in 2005 when the government there ended the agreement allowing for a US base; this was in response to US criticisms of a crackdown on critics of the regime.[32] Another setback for the United States occurred in Mongolia in January 2006 when excommunists ousted the prodemocratic government there in a parliamentary vote. While President George W. Bush had previously lauded this government, both Russia and China looked favorably on the change.[33]

Economic objectives. Russia's economic involvement in Asia Pacific entails at least two dimensions. One is the general interest that Russia has in developing economic relations with the countries of Northeast Asia, particularly with trade and investment. The other is the more specific situation of the RFE. This too involves the development of trade and investment relations with neighboring countries. In general the specific interests of the RFE coincide with broader Russian interests, but this is not necessarily the case and one should not confuse the two.

While the European Union is Russia's leading trade partner, accounting for over half of Russia's trade, China comes second, with Japan sixth, and

South Korea tenth (see Table 12.2). For the RFE Japan has been the major export destination, with the United States the major source of imports; China and South Korea are also important trading partners. While the RFE's trade has been slow to develop, for January to July 2005 the major trading partners in order were the United States (US$4.4 billion), China (US$1.2 billion), Japan (US$1.1 billion), and South Korea US$0.68 billion).[34]

In addition to the trade focus, Russia has an interest in attracting investment from Northeast Asian countries. The RFE might be a particular focus for such investment, but it could extend to Siberia and other parts of Russia. In the RFE foreign investment would assist in the development of extractive industries; improving infrastructure such as transport facilities is an important part of this. Japan is the most important source of investment, but South Korea also plays a role and there is some interest from US sources.

The RFE provides about 6 percent of Russian GDP,[35] with an emphasis on the exploitation of natural resources. These include minerals such as gold and diamonds, coal, fisheries, and timber. There are many different mineral resources, and oil and gas reserves that could be developed economically with further investment.[36] Existing extractive industries could also benefit from additional investment. Apart from improving efficiency, there could be scope for some refining of products to occur before the raw materials are exported. The uncertain political and legal environment is a deterrent to foreign investment. The loss of Soviet subsidies to the RFE and the failure to attract sufficient investment have had an adverse effect on the economy of the region.

Proposals to build a pipeline to export oil from the East Siberian oil fields near Irkutsk provide an interesting example of the way politics and economics interact in relation to Russian policies in Asia Pacific.[37] During the 1990s a plan had been promoted by China in conjunction with Yukos, the Russian oil company, to build a 2,400-kilometer pipeline that would

Table 12.2   Major Russian Trade Partners in Northeast Asia, 2004 (percentage)

	Imports to Russia	Exports from Russia	Total Trade
China	7.1	6.5	6.7
Japan	4.5	2.7	3.2
South Korea	2.0	1.1	1.4
Total	13.6	10.3	11.3

Source: Europa, "Russia—Trade Statistics: Russia's Trade Balance with Major Partners (2004)," http://trade-info.cec.eu.int/doclib/cfm/doclib_section.cfm?sec=138&lev=2&order =date, accessed 10 February 2006.

terminate at Daqing in northeastern China. Prime Minister Koizumi Junichiro of Japan, however, put forward an alternative proposal during his visit to Moscow in January 2003. This would involve the pipeline being extended for 800 kilometers to Nakodhka on the Sea of Japan near Vladivostok. Russia postponed its original acceptance of the Chinese plan and shifted toward the Japanese proposal. The latter involved additional investment for the development of the oil industry in Russia, as well as providing more export opportunities, given Nakodhka's location as a port. Having played China and Japan against each other on this issue, Putin announced Russia's acceptance of the Japanese proposal during his visit to Japan in November 2005.[38]

■ Australia

As in the Russian case, we can approach Australian involvement in Asia Pacific by reviewing first of all the historical context, and then giving particular attention to the political-strategic and economic dimensions of that involvement in the post–Cold War era. A continuing theme throughout Australian history has been the issue of how a Western country located on the edge of Asia comes to terms with its environment. In the contemporary era, while this general theme persists, the major focus has been on how Australia as a "middle power" pursues its political-strategic and economic objectives within Asia Pacific.

Historical Context

Australia began its European history with the establishment of New South Wales (NSW) as a British colony in 1788. Subsequently other British colonies were established, either through separation from NSW or as new colonies from the beginning. Most of these colonies were self-governing by the mid-nineteenth century, with Britain retaining responsibility for foreign and defense policy. All of the Australian mainland colonies and Tasmania federated to form the Commonwealth of Australia within the British Empire in 1901. Although involved in the early federation discussions, New Zealand remained outside the new federation. Britain continued to retain ultimate responsibility for foreign policy and defense (acting on behalf of the British Empire), although Australian governments could lobby on issues of particular concern to Australia.[39]

Rivalry among the European powers was one of the factors affecting the position of the Australian colonies from the late eighteenth century and during the nineteenth century. Rivalry with France had been important in 1788 and then continued during the Napoleonic wars. In the second half of the nineteenth century the main concerns were France, Germany, and Russia, depending on the relationship between Britain and these powers in Europe and elsewhere. Colonial expansion by France and Germany in the South Pacific sometimes alarmed the Australian colonists. The Australian colonies believed that distance from Britain made them vulnerable.[40] In the latter part of the nineteenth century the emergence of Japan as another significant power in the region added to Australian concerns about vulnerability. Apart from these various concerns relating to external security, there was also insecurity in the Australian colonies about protecting the British-derived way of life being established there. At the time of the gold rushes in the mid-nineteenth century there had been hostility expressed to Chinese miners, and loss of life occurred in some anti-Chinese riots. Similar attitudes prevailed in 1901, with Pacific islanders working on sugar plantations in Queensland being another source of concern. Protecting Australian living standards was a major objective for the fledgling labor movement but these attitudes were shared across the political spectrum. Hence the Immigration Restriction Act, the embodiment of the White Australia Policy, was the first major piece of legislation passed by the new Commonwealth parliament in 1901.[41] British objections, based on the principle that there should be free movement within the British Empire, and motivated also by concerns about the impact on relations with Japan, were overridden.

At a geopolitical level, Australia's concerns in the "Far East" from 1901 to 1945 centered on Japan. While Britain retained the primary responsibility for foreign policy, there was always a fear that the British agenda would not necessarily coincide with the Australian agenda. Japan was a concern for Britain, but it was only one issue among many. For Australia Japan was more of a preoccupation. Australian fears were assuaged to some extent by the conclusion of the Anglo-Japanese alliance in 1902. The alliance provided that the two parties would remain neutral in the event of conflict with a third party, but provide support if the conflict were with two or more parties.

At the time of World War I Japan became involved as a British ally, occupying German islands north of the Equator and escorting Australian troop ships across the Indian Ocean on their way to the Middle East and Europe. Billy Hughes (Australian prime minister, 1915–1923) was concerned that Japan be kept north of the equator in any territorial settlement. He argued this case at the Paris Peace Conference in 1919 where Australia was represented as part of the British Empire delegation. Hughes also managed to offend the Japanese by successfully opposing the inclusion of a clause on racial equality in the covenant for the new League of Nations. Domestically the White Australia Policy remained secure as one of the founding principles of the Australian federation.

Australian fears about Japan acquired more substance in light of Japan's expansionist moves in the 1930s: the establishment of a puppet state in Manchuria (renamed Manchukuo) in 1931, and then the launching of war against China in 1937. Concurrently Australia gradually developed an independent foreign policy as a consequence of the passage of the Statute of Westminster in 1931 (granting independence to the self-governing dominions such as Australia, although enacting legislation by the dominions was also required). By April 1939 conservative prime minister Robert Menzies could describe Britain's Far East as Australia's "near north." Conservative governments in Australia during the 1930s pursued a policy of appeasement in relation to Japan, generally preferring to avoid confrontation in the hope that this would divert Japan from any southward designs.

This policy collapsed with Japan's attack on Pearl Harbor in December 1941. Concurrently Japan launched attacks in Southeast Asia. Singapore, supposedly the linchpin for the defense of the British Empire in the Far East, fell to the advancing Japanese in February 1942. Following Pearl Harbor, Labor prime minister John Curtin turned to the United States for assistance; US forces under General Douglas MacArthur based themselves in Australia from 1942 as part of the US strategy for waging war against Japan. Britain remained important to Australia but henceforth had a secondary strategic role compared to the United States.

In the aftermath of the Pacific War Australia supported the imposition of a harsh settlement on Japan. Australian governments were intent on placing the security relationship with the United States on a long-term basis, achieving some success in this respect with the conclusion of the ANZUS (Australia–New Zealand–United States) Treaty in 1951. However, from the US perspective this treaty was essentially a quid pro quo for Australia (and New Zealand) agreeing to the relatively lenient peace treaty with Japan. From about 1947 the United States had decided that it was more important to ensure that Japan became an ally in the Cold War than to impose a more stringent peace settlement. In Asia Pacific the US strategy of containment focused particularly on China. Australia generally adhered to the US position, although not invariably (selling wheat to China in the 1960s for example, whereas the United States maintained a trade embargo). Australian forces fought alongside those of the United States in the major Cold War conflicts in the region: the Korean War (1950–1953) and then the Vietnam War (1965 to early 1970s). Australian governments were keen to have US forces committed in Southeast Asia, and supported a hawkish position in relation to Vietnam in the mid-1960s. Australia also supported a continuing position for British forces in Southeast Asia. On this basis Australian forces became involved in the conflict with communist guerrillas in Malaya in the 1950s, and then supported Britain and Malaysia in opposition to Indonesia's "Konfrontasi"—or confrontation— of the new Malaysian federation from 1963 to 1966. Support for both US and British forces in Southeast Asia, including a willingness to commit Australian forces in a junior role, was known as "forward defense."

Australian policy in Asia Pacific in the 1950s and 1960s was not shaped simply by the Cold War context. Policy toward Japan began to shift, particularly with the perception that Japan's economic recovery could make that country an important economic partner. This perception was the major motivation for the conclusion of the Australia-Japan commerce agreement in 1957. By the late 1960s Japan had replaced Britain as the most important destination for Australian exports. Australia also developed an important political relationship with Indonesia. Support from the Labor government in the late 1940s for Indonesian independence from the Netherlands enhanced Australia's reputation with Indonesian nationalists. With international recognition of Indonesian independence from 1949, Australia generally had a strong political relationship with Indonesia although there were differences over some issues. Australia supported continued Dutch rule in West New Guinea, and then the establishment of Malaysia in 1963. On the first issue Australia found itself isolated when the Kennedy administration pressured the Netherlands after 1961 to transfer West New Guinea to Indonesia (this happened in 1963 after a short period of UN tutelage). In relation to Malaysia, Australian support was low-key in order to minimize conflict with Indonesia. The inauguration of the New Order in Indonesia under Suharto made the pursuit of Australian objectives in relation to that country much easier; little was heard about the bloodbath accompanying this transition when large numbers of alleged communists were massacred.

There was an important shift in Australian involvement in Asia Pacific from the early 1970s.[42] There were important developments occurring at the geopolitical and economic levels, but change was also occurring within Australian society. Geopolitically the main change was the achievement of rapprochement between China and the United States as signified in the Shanghai Communiqué of February 1972. Sino-US confrontation, the main dimension of the Cold War in Asia Pacific, came to an end. This made it easier for the United States to disengage from Vietnam, as happened with the Paris accords in 1973. With the end of intense Sino-US conflict there was much greater fluidity in the international politics of the region, and this made it easier for US allies such as Australia to pursue more independent policies. This situation coincided with the election of a Labor government in Canberra for the first time in twenty-three years. Led by Gough Whitlam, this government was committed to the development of a more independent foreign policy for Australia, which was seen as not inconsistent with maintaining a strong relationship with the United States. Australia moved to extend diplomatic recognition to China and also withdrew the last remaining Australian advisers in South Vietnam (most Australian troops had left under the previous conservative government). Indonesia was an important focus for Australian policy, leading Whitlam to acquiesce in the Indonesian occupation of Portuguese (East) Timor in December 1975, despite the fact that no agreed act of self-determination had been carried out.

China, Indonesia, and the United States were the countries in Asia Pacific of greatest strategic concern to Australia. Under the conservative Coalition government led by Malcolm Fraser (1975–1983) there was a shift toward a stronger alignment with China. Whereas Whitlam attempted to be even handed between China and the USSR, Fraser was more strongly anti-Soviet. This also led Fraser to oppose Vietnam's intervention in Cambodia in late 1978 against the Khmer Rouge regime; Fraser regarded Soviet support for Vietnam as part of a pattern of renewed Soviet expansionism at this time. Under both Fraser and Bob Hawke (Labor prime minister, 1983–1991) Australia continued the support for the New Order in Indonesia, including the incorporation of East Timor into Indonesia; the perception of Indonesia's strategic importance overrode any concerns about human rights violations. Fraser was prepared to pressure the United States over issues such as policy toward the USSR, including its regional manifestations. Hawke was less attached to a particular view of global strategy, and more inclined to accommodate US positions should Australia be in a position to have some influence. The Treaty of Rarotonga in 1985, establishing the South Pacific Nuclear Free Zone (SPNFZ), was crafted in such a way that US nuclear activities in the region would not be impeded. Hawke also supported the United States in the US–New Zealand nuclear ships dispute, a conflict that developed after the 1984 election of a Labour government in New Zealand with a commitment to banning visits by nuclear-armed or nuclear-powered ships.

In the 1970s and 1980s Japan was the most important focus for Australian economic involvement in Asia Pacific. As an export destination for Australia, Japan was at a peak in the 1970s with Australian raw materials providing an important basis for the development of heavy industry. Subsequently the shift in Japan's economy in a more high-tech direction meant less emphasis on the provision of raw materials than had previously been the case. Nevertheless Japan remained as the single most important destination for Australian exports. Improved relations with China also facilitated the export of raw materials there, and this became even more the case with the implementation of economic reforms in China in the post-Mao period. In Northeast Asia the three newly industrializing economies of South Korea, Taiwan, and Hong Kong also assumed an increasingly important role as export destinations for Australia. With lower tech industries moving from Japan to South Korea, Taiwan, and China these economies generated an increasingly stronger demand for Australian raw materials. The importance of Northeast Asia for the Australian economy was recognized in a report commissioned by the Hawke government. Entitled *Australia and the Northeast Asian Ascendancy* and known as the Garnaut Report for short (after Professor Ross Garnaut, its author), this report argued that Australia could build on its economic links with Northeast Asia by further liberalizing its economy.[43] Neoliberal economic changes had been one of the major features of economic policy under the Hawke government, with tariff minimization as one aspect. Garnaut's argument was that further liberalization would encourage governments in Northeast Asia to move in a similar direction, thus enhancing the opportunities for Australian exports. Rather than developing manufacturing industries catering to a protected home market, Australia should concentrate on the development of areas of expertise where it could compete regionally and globally.

Apart from these economic changes that developed during the 1980s, Australia was experiencing other changes that affected the way the country related to Asia Pacific. The abandonment of the White Australia Policy was one such change. Changes introduced in 1966 at an administrative level prepared the way for the demise of this policy. Although the changes were far reaching in their consequences there was no major fanfare for fear of an adverse public reaction. The strengthening of more liberal attitudes in Australian society made it difficult to justify a racially discriminatory immigration policy; Australia also had to consider its wider international reputation. A racially discriminatory immigration policy would have an adverse effect on Australia's ability to promote other objectives, not the least of which was the strengthening of its political and economic links with Asia Pacific countries.

The abandonment of the White Australia Policy made it easier for immigrants from Asian countries to come to Australia, and over the following decades an increased proportion did. By 2002 over 4 percent of the Australian population was born in East or South Asia.[44] Refugees from

Vietnam were an important component of the increasing number of Asians in Australia. Malcolm Fraser played an important role in winning acceptance for these refugees, an issue that achieved some prominence in the late 1970s and early 1980s when there were large numbers fleeing Vietnam's shores. International arrangements were put in place to facilitate the resettlement of asylum seekers from Vietnam, including the boat people. Statistics show that 170,994 people from Vietnam settled in Australia between 1973–1974 and 1999–2000.[45] The increasing number of Asians in Australia contributed to the country's greater cultural diversity, sometimes promoted as "multiculturalism." Whatever term is used to characterize the change that occurred, the cultural gap between Australia and Asia was reduced. Asians were increasingly part of Australian society.

Post–Cold War

The end of the Cold War was a less traumatic development for Australia than it was for Russia and the other successor states of the USSR.[46] The basic direction of Australian involvement in Asia Pacific had been set in the circumstances of the changed regional environment in the early 1970s. The greatest impact of the collapse of the USSR was in Europe, but this development also augmented the fluidity of international politics in Asia Pacific. From the Australian perspective this was another factor that had to be considered when determining the development of regional policies, but it did not result in any fundamental reorientation. In relation to Australian domestic politics, the post–Cold War era has seen both Labor and conservative Coalition governments in office. Paul Keating replaced Bob Hawke as Labor prime minister in 1991. The Coalition (combining the right-of-center Liberal Party and the smaller, rural-based National Party) won office in March 1996, and John Howard became prime minister; the Coalition won further elections in 1998, 2001, and 2004. While both Labor and Coalition governments regarded Australian engagement in Asia Pacific as a major priority and their policies overlapped in many respects, there were also some differences of emphasis. This will become clear when we examine the major developments affecting Australia's political-strategic and economic involvement in Asia Pacific under the two governments.

As far as the domestic context of Australian engagement in Asia Pacific is concerned, it is worth noting some of the significant developments under the Keating Labor government (1991–1996) and the Howard Coalition government (1996–). Under Keating, supported strongly by foreign minister Gareth Evans, there was some attempt to integrate Australia more strongly with Asia Pacific.[47] Australia took a lead in the establishment and development of APEC, which began its annual leaders' summits in 1993. Australia was also active in supporting the ASEAN Regional Forum, which began meeting on an annual basis in 1994 to discuss Asia Pacific security issues. Australia never claimed to be "part of Asia" or an "Asian country," although Gareth Evans on one occasion argued that Australia was part of the "East Asian hemisphere."[48] Asia Pacific terminology (favored also by the United States) provided a means for legitimizing Australian (and US) involvement in East Asian affairs. There were practical security and economic benefits for Australia in becoming more accepted within the region. The Labor government believed that some adaptation of Australian identity would help in achieving the goal of repositioning Australia within the Asia Pacific region. This was part of the reason for Keating's support of republicanism, signaling to the world that Australia was clearly an independent country and committed to a future in Asia Pacific. Keating was also a strong advocate of multiculturalism and reconciliation with the indigenous people. He saw these goals as worthwhile in themselves but they also provided an indication to the world, and Asia Pacific in particular, about Australia's political direction.

Under the Howard government there has been some shift of emphasis even though involvement in the region as a means for achieving Australia's security and economic objectives has remained central. Howard rejected any attempt to remake Australian identity, believing that Keating's approach smacked of social engineering. Australia's regional objectives could be advanced through supporting "practical regionalism" rather than "cultural regionalism." Regional cooperation on a pragmatic basis would be supported, but not any steps that implied that Australia was culturally part of Asia. Howard wanted more emphasis on the relationship with the United States, believing that the alliance had been undermined by Labor's "Asia first" approach. While multilateral cooperation continued in many contexts, there was also some shift toward bilateralism. Relationships with Asian countries were important, but links with other regions should not be neglected.

In the late 1990s the Howard government had to contend with a conservative populist movement known as Hansonism.[49] This movement was focused on certain domestic issues but also had implications for Australia's relations with Asian countries. It took its name from Pauline Hanson, a disendorsed Liberal candidate who was elected as an independent for the Queensland seat of Ipswich in the 1996 federal elections. Hansonism, organized politically as One Nation, reached its peak in the 1998 Queensland state elections when it won about a quarter of the vote. Hansonism portrayed itself as representing the "old Australia," supporting economic protection and a more restrictive approach to immigration. It preferred assimilation to multiculturalism, would limit the acceptance of refugees and opposed any special benefits for indigenous people. Relations with Asian countries were affected because of One Nation's hostility to Asian immigration and suspicion of moves to strengthen links with Asian countries. One Nation had the potential to damage Australia's position within Asia Pacific, while also damaging the Coalition's political base, especially in rural areas. While the Coalition argued against most of One Nation's positions, it also adopted a conservative stance on some issues to protect its own base. The most obvious example of this was in relation to the issue of asylum seekers, where "boat people" were automatically detained. After the *Tampa* incident in August 2001, when would-be asylum seekers were prevented from landing on Australian soil, the Coalition went to the electorate on the issue of border protection. It won a convincing victory.[50] While One Nation essentially imploded as a political force, Howard's ability to take some of its policies and repackage them in an acceptable way was also a factor in its loss of support. Hansonism was removed as a threat to Australian involvement in Asia Pacific, thus making it easier for the Coalition government to engage with the region on its own terms.

Political-strategic objectives. Keeping in mind the domestic context affecting Australian involvement in Asia Pacific in the post–Cold War era, we focus next on the substance of political-strategic and economic engagement under both the Keating and Howard governments. For both governments it has been a matter of how best to advance Australian interests on the basis of the limited resources available to a middle power. In practice the general direction pursued by the two governments has been similar, although there have been some differences in terms of emphasis and rhetoric. Particular international events have also had an impact, especially in the case of the Coalition.

The political-strategic dimension was an important aspect of Australia's Asia Pacific engagement under the Keating government. Labor favored a "cooperative security" approach, emphasizing security "with" rather than security "against." Arrangements such as the ASEAN Regional Forum received favorable attention, and Australia also took a leading role in the UN peacekeeping operation in Cambodia in 1992–1993 (helping bring an end to a conflict that had begun with Vietnamese intervention against the Khmer Rouge government in 1978). While Australia continued to relate to a range of countries in the region, particular attention was given to Indonesia. Keating declared "No country is more important to Australia than Indonesia."[51] Australia continued its support for Indonesia's incorporation of East Timor, arguing that the best way to advance human rights in that territory was to maintain a good relationship with Indonesia. The close relationship between the two countries was symbolized in a security agreement concluded in 1995. The relationship with the United States remained important as one element of Australia's political-strategic engagement in Asia Pacific. The Labor government saw this relationship as providing opportunities for advancing Australia's goals in the region; the aim was to win US support for Australian policies on various issues, Indonesia being a notable example (the United States was generally more critical of the human rights situation in Indonesia than was Australia).

Under the Howard government from 1996 (with Alexander Downer as foreign minister) there was an attempt to put more emphasis on the relationship with the United States.[52] The Coalition argued that Labor had lost sight of the fact that the US alliance was the central feature of Australian foreign policy. An early example was the strong support given to the United States in the Taiwan Strait crisis of March 1996. Over time, however, the Coalition became more nuanced in its approach to the alliance, at least in the Asia Pacific region. Too strong an identification with the United States could sometimes undermine Australian relations with other Asia Pacific countries, most notably China.

A crisis arose in the relationship with Indonesia in 1999. Howard had initially continued the Keating approach in a low-key way. With democratization occurring in Indonesia after Suharto's fall in 1998, a decision was made to hold a referendum on self-determination in East Timor. Australia went along with this decision, while believing that the best outcome would be a pro-Indonesian vote. When the vote was strongly in favor of independence but Indonesia (and particularly the military) appeared reluctant to accept this situation, the Howard government came under strong public pressure to intervene on the side of the East Timorese. The UN Security Council approved the necessary resolution and US pressure won Indonesian acquiescence. Australia led a UN-authorized force to restore order, and then contributed to the UN force that oversaw East Timor's transition to independence, a goal achieved in 2002. While Australia's motivation was primarily humanitarian, the episode contributed to a deterioration in Australian-Indonesian relations. The security treaty was abrogated, with many Indonesians portraying the intervention as evidence of Australian expansionism.

Another event affecting Australia's political-strategic involvement in Asia Pacific was the terrorist attacks in New York and Washington on September 11, 2001. Australia became a strong supporter of the war on terrorism, and contributed forces in Afghanistan. Australia also participated in the initial attack on Iraq in 2003, and from 2005 stationed a small force in southern Iraq. The Howard government's perception of the US alliance was an important consideration in the policies it followed, particularly in Iraq, while it also argued that solidarity against terrorism was a moral imperative. Australia's position on these issues created difficulties in its relations with predominantly Muslim countries in Southeast Asia such as Indonesia and Malaysia. Nevertheless there was strong cooperation between Indonesia and Australia in the aftermath of the Bali bombings in October 2002 when 202 people (including eighty-eight Australians) were killed. The election of Susilo Bambang Yudhoyono as president of Indonesia in 2004 provided an opportunity for Australia to improve relations with Indonesia. Australia also became the major contributor of relief funds to Indonesia after the tsunami hit the shores of Aceh on Boxing Day 2004.

The relationship with China was an important focus for the Howard government. After the tensions over Taiwan in 1996, the government became more sensitive to the Chinese position on a range of issues. A key consideration was China's growing economic strength, and Australia's wish to benefit from that expansion (see below). This increased China's bargaining power in relation to Australia. On the Taiwan issue, for example, Australia indicated that it would not necessarily support the US position in the event of conflict.[53] The US alliance remained central to the Howard government's foreign policy, but Australia was also accommodating to China's increasing economic and strategic strength. An important symbolic occasion occurred in October 2003 when presidents George W. Bush and Hu Jintao visited Canberra on successive days, with both men addressing the Australian parliament.

Australia in some respects was pursuing a hedging strategy in Asia Pacific, maintaining the alliance with the United States but also cooperating with China. Another element of this strategy was the development of a stronger security relationship with Japan. Although the Australian-Japanese relationship was concerned mainly with economic issues, low-key security cooperation and more high-level political exchanges also developed. An important consideration was to avoid any impression that these developments were directed against China. By maintaining and developing substantive relationships with all the major powers in Asia Pacific, Australia was maximizing its ability to act independently in the region. In this respect there was substantial continuity in approach between the Keating and Howard governments.

Economic objectives. The economic dimension was fundamental to Australian engagement in Asia Pacific under both the Keating and Howard governments. This was a continuation of the situation that had developed since at least the 1970s. East Asia, and particularly Northeast Asia, was the most important destination for Australian exports. In the period covered by these two governments, well over half of Australia's exports went to East Asia. The general pattern was for Australia to export raw materials such as coal and iron ore, and to import manufactured goods. Such goods could be low cost items such as clothing and footwear from countries with low labor costs, or more high tech in the case of Japan (cars, for example). (See Table 12.3.)

The question for Australian governments was how best to maintain and develop their economic relationships with the East Asian countries. As with the political-strategic dimension of Australian engagement, there has been substantial continuity between the Keating and Howard govern- ments, but also some differences of emphasis.

During the Keating period the dominant perception of East Asia was that of the "Asian economic miracle." The major economies of Northeast Asia (Japan, China, South Korea, Taiwan, Hong Kong) were all experienc- ing high rates of economic growth, and this pattern was also evident with some of the Southeast Asian countries (Singapore, Malaysia, Thailand). The Keating government continued to follow neoliberal economic policies in Australia. Following the arguments of the Garnaut Report of 1989, it also hoped that Australia's example would encourage East Asian countries to

Table 12.3 Australia's Trade with Asia Pacific (percentages)

	Exports from Australia	Imports to Australia	Total Australian Trade
Japan	19.7	11.5	15.2
China	10.2	13.3	11.9
South Korea	7.7	3.3	5.3
Taiwan	3.9	2.4	3.1
Hong Kong	2.1	0.8	1.4
Total, Northeast Asia	43.6	31.3	36.9
Singapore	2.6	4.9	3.8
Malaysia	2.0	4.0	3.1
Thailand	3.1	2.8	2.9
Indonesia	2.7	2.2	2.4
Philippines	0.7	0.5	0.6
Total, ASEAN-5	11.1	14.4	12.8
Total, Northeast Asia and ASEAN-5	54.7	45.7	49.7

Source: Country Fact Sheets, Department of Foreign Affairs and Trade, Australia, www.dfat.gov.au, accessed 10 February 2006.

Note: ASEAN-5: Thailand, Malaysia, Indonesia, Philippines, Singapore.

move in a similar direction. Countries such as Japan and South Korea, for example, maintained tariffs on various agricultural imports to protect their own farmers. Australia was also active within APEC, seeing this forum as another means for encouraging regional countries to move in a neoliberal direction. The favored approach was "open regionalism" whereby APEC countries would reduce economic barriers among themselves but not in a way to discriminate against nonmembers.

The Howard government also maintained Australia's neoliberal economic direction, going further in some respects such as industrial relations. Economic engagement with East Asia remained important but there were some complications. Perhaps the major one was the Asian economic crisis of 1997, leading to the collapse of financial institutions in a number of countries. The worst affected countries were South Korea, Thailand, and Indonesia, but there was also a broader regional impact. With the reduced economic capacity of the affected countries their ability to purchase from trading partners such as Australia was also affected. Australia supported measures to facilitate recovery from the financial crisis, generally arguing in favor of more generous conditions than those imposed by the International Monetary Fund.[54] The Asian Monetary Fund proposed by Japan did not eventuate. Japan's sluggish economic performance from the mid-1990s also represented a shift from the Asian economic miracle.

During the Howard period there was a shift from multilateralism as a way of pursuing Australian economic interests. This shift mirrored changes occurring in the international environment. APEC continued as a forum for furthering economic cooperation but did not become an instrument for transforming economic relations in the region; APEC's annual summit meetings were an important part of diplomacy in Asia Pacific. The WTO was the major setting for negotiating about trade on a global level, and Australia participated in the Doha Round after 2001. Supplementing or competing with multilateralism, there was an increasing emphasis on bilateralism. Frustrated with the slow progress in multilateral negotiations, many countries believed they could better position themselves by concluding bilateral agreements. The drawback was that such agreements might further impede progress in multilateral negotiations that generally promised more overall in the long term. The most significant bilateral agreement Australia concluded was the free trade agreement with the United States (agreed 2004, implemented 2005).[55] Other significant Australian agreements were with Singapore (2003) and Thailand (effective 2005). Negotiations were taking place with China, Malaysia, and ASEAN (in conjunction with New Zealand), and preliminary discussions were being held with Japan. China's booming economy was of particular interest to Australia, with China a major market for Australian iron ore, alumina and aluminium, oil, coal, and agricultural products (such as wool); export of liquefied natural gas began on a large scale in 2006.[56]

Despite the shift toward bilateralism, Australia took an interest in any regional initiatives that had implications for its own economic engagement. Following the Asian economic crisis, ASEAN Plus Three (the ten ASEAN countries plus China, Japan, and South Korea) (APT) emerged as a response to the failure of the East Asian countries to develop regional initiatives for dealing with the crisis. There were discussions about establishing this grouping as an East Asian Community. While the United States was not regarded as eligible for membership (unlike the situation with APEC), there was debate among East Asian countries about inviting Australia, New Zealand, and India. Australia was invited to the summit meeting of the nascent community held in Kuala Lumpur in December 2005 (resulting in a decision to hold a regular East Asia Summit). While the significance of the proposed community remained unclear, it was in Australia's interests to participate in any development that might affect its economic and political engagement in Asia Pacific.

While the Howard government put more emphasis on bilateralism than on multilateralism in pursuing Australian economic engagement in Asia Pacific, there remained significant overlap with the policies of the Keating government. The shift away from multilateralism was partly a response to the perceived limitations of that approach, but this was not a denial of the need to pursue multilateralism where appropriate. As in the case of the political-strategic dimension, the picture that emerges is one of significant continuities between the two governments, but with some differences in emphasis and rhetoric.

Comparisons

Clearly both Russia and Australia have a strong interest in engaging in Asia Pacific affairs. It is interesting in conclusion to make some comparisons about the way they have pursued engagement. These comparisons cover both the historical context of their involvement, and the basis of their contemporary engagement.

Both Russia and Australia may be regarded as settler states within the region. If we take the RFE as the focus for Russian involvement in the region, most of its population is Russian. In the Australian case most settlers were from Britain or Ireland and, despite the development of greater cultural diversity in recent years, people of Anglo-Celtic background still form a clear majority of the Australian population. In both Australia and the RFE, European expansion came at the expense of the indigenous population. One difference between the RFE and Australia was that Australia was not only geographically distant from Britain, the home country, but also geographically distinct. The RFE might have been geographically distant from European Russia but Russia was one continuous territory from the Baltic to the Pacific. Politically Australia developed as a series of self-governing British colonies, later federating into one country, and evolving to full independence by the time of World War II (but with strong links remaining with Britain). The RFE was governed as an integral part of Russia from Tsarist times, through the Soviet period, and now as part of the post-Soviet Russian Federation. Russian policy toward Asia Pacific is determined in Moscow, although frequently influenced by concerns emanating from the RFE. Australian policy in the region is that of an independent state, wholly within Asia Pacific, although not necessarily part of Asia.

If we compare Russia and Australia in terms of their contemporary engagement one aspect is the political-strategic dimension. Here Russia is mainly focused on Northeast Asia, particularly in terms of its relations with China, Japan, and the United States; it is also directly involved in the Korean issue, and has important links with both North and South Korea. Developments in Central Asia have a bearing on Russian relations with China and the United States. Australia has a strong interest in Northeast Asia, relating both to its economic ties and to the fact that this area is a fulcrum for relations among the major powers. However, Australia also has a major interest in areas adjoining its own territory: Southeast Asia, especially Indonesia, and the South Pacific.

In terms of the economic dimension, the main interest for both Russia and Australia is Northeast Asia. Potentially Russia could be a competitor to Australia as a supplier of raw materials to the major economies in that area.[57] The overall significance of Northeast Asia, and Asia Pacific more broadly, is less for Russia than for Australia. For the RFE alone, however, Northeast Asia is of greater significance than for Australia. Australia also has important economic interests in Southeast Asia, but less than those in Northeast Asia. Broadly speaking, Australia is an important industrialized economy but outside the Group of Eight (G8); its greatest significance in terms of the world economy is as an exporter of minerals and agricultural produce. Russia is also an industrialized economy but within the G8 (although largely for political reasons). However, Russia also has major problems as a post-Soviet transitional economy. These include establishing a capitalist system while also achieving equity, modernizing infrastructure, and combating crime and corruption. Many of these issues can be seen in a concentrated form in the RFE; this region in many respects is comparable to a developing country.

Australia's engagement with Asia Pacific is facilitated by the fact that it is an independent country focused on that region. Russian engagement in Asia Pacific is also important but, whatever the interests of the RFE, that engagement tends to have a lower priority in Russia's international agenda as compared with other matters. The concerns of European Russia come first, and that means a strong emphasis on the Soviet successor states, Europe more broadly, and the transatlantic context.

▦ Notes

1. Davis, *The Russian Far East,* p. 24.
2. Ibid., p. 3.
3. A good history of the Russian Far East is Stephan, *The Russian Far East.*
4. Davis, *The Russian Far East,* p. 7.
5. Ibid., p. 9.
6. Ibid., p. 10.
7. Ibid., p. 15.
8. Ibid.
9. Thornton and Ziegler, "The Russian Far East in Perspective," p. 19.
10. A detailed assessment of Russian military forces in Asia is Austin and Muraviev, *The Armed Forces of Russia in Asia.*
11. Figures are from *The Military Balance 2005–2006,* pp. 165, 167.
12. Davis, *The Russian Far East,* p. 125.
13. Ibid., pp. 116–117.
14. MacFarlane, "The 'R' in BRICs," p. 44. This point is based on World Bank figures. Figures from the International Institute for Strategic Studies suggest the difference is not as great as this.
15. Davis, *The Russian Far East,* p. 91.
16. Kimura, "Russia and the CIS in 2004," pp. 63–64.
17. Davis, *The Russian Far East,* p. 91.
18. Hasegawa, "Japan," p. 110.
19. Miu Okikawa Dieter, "Japan Is Overtly Satisfied with Yeltsin Visit," *Japan Times* (Weekly International Edition), 25–31 October 1993, p. 3.
20. "Putin, Koizumi Pledge to Work on Island Dispute," Radio Free Europe/ Radio Liberty, 21 November 2005, www.rferl.org/featuresarticle/2005/11/ 21393694-bad8-4bea-a613-38480b8b57ac.html (accessed 10 February 2006).
21. Davis, *The Russian Far East,* p. 15. See further Okada, "The Japanese Economic Presence in the Russian Far East."
22. For the text of this treaty, see "Treaty on Basic Relations Between the Republic of Korea and the Russian Federation," in *Korea and World Affairs* 16, no. 4 (Winter 1992), pp. 744–748.
23. Davis, *The Russian Far East,* p. 98.
24. Ibid.

25. For background on Central Asia's position in international politics, see for example, Rumer, "The Powers in Central Asia"; Menon, "The New Great Game in Central Asia."

26. See further Akbarzadeh, *Uzbekistan and the United States.*

27. Buszynski, "Russia and the Commonwealth of Independent States in 2002," p. 21.

28. Buszynski, "Russia and the CIS in 2003," p. 163.

29. Ibid., p. 162.

30. Ibid., p.163.

31. Ibid., p. 161.

32. "US Confirms Uzbek Base Departure," BBC News, Asia-Pacific, 27 September 2005, http://news.bbc.co.uk/2/hi/asia-pacific/4288280.stm (accessed 10 February 2006).

33. Jonathan Watts, "Colour of Revolution in Mongolia Turns Red Again," *Guardian Weekly,* 20–26 January 2006, p. 8.

34. "Economic Cooperation Between the Russian Far East and Foreign Countries in 2004–2005," November 2005, p. 2, www.bisnis.doc.gov/bisnis/bisdoc/0511rfecoop.htm (accessed 12 February 2006).

35. Davis, *The Russian Far East,* p. 59.

36. See Australian Department of Foreign Affairs and Trade, East Asia Analytical Unit, *Pacific Russia,* Appendix II. See also Davis, *The Russian Far East,* chapter 4, for an overview of the economy of the RFE.

37. See Buszynski, "Russia and the CIS in 2003," pp. 165–166; Kimura, "Russia and the CIS in 2004," pp. 64–65.

38. Ron Synovitz, "Russia: Putin Says Oil Pipeline Will Reach Far East Coast," Radio Free Europe/Radio Liberty, 21 November 2005, www.rferl.org/featuresarticle/2005/11/880fdc55-d2da-41f5-8efc-ff49e639d554.html (accessed 10 February 2006).

39. For a useful collection of documents on the history of Australian foreign policy from the 1870s to the 1970s, see Meaney, ed., *Australia and the World.*

40. This sense of vulnerability is discussed further in Cheeseman, "Australia," and Burke, *In Fear of Security.*

41. See Tavan, *The Long, Slow Death of White Australia.*

42. A good reference work on Australia's Asian engagement from the 1970s to 2000 is Edwards and Goldsworthy, ed., *Facing North.*

43. Garnaut, *Australia and the Northeast Asian Ascendancy.*

44. Based on "Table 5.34 Main Countries of Birth of the Population," *Year Book Australia, 2005,* www.abs.gov.au/ausstats/abs@.nsf/94713ad445ff1425ca25682000192af2/2D7A4BF79F53D825CA256F7200832F90?opendocument (accessed 10 February 2006). This table only includes the main source countries. Descendants of people born in these countries are not included.

45. Quilty, "Immigration and Multiculturalism," p. 313.

46. The series on "Australia in World Affairs," produced under the auspices of the Australian Institute of International Affairs, is a useful reference. The relevant volumes for the post–Cold War period are Cotton and Ravenhill, ed., *Seeking Asian Engagement,* and Cotton and Ravenhill, ed., *The National Interest in a Global Era.* General books that are useful include McDougall, *Australian Foreign Relations,* and Firth, *Australia in International Politics.*

47. Keating, *Engagement.*

48. B. Whiteman, "Australia Part of East Asia: Foreign Minister," *Insight* (Australian Department of Foreign Affairs and Trade) 4, no. 4 (4 April 1995), p. 12.

49. For a succinct analysis of Hansonism, see Markus, *Race,* chapter 6.

50. Marr and Wilkinson, *Dark Victory.*

51. Paul Keating, speech at launch of "Australia Today Indonesia '94" promotion, 16 March 1994, *Ministerial Document Service* (Australia), 17 March 1994, no. 146/93-4, pp. 4987–4994.

52. For a positive appraisal of the Howard government's Asia Pacific policies, see Tow, "Evolving Australian Security Interests in the Asia-Pacific."

53. See transcript of media conference with Alexander Downer in Beijing, 17 August 2004, www.foreignminister.gov.au/transcripts/2004/040817_ds_beijing .html (accessed 10 February 2006).

54. See Beeson and Bell, "Australia in the Shadow of the Asian Crisis."

55. For critical perspectives on the Australia-US free trade agreement, see Capling, *All the Way with the USA,* and Weiss et al., *How to Kill a Country.*

56. "People's Republic of China Country Brief—September 2005," Department of Foreign Affairs and Trade (Australia), www.dfat.gov.au/geo/china/cb_ index.html (accessed 10 February 2006).

57. See Australia, Department of Foreign Affairs and Trade, East Asia Analytical Unit, *Pacific Russia,* chapter 7.

International
Organizations

P revious chapters in this book have given particular attention to the role of states in the international politics of Asia Pacific. We have seen how there is much variation among the states in the region. They include the major powers of the United States, China, and Japan in Northeast Asia, the contested situations in Taiwan and Korea, the frequently weak states in Southeast Asia (exemplified by Indonesia), Russia as a declining power, and Australia as a middle power. Apart from the broad categories, each state also has its own characteristics. In this chapter we will examine international organizations as another dimension of international politics in Asia Pacific, thus adding to the picture of complexity within the region.

International organizations can be viewed from various perspectives. One view is that they are just another context in which states operate in the international arena. In other words, the focus remains very much on states, and international organizations are not viewed as actors in their own right. An alternative view is that, whatever the circumstances leading to the establishment of international organizations, such organizations usually acquire some autonomy during the course of their development. Secretariats and the bureaucracy associated with organizations can be part of this. Norms can develop within organizations and these in turn affect the behavior of states. From this perspective international organizations and states function alongside each other, while also interacting. This chapter takes the latter view; that is, that international organizations generally develop some autonomy, while at the same time both influencing and being influenced by states. The focus here is on intergovernmental organizations but there are also many international nongovernmental organizations (INGOs). INGOs are very important in relation to a number of issues in Asia Pacific. They frequently interact with both states and international (intergovernmental) organizations. In this chapter, however, only passing reference will be made to INGOs.[1]

Given this understanding of international organizations, we can think about their role in Asia Pacific in terms of a number of levels. As we have seen, Asia Pacific encompasses various subregions. The most significant of the subregions in relation to the role of international organizations is Southeast Asia. The Association of Southeast Asian Nations is the most highly developed of the international organizations in Asia Pacific. If we consider Asia Pacific as a whole, two organizations stand out. One is Asia-Pacific Economic Cooperation (APEC), which is, strictly speaking, a forum or grouping rather than an international organization. APEC's original focus was economic, but it has also assumed a more broadly political role. The other Asia Pacific entity is the ASEAN Regional Forum (ARF), which is also a forum rather than an international organization; ARF focuses on security matters. As an alternative to the Asia Pacific focus there are also some groupings (and potentially organizations) that have an East Asian focus (Northeast and Southeast Asia). In the aftermath of the 1997 Asian financial crisis a grouping known as ASEAN Plus Three emerged (the ten ASEAN members plus China, Japan, and South Korea). This grouping (less Burma, Cambodia, and Laos) has also been the basis for the Asian component of the Asia-Europe Meeting (ASEM), which commenced in 1996 (the European Union members constituting the European component). By 2005 there were also moves to broaden ASEAN Plus Three to constitute an East Asian Community.

As well as the international organizations in Asia Pacific that have a regional basis, there are also many globally based organizations that operate in this region. Most obvious in this respect are the United Nations and its various programs and agencies, including the International Monetary Fund and the World Bank. In examining the role of international organizations in the international politics of Asia Pacific it is clearly important to include this global dimension.

This chapter focuses first of all on the regional level, asking why regional organizations or groupings have emerged and what their significance has been. From this perspective we will examine ASEAN as the preeminent example of a subregional organization. Then we will turn to the Asia Pacific groupings, APEC and ARF, asking essentially the same questions. We also need to examine the emergence of the East Asian grouping, ASEAN Plus Three, and the nascent East Asian Community, from a similar perspective. Finally, we will give our attention to the role of global organizations, specifically the United Nations and its agencies, asking what their scope and significance have been. An interesting question to ask is whether these various developments indicate that forms of regional and global governance are emerging in Asia Pacific, with implications in turn for the role of states in the international politics of the region.

■ The Subregional Level: ASEAN

Whether focusing on regionalism in general or specific manifestations of regionalism, it is important to examine the factors that have led to the emergence of this phenomenon. Regionalism is often viewed as a response to globalization. According to this view, states come together in regional organizations or groupings to strengthen their position in relation to the global arena. Insofar as states within a particular region have some common interests, they will be in a better position to advance those interests when they work together. There can also be issues within a particular region that lead states to come together. A regional organization can be a means for regional states to deal with matters affecting their region.

As far as ASEAN is concerned, its origins relate mainly to circumstances prevailing in Southeast Asia in the 1960s.[2] Most germane in this respect was Indonesia's Confrontation (Konfrontasi) of the new Malaysian federation from 1963 to 1966. Indonesia, under the leadership of Sukarno, believed that Malaysia was a neocolonial creation designed to perpetuate British influence in the area. With Sukarno's fall from power after 1965, and the emergence of the New Order under Suharto, there were greater opportunities for promoting harmonious relations among the major noncommunist states of Southeast Asia. The establishment of a new organization incorporating Indonesia would minimize the risks of Indonesia becoming involved in another conflict comparable to Confrontation. The ASEAN Declaration (Bangkok Declaration) of August 1967 did not spell out ASEAN's security role explicitly. While the declaration focused mainly on the promotion of economic and cultural cooperation, however, clearly the organization's broader political and security role was very important. This continued to be the case over subsequent decades. Apart from Indonesia, the founding ASEAN members were Malaysia, the Philippines, Singapore, and Thailand (ASEAN-5). Brunei joined in 1984 (hence ASEAN-6). A major expansion occurred in the 1990s, with Vietnam joining in 1995, Burma and Laos in 1997, and Cambodia in 1999 (ASEAN-10). Intra-Southeast Asian issues have remained important in the different phases in Southeast Asia's development. At the same time ASEAN has played a role in helping to position the region in relation to the world more generally, with reference to both political-security and economic dimensions.[3]

In ASEAN's early years meetings were usually held at foreign minister level. This changed at the Bali summit in February 1976, the first meeting involving heads of government. Circumstances in Southeast Asia were again of particular relevance. With the fall of Saigon to advancing communist forces in April 1975, and the subsequent reunification of Vietnam, the political landscape in Southeast Asia had changed significantly. Even before this development the United States had signaled a reduced involvement in Southeast Asian affairs. ASEAN's declaration of Southeast Asia as a Zone of Peace, Freedom, and Neutrality (ZOPFAN) in 1971 had indicated an aspiration to conduct the affairs of Southeast Asia without outside interference. By 1975–1976 the perception among ASEAN governments was that some substance needed to be given to this aspiration. Strengthening ASEAN was the chosen means. The ASEAN leaders adopted two new statements designed to strengthen the organization, and established a permanent secretariat based in Jakarta. The two statements were the Treaty of Amity and Cooperation in Southeast Asia, and the Declaration of ASEAN Concord. These statements provided much more detail than the Bangkok Declaration of 1967. Although security cooperation was supposed to be on a non-ASEAN basis, cooperation under the new framework would cover virtually the whole range of governmental activities. Under the Treaty of Amity and Cooperation there was provision for the peaceful settlement of disputes (Article 2), as well as cooperation relating to the promotion of "international peace and stability in the region" (Article 4). The "ASEAN way" was to be based on the peaceful resolution of disputes and noninterference in the domestic affairs of member states.

An early challenge for ASEAN in the post-1976 era was the Third Indochina War. This conflict commenced in late 1978 when Vietnamese forces entered Cambodia to depose the Khmer Rouge regime. Vietnam's motivation was not so much to halt the genocide perpetrated by the Khmer Rouge as to counter Pol Pot's anti-Vietnamese position over various issues. Within ASEAN, Thailand was the member that felt most threatened by this development. Thailand and Vietnam were traditionally rivals for influence in Cambodia. Given this situation it was incumbent on ASEAN members to give support to Thailand. Failure to do so would have suggested that ASEAN was impotent in such situations. Nevertheless there was some variation among the ASEAN countries in terms of their approach to this conflict. Singapore was probably most strongly behind Thailand. Malaysia and Indonesia were more willing to pursue accommodation with Vietnam, although neither country breached ASEAN unity on this matter. China was in fact the Khmer Rouge's main backer, but ASEAN and the United States also gave support. Opposition to Vietnam (and the USSR as its main supporter) meant the human rights abuses of the Khmer Rouge were over-looked. While there were differences of emphasis among ASEAN members during the conflict, ASEAN unity was generally maintained. Nevertheless ASEAN was not a major player in this conflict. The most important parties were Vietnam, the pro-Vietnamese government in Cambodia, the Khmer Rouge and other anti-Vietnamese Cambodian groups, China, and the USSR. The resolution of the conflict came about at an external level when agreement was reached between the USSR and China in 1989. This was followed by a UN-brokered agreement among the various Cambodian parties (including the pro-Vietnamese government) in 1991. With ASEAN no longer arrayed against Vietnam, the way was open for the establishment of a more comprehensive organization in the 1990s.

Alongside ASEAN's involvement in Southeast Asian issues, the organization has also played some role in helping its members to position themselves better in relation to the forces of globalization, particularly at an economic level. One way this has been done is through establishing relationships with various countries and organizations as "dialogue partners." In the late 1970s and early 1980s dialogue partners included Japan, the United States, the European Community (now Union), Australia, New Zealand, Canada, and the UN Development Programme. In the 1990s dialogue partner status was extended to South Korea, India, China, and Russia. The ASEAN Post-Ministerial Conferences are an important venue for the discussion of matters of mutual interest with dialogue partners. ASEAN members have generally been able to work on the basis of their collective interests in these discussions.

Achieving economic cooperation in relation to the intra-ASEAN dimension has been more difficult. It has been difficult to establish a common market because most of the ASEAN economies are competitive rather than complementary. Most ASEAN countries have been significant as exporters of raw materials, but with attention increasingly shifting to export-oriented manufacturing industries. Singapore as a commercial entrepôt and Brunei as a small oil state are in a different category again. Schemes for promoting intra-ASEAN economic cooperation have faced the problem that member states do not want to specialize in particular areas if that means giving up or reducing some area of economic activity that they see as promising. Nevertheless an agreement for an ASEAN free trade area (AFTA) was concluded in 1992. This promised phased reductions on tariffs on manufactured goods within the ASEAN area.

While AFTA was significant, the major development affecting ASEAN was the expansion of its membership during the 1990s. Again, this was primarily a response to Southeast Asian circumstances. With the end of the Third Indochina War there was an opportunity to expand ASEAN to make it a comprehensive Southeast Asian organization. Instead of having Southeast Asia riven by war, the goal of settling disputes peacefully among the Southeast Asian countries might finally mean something. By expanding to Vietnam in the first instance, and then taking in Burma, Laos, and Cambodia, it was hoped that the economic development and political stability of these countries would be facilitated. According to the dominant view within ASEAN, contentious issues such as human rights in Burma were best dealt with by a policy of engagement. The new ASEAN members had a traditional view of sovereignty, aiming to minimize external involvement in what they regarded as domestic affairs. At the same time there was a push in the late 1990s, supported particularly by Thailand and the Philippines, for "flexible engagement" as a means of dealing with the increasing number of issues that transcended national boundaries.[4] Apart from human rights issues, another example was the smoke haze generated by illegal forest fires in Sumatra, and affecting not just Indonesia but also Malaysia and Singapore. While ASEAN members in the end supported a more restrictive approach, the very nature of many of the problems in the region has led to more flexibility in practice.

ASEAN has had a role not just in helping to position its members better in relation to the forces of globalization, but also in the context of broader developments in Asia Pacific. ASEAN has had a role in shaping the form of both APEC and ARF, which are discussed in the next section of this chapter. ASEAN has had an influence as the most highly organized of the regional organizations. This in turn means that the Southeast Asian countries as a group have more influence than might otherwise be the case.

Despite the influence that ASEAN has in this organizational context, the role that it has played in many of the crises affecting the region in recent times has been less than one might assume. Although it is the most highly organized of the Asia Pacific regional organizations, this does not necessarily mean that it has the collective resources available when they are needed. ASEAN members are often very sensitive about respecting the sovereignty of fellow members and not acting against the perceived interests of members. In the Asian financial crisis of 1997 a number of ASEAN countries were affected, but ASEAN lacked the wherewithal to respond effectively. The main response came from the global level (see below). In the case of the East Timor crisis in 1999, ASEAN members again lacked the resources to respond, but more particularly did not wish to offend Indonesia.[5] Nevertheless some ASEAN members, particularly Thailand and the Philippines, did contribute significantly to the peacekeeping operation in East Timor. In the aftermath of the tsunami of Boxing Day 2004, the most effective response came from external powers and the United Nations rather than from ASEAN. The question of having the necessary resources and the ability to deploy them was most relevant in this instance.

ASEAN's lack of effectiveness in dealing with recent crises does not mean that the organization should be written off. While not being decisive in these situations, it has helped to facilitate the response that has occurred. ASEAN has helped its members in responding to globalization and other external forces impinging on Southeast Asia. Perhaps most importantly it has provided the basis for a security community in Southeast Asia.[6] This has done much to enhance security in Southeast Asia at the interstate level. Contrary to the situation that frequently prevailed in Southeast Asia up to the 1980s it is now virtually unthinkable that armed conflict would occur among states in Southeast Asia. State-society tensions remain, of course, but the practical import of the ASEAN way has been to reduce, and perhaps eliminate, interstate conflict in Southeast Asia.

▓ The Asia Pacific Level: APEC and the ASEAN Regional Forum

At the Asia Pacific level the development of regional institutions has been relatively weak. This reflects the weakness of "Asia Pacific" as a regional identity, which in turn makes it more difficult to strengthen the sense of attachment to this region. These observations can be borne out by examining the two major instances of regionalism in Asia Pacific: APEC and the ASEAN Regional Forum.

Asia-Pacific Economic Cooperation

When it was formed in 1989 APEC was the culmination of attempts to promote an Asia Pacific economic regionalism extending back over two decades. The most significant earlier grouping was the Pacific Economic Cooperation Conference (later Council) (PECC) involving representatives from government, business, and academia. Although the specific call for the inaugural meeting of APEC came from Prime Minister Bob Hawke of Australia in 1989, Japanese support for this initiative was crucial.[7] From Japan's perspective APEC provided a means for broadening and strengthening its relations with other Asia Pacific countries. The United States was concerned that it could be excluded from such an important development and lobbied for inclusion in APEC. The inaugural members of APEC were thus Australia, Japan, and the United States, together with Canada, New

Zealand, South Korea, and the then six members of ASEAN. In 1991 China became a member, along with Taiwan and Hong Kong as "economies." Membership expanded further in 1993 with the admission of Mexico and Papua New Guinea, followed by Chile in 1994, and then Peru, Russia, and Vietnam in 1997.

APEC's objectives focused on trade liberalization both within the region and on a global level. Among member countries APEC sought to reduce trade barriers according to the principles of "open regionalism." This meant that any reductions would also be available to nonmember countries. APEC did not envisage itself as simply another trading bloc. At a global level APEC was relevant in the context of the Uruguay Round of GATT. The Uruguay Round lasted from 1986 to 1993 and culminated in the establishment of the World Trade Organization as the successor to GATT. By working together APEC members could augment the campaign in favor of greater trade liberalization.

APEC's political profile was strengthened from the time of its Seattle meeting in 1993 when President Clinton arranged that the annual summits would be meetings of "economic leaders" (meaning heads of government except in the cases of Taiwan and Hong Kong). With the conclusion of the Uruguay Round, APEC's attention focused more exclusively on the promotion of trade liberalization among its own members. An important statement was the Bogor Declaration in 1994, committing members to free trade by 2010 for the industrialized economies, and by 2020 for the developing economies. In practice this appeared to be more of a statement of desirable aims than a binding agreement to be implemented. Domestic pressures in member countries frequently undermined attempts to liberalize trade. An instance of this was when Japan refused to take part in two sectors of APEC's program for Early Voluntary Sector Liberalization (EVSL) in 1997: fish and fish products, and forestry products.[8] This was symptomatic of APEC's inability to deliver. At the same time APEC was not significantly involved in dealing with the big issue of the time, the Asian financial crisis. APEC's weakness in providing concrete benefits to members was a factor in the increasing popularity of proposals for bilateral trade agreements. If multilateralism was not working, then members would look at alternatives. Multilateral agreements were more difficult to achieve but were more beneficial in the long term. Governments, however, were frequently influenced by short-term factors and the need to demonstrate concrete gains.

Given that APEC has not delivered what it originally promised, its summit meetings remain significant as the only occasion when the leaders of the Asia Pacific countries can consult broadly on the political issues facing the region. The Auckland summit in September 1999 was fortuitously at the same time that the crisis in East Timor was running out of control. Diplomacy at the summit assisted greatly in winning the political support necessary for international intervention to occur in East Timor with the authorization of the United Nations. The Shanghai summit in October 2001, just after the September 11 attacks, provided a good platform for President George W. Bush to mobilize support for the war on terrorism from the Asia Pacific countries. Low-level economic cooperation will continue in APEC, but it appears unlikely to fulfill its original potential for a more ambitious form of economic regionalism.

The ASEAN Regional Forum

ARF is explicitly concerned with Asia Pacific security.[9] While Asia Pacific in scope, this is not reflected in its title. It functions as a multilateral security forum under the auspices of ASEAN. This reflects ASEAN's major role in the founding of the forum. In the early 1990s there were various proposals to establish a multilateral security arrangement in Asia Pacific. In July 1990 Gareth Evans, the Australian foreign minister, proposed an Asian version of the Organization for Security and Cooperation in Europe (OSCE); Joe Clark, the Canadian foreign minister, had a similar proposal. Critics argued that this type of organization would have been too highly structured for Asian circumstances; in addition, Australia and Canada as middle powers lacked the political weight of other actors in the region. In July 1991 the Japanese foreign minister, Nakayama Taro, suggested a multilateral security forum based on the ASEAN Post-Ministerial Conference. Both the United States and China were skeptical. The United States believed such arrangements might undermine its various bilateral security alliances in the region. China saw multilateralism as a device for containing its own role in the region. The United States and China were therefore unlikely to propose any multilateral arrangement themselves. A proposal emanating from Japan would encounter opposition from the other major powers, as well as reviving anti-Japanese memories from the Pacific war in a number of countries. A proposal from ASEAN was least likely to attract opposition. The organization could not be accused of seeking regional domination, and ASEAN already had dialogue relationships with a number of relevant powers. From ASEAN's perspective a new security forum would be a way of enhancing its ability to influence developments within its own region, and within the wider Asia Pacific. In the post–Cold War situation there was an increasing awareness that Southeast Asia was part of a wider region.

Motivated by this kind of thinking, and with the support of a number of relevant countries, ASEAN was successful in winning support for the establishment of the new forum, with the first meeting being held in Bangkok in July 1994. Meetings were subsequently held on an annual basis, rotating among the different ASEAN members, and with the foreign minister of the host country acting as chair. The original membership consisted of the ASEAN-6, together with ASEAN's dialogue partners and other significant regional countries. By the end of the 1990s membership extended to the ASEAN-10, Australia, Canada, China, the European Union, India, Japan, Mongolia, New Zealand, Papua New Guinea, Russia, South Korea, and the United States; North Korea became a member in 2000.[10]

With ASEAN in the driver's seat, the ASEAN Regional Forum was to function on the basis of ASEAN principles, that is, primarily through consultation and dialogue. The 1995 meeting envisaged three stages in the development of the forum's role in regional security measures: confidence building measures, preventive diplomacy, and conflict resolution. In practice the emphasis has been on dialogue, promoting opportunities for exchanges among parties involved in security issues in the region. This has not included the Taiwan issue, however, given that China regards this conflict as a domestic matter. ARF has not played a significant role in relation to the Korean issue. The forum has never pretended that it could intervene in a decisive way in relation to any of the conflicts in the region. Despite their initial skepticism, both China and the United States have seen some positive roles for the forum. From China's perspective, provided that Taiwan is kept off the agenda, the forum provides a venue for building bridges with its regional neighbors. The United States has seen a role for the forum in complementing US involvement in the region through other means, particularly the US-centered network of bilateral alliances. ARF contributes at a low level to a sense of Asia Pacific identity, in this case centered on ASEAN itself, but its significance should not be exaggerated.

▨ The East Asian Alternative

The alternative to "Asia Pacific" as a regional construct is one based on East Asia. In December 1990 Mahathir, the prime minister of Malaysia, had argued in favor of establishing an East Asian Economic Group.[11] Mahathir believed that such a group would be better than APEC in protecting the interests of East Asian countries. The proposed group would have excluded the United States and other Western countries, such as Australia and New Zealand. Japan in particular was not prepared to go in this direction for fear of damaging its relationship with the United States; many other East Asian countries were unenthusiastic too. Mahathir adjusted his proposal to focus on an East Asian Economic Caucus that could function on an informal level in the context of broader regional groupings such as APEC. The idea of an East Asian grouping did not die and came to the fore again in different circumstances in the late 1990s.[12]

The establishment of the ASEM in 1996 provided an opportunity for East Asian countries (ASEAN-7, China, Japan, South Korea) to come together in an organizational setting without the involvement of the United States. More significant, however, in the emergence of an East Asian grouping, was the Asian financial crisis of 1997. APEC was of little importance in dealing with this crisis, while there was also a widespread perception in East Asia that the United States and the International Monetary Fund had been unsympathetic to regional concerns in their response. Japanese proposals for an Asian Monetary Fund to offer assistance on more generous terms received short shrift from the United States.

The development of an East Asian grouping focused on meetings between ASEAN and China, Japan, and South Korea, known as ASEAN Plus Three (APT).[13] APT began as an informal meeting of heads of government at the ASEAN summit meeting in Kuala Lumpur in 1997.[14] Its main concrete achievement to date has been the conclusion of a currency swap agreement by APT finance ministers. This agreement, known as the Chiang Mai Initiative (CMI), was reached in May 2000 at the time of the annual meeting of the Asian Development Bank.[15] APT countries would assist each other with currency transfers in the event the currency of a member country came under threat in the context of international financial markets; assistance from Japan would be most relevant in this respect. APT has also provided a forum for considering the future direction of East Asian regionalism. There has been some perception of a need to compete with regional groupings such as the European Union and the North American Free Trade Agreement. In 1998 the second APT summit meeting in Hanoi appointed an East Asian Vision Group to assess future directions. Reporting in 2001, this group proposed an East Asia Summit in 2005, with a view to establishing an East Asian Community.[16] The summit took place in Kuala Lumpur in December 2005, but did not lead to the declaration of a new community as such; the main commitment was to hold a regular East Asia Summit.[17]

With these various developments occurring, it is important to assess the prospects for APT and the proposed East Asian Community. While various factors have contributed to the enhanced significance of APT, is it likely to do any better than a grouping such as APEC, or indeed ASEAN?

Problems arising from competing interests are likely to be a major constraint with APT, as with APEC and ASEAN. The ability to overcome these differences is often limited. Competition between China and Japan is one important limiting factor; the position adopted by the United States is another. Nor can one say that the ASEAN countries are necessarily united on the future development of APT.

Japan needs to be involved in APT to ensure that it maintains its influence in Southeast Asia; the grouping also has some significance for Japan's relations with its Northeast Asian neighbors.[18] Japan wants to make sure that it is not disadvantaged vis-à-vis China in relations with the ASEAN countries. China and ASEAN agreed in 2001 to pursue discussions on establishing a China-ASEAN FTA. Japan's preference has been to negotiate FTAs with individual Southeast Asian countries (most notably with Singapore, and potentially with Malaysia, the Philippines, and Thailand).[19] Although ASEAN announced in 2005 that it would commence negotiations for a Japan-ASEAN FTA, Japan appears to have no interest in a closed economic regionalism. If there is to be an East Asian FTA it should be based on the concept of open regionalism and not damage Japan's relations with the United States. Japan favored expanding APT to include Australia, New Zealand, and India; it was agreed that the East Asia Summit in 2005 would include these countries.

From China's perspective APT offers opportunities to expand its influence in relation to Southeast Asia and to appear as a leader of East Asian regionalism.[20] The proposed China-ASEAN FTA would mainly benefit China given its cheap labor costs and other production advantages. Among the ASEAN countries, Singapore and Thailand appear most interested in the proposed FTA; other members have become more aware of the disadvantages as discussion has proceeded.[21]

The United States would oppose the development of an East Asian bloc where it believed its own interests were being disadvantaged.[22] A grouping that was based on open regionalism and developed in partnership with the United States would be preferred. Hence the United States preferred the approach supported by Japan rather than more restrictive proposals. If there is a move in the direction of a closed East Asian regionalism, the United States is likely to try to subvert such a scheme. It would use its influence with key players, and possibly also try to revive APEC. Another approach would be to give increased attention to promoting global multilateralism through the World Trade Organization. One of the reasons for the growth of FTAs and a more restrictive regionalism has been the lack of progress in liberalizing conditions of trade at a world level through the WTO.

■ The Global Dimension:
The United Nations and Its Agencies

Turning from the regionally based international organizations, we also need to examine the role of global organizations in Asia Pacific. As with the regional level, the focus is on intergovernmental organizations rather than international nongovernmental organizations. This means giving particular attention to the United Nations and its agencies. We begin with an overview of the United Nations system, and then assess the nature and significance of that system's involvement in relation to security, economic, and social issues in Asia Pacific.[23]

The United Nations, founded in 1945, at the end of World War II, is a complex organization.[24] Public attention often focuses on the role of the General Assembly, the Security Council, and the Secretary-General, but there are many other aspects to the UN. The UN's principles, structure, and rules are to be found in its charter. The General Assembly and the Security Council are among the UN's principal organs. The General Assembly is the UN's representative body, with all member states having one vote. The General Assembly can pass resolutions and establish subsidiary bodies, but when a crisis arises it is far less significant than the Security Council. The Security Council was intended by the UN's founders to give teeth to the organization. Resolutions passed by the council would be binding on all UN members. However, the five permanent members of the Security Council (China, France, Russia, the United Kingdom, and the United States) can veto resolutions. (There are also ten nonpermanent members that do not have this veto power.) The Secretary-General's role is to implement the decisions of the Security Council and the General Assembly, but he also acts as a troubleshooter and facilitator in relation to many issues. The Secretary-General heads the UN Secretariat, the main element in the UN bureaucracy, which in turn consists of many departments organized to carry out the UN's role. Apart from the General Assembly, the Security Council, and the Secretariat, other principal organs include the Trusteeship Council (now defunct), the Economic and Social Council (ECOSOC), and the International Court of Justice (ICJ). ECOSOC consists of fifty-four state members elected by the General Assembly for overlapping terms of three years. The economic and social functions of the UN are focused in this body, which also exercises oversight over functional commissions (such as the Commission on Human Rights) and the various regional commissions (in Asia Pacific the Economic and Social Commission for Asia and the Pacific [ESCAP]). The ICJ embodies the UN's judicial function, with fifteen judges chosen for nine year terms by the General Assembly and the Security Council (but with permanent members not having a veto); it sits in The Hague.

The UN does not just consist of principal organs, but also of many programs and funds, and specialized agencies. Programs and funds usually have a more direct relationship with the principal organs, in particular ECOSOC. Examples include the United Nations Development Programme (UNDP), the United Nations Environment Programme (UNEP), and the United Nations High Commissioner for Refugees (UNHCR). Specialized agencies also report to ECOSOC, but in practice they are more autonomous than the programs and funds. Many major international organizations are UN specialized agencies. Examples include the International Monetary Fund (IMF), the World Bank Group, the International Labour Organization (ILO), the Food and Agriculture Organization (FAO), the World Health Organization (WHO), and the United Nations Educational, Scientific and Cultural Organization (UNESCO). The IMF and World Bank are also known as the Bretton Woods institutions, after the conference that led to their founding. In 1995 they were joined by the World Trade Organization (WTO), which replaced the earlier General Agreement on Tariffs and Trade (GATT). The WTO is usually described as a "related organization" of the UN.

Security Issues

Keeping in mind the complexities of the UN as an organization or system, we can assess its significance for Asia Pacific first of all in relation to security issues.[25] Here we are concerned most of all with the involvement of the Security Council, the General Assembly, and the Secretary-General both in relation to specific crises and ongoing issues. At this level the UN has played a minor but not insignificant role in Asia Pacific. One factor lessening the significance of the UN is that three of the Permanent Five (P-5) members of the Security Council are directly engaged in Asia Pacific (China, Russia, and the United States). These powers can veto (or threaten to veto) UN involvement in issues that directly affect their own position. The most significant involvement of the UN in Asia Pacific security was at the time of the Korean War (1950–1953). The response to the North Korean attack in June 1950 was under UN auspices but only because the Soviet Union was boycotting the Security Council at the time in support of the claim by the People's Republic of China to occupy the Chinese seat (rather than the Nationalist government, the Republic of China). Since neither the Soviet Union nor China (the Communist government) was involved in the Security Council, the United States was able to use the UN for its own ends. This certainly helped to legitimize the US-led counterattack, but it was predominantly a US operation.

Subsequently, in terms of the major security issues in Asia Pacific, the involvement of the UN was generally only a minor aspect or perhaps not a feature at all. China has vehemently opposed any UN involvement in relation to the Taiwan issue, since it regards that issue as a domestic matter. The same constraint applies in relation to issues such as Tibet. As far as the Korean issue is concerned, the major powers have generally preferred to deal with that matter on their own or in conjunction with the two Korean states, although there is a residual UN involvement. The UN did not have significant involvement in relation to the Vietnam War during the 1960s and early 1970s, or in relation to the Cambodian conflict after 1978 and during the 1980s (Third Indochina War). US involvement was the major constraint in the first instance, while Soviet backing for Vietnam was most significant in the second.

In the case of the Cambodian conflict the situation began to change once Vietnam, supported by the Soviet Union, sought a settlement. With the major powers agreed on the need to end the conflict, there was scope for the UN to become involved in facilitating and implementing agreement among the various Cambodian parties. Following the Paris peace agreement in October 1991 between the pro-Vietnamese Hun Sen government and the three anti-Vietnamese parties, the UN became involved in overseeing transitional arrangements in 1992–1993 leading to elections in May 1993. At its height the United Nations Transitional Authority in Cambodia (UNTAC) had about 16,000 military personnel and 3,500 civilian police, with some forty-five countries contributing. UNTAC's leader was Yasushi Akashi, special representative of the UN Secretary-General; the leader of the military component was General John Sanderson of Australia. Although the Hun Sen party won fewer votes than the Sihanoukists (royalists), the former group used its dominant position in government to control the coalition that was set up after the election. The outcome was not necessarily democratic, and some instability continued. However, Cambodia was no longer a war zone and was clearly more stable than it had been.

The other major contribution by the UN to Asia Pacific security in recent times has been in relation to East Timor. Again this was a situation where the major powers did not have their own interests directly at stake. There was thus more scope for UN involvement if other circumstances were also favorable. The UN had been involved in facilitating discussions between Indonesia and Portugal over East Timor since 1982. These discussions became more significant after Suharto fell from power in 1998 and interim president B. J. Habibie then committed himself to a vote on the issue of autonomy versus independence for East Timor. The UN was involved in organizing the vote, held on 30 August 1999, through the United Nations Mission in East Timor (UNAMET). The issue of military intervention in

East Timor arose when violence, orchestrated by the Indonesian military, erupted in response to the strongly proindependence vote. A UN-authorized force, known as International Force East Timor (INTERFET), was dispatched to the territory by late September. Leadership of the force, and the major military contribution, came from Australia. The United Nations Transitional Administration in East Timor (UNTAET) subsequently replaced INTERFET, assuming not just the security function but the whole array of tasks required to prepare East Timor for independence. The UN became the sovereign power in East Timor, with Sergio Vieira de Mello of Brazil as UNTAET's administrator. Although East Timor is smaller than Cambodia in all respects, the scope of UN involvement was much more ambitious. It went beyond peacekeeping to become an exercise in peace building. Although the UN has been criticized for lacking the capacity to carry out its tasks in East Timor adequately, independence did come in May 2002. The UN remained involved for a few years through the United Nations Mission of Support in East Timor (UNMISET). East Timor is no longer a center of international contention in the way that it was before 1999, but continues to face many problems of its own (highlighted by the mid-2006 crisis).

UN involvement in security issues in Asia Pacific in the future is most likely to occur in situations where the interests of the major powers are not directly involved. This means that Southeast Asia would be a more likely arena than Northeast Asia. At the same time most Southeast Asian countries have a traditional view of sovereignty, adhering strictly to the principle of nonintervention. For external intervention to occur, under UN auspices or any other auspices for that matter, there would have to be a very serious humanitarian crisis, involving loss of life on a very large scale. Even then it is worth recalling that the genocide in Cambodia under the Khmer Rouge between 1975 and 1978 did not lead to UN or any other form of international intervention. When Vietnam intervened in 1978 it did not use humanitarian arguments to justify its actions; the emphasis was on the need to counter the anti-Vietnamese policies of Pol Pot. Similarly, the loss of life in East Timor under Indonesian rule did not lead to international intervention until the very specific circumstances of September 1999 arose. While there are many situations in Southeast Asia where lives are being lost, these relate to regional conflicts of different kinds (as in Indonesia) or occasional outbursts by military regimes (as in Burma). There are no "killing fields" that might provide the basis for UN intervention.

Economic Issues

In relation to economic issues, we can make a distinction between financial and trade issues on the one hand, and issues of development on the other. The IMF and the WTO are particularly relevant to the first aspect; various specialized agencies and programs are relevant to the second.

The IMF attracted a lot of publicity in Asia Pacific at the time of the Asian financial crisis in 1997. Its general brief is to promote stability in the international monetary system. If the currency of a particular country comes under pressure, then the IMF can offer assistance. This assistance will normally be offered subject to the recipient country undertaking economic restructuring of various kinds. The restructuring represents the IMF prescription for avoiding a recurrence of the problem. Voting power in the IMF is based on the contributions made by members, which means that the United States is the single most important member with normally almost 20 percent of the voting strength. Structural adjustment packages offered by the IMF are financed on the basis of voluntary contributions; again this normally means that the United States has the greatest influence. At the time of the Asian financial crisis the IMF offered assistance to Indonesia, South Korea, and Thailand as the most affected countries. The United States was most influential in determining the shape of the rescue packages. Asian countries were critical of the conditions imposed, arguing that the social consequences would be too severe. However, the United States scotched proposals for an Asian Monetary Fund that would have been more generous in the terms it offered. The subsequent development of a more strongly East Asian regionalism, most clearly evident in ASEAN Plus Three, has been partly in response to the previous experience with the IMF. However, these regional initiatives are unlikely to reduce the significance of the IMF.

Many regional organizations or groupings, whether centered on East Asia, Asia Pacific, or Southeast Asia, have a major focus on trade issues. At the same time most Asia Pacific countries, including China most significantly since 2001, are members of the WTO (Russia and Vietnam are important nonmembers). While regional groupings have frequently sought to promote economic cooperation among their members, they have also functioned as caucuses or lobby groups in relation to global trade negotiations. This was the case with APEC in the Uruguay Round of GATT (1986–1994, although APEC was not formed until 1989). In the case of the WTO the Doha Round was initiated in 2001, but progress has been slow. Key players have been unwilling to make the concessions necessary for further trade liberalization to occur. Domestic pressures are often the most significant factor in this respect. Groups such as APEC, ASEAN Plus Three, and ASEAN can act as lobby groups within the global trade negotiations. However, because of the slow progress, there has been a shift of emphasis toward bilateral and regional free trade agreements. While it is understandable that such jockeying for advantage occurs, in the long term these agreements are unlikely to offer the same gains as an agreement negotiated on a global basis; not only that, but they are likely to impede such an agreement and, at worst, encourage the development of closed rival trading blocs.

Apart from the issues of finance and trade, Asia Pacific is also a major center for global organizations concerned with development. Many Asia Pacific countries have (or had) Third World economies, and hence have a vital interest in development issues. Among the specialized agencies, the World Bank is involved in offering loans on a concessional basis to assist development (at a regional level the activities of the Asian Development Bank should also be mentioned[26]). Among the UN programs, the UNDP is most relevant as a channel for development cooperation. With a Regional Bureau for Asia and the Pacific based in Kuala Lumpur, the UNDP also has country offices based in most of the states of the region. It has a number of regionally based programs, and works closely with regional organizations such as ASEAN.

Social Issues

Development issues link closely with social issues more broadly. Development involves more than achieving economic growth, but also has an important social dimension; quality of life issues are involved. Security also has an important social dimension, as the concept of human security makes clear; any matter affecting the well-being of an individual can be seen as relevant to human security. Keeping in mind this broad context, examples of social issues in Asia Pacific that have involved the UN system are health, drug trafficking, and refugees. The UN has also become involved in dealing with natural disasters such as the tsunami of Boxing Day 2004.

Health issues have been highlighted in recent years through the impact of pandemics such as HIV/AIDS and SARS (severe acute respiratory syndrome); concerns about avian influenza (bird flu) raise similar issues. Although Asia Pacific as a region has been less affected by HIV/AIDS than Africa, it has had a big impact in certain countries (see the discussion in Chapter 10). In per capita terms, Cambodia, Thailand, and Burma have been the worst affected among the East Asian countries (and Papua New Guinea in the Pacific Islands region); the issue has also become more serious in Vietnam, China, and Indonesia. SARS was a major issue affecting Asia Pacific countries in 2002–2003, with major outbreaks in southern China, Vietnam, Hong Kong, Singapore, Taiwan, and Toronto (Canada). Bird flu, with its potential to infect humans, was detected in Hong Kong in 2003 and some Southeast Asian countries from 2004. In all these situations the World Health Organization, in conjunction with local health authorities, has played a major role in leading and coordinating the response. In relation to HIV/AIDS, there is also a specialized program, the Joint United Nations Programme on HIV/AIDS (UNAIDS). Bird flu involves not just the WHO, but organizations concerned with animal issues: the Food and Agriculture Organization (FAO) and the World Organization for Animal Health (known as OIE after its French name, Office International des Epizooties).[27]

Drug trafficking is a major issue in Asia Pacific, as in many other regions of the world. A particular area of concern is the Golden Triangle linking Burma with parts of neighboring Thailand and Laos. Heroin derived from opium production in Burma is shipped through Thailand and Laos to markets throughout Asia Pacific and other parts of the world. Although Burma claims to be antidrugs, there is a widespread perception that its military regime profits from drug trafficking. Action against the drug trade involves cooperation among various countries, with the UN taking a leading role through the United Nations Office on Drugs and Crime (UNODC), part of the Secretariat.[28]

In relation to refugees, UN involvement is mainly through the United Nations High Commissioner for Refugees (UNHCR).[29] In the post-1945 period conflicts such as the Chinese civil war, the Korean War, and the Vietnam War were a major source of refugees. In the late 1970s and early 1980s many people fled Vietnam and Cambodia, responding to changes in those countries (unification under communist auspices in Vietnam, and the rule of the Khmer Rouge in Cambodia). In the 1990s Cambodia, East Timor, and Burma were important sources of refugees. In current circumstances Burma is the main source of refugees in the region. However, there are also situations involving displaced persons, with over one million in Indonesia because of the regional conflicts there. Displaced people only become refugees when they cross an international border, apply for asylum, and are accepted as meeting the criteria set down in the 1951 Refugee Convention. The UNHCR's brief is to care for refugees rather than for displaced persons. While refugees from Burma are the main concern for UNHCR in Asia Pacific currently, the situations in Indonesia and North Korea also have the potential to generate refugees.

A good example of UN involvement in dealing with natural disasters is the tsunami of Boxing Day 2004. The worst affected region was Aceh in Indonesia with about 130,000 killed, although Thailand and Burma also suffered among the Southeast Asian countries (and, further west, India, Sri Lanka, and the Maldives). While several UN agencies were involved in dealing with various aspects of the disaster, the major coordinating body was the Office for the Coordination of Humanitarian Affairs, located in the Secretariat and headed by Under Secretary-General for Humanitarian Affairs and

Emergency Relief Jan Egeland. Initially the United States established a core group, consisting of itself, Japan, India, and Australia (and later the Netherlands and Canada), to organize an immediate response to the situation. This action was motivated by a perceived slowness on the part of the UN, but following a summit meeting in early January 2005, the UN resumed the main coordinating role.[30] Nevertheless the countries of the core group, together with others such as Germany, played a major role in contributing funds and other resources (such as personnel and equipment) to deal with the crisis. The particular example of the 2004 tsunami might be taken as illustrating how the UN becomes involved in dealing with complex human emergencies. Sometimes these emergencies might relate more obviously to security situations, but clearly natural disasters have major implications for human security.[31]

*   *   *

Does the role of regional and global organizations in Asia Pacific international politics suggest that regional governance and global governance[32] are emerging as important features of the region? As a term, "governance" is broader in scope than "government." Government refers to the body that exercises formal authority within a state; in a federal system authority is divided between the national and subnational levels of government (the latter confusingly often termed "states," as in the United States or Australia). If world government were ever to arise, it would be in the context of a situation where existing national states had ceded authority to a world state. Governance is a term suggesting that "governing" can encompass a variety of actors: not just states, but also international organizations of various kinds, and indeed nongovernment actors in some instances. Another term used is "regime."[33] A regime refers to how issues of a particular kind are handled by the various actors involved; it will entail implicit "rules." One can talk about an international refugee regime or a nuclear nonproliferation regime, for example.

Relating these terms to Asia Pacific, regional governance would mean that a situation had arisen where regional institutions had become so significant that they now shared the task of governing with the various regional states. However, regional institutions are generally so weak that the term "regional governance" is not really applicable. This is certainly the situation when thinking in terms of broad regional categories such as Asia Pacific or East Asia. Even in Southeast Asia, where ASEAN is well established, the organization is too weak to warrant the use of regional governance as a concept. It is more accurate to think in terms of states being the preeminent actors (taking account of the range of states), with regional organizations constituting another set of relevant actors. These organizations might have limited autonomy in some respects, but are generally subordinate to states.

Assessing the relevance of global governance in Asia Pacific raises issues similar to those involved in assessing regional governance. Certainly a range of global organizations, mainly from the UN system, is involved in the region, and contributes to the task of governing. However, as with the regional organizations, the shift of authority from states to global organizations is generally too limited to justify claims that Asia Pacific has become part of a system of global governance.

Rather than using terms such as regional governance and global governance, it might be more helpful to delineate the various kinds of regimes that exist in Asia Pacific. For any given issue it is possible to define the roles played by states, international organizations, and other actors. Part of the task would involve characterizing the rules and norms that determine how issues are dealt with. Such an approach would generally indicate that while states are mostly preeminent in the various regimes affecting Asia Pacific, there is also increasing scope for both regional and global organizations to play a role.

▓ Notes

1. A reference work on international organizations (governmental and nongovernmental) in Asia Pacific is McDougall, *Historical Dictionary of International Organizations in Asia and the Pacific.* See also Wesley, ed., *The Regional Organizations of the Asia-Pacific.*

2. For background on the international politics of Southeast Asia, see Chapter 10 of this book.

3. A comprehensive reader on ASEAN is Siddique and Kumar, comp., *The 2nd ASEAN Reader.*

4. See Henderson, *Reassessing ASEAN,* pp. 48–55.

5. See Dupont, "ASEAN's Response to the East Timor Crisis."

6. See Acharya, *Constructing a Security Community in Southeast Asia.*

7. See Terada, "The Genesis of APEC."

8. See Ravenhill, *APEC and the Construction of Pacific Rim Regionalism,* pp. 180–184; Wesley, "APEC's Mid-Life Crisis?"

9. An early assessment of the ASEAN Regional Forum is Leifer, *The ASEAN Regional Forum.* More recent assessments include Garofano, "Power, Institutions, and the ASEAN Regional Forum"; Heller, "The Relevance of the ASEAN Regional Forum (ARF) for Regional Security in the Asia-Pacific"; Emmers, *Cooperative Security and the Balance of Power in ASEAN and the ARF,* chapters 1 and 5; Caballero-Anthony, *Regional Security in Southeast Asia,* chapter 4.

10. Caballero-Anthony, *Regional Security in Southeast Asia,* p. 128.

11. See Higgott and Stubbs, "Competing Conceptions of Economic Regionalism," pp. 516–535.

12. Book-length studies on recent developments in East Asian regionalism include Lincoln, *East Asian Economic Regionalism,* and Pempel, ed., *Remapping East Asia.*

13. On ASEAN Plus Three, see Stubbs, "ASEAN Plus Three"; Beeson, "ASEAN Plus Three and the Rise of Reactionary Regionalism"; Webber, "Two Funerals and a Wedding?" especially pp. 356–365; Hund, "ASEAN Plus Three."

14. Stubbs, "ASEAN Plus Three," p. 443.

15. Ibid., p. 449.

16. Ibid., p. 443; Zhang Yunling, "Emerging New East Asian Regionalism," pp. 59–60, 62.

17. Kuala Lumpur Declaration, 14 December 2005, www.aseansec.org/18098 .htm (accessed 18 February 2006).

18. On Japan's approach to APT, see Hund, "ASEAN Plus Three," pp. 393–394, 398–402; Gilson, "Complex Regional Multilateralism," pp. 84–87.

19. Zhang Yunling, "Emerging New East Asian Regionalism," pp. 57, 58.

20. On China's approach to APT, see Hund, "ASEAN Plus Three," pp. 394–395, 402–404; Ahn, "The Rise of China and the Future of East Asian Integration."

21. See Hund, "ASEAN Plus Three," pp. 396–397.

22. For a recommended US approach to East Asian regionalism, see Lincoln, *East Asian Economic Regionalism,* chapter 10.

23. A useful reference on the United Nations in Southeast Asia and the South Pacific is Alley, *The United Nations in Southeast Asia and the South Pacific.*

24. A useful general reference on the United Nations is Mingst and Karns, ed., *The United Nations in the Post–Cold War Era.*

25. See Foot, "The UN System's Contribution to Asia-Pacific Security Architecture"; "UN Peace Operations and Asian Security."

26. See Kappagoda, *The Asian Development Bank.*

27. For further information on these health issues, refer to the Web sites of relevant organizations, especially the World Health Organization (www.who.int) and the Joint United Nations Programme on HIV/AIDS (www.unaids.org).

28. See United Nations Office on Drugs and Crime, www.unodc.org.

29. On the issue of refugees, see the discussion of unregulated people movements in Chapter 10.

30. Huxley, "The Tsunami and Security," pp. 124–125.

31. See Kent, "International Humanitarian Crises."

32. A useful reference on global governance is Held and McGrew, ed., *Governing Globalization.*

33. See Krasner, ed., *International Regimes.*

Part 5
Conclusion

Emerging Themes | 14

The first chapter of this book outlined some approaches to explaining the dynamics of international politics, giving attention to realism, liberalism (or liberal institutionalism), various critical approaches, and a culturalistic approach. At this point it is useful to review these approaches in terms of how they contribute to an understanding of Asia Pacific international politics, particularly in light of the topics that have been discussed. This will also provide a starting point for assessing likely future directions in Asia Pacific international politics.

■ Reviewing Approaches

Throughout this book there has been a strong focus on the role of states, and particularly the major powers (United States, China, Japan). This might suggest an essentially realist analysis. Insofar as realism is an important underlying theme, however, it is subject to various modifications. It is a realism that is historically grounded, rather than deriving from the neorealist perspective with its assumptions about states behaving primarily on the basis of the position they occupy in the international system. The argument presented in this book is that an understanding of the role and interactions of the major powers can provide a significant insight into the dynamics of international politics in the region as a whole. In understanding the role of each power it is important to take account of the impact of historical experience and domestic politics. Perceptions are important. Each state might be influenced by various material factors, but its international trajectory is by no means predetermined. The emphasis on the political-strategic dimension in discussing the role of each power might suggest the influence of realism, but there is also some emphasis on economics and other issues such as human rights.

Moving beyond the direct focus on the major powers, assessing the significance of realism becomes more complex. In relation to the two flashpoints of Northeast Asia, Taiwan and Korea, we saw that the major powers were directly involved but that local factors were also very important. China regards the Taiwan question as simply a domestic matter. Nevertheless Taiwan has most of the characteristics of a state, even though it does not receive wide international recognition. Developments in Taiwan itself have a big impact on this particular issue. This is also the case with the Korean problem, not just in relation to North Korea but also with South Korea. With both Taiwan and the two Koreas it is important to assess the impact of domestic developments, rather than focusing on government policy alone. While both situations can be seen as traditional security issues in many senses, they are not simply state-to-state matters; the fate of millions of people is at stake and human security is clearly relevant.

In discussing international politics in Southeast Asia the point was made that relations among states are just one dimension of the situation. While the major powers are involved in this region, their significance is less than in Northeast Asia. Southeast Asian states often face challenges from within; their domestic situations frequently have important international implications. Realism requires important modifications when applied to Southeast Asia.

Similarly, when one assesses the role of international organizations, the realist position that these bodies are merely vehicles for states to act together seems oversimplified. International organizations, whether regional or global, often develop some autonomy; nevertheless they are not independent organizations and state behavior is the main factor influencing their role.

Liberalism or liberal institutionalism also places a strong emphasis on the role of states. However, it is more open to the role of other actors, and sees states as frequently porous in the way they respond to both internal and external influences. Whereas realism focuses on high politics, giving particular attention to traditional security issues, liberalism puts more emphasis on low politics. This accommodates a range of economic and social issues, including the new international agenda. The approach adopted in this book is quite compatible with the main tenets of liberalism. While there is a strong emphasis on the role of states, this is not an exclusive emphasis. Attention is drawn to the range of influences on states, and to the roles of actors such as international organizations. Similarly while security plays a prominent role in the discussion, security is viewed broadly, and a range of economic and other issues come under scrutiny.

In referring to critical perspectives a key point is the way in which many of these approaches are explicit about their underlying values. Their foci in terms of explaining international dynamics can vary. In their approach to international politics most states in the Asia Pacific region put a high value on security. Critical perspectives ask us to consider what is meant by terms such as "states" and "security." The discussion in this book has attempted to take an open-minded approach to such matters, emphasizing evolution over time. There has also been attention to other goals pursued by states in relation to issues such as economics and human rights. The emergence of new ways of organizing the region, such as through regionalism and global multilateralism, has also received attention. It is important to remain open to the range of ways of organizing human affairs; human welfare should be the central consideration. The virtue of constructivism is that it emphasizes that people make their own history. While we cannot be oblivious to the role of material factors, there is scope for changing perceptions through political and other means to achieve better human outcomes.

In relation to the culturalistic approach, the perspective adopted in this book has been to emphasize the importance of the historical context in understanding the behavior of the various actors involved in Asia Pacific international politics. It is important to be aware of the particularities of situations. However, this is not to say that generalizations in relation to underlying dynamics should not be attempted. The various Western approaches offer insight into the dynamics of various aspects of Asia Pacific international politics. At the same time it is important to be aware of how the role of states is affected by the outlook of people within those states, particularly the key decisionmakers. That outlook can be shaped by long historical experience. This is most clear in relation to China, but Japan, Korea, and Vietnam provide other good examples. At a broad level the universal theories are relevant but there is scope within that framework to allow for differences deriving from particular cultural influences.

■ Future Directions

Given the analysis presented in this book, as highlighted by the review of relevant theories, what might be said about likely future directions in Asia Pacific international politics? The major themes developed provide a good starting point: the role of the major powers, and particularly the way they relate to each other; Taiwan and Korea as the flashpoints of Northeast Asia; developments in Southeast Asia; and the role of international organizations. The roles of Russia and Australia are also relevant.

Developments affecting the United States, China, and Japan will be central to the future of international politics in Asia Pacific, especially in Northeast Asia. In the post-9/11 era the United States has been preoccupied with issues concerning the war on terrorism and Iraq. These issues are likely to remain part of the agenda for the United States but also to diminish in importance. A major issue for the United States is whether it remains engaged in Asia Pacific in more or less the same way. Will it remain as the regional hegemon, as suggested by John Ikenberry for example,[1] or will there be a more even situation among the three major powers?

Part of the answer to this question depends on what happens with China. "Rising China" is a key feature of Asia Pacific international politics in the post-9/11 era. At one level this is simply recognition of the economic growth occurring in China and the impact this is having on the political and economic landscape of the region. The success of its strategy of economic modernization means that China will carry greater political clout within the region. However, there are various possibilities as to how China will use this weight. A confrontationist course on some issues could lead to clashes with other powers. At the very least China will insist on having a major influence on the issues that are its most direct concern. Another consideration, of course, is that economic modernization will lead to large-scale political change in China. So far China has been able to maintain its authoritarian political system, but whether that system is compatible with economic modernization in the long term remains to be seen. Pressure for increased political expression from the growing middle class is likely to become stronger. If instability results, this will then weaken China's international voice, at least in the short term.

In Japan's case the key question is whether it will become a "normal power." In the post–Cold War period Japan's military strength has steadily grown, augmenting its position as the world's second most important economic power. Japan's preparedness to use its military power has grown too, but there are still many legal and political constraints. Nevertheless the trajectory seems clear. So far Japan has worked within the context of the US-Japan alliance, while steadily becoming more independent. Should the nationalist right grow in strength in Japan, the independent direction is likely to become more marked. This could lead to clashes with China, and there could also be tensions with the United States.

Developments relating to the major powers are likely to play out at one level in relation to the Taiwan and Korean issues. China will have greater leverage in relation to Taiwan. At the same time democratization has reinforced sentiment in Taiwan in favor of independence. Democratization has strengthened Taiwan's position in the eyes of the United States, but not to the extent of supporting provocative behavior by Taiwan. The United States also has to balance its interest in having the Taiwan issue dealt with peacefully against its need for Chinese support on a range of issues. "Strategic ambiguity" is likely to continue as the main theme in the US position on this matter. Whether China would be prepared to use its greater leverage to act more forcefully regarding Taiwan remains unclear; however, it has made clear that it could act if there were attempts to change Taiwan's status in favor of independence.

China is a major influence in relation to the two Korean states. It has been playing essentially the role of mediator in the crisis that has developed in US-DPRK relations since 2001. Whatever the outcome of that crisis, the United States is likely to continue as a major factor in Korean affairs. Nevertheless US influence in relation to South Korea has declined, partly because of the progressive ascendancy in South Korean politics, but also because of a perception that US strategy toward North Korea has been too provocative. Japan too has generally preferred a more conciliatory approach. The question of North Korea's future is the main issue for Korean affairs and the various powers involved. The general preference has been for the soft landing, propping up the DPRK if necessary to avoid the human costs of its collapse; South Korea would also find it difficult to cope with a political and economic collapse of its northern neighbor. The main problem in implementing the soft landing strategy has been US distaste for the North Korean regime, especially during the George W. Bush administration. Republicans in particular have argued that the regime is tyrannical and should not be rewarded for blackmail; the DPRK's attempt to acquire nuclear weapons is dangerous and should be blocked. The very fact that North Korea could go nuclear, not to mention its ability to launch an attack across the 38th parallel, is likely to encourage a conciliatory approach to this issue in the long term. China, Japan, Russia, and South Korea all favor this approach, as did the United States under the Clinton administration. Under George W. Bush the United States has been more aggressive, but the risks involved are likely to bring about some modification of the US approach in the long term; the United States also needs to avoid being too isolated on this issue. Isolation could jeopardize other US objectives in the region.

Southeast Asia will continue as a region where all three major powers are involved, but where local factors are frequently preeminent. China is likely to continue expanding its influence, particularly in mainland Southeast Asia, but not confined to there. As China's economic power grows it will be in a position to exert stronger influence in maritime Southeast Asia too.[2] Nevertheless, in the near future at least, Japan is likely to continue as the most significant economic partner for most of the Southeast Asian countries. The United States also has important economic links in a number of cases. Southeast Asian countries could be important to the United States in countering China's expanding role; issues from the war on terrorism are likely to continue too but at a minor level.

State-society tensions will continue in many Southeast Asian countries, thus weakening the states involved. This is most evidently the case in Indonesia where democratization has unleashed many contending forces, with weak government as the consequence. The separation of Aceh and West Papua is unlikely, but there could be continuing tensions in those areas (the 2005 Aceh settlement notwithstanding). Tensions in areas such as the southern Philippines and the Burmese border regions are likely to continue. The struggle for democracy in Burma does not appear to be set for early resolution. Frequently these various kinds of conflicts will manifest themselves at the international level, as external powers and nongovernmental organizations take an interest and the antigovernment groups campaign for support. While there will be differences over various issues among the Southeast Asian states, it is unlikely that there will be major conflicts.

This last point relates to the success of ASEAN as a regional organization in Southeast Asia. While it has not fulfilled all of the ambitions held for it, it has functioned relatively well as a security community and this is likely to continue. Other regional organizations are much weaker. At the Asia Pacific level, APEC has been disappointing and the ASEAN Regional Forum has only played a minor role. Both groupings are likely to continue as part of the web of international organizations in the region. The "East Asia" dimension is likely to become stronger through ASEAN Plus Three and now the nascent East Asian Community. In the long term, however, these groupings are unlikely to have significant teeth.

A consequence of weak regionalism is that global organizations, particularly the UN system, are frequently involved in dealing with Asia Pacific issues. This occurs sometimes with specific security issues, but perhaps more frequently with economic issues and the new international agenda. This pattern is likely to continue, with the UN either complementing or filling the gap left by regional organizations.

Apart from international organizations, Russia and Australia were also considered as "other actors." On the basis of the recent trajectory Russia's influence in the region is likely to continue to decline. The situation of the Russian Far East might improve if its role as an energy supplier develops, but generally the prospects for this region look bleak. Australia's engagement with Asia Pacific can be expected to continue, although its overall influence on regional affairs will be modest.

As the twenty-first century proceeds we can expect the various issues discussed in this book to continue in importance. Understanding the historical context (both the recent past and the more distant past) helps us to assess where the region is likely to go in the future. Clearly there can be wild cards, such as the collapse of the USSR or September 11, but a focus on the key factors affecting the most significant actors in the region does provide a good starting point. Prediction is not simply an act of the imagination. We have canvassed a range of possibilities. By the time these words are published, readers will be able to add their own postscript, indicating which of these possibilities have come to pass and why. Whatever the variations in terms of the significance of actors and issues, Asia Pacific will continue its role as one of the key regions in world politics.

Notes

1. Ikenberry, "American Hegemony and East Asia."
2. Indicative of this trend is "Chinese Missile Aid for Indonesia."

Acronyms and Abbreviations

ABM	Anti-Ballistic Missile (Treaty)
ABRI	Angkatan Bersenjata Republik Indonesia (Indonesian Armed Forces)
ADB	Asian Development Bank
AFTA	ASEAN free trade area
AMF	Asian Monetary Fund
ANZUS	Australia-New Zealand-United States Treaty
APEC	Asia-Pacific Economic Cooperation
APT	ASEAN Plus Three
ARF	ASEAN Regional Forum
ARMM	Autonomous Region of Muslim Mindanao (Philippines)
ASEAN	Association of Southeast Asian Nations
ASEM	Asia-Europe Meeting
CCP	Chinese Communist Party
CE	Common Era
CMI	Chiang Mai Initiative
CNOOC	China National Offshore Oil Corporation
DC	District of Columbia
DMZ	Demilitarized Zone (Korea)
DPP	Democratic Progressive Party (Taiwan)
DPR	Dewan Perwakilan Rakyat (House of Representatives) (Indonesia)
DPRK	Democratic People's Republic of Korea
EASI	East Asia Strategy Initiative
EASR I	*The United States Security Strategy for the East Asia-Pacific Region,* 1995 (Nye Report)

EASR II	*The United States Security Strategy for the East Asia-Pacific Region,* 1998
ECOSOC	Economic and Social Council
EEC	Eurasian Economic Community
EEZ	exclusive economic zone
ESCAP	Economic and Social Commission for Asia and the Pacific
ETIM	East Turkestan Islamic Movement
EVSL	Early Voluntary Sector Liberalization
FAO	Food and Agriculture Organization
FKM	Front Kedaulatan Maluku (Maluku Sovereignty Front) (Indonesia)
FMS	Foreign Military Sales
Fretilin	Frente Revolucionária de Timor Leste Independente (Revolutionary Front for an Independent East Timor)
FSX	Fighter Experience (fighter aircraft)
FTA	free trade area
FULRO	United Front for the Struggle of the Oppressed Races (Vietnam)
FY	fiscal year
G7	Group of Seven
G8	Group of Eight
GAM	Gerakan Aceh Merdeka (Free Aceh Movement) (Indonesia)
GATT	General Agreement on Tariffs and Trade
GDP	gross domestic product
Golkar	Sekretariat Bersama Golongan Karya (Joint Secretariat of Functional Groups) (Indonesia)
GPA	Global Program on AIDS
GRP	gross regional product
GULAG	Glavnoe Upravlenie Lagerei (Main Directorate for Corrective Labor Camps) (USSR)
GUUAM	Georgia-Ukraine-Uzbekistan-Azerbaijan-Moldova
HIV/AIDS	human immunodeficiency virus/acquired immunodeficiency syndrome
IAEA	International Atomic Energy Agency
IBRD	International Bank for Reconstruction and Development (World Bank)
ICJ	International Court of Justice
ICMI	Ikatan Cendekiawan Muslem se Indonesia (Indonesian Association of Muslim Intellectuals)

IDPs	internally displaced people
ILO	International Labour Organization
IMF	International Monetary Fund
INGO	international nongovernmental organization
INTERFET	International Force East Timor
JCP	Japan Communist Party
JDA	Japan Defense Agency
JI	Jemaah Islamiah (Indonesia)
JSP	Japan Socialist Party
KEDO	Korean Peninsula Energy Development Organization
Keidanren	Federation of Economic Organizations (Japan)
KMT	Kuomintang (Guomindang)
KNIL	Koninklijk Nederlands-Indisch Leger (Royal Netherlands Indies Army)
Kostrad	Komando Stregis Angkatan Darat (Strategic Reserve Command, Indonesian Army)
LDP	Liberal Democratic Party (Japan)
MALSINDO	Malacca Straits Coordinated Patrols (Malaysia-Singapore-Indonesia)
Masyumi	Consultative Council of Muslims (Indonesia)
METI	Ministry of Economy, Trade, and Industry (Japan)
MFA	Ministry of Foreign Affairs (China)
MFN	Most Favored Nation
MILF	Moro Islamic Liberation Front (Philippines)
MITI	Ministry of International Trade and Industry (Japan)
MNLF	Moro National Liberation Front (Philippines)
MOF	Ministry of Finance (Japan)
MOFA	Ministry of Foreign Affairs (Japan)
MOFTEC	Ministry of Foreign Trade and Economic Cooperation (China)
MPR	Majelis Permusyawaratan Rakyat (People's Consultative Assembly) (Indonesia)
MTCR	Missile Technology Control Regime
NATO	North Atlantic Treaty Organization
NEFOs	New Emerging Forces
NGO	nongovernmental organization
NICs	newly industrializing countries
NIEs	newly industrializing economies
NKAG	North Korea Advisory Group
NLD	National League for Democracy (Burma)
NMD	national missile defense

Nokyo	Agricultural Cooperative Association (Japan)
NSW	New South Wales
NU	Nahdlatul Ulama (Indonesia)
OECD	Organisation for Economic Cooperation and Development
OIE	Office International des Epizooties (World Organization for Animal Health)
OLDEFOs	Old Established Forces
ONUMOZ	Opération des Nations Unies au Mozambique (United Nations Operation in Mozambique)
ONUVEN	Mission d'Observation des Nations Unies chargée de la Vérification du Processus Électoral au Nicaragua (United Nations Observer Mission in Nicaragua)
OPM	Organisasi Papua Merdeka (Free Papua Movement)
OSCE	Organization for Security and Cooperation in Europe
P-5	Permanent Five Members of the UN Security Council
PAN	Partai Amanat Nasional (National Mandate Party) (Indonesia)
PAS	Parti Islam Se-Malaysia
PCB	Program Coordinating Board (for UNAIDS)
PDI	Partai Demokrasi Indonesia (Democratic Party of Indonesia)
PDI-P	Partai Demokrasi Indonesia - Perjuangan (Indonesian Democratic Party of Struggle)
PECC	Pacific Economic Cooperation Conference
Peta	Pembela Tanah Air (Protectors of the Fatherland) (Indonesia)
PKB	Partai Kebangkitan Bangsa (National Awakening Party) (Indonesia)
PKI	Partai Komunis Indonesia (Indonesian Communist Party)
PKO	peacekeeping operations
PLA	People's Liberation Army
PLWHA	People Living with HIV/AIDS
PNI	Partai Nasional Indonesia (Indonesian Nationalist Party)
PNTR	permanent normal trade relations
PPP	parity purchasing power
PPP	Partai Persatuan Pembangunan (United Development Party) (Indonesia)
PRC	People's Republic of China
PULO	Pattani United Liberation Organization (Thailand)
QDR 1997	*Report of the Quadrennial Defense Review,* 1997

QDR 2001	*Quadrennial Defense Review Report,* 2001
QDR 2006	*Quadrennial Defense Review Report,* 2006
Rengo	Japanese Trade Union Council
RFE	Russian Far East
ROC	Republic of China
ROK	Republic of Korea
RUSI	Republic of the United States of Indonesia
SARS	severe acute respiratory syndrome
SBY	Susilo Bambang Yudhoyono (Indonesian president from 2004)
SCO	Shanghai Cooperation Organization
SDF	Self-Defense Forces
SEATO	Southeast Asia Treaty Organization
SII	Structural Impediments Initiative
SLORC	State Law and Order Restoration Council (Burma)
Sohyo	General Council of Japanese Trade Unions
SPDC	State Peace and Development Council (Burma)
SPNFZ	South Pacific Nuclear Free Zone
TMD	theater missile defense
TNI	Tentara Negara Indonesia (Indonesian National Army)
UMNO	United Malays National Organization
UN	United Nations
UNAIDS	United Nations Programme on HIV/AIDS
UNAMET	United Nations Mission in East Timor
UNCLOS	United Nations Convention on the Law of the Sea
UNDOF	United Nations Disengagement Observer Force (between Syria and Israel)
UNDP	United Nations Development Programme
UNEP	United Nations Environment Programme
UNESCO	United Nations Educational, Scientific and Cultural Organization
UNGOMAP	United Nations Good Offices Mission in Afghanistan and Pakistan
UNHCR	United Nations High Commissioner for Refugees
UNICEF	United Nations Children's Fund
UNIFIL	United Nations Interim Force in Lebanon
UNIIMOG	United Nations Iran-Iraq Military Observer Group
UNMIK	United Nations Mission in Kosovo
UNMISET	United Nations Mission of Support in East Timor
UNODC	United Nations Office on Drugs and Crime
UNTAC	United Nations Transitional Authority in Cambodia

UNTAET	United Nations Transitional Administration in East Timor
UNTAG	United Nations Transition Assistance Group in Namibia
UPMs	unregulated people movements
USSR	Union of Soviet Socialist Republics
VOC	Vereenigde Ooste-Indische Compagnie (Dutch United East India Company)
WHO	World Health Organization
WMD	weapons of mass destruction
WTO	World Trade Organization
ZOPFAN	Zone of Peace, Freedom, and Neutrality

Bibliography

Acharya, Amitav. *Constructing a Security Community in Southeast Asia: ASEAN and the Problem of Regional Order.* London: Routledge, 2001.

———. *The Quest for Identity: International Relations of Southeast Asia.* Singapore: Oxford University Press, 2000.

Ahn, Byung-joon. "The Rise of China and the Future of East Asian Integration," *Asia-Pacific Review* 11, no. 2 (2004), pp. 18–35.

Ahn, Yinhay. "North Korea in 2001: At a Crossroads," *Asian Survey* 42, no. 1 (January/February 2002), pp. 46–55.

———. "North Korea in 2002: A Survival Game," *Asian Survey* 43, no. 1 (January/February 2003), pp. 49–63.

Akaha, Tsuneo. "Japan's Comprehensive Security Policy: A New East Asian Environment," *Asian Survey* 31, no. 4 (April 1991), pp. 324–340.

Akbarzadeh, Shahram. *Uzbekistan and the United States.* London: Zed, 2005.

Alley, Roderic. *The United Nations in Southeast Asia and the South Pacific.* New York: St. Martin's, 1998.

Almond, Gabriel. *The American People and Foreign Policy.* New York: Praeger, 1960.

Altman, Dennis. "AIDS and Questions of Global Governance," *Pacifica Review* 11, no. 2 (June 1999), pp. 195–211.

Arnold, Walter. "Japan and China," in Robert S. Ozaki and Walter Arnold, ed., *Japan's Foreign Relations: A Global Search for Economic Security.* Boulder, CO: Westview, 1985, pp. 102–116.

———. "Political and Economic Influences in Japan's Relations with China Since 1978," *Millennium* 18, no. 3 (Winter 1989), pp. 415–434.

Aspinall, Edward, and Mark T. Berger. "The Break-up of Indonesia? Nationalisms After Decolonisation and the Limits of the Nation-State in Post–Cold War Southeast Asia," *Third World Quarterly* 22, no. 6 (2001), pp. 1003–1024.

Austin, Greg, and Alexey D. Muraviev. *The Armed Forces of Russia in Asia.* London: I.B. Tauris, 2000.

Australian Department of Foreign Affairs and Trade, East Asia Analytical Unit. *Asia's Global Powers: China-Japan Relations in the 21st Century.* Canberra, 1996.

———. *Pacific Russia: Risks and Rewards.* Canberra, 1996.

Baker, James A., III. "America in Asia: Emerging Architecture for a Pacific Community," *Foreign Affairs* 70, no. 5 (1991), pp. 1–18.

Battersby, Paul. "Border Politics and the Broader Politics of Thailand's International Relations in the 1990s: From Communism to Capitalism," *Pacific Affairs* 71, no. 4 (Winter 1998–1999), pp. 473–488.

Baum, Julian, and Louise do Rosario. "Taiwan: The Sumo Neighbour," in Nigel Holloway, ed., *Japan in Asia: The Economic Impact on the Region.* Hong Kong: Review Publishing, 1991, pp. 52–65.

Beeson, Mark. "ASEAN Plus Three and the Rise of Reactionary Regionalism," *Contemporary Southeast Asia* 25, no. 2 (August 2003), pp. 251–268.

———, ed. *Contemporary Southeast Asia: Regional Dynamics, National Differences.* New York: Palgrave Macmillan, 2004.

Beeson, Mark, and Stephen Bell. "Australia in the Shadow of the Asian Crisis," in Richard Robison, Mark Beeson, Kanishka Jayasuriya, and Hyuk-Rae Kim, ed., *Politics and Markets in the Wake of the Asian Crisis.* London: Routledge, 2000, pp. 297–312.

Bernstein, Richard, and Ross H. Munro. *The Coming Conflict with China.* New York: Alfred A. Knopf, 1997.

Bertrand, Jacques. *Nationalism and Ethnic Conflict in Indonesia.* Cambridge: Cambridge University Press, 2004.

Beyrer, Chris. *War in the Blood: Sex, Politics, and AIDS in Southeast Asia.* London: Zed, 1998.

Brennan, Frank. *Tampering with Asylum: A Universal Humanitarian Problem.* St. Lucia, Qld.: University of Queensland Press, 2003.

Bridges, Brian. *Korea After the Crash: The Politics of Economic Recovery.* London: Routledge, 2001.

Brock, David. "The Theory and Practice of Japan-Bashing," *National Interest,* no. 17 (Fall 1989), pp. 29–40.

Buckley, Roger. *The United States in the Asia-Pacific Since 1945.* Cambridge: Cambridge University Press, 2002.

Burchill, Scott, Richard Devetak, Andrew Linklater, Matthew Paterson, Christian Reus-Smit, and Jacquie True. *Theories of International Relations,* 2nd ed. Houndmills: Palgrave, 2001.

Burke, Anthony. *In Fear of Security: Australia's Invasion Anxiety.* Annandale, NSW: Pluto, 2001.

Buszynski, Leszek. "Russia and the CIS in 2003: Regional Reconstruction," *Asian Survey* 44, no. 1 (January/February 2004), pp. 158–167.

———. "Russia and the Commonwealth of Independent States in 2002: Going Separate Ways," *Asian Survey* 43, no. 1 (January/February 2003), pp. 15–24.

Buzan, Barry. "The Asia-Pacific: What Sort of Region in What Sort of World?" in Anthony McGrew and Christopher Brook, ed., *Asia-Pacific in the New World Order.* London: Routledge, 1998, in association with the Open University, pp. 68–87.

Buzo, Adrian. *The Making of Modern Korea.* London: Routledge, 2002.

Caballero-Anthony, Mely. *Regional Security in Southeast Asia: Beyond the ASEAN Way.* Singapore: Institute of Southeast Asian Studies, 2005.

Campbell, Kurt M., and Yuki Tatsumi. "In the Aftermath of the Storm: US Foreign Policy in the Wake of 9/11 and Its Implications for the Asia-Pacific Region," *Asia-Pacific Review* 9, no. 2 (November 2002), pp. 31–44.

"Can North Korea Be Engaged? An Exchange Between Victor D. Cha and David C. Kang," *Survival* 46, no. 2 (Summer 2004), pp. 89–108.

Capling, Ann. *All the Way with the USA: Australia, the US and Free Trade,* Briefings series. Sydney: University of New South Wales Press, 2005.

Carr, E.H., edited by Michael Cox. *The Twenty Years' Crisis, 1919–1939: An Introduction to the Study of International Relations.* New York: Palgrave Macmillan, 2001.

Cha, Victor D. "South Korea in 2004: Peninsular Flux," *Asian Survey* 45, no. 1 (January/February 2005), pp. 33–40.

Cha, Victor D., and David C. Kang. *Nuclear North Korea: A Debate on Engagement Strategies.* New York: Columbia University Press, 2003.

Chalk, Peter. *Grey-Area Phenomena in Southeast Asia: Piracy, Drug Trafficking and Political Terrorism,* Canberra Papers on Strategy and Defence no. 123, Strategic and Defence Studies Centre, Research School of Pacific and Asian Studies, Australian National University, Canberra, 1997.

Chan, Gerald. *Chinese Perspectives on International Relations: A Framework for Analysis.* London: Macmillan, 1999.

Chan, Steve. "Taiwan in 2004: Electoral Contests and Political Stasis," *Asian Survey* 45, no. 1 (January/February 2005), pp. 54–58.

Chapman, J.W.M., Reinhard Drifte, and I.T.M. Gow. *Japan's Quest for Comprehensive Security.* London: Frances Pinter, 1983.

Cheeseman, Graeme. "Australia: The White Experience of Fear and Dependence," in Ken Booth and Russell Trood, ed., *Strategic Cultures in the Asia-Pacific Region.* Houndmills: Macmillan, 1999, pp. 273–298.

"China's Military Modernisation: A Confluence of Improvements," *Strategic Comments* 9, no. 6 (August 2003).

"Chinese Missile Aid for Indonesia: How Strategic a Partnership?" *Strategic Comments* 11, no. 6 (August 2005).

Coppel, Charles A. *Indonesian Chinese in Crisis.* Kuala Lumpur: Oxford University Press, 1983.

Cotton, James, and John Ravenhill, ed. *The National Interest in a Global Era: Australia in World Affairs, 1996–2000.* South Melbourne, Victoria: Oxford University Press, for the Australian Institute of International Affairs, 2001.

———, ed. *Seeking Asian Engagement: Australia in World Affairs, 1991–1995.* Melbourne: Oxford University Press, for the Australian Institute of International Affairs, 1997.

Cribb, Robert. "Not the Next Yugoslavia: Prospects for the Disintegration of Indonesia," *Australian Journal of International Affairs* 53, no. 2 (July 1999), pp. 169–178.

Crowe, William J., Jr., and Alan D. Romberg. "Rethinking Security in the Pacific," *Foreign Affairs* 70, no. 2 (Spring 1991), pp. 123–140.

Cumings, Bruce. "Decoupled from History: North Korea in the 'Axis of Evil,'" in Bruce Cumings, Ervand Abrahamian, and Moshe Ma'oz, *Inventing the Axis of Evil: The Truth About North Korea, Iran, and Syria.* New York: New Press, 2004, pp. 1–91.

————. *Korea's Place in the Sun: A Modern History.* New York: W.W. Norton, 1997.

————. *The Origins of the Korean War,* 2 vols. Princeton: Princeton University Press, 1981, 1990.

Dauvergne, Peter. "The Political Economy of Indonesia's 1997 Forest Fires," *Australian Journal of International Affairs* 52, no. 1 (April 1998), pp. 13–17.

Davis, Sue. *The Russian Far East: The Last Frontier?* London: Routledge, 2003.

Delfs, Robert, and Louise do Rosario. "China: Sense or Sensibility," in Nigel Holloway, ed., *Japan in Asia: The Economic Impact on the Region.* Hong Kong: Review Publishing, 1991, pp. 37–51.

Deng, Yong. "Hegemon on the Offensive: Chinese Perspectives on US Global Strategy," *Political Science Quarterly* 116, no. 3 (Fall 2001), pp. 343–365.

Deng, Yong, and Fei-Ling Wang, ed. *China Rising: Power and Motivation in Chinese Foreign Policy.* Lanham, MD: Rowman and Littlefield, 2005.

Destler, I.M., and Michael Nacht. "US Policy Toward Japan," in Robert J. Art and Seyom Brown, ed., *US Foreign Policy: The Search for a New Role.* New York: Macmillan, 1993, pp. 289–314.

Dibb, Paul. "Indonesia: The Key to South-East Asia's Security," *International Affairs* 77, no. 4 (2001), pp. 829–842.

Dirlik, Arif, ed. *What Is in a Rim? Critical Perspectives on the Pacific Region Idea,* 2nd ed. Lanham, MD: Rowman and Littlefield, 1998.

Drifte, Reinhard. *Japan's Foreign Policy,* Chatham House Papers. London: Routledge, for the Royal Institute of International Affairs, 1990.

————. *Japan's Foreign Policy in the 1990s: From Economic Power to What Power?* New York: St. Martin's, in association with St. Antony's College, Oxford, 1996.

————. *Japan's Security Relations with China Since 1989: From Balancing to Bandwagoning?* London: RoutledgeCurzon, 2003.

Drysdale, Peter, and Dong Dong Zhang, ed. *Japan and China: Rivalry or Cooperation in East Asia?* Canberra: Asia Pacific, 2000.

Dupont, Alan. "ASEAN's Response to the East Timor Crisis," *Australian Journal of International Affairs* 54, no. 2 (July 2000), pp. 163–170.

————. *East Asia Imperilled: Transnational Challenges to Security.* Cambridge: Cambridge University Press, 2001.

East Asian Strategic Review 2002. Tokyo: National Institute for Defense Studies, 2002.

Edwards, Peter, and David Goldsworthy, ed. *Facing North: A Century of Australian Engagement with Asia,* vol. 2, *1970s to 2000.* Melbourne: Melbourne University Press, 2003.

Emmers, Ralf. *Cooperative Security and the Balance of Power in ASEAN and the ARF.* London: RoutledgeCurzon, 2003.

Emmerson, Donald K. "Will Indonesia Survive?" *Foreign Affairs* 79, no. 3 (2000), pp. 95–107.

Fallows, James. *Looking at the Sun: The Rise of the New East Asian Economic and Political System.* New York: Pantheon, 1994.

Feith, Herbert. *The Decline of Constitutional Democracy in Indonesia.* Ithaca, NY: Cornell University Press, 1962.

Firth, Stewart. *Australia in International Politics: An Introduction to Australian Foreign Policy,* 2nd ed. Crows Nest, NSW: Allen and Unwin, 2005.

Foot, Rosemary. "Bush, China and Human Rights," *Survival* 45, no. 2 (Summer 2003), pp. 167–186.

———. *The Practice of Power: US Relations with China Since 1949.* New York: Oxford University Press, 1995.

———. *Rights Beyond Borders: The Global Community and the Struggle over Human Rights in China.* Oxford: Oxford University Press, 2000.

———. "The UN System's Contribution to Asia-Pacific Security Architecture," *Pacific Review* 16, no. 2 (2003), pp. 207–230.

Freeman, Nick J. "Laos: Timid Transition," in John Funston, ed., *Government and Politics in Southeast Asia.* London: Zed, 2001, pp. 120–159.

Friedberg, Aaron L. "11 September and the Future of Sino-American Relations," *Survival* 44, no. 1 (Spring 2002), pp. 33–49.

Garnaut, Ross. *Australia and the Northeast Asian Ascendancy: Report to the Prime Minister and the Minister for Foreign Affairs and Trade.* Canberra: Australian Government Publishing Service, 1989.

Garofano, John. "Power, Institutions, and the ASEAN Regional Forum," *Asian Survey* 42, no. 3 (May/June 2002), pp. 502–521.

Garrison, Jean A. *Making China Policy: From Nixon to G.W. Bush.* Boulder, CO: Lynne Rienner, 2005.

Gertz, Bill. *The China Threat: How the People's Republic Targets America.* Washington, DC: Regnery, 2000.

Gilson, Julie. "Complex Regional Multilateralism: 'Strategising' Japan's Responses to Southeast Asia," *Pacific Review* 17, no. 1 (March 2004), pp. 71–94.

Goldstein, Avery. *Rising to the Challenge: China's Grand Strategy and International Security.* Stanford: Stanford University Press, 2005.

Goldstein, Carl, and Anthony Rowley. "Hong Kong: Shogun Wedding," in Nigel Holloway, ed., *Japan in Asia: The Economic Impact on the Region.* Hong Kong: Review Publishing, 1991, pp. 66–79.

Gordon, Bernard K. *The Dimensions of Conflict in Southeast Asia.* Englewood Cliffs, NJ: Prentice-Hall, 1966.

———. "Japan: Searching Once Again," in James C. Hsiung, ed., *Asia Pacific in the New World Politics.* Boulder, CO: Lynne Rienner, 1993, pp. 49–70.

Green, Michael Jonathan. *Japan's Reluctant Realism: Foreign Policy Challenges in an Era of Uncertain Power.* New York: Palgrave, 2001.

Grimes, William W. "Economic Performance," in Steven K. Vogel, ed., *US-Japan Relations in a Changing World.* Washington, DC: Brookings Institution Press, 2002, pp. 35–62.

Halliday, Fred. "International Relations: Is There a New Agenda?" *Millennium* 20, no. 1 (Spring 1991), pp. 57–72.

Harding, Harry. "China's American Dilemma," *Annals of the American Academy of Political and Social Science* 519 (January 1992), pp. 12–25.

———. *A Fragile Relationship: The United States and China Since 1972.* Washington, DC: Brookings Institution, 1992.

Harrison, Selig. "Did North Korea Cheat?" *Foreign Affairs* 84, no. 1 (January/February 2005), pp. 99–110.

———. *Korean Endgame: A Strategy for Reunification and US Disengagement.* Princeton: Princeton University Press, 2002.

Harrison, Selig, and Clyde V. Prestowitz Jr. "Pacific Agenda: Defense or Economics?" *Foreign Policy,* no. 79 (Summer 1990), pp. 56–76.

Hasegawa, Tsuyoshi. "Japan," in Ramesh Thakur and Carlyle A. Thayer, ed., *Reshaping Regional Relations: Asia-Pacific and the Former Soviet Union.* Boulder, CO: Westview, 1993, pp. 101–123.

Hatch, Walter, and Kozo Yamamura. *Asia in Japan's Embrace: Building a Regional Production Alliance.* Cambridge: Cambridge University Press, 1996.

Hefner, Robert W. "Islam and Nation in the Post-Suharto Era," in Adam Schwarz and Johnathan Paris, ed., *The Politics of Post-Suharto Indonesia.* New York: Council on Foreign Relations Press, 1999, pp. 40–72.

Held, David, and Anthony McGrew, ed. *Governing Globalization: Power, Authority and Global Governance.* Cambridge: Polity, 2002.

Held, David, Anthony McGrew, David Goldblatt, and Jonathan Perraton. *Global Transformations: Politics, Economics and Culture.* Cambridge: Polity, 1999.

Heller, Dominik. "The Relevance of the ASEAN Regional Forum (ARF) for Regional Security in the Asia-Pacific," *Contemporary Southeast Asia* 27, no. 1 (2005), pp. 123–145.

Henderson, Jeannie. *Reassessing ASEAN,* Adelphi Paper no. 328, May 1999, pp. 48–55.

Higgott, Richard, and Richard Stubbs. "Competing Conceptions of Economic Regionalism: APEC Versus EAEC," *Review of International Political Economy* 2, no. 3 (1995), pp. 516–535.

Hill, Hal. *The Indonesian Economy,* 2nd ed. Cambridge: Cambridge University Press, 2000.

———. *The Indonesian Economy in Crisis: Causes, Consequences and Lessons.* Singapore: Institute of Southeast Asian Studies, 1999.

Hoare, James, and Susan Pares. *Conflict in Korea: An Encyclopedia.* Santa Barbara, CA: ABC-CLIO, 1999.

Holland, Harrison M. *Japan Challenges America: Managing an Alliance in Crisis.* Boulder, CO: Westview, 1992.

Hook, Glenn D., Julie Gilson, Christopher W. Hughes, and Hugo Dobson. *Japan's International Relations: Politics, Economics and Security.* London: Routledge, 2001.

Huan, Guo-cang. "Taiwan: A View from Beijing," *Foreign Affairs* 63, no. 5 (Summer 1985), pp. 1064–1080.

Hughes, Christopher W. *Japan's Security Agenda: Military, Economic, and Environmental Dimensions.* Boulder, CO: Lynne Rienner, 2004.

Hughes, Neil C. "A Trade War with China?" *Foreign Affairs* 84, no. 4 (July–August 2005), pp. 94–106.

Hund, Markus. "ASEAN Plus Three: Towards a New Age of Pan–East Asian Regionalism? A Skeptic's Appraisal," *Pacific Review* 16, no. 3 (2003), pp. 383–417.

Huntington, Samuel S. *The Clash of Civilizations and the Remaking of World Order.* New York: Simon and Schuster, 1996.

Huxley, Tim. *Disintegrating Indonesia? Implications for Regional Security,* Adelphi Paper no. 349, 2002.

———. "The Tsunami and Security: Asia's 9/11?" *Survival* 47, no. 1 (Spring 2005), pp. 123–132.

Ijiri, Hidenori. "Sino-Japanese Controversy Since the 1972 Diplomatic Normal-ization," *China Quarterly,* no. 124 (December 1990), pp. 639–661.

Ikenberry, John. "American Hegemony and East Asia," *Australian Journal of International Affairs* 58, no. 3 (September 2004), pp. 353–367.

International Crisis Group. "Aceh: A Fragile Peace," Asia Report no. 47, 27 February 2003.

————. "Aceh: How Not to Win Hearts and Minds," Indonesia Briefing, 23 July 2003.

————. "Aceh: A New Chance for Peace," Asia Briefing no. 40, 15 August 2005.

————. "Communal Violence in Indonesia: Lessons from Kalimantan," Asia Report no. 19, 27 June 2001.

————. "Dividing Papua: How Not to Do It," Indonesia Briefing, 9 April 2003.

————. "Indonesia Backgrounder: Jihad in Central Sulawesi," Asia Report no. 74, 3 February 2004.

————. "Indonesia: Ending Repression in Irian Jaya," Asia Report no. 23, 20 September 2001.

————. "Indonesia: Resources and Conflict in Papua," Asia Report no. 39, 13 September 2002.

————. "Indonesia: The Search for Peace in Maluku," Asia Report no. 31, 8 February 2002.

————. "Japan and North Korea: Bones of Contention," Asia Report no. 100, 27 June 2005.

Iriye, Akira. "Chinese-Japanese Relations, 1945–90," *China Quarterly,* no. 124 (December 1990), pp. 624–638.

"Japan's Push for Missile Defence: Benefits, Costs, Prospects," *Strategic Comments* 9, no. 8 (October 2003).

Jiang Zemin and Li Peng on Taiwan Question. China Intercontinental, 1996.

Johnson, Chalmers. *Blowback: The Costs and Consequences of American Empire.* London: Time Warner Paperback, 2002.

————. "History Restarted: Japanese-American Relations at the End of the Century," in Richard Higgott, Richard Leaver, and John Ravenhill, ed., *Pacific Economic Relations in the 1990s: Cooperation or Conflict?* St. Leonards, NSW: Allen and Unwin, 1993, pp. 39–61.

————. "Japanese-Chinese Relations, 1952–1982," in Herbert J. Ellison, ed., *Japan and the Pacific Quadrille: The Major Powers in East Asia.* Boulder, CO: Westview, 1987, pp. 107–134.

————. *MITI and the Japanese Miracle: The Growth of Industrial Policy, 1925–1975.* Stanford: Stanford University Press, 1982.

Kan, Shirley A. *China and Proliferation of Weapons of Mass Destruction and Missiles: Policy Issues.* Washington, DC: Report for Congress, Congressional Research Service, 4 December 2002, www.fas.org/spp/starwars/crs/RL31555.pdf (accessed 7 October 2005).

Kang, David C. "Getting Asia Wrong: The Need for New Analytical Frameworks," *International Security* 27, no. 4 (Spring 2003), pp. 57–85.

Kappagoda, Nihal. *The Asian Development Bank.* Boulder, CO: Lynne Rienner, 1995.

Keating, Paul. *Engagement: Australia Faces the Asia-Pacific.* Sydney: Pan Macmillan Australia, 2000.

Kent, Randolph C. "International Humanitarian Crises: Two Decades Before and Two Decades Beyond," *International Affairs* 80, no. 5 (October 2004), pp. 851–869.

Keohane, Robert O., and Joseph S. Nye. *Power and Interdependence,* 3rd ed. New York: Longman, 2001.

Kesavan, K. V. "Japan and the Tiananmen Square Incident: Aspects of the Bilateral Relationship," *Asian Survey* 30, no. 7 (July 1990), pp. 669–681.

Kiernan, Ben. "The Demography of Genocide in Southeast Asia: The Death Tolls in Cambodia, 1975–1979, and East Timor, 1975–1980," *Critical Asian Studies* 35, no. 4 (2003), pp. 585–597.

Kihl, Young Whan, ed. *Korea and the World: Beyond the Cold War.* Boulder, CO: Westview, 1994.

Kimura, Hiroshi. "Russia and the CIS in 2004: Putin's Offensive and Defensive Actions," *Asian Survey* 45, no. 1 (January/February 2005), pp. 59–66.

Kingsbury, Damien. *The Politics of Indonesia,* 2nd ed. South Melbourne, Victoria: Oxford University Press, 2002.

———. *South-East Asia: A Political Profile.* South Melbourne, Victoria: Oxford University Press, 2001.

Kipp, Rita Smith. "Indonesia in 2003: Terror's Aftermath," *Asian Survey* 44, no. 1 (January/February 2004), pp. 62–69.

Klien, Susanne. *Rethinking Japan's Identity and International Role: An Intercultural Perspective.* New York: Routledge, 2002.

Kornberg, Judith F., and John R. Faust. *China in World Politics: Policies, Processes, Prospects.* Boulder, CO: Lynne Rienner, 2004.

Krasner, Stephen D., ed. *International Regimes.* Ithaca, NY: Cornell University Press, 1983.

Krauthammer, Charles. "Democratic Realism: An American Foreign Policy for a Unipolar World," Irving Kristol Lecture, American Enterprise Institute for Public Policy Research, Washington, DC, 10 February 2004, www.aei.org/publications/pubID.19912,filter.all/pub_detail.asp (accessed 5 October 2005).

Kreisberg, Paul H. "The U.S. and Asia in 1990," *Asian Survey* 31, no. 1 (January 1991), pp. 1–13.

Lam, Willy. "Hu Jintao's Move to Consolidate Power," *China Brief* (Jamestown Foundation), 4, no. 19 (30 September 2004), pp. 1–3, www.jamestown.org/images/pdf/cb_004_019.pdf (accessed 6 October 2005).

Lampton, David M. "China's Foreign and National Security Policy-Making Process: Is It Changing, and Does It Matter?" in David M. Lampton, ed., *The Making of Chinese Foreign and Security Policy in the Era of Reform, 1978–2000.* Stanford: Stanford University Press, 2001, pp. 1–36.

———. *Same Bed, Different Dreams: Managing US-China Relations, 1989–2000.* Berkeley: University of California Press, 2001.

Lardy, Nicholas R. *Integrating China into the Global Economy.* Washington, DC: Brookings Institution Press, 2002.

Lee, Hong Yung. "South Korea in 2002: Multiple Political Dramas," *Asian Survey* 43, no. 1 (January/February 2003), pp. 64–77.

———. "South Korea in 2003: A Question of Leadership?" *Asian Survey* 44, no. 1 (January/February 2004), pp. 130–138.

Lee Lai To, *China and the South China Sea Dialogues.* Westport, CT: Praeger, 1999.

Legge, John D. *Sukarno: A Political Biography,* 2nd ed. Sydney: Allen and Unwin, 1984.

Leifer, Michael. *The ASEAN Regional Forum,* Adelphi Paper no. 302, July 1996.

———. *Dictionary of the Modern Politics of South-East Asia,* 3rd ed. London: Routledge, 2001.

———. *Singapore's Foreign Policy: Coping with Vulnerability.* London: Routledge, 2000.

Lijun, Sheng. *China and Taiwan: Cross-Strait Relations Under Chen Shui-bian.* London: Zed, 2002.

Lin Piao. "Long Live the Victory of People's War!" in K. Fan, ed., *Mao Tse-tung and Lin Piao: Post-Revolutionary Writings.* Garden City, NY: Anchor, 1972, pp. 357–412.

Lincoln, Edward J. *East Asian Economic Regionalism.* Washington, DC: Brookings Institution Press, for the Council on Foreign Relations, New York, 2004.

Lo, Chi-kin. *China's Policy Towards Territorial Disputes: The Case of the South China Sea Islands.* London: Routledge, 1989.

Lord, Winston. "A New Pacific Community: Ten Goals for American Policy," *Foreign Policy Bulletin* 3 no. 6 (May/June 1993), pp. 49–53.

Macdonald, Donald Stone. *The Koreans: Contemporary Politics and Society,* 3rd ed. Boulder, CO: Westview, 1996.

MacFarlane, S. Neil. "The 'R' in BRICs: Is Russia an Emerging Power?" *International Affairs* 82, no. 1 (January 2006), pp. 41–57.

Mackerras, Colin, ed. *Eastern Asia: An Introductory History,* 3rd ed. Sydney: Longman, 2000.

Malik, J. Mohan. "Dragon on Terrorism: Assessing China's Tactical Gains and Strategic Losses After 11 September," *Contemporary Southeast Asia* 24, no. 2 (August 2002), pp. 252–293.

———. *The Gulf War: Australia's Role and Asian-Pacific Responses,* Canberra Papers on Strategy and Defence no. 90. Canberra: Strategic and Defence Studies Centre, Research School of Pacific Studies, Australian National University, 1992.

———. "The Proliferation Axis: Beijing-Islamabad-Pyongyang," *Korean Journal of Defense Analysis* 15, no. 1 (Spring 2003), pp. 57–100.

Malley, Michael S. "Indonesia in 2001: Restoring Stability in Jakarta," *Asian Survey* 42, no. 1 (January/February 2002), pp. 124–132.

———. "Indonesia in 2002: The Rising Cost of Inaction," *Asian Survey* 43, no. 1 (January/February 2003), pp. 135–146.

Mann, Jim. *About Face: A History of America's Curious Relationship with China, from Nixon to Clinton.* New York: Alfred A. Knopf, 1999.

Mares, Peter. *Borderline: Australia's Response to Refugees and Asylum Seekers in the Wake of the Tampa,* 2nd ed. Sydney: University of New South Wales Press, 2002.

Markus, Andrew. *Race: John Howard and the Remaking of Australia.* Crows Nest, NSW: Allen and Unwin, 2001.

Marr, David, and Marian Wilkinson. *Dark Victory: How a Government Lied Its Way to Political Triumph.* Crows Nest, NSW: Allen and Unwin, 2004.

Marshall, Patrick G. "The US and Japan," *CQ Researcher,* 31 May 1991, pp. 327–347.

Mastanduno, Michael. "Incomplete Hegemony and Security Order in the Asia-Pacific," in G. John Ikenberry, ed., *America Unrivaled: The Future of the Balance of Power.* Ithaca, NY: Cornell University Press, 2002, pp. 181–210.

McCormack, Gavan. *Target North Korea: Pushing North Korea to the Brink of Nuclear Catastrophe.* New York: Thunder's Mouth/Nation, 2004.

McDougall, Derek. "Asia-Pacific Security Regionalism: The Impact of Post-1997 Developments," *Contemporary Security Policy* 23, no. 2 (August 2002), pp. 113–134.

———. *Australian Foreign Relations: Contemporary Perspectives.* South Melbourne, Victoria: Addison-Wesley Longman, 1998.

———. *Historical Dictionary of International Organizations in Asia and the Pacific.* Lanham, MD: Scarecrow, 2002.

———. *Studies in International Relations: The Asia-Pacific, the Nuclear Age, Australia,* 2nd ed. Rydalmere, NSW: Hodder Headline, 1997.

McLaurin, Ronald D., and Chung-in Moon. *The United States and the Defense of the Pacific.* Boulder, CO: Westview, 1989.

Meaney, Neville, ed. *Australia and the World: A Documentary History from the 1870s to the 1970s.* Melbourne: Longman Cheshire, 1985.

Meeting the North Korean Nuclear Challenge: Report of an Independent Task Force Sponsored by the Council on Foreign Relations. New York: Council on Foreign Relations, 2003.

Menon, Rajan. "The New Great Game in Central Asia," *Survival* 45, no. 2 (Summer 2003), pp. 187–204.

The Military Balance 1996–1997. London: Oxford University Press, for the International Institute for Strategic Studies, 1996.

The Military Balance 2002–2003. London: Oxford University Press, for the International Institute for Strategic Studies, 2002.

The Military Balance 2003–2004. London: Oxford University Press, for the International Institute for Strategic Studies, 2003.

The Military Balance 2004–2005. London: Oxford University Press, for the International Institute for Strategic Studies, 2004.

The Military Balance 2005–2006. London: Routledge, for the International Institute for Strategic Studies, 2005.

Miller, John H. "The Glacier Moves: Japan's Response to US Security Policies," *Asian Affairs* 30, no. 2 (Summer 2003), pp. 132–141.

Mingst, Karen A., and Margaret P. Karns, ed. *The United Nations in the Post–Cold War Era,* 2nd ed. Boulder, CO: Westview, 2000.

Mochizuki, Mike M. "To Change or to Contain: Dilemmas of American Policy Toward Japan," in Kenneth A. Oye, Robert J. Lieber, and Donald Rothchild, ed., *Eagle in a New World: American Grand Strategy in the Post–Cold War Era.* New York: HarperCollins, 1992, pp. 335–359.

Morgenthau, Hans J., revised by Kenneth W. Thompson. *Politics Among Nations: The Struggle for Power and Peace.* New York: McGraw-Hill, 2003.

Mukundan, P. "Scourge of Piracy in Southeast Asia—Any Improvements in 2004?" in Michael Richardson and P. Mukundan, *Political and Security Outlook 2004: Maritime Terrorism and Piracy,* Trends in Southeast Asia Series: 3 (2004), pp. 9–18. Singapore: Institute of Southeast Asian Studies.

Murphey, Rhoads. *A History of Asia,* 5th ed. New York: Longman, 2005.

Nathan, Andrew J., and Robert S. Ross. *The Great Wall and the Empty Fortress: China's Search for Security.* New York: W.W. Norton, 1997.

A National Security Strategy for a New Century, May 1997, p. 7, http://clinton2.nara.gov/wh/eop/nsc/strategy (accessed 17 February 2003).

The National Security Strategy of the United States of America (September 2002).

Neher, Clark D. *Southeast Asia in the New International Era,* 4th ed. Boulder, CO: Westview, 2002.

Newby, Laura. *Sino-Japanese Relations: China's Perspective.* London: Routledge, for the Royal Institute of International Affairs, 1988.

Noland, Marcus. *Korea After Kim Jong-il.* Washington, DC: Institute for International Economics, 2004.

———. "US-China Economic Relations," in Robert S. Ross, ed., *After the Cold War: Domestic Factors and US-China Relations.* Armonk, NY: M.E. Sharpe, 1998, pp. 107–147.

Nye, Joseph S., Jr. "East Asian Security: The Case for Deep Engagement," *Foreign Affairs* 74, no. 4 (July/August 1995), pp. 90–102.

———. "The 'Nye Report': Six Years Later," *International Relations of the Asia-Pacific* 1, no. 1 (2001), pp. 95–103.

———. *Soft Power: The Means to Success in World Politics.* New York: Public Affairs, 2004.

Oberdorfer, Don. *The Two Koreas: A Contemporary History.* London: Warner, 1999.

Odgaard, Liselotte. "Deterrence and Cooperation in the South China Sea," *Contemporary Southeast Asia* 23, no. 2 (August 2001), pp. 292–306.

O'Hanlon, Michael, and Mike Mochizuki. *Crisis on the Korean Peninsula: How to Deal with a Nuclear North Korea.* New York: McGraw-Hill, 2003.

———. "Toward a Grand Bargain with North Korea," *Washington Quarterly* 26, no. 4 (Autumn 2003), pp. 7–18.

Oishi, Mikio, and Fumitaka Furuoka. "Can Japanese Aid Be an Effective Tool of Influence? Case Studies of Cambodia and Burma," *Asian Survey* 43, no. 6 (November/December 2003), pp. 890–907.

Okada, Kunio. "The Japanese Economic Presence in the Russian Far East," in Judith Thornton and Charles E. Ziegler, ed., *Russia's Far East: A Region at Risk.* Seattle: National Bureau of Asian Research, in association with University of Washington Press, 2002, pp. 419–440.

Okamoto, Yukio. "Japan and the United States: The Essential Alliance," *Washington Quarterly* 25, no. 2 (Spring 2002), pp. 59–72.

"The One-China Principle and the Taiwan Issue," China White Paper, February 2000, www.chinaembassy.org/eng/zt/twwt/White%20Papers/t36705.htm (accessed 10 October 2005).

Pangestu, Mari. "East Kalimantan: Beyond the Timber and Oil Boom," in Hal Hill, ed., *Unity and Diversity: Regional Economic Development in Indonesia Since 1970.* Singapore: Oxford University Press, 1991, pp. 151–175.

Park, Kyung-Ae. "North Korea in 2003: Pendulum Swing Between Crisis and Diplomacy," *Asian Survey* 44, no. 1 (January/February 2004), pp. 139–146.

———. "North Korea in 2004: From Brisk Diplomacy to Impasse," *Asian Survey* 45, no. 1 (January/February 2005), pp. 14–20.

Pempel, T.J., ed. *Remapping East Asia: The Construction of a Region.* Ithaca, NY: Cornell University Press, 2005.

Peng,Yuan. "The Taiwan Issue in the Context of New Sino-US Strategic Cooperation," Center for Northeast Asian Policy Studies, Brookings Institution, Washington, DC, Summer 2004, p. 12, www.brookings.edu/fp/cnaps/papers/yuan2004.pdf (accessed 10 October 2005).

Peterson, Andrew. "Dangerous Games Across the Taiwan Strait," *Washington Quarterly* 27, no. 2 (Spring 2004), pp. 23–41.

"Philippines' Claim to Sabah," in Michael Leifer, *Dictionary of the Modern Politics of South-East Asia,* 3rd ed. London: Routledge, 2001, pp. 222–223.

"Piracy and Maritime Terror in Southeast Asia," *Strategic Comments* 10, no. 6 (July 2004).

Pollack, Jonathan D. "The United States and Asia in 2003: All Quiet on the Eastern Front?" *Asian Survey* 44, no. 1 (January/February 2004), pp. 1–13.

———. "The United States and Asia in 2004: Unfinished Business," *Asian Survey* 45, no. 1 (January/February 2005), pp. 1–13.

Polomka, Peter. "Towards a 'Pacific House,'" *Survival* 33, no. 2 (March/April 1991), pp. 173–182.

Prestowitz, Clyde V., Jr. *Trading Places: How We Allowed Japan to Take the Lead.* New York: Basic, 1988.

Purdey, Jemma. "Anti-Chinese Violence and Transitions in Indonesia: June 1998–October 1999," in Tim Lindsey and Helen Pausacker, ed., *Chinese Indonesians: Remembering, Distorting, Forgetting*. Clayton, Victoria: Monash Asia Institute, with Institute of Southeast Asian Studies, 2005, pp. 14–40.

Purrington, Courtney. "Tokyo's Policy Responses During the Gulf War and the Impact of the 'Iraqi Shock' on Japan," *Pacific Affairs* 65, no. 2 (Summer 1992), pp. 161–181.

Purrington, Courtney, and A.K. "Tokyo's Policy Responses During the Gulf Crisis," *Asian Survey* 31, no. 4 (April 1991), pp. 307–323.

Pye, Lucian W. *Asian Power and Politics: The Cultural Dimensions of Politics.* Cambridge: Belknap Press of Harvard University Press, 1985.

Quansheng, Zhao. "Domestic Factors of Chinese Foreign Policy: From Vertical to Horizontal Authoritarianism," *Annals of the American Academy of Political and Social Science* 519 (January 1992), pp. 158–175.

Quilty, Mary. "Immigration and Multiculturalism," in Peter Edwards and David Goldsworthy, ed., *Facing North: A Century of Australian Engagement with Asia,* vol. 2, *1970s to 2000.* Melbourne: Melbourne University Press, 2003, pp. 297–324.

Quimpo, Nathan Gilbert. "Options in the Pursuit of a Just, Comprehensive, and Stable Peace in the Southern Philippines," *Asian Survey* 41, no. 2 (March/April 2001), pp. 271–289.

Ravenhill, John. *APEC and the Construction of Pacific Rim Regionalism.* Cambridge: Cambridge University Press, 2001.

Reid, Anthony. "War, Peace and the Burden of History in Aceh," *Asian Ethnicity* 5, no. 3 (October 2004), pp. 301–314.

Rice, Condoleezza. "Campaign 2000—Promoting the National Interest," *Foreign Affairs* 79, no. 1 (January–February 2000), pp. 45–62.

Richardson, Michael. *A Time Bomb for Global Trade: Maritime-Related Terrorism in an Age of Weapons of Mass Destruction.* Singapore: Institute of Southeast Asian Studies, 2004.

Ricklefs, M.C. *A History of Modern Indonesia Since c. 1200,* 3rd ed. Stanford: Stanford University Press, 2001.

Rigger, Shelley. "Taiwan in 2002: Another Year of Political Droughts and Typhoons," *Asian Survey* 43, no. 1 (January/February 2003), pp. 41–48.

Rix, Alan. "Japan and the Region: Leading from Behind," in Richard Higgott, Richard Leaver, and John Ravenhill, ed., *Pacific Economic Relations in the 1990s: Cooperation or Conflict?* St. Leonards, NSW: Allen and Unwin, 1993, pp. 62–82.

Ross, Robert S. "National Security, Human Rights, and Domestic Politics: The Bush Administration and China," in Kenneth A. Oye, Robert J. Lieber, and Donald Rothchild, ed., *Eagle in a New World: American Grand Strategy in the Post–Cold War Era.* New York: HarperCollins, 1992, pp. 281–313.

———. "US Policy Toward China," in Robert J. Art and Seyom Brown, ed., *US Foreign Policy: The Search for a New Role.* New York: Macmillan, 1993, pp. 338–357.

Roy, Denny. "China and the War on Terrorism," *Orbis* 46, no. 3 (Summer 2002), pp. 511–521.

———. *China's Foreign Relations.* Houndmills: Macmillan, 1998.

———. "China's Reaction to American Predominance," *Survival* 45, no. 3 (Autumn 2003), pp. 57–78.

———. "The Sources and Limits of Sino-Japanese Tensions," *Survival* 47, no. 2 (Summer 2005), pp. 191–214.

———. *Taiwan: A Political History.* Ithaca, NY: Cornell University Press, 2003.

———. "Tensions in the Taiwan Strait," *Survival* 42, no. 1 (Spring 2000), pp. 76–96.

Rumer, Boris. "The Powers in Central Asia," *Survival* 44, no. 3 (Autumn 2002), pp. 57–68.

Saich, Tony. *Governance and Politics of China.* Houndmills: Palgrave, 2001.

Sakai, Minako. "Resisting the Mainland: The Formation of the Province of the Bangka-Belitung (Babel)," in Damien Kingsbury and Harry Aveling, ed., *Autonomy and Disintegration in Indonesia.* London: RoutledgeCurzon, 2003, pp. 188–200.

SBS World Guide, 9th ed. South Yarra, Victoria: Hardie Grant, 2001.

Scalapino, Robert A. "Cross-Strait Relations and the United States," in Donald S. Zagoria, ed., *Breaking the China-Taiwan Impasse.* Westport, CT: Praeger, 2003, pp. 3–9.

Segal, Gerald. *The Fate of Hong Kong.* London: Simon and Schuster, 1993.

Shambaugh, David. *Beautiful Imperialist: China Perceives America, 1972–1990.* Boulder, CO: Westview, 1992.

———. "China and the Korean Peninsula: Playing for the Long Term," *Washington Quarterly* 26, no. 2 (Spring 2003), pp. 43–56.

———, ed. *Is China Unstable? Assessing the Factors.* Armonk, NY: M.E. Sharpe, 2000.

———. "A Matter of Time: Taiwan's Eroding Military Advantage," *Washington Quarterly* 23, no. 2 (Spring 2000), pp. 119–133.

———. *Modernizing China's Military: Progress, Problems, and Prospects.* Berkeley: University of California Press, 2002.

Shinohara, Miyohei. "Japan as a World Economic Power," *Annals of the American Academy of Political and Social Science* 513 (January 1991), pp. 12–24.

Shintaro Ishihara. *The Japan That Can Say No.* New York: Simon and Schuster, 1991.

Shiraishi, Takashi. "The Indonesian Military in Politics," in Adam Schwarz and Johnathan Paris, ed., *The Politics of Post-Suharto Indonesia.* New York: Council on Foreign Relations Press, 1999, p. 73–86.

Siddique, Sharon, and Sree Kumar, comp. *The 2nd ASEAN Reader.* Singapore: Institute of Southeast Asian Studies, 2003.

Sigal, Leon V. *Disarming Strangers: Nuclear Diplomacy with North Korea.* Princeton: Princeton University Press, 1998.

Smith, Anthony L. "Indonesia: Transforming the Leviathan," in John Funston, ed., *Government and Politics in Southeast Asia.* London: Zed, 2001, pp. 74–119.

Smith, Heather, and Sandra Eccles. "Lessons from Korea's Crisis," in Heather Smith, ed., *Looking Forward: Korea After the Economic Crisis.* Canberra: Asia Pacific, 2000, pp. 1–22.

Söderberg, Marie, ed. *Chinese-Japanese Relations in the Twenty-first Century: Complementarity and Conflict.* London: Routledge, 2002.

Soesastro, Hadi, Anthony L. Smith, and Han Mui Ling, ed. *Governance in Indonesia: Challenges Facing the Megawati Presidency.* Singapore: Institute of Southeast Asian Studies, 2003.

Solomon, Richard H. "Political Culture and Diplomacy in the Twenty-first Century," in Richard J. Samuels and Myron Weiner, ed., *The Political Culture of Foreign Area and International Studies: Essays in Honor of Lucian W. Pye.* Washington, DC: Brassey's (US), 1992, pp. 141–154.

Stephan, John J. *The Russian Far East: A History.* Stanford: Stanford University Press, 1994.

Stockwin, J.A.A. *Dictionary of the Modern Politics of Japan.* London: Routledge-Curzon, 2003.

———. *Governing Japan: Divided Politics in a Major Economy,* 3rd ed. Oxford: Blackwell, 1999.

A Strategic Framework for the Asian Pacific Rim: Report to Congress 1992. Washington, DC: Department of Defense, 1992.

Strategic Survey 1995–1996. London: Oxford University Press, for the International Institute for Strategic Studies, 1996.

Strategic Survey 2002–2003. London: Oxford University Press, for the International Institute for Strategic Studies, 2003.

Strategic Survey 2003–2004. London: Oxford University Press, for the International Institute for Strategic Studies, 2004.

Stubbs, Richard. "ASEAN Plus Three: Emerging East Asian Regionalism?" *Asian Survey* 42, no. 3 (May/June 2002), pp. 440–455.

Suettinger, Robert L. *Beyond Tiananmen: The Politics of US-China Relations, 1989–2000.* Washington, DC: Brookings Institution Press, 2003.

Sukma, Rizal. "Aceh in Post-Suharto Indonesia: Protracted Conflict Amid Democratisation," in Damien Kingsbury and Harry Aveling, ed. *Autonomy and Disintegration in Indonesia.* London: RoutledgeCurzon, 2003, pp. 148–156.

Sutter, Robert G. *China's Rise in Asia: Promises and Perils.* Lanham, MD: Rowman and Littlefield, 2005.

Talbott, Strobe. "US-China Relations in a Changing World," in Christopher Marsh and June Teufel Dreyer, ed., *US-China Relations in the Twenty-First Century:*

Policies, Prospects, and Possibilities. Lanham, MD: Lexington, 2003, pp. 1–12.

Tan, Qingshan. "US-China Nuclear Cooperation Agreement: China's Nonproliferation Policy," *Asian Survey* 29, no. 9 (September 1989), pp. 870–882.

Tavan, Gwenda. *The Long, Slow Death of White Australia.* Carlton North, Victoria: Scribe, 2005.

Terada, Takashi. "The Genesis of APEC: Australia-Japan Political Initiatives," Pacific Economic Paper no. 298, Australia-Japan Research Centre, Australian National University, Canberra, December 1999.

Terrill, Ross. *The New Chinese Empire: And What It Means for the United States.* New York: Basic, 2003.

Tetsuya, Umemoto. "Comprehensive Security and the Evolution of the Japanese Security Posture," in Robert A. Scalapino, Seizaburo Sato, Jusuf Wanandi, and Sung-joo Han, ed., *Asian Security Issues: Regional and Global.* Berkeley: Institute of East Asian Studies, University of California, 1988, pp. 28–49.

Thornton, Judith, and Charles E. Ziegler. "The Russian Far East in Perspective," in Judith Thornton and Charles E. Ziegler, ed., *Russia's Far East: A Region at Risk.* Seattle: National Bureau of Asian Research, in association with University of Washington Press, 2002, pp. 3–34.

"Time to Deliver: A Survey of Indonesia," *The Economist,* 11–17 December 2004, pp. 1–16.

Tipton, Frank B. *The Rise of Asia: Economics, Society and Politics in the Industrial Age.* Honolulu: University of Hawaii Press, 1998.

Tow, William T. *Asia-Pacific Strategic Relations: Seeking Convergent Security.* Cambridge: Cambridge University Press, 2001.

———. "Evolving Australian Security Interests in the Asia-Pacific: Policy Coherence or Disjunction?" in Derek McDougall and Peter Shearman, ed., *Australian Security After 9/11: New and Old Agendas.* Aldershot: Ashgate, 2006, pp. 87–103.

Tucker, Nancy Bernkopf, ed. *Dangerous Strait: The US-Taiwan-China Crisis.* New York: Columbia University Press, 2005.

Turner, Mark. "Terrorism and Secession in the Southern Philippines: The Rise of the Abu Sayaff," *Contemporary Southeast Asia* 17, no. 1 (June 1995), pp. 1–19.

Turner, Mark, and Owen Podger, with Maria Sumardjono and Wayan K. Tirthayasa. *Decentralisation in Indonesia: Redesigning the State.* Canberra: Asia Pacific, 2003.

"The United States and Japan: Advancing Toward a Mature Partnership," INSS Special Report, Institute for National Strategic Studies, National Defense University, Washington, DC, 11 October 2000, www.ndu/inss/press/Spelreprts/sr_japan.html (accessed 15 December 2003).

United States, Department of Defense. *Quadrennial Defense Review Report,* September 30, 2001.

———. *A Strategic Framework for the Asian Pacific Rim: Report to Congress 1992.* Washington, DC: Department of Defense, 1992.

———. *The United States Security Strategy for the East Asia–Pacific Region 1995.*

———. *The United States Security Strategy for the East Asia–Pacific Region 1998,* www.defenselink.mil/pubs/easr98 (accessed 17 February 2003).

"UN Peace Operations and Asian Security," *International Peacekeeping* 12, no. 1 (Spring 2005, special issue).

Valencia, Mark J. *China and the South China Sea Disputes,* Adelphi Paper no. 298, October 1995.

Van Wolferen, Karel. *The Enigma of Japanese Power: People and Politics in a Stateless Nation.* New York: Knopf, 1989.

Vaqsavakul, Thaveeporn. "Vietnam: *Doi Moi* Difficulties," in John Funston, ed., *Government and Politics in Southeast Asia.* London: Zed, 2001, pp. 372–410.

Vogel, Steven K., ed. *US-Japan Relations in a Changing World.* Washington, DC: Brookings Institution Press, 2002.

Waltz, Kenneth. *Theory of International Politics.* Reading, MA: Addison-Wesley, 1979.

Wang, Jianwei, and Zhimin Lin. "Chinese Perceptions in the Post–Cold War Era: Three Images of the United States," *Asian Survey* 32, no. 10 (October 1992), pp. 902–917.

Ward, Adam. "China and America: Trouble Ahead?" *Survival* 45, no. 3 (Autumn 2003), pp. 35–56.

Weatherbee, Donald E., with Ralf Emmers, Mari Pengestu, and Leonard C. Sebastian. *International Relations in Southeast Asia: The Struggle for Autonomy.* Lanham, MD: Rowman and Littlefield, 2005.

Webber, Douglas. "Two Funerals and a Wedding? The Ups and Downs of Regionalism in East Asia and Asia-Pacific After the Asian Crisis," *Pacific Review* 14, no. 3 (2001), pp. 339–372.

Weeks, Stanley B., and Charles A. Meconis. *The Armed Forces of the USA in the Asia-Pacific Region.* St. Leonards, NSW: Allen and Unwin, 1999.

Weiss, Linda, Elizabeth Thurbon, and John Mathews. *How to Kill a Country: Australia's Devastating Trade Deal with the US.* Crows Nest, NSW: Allen and Unwin, 2004.

Wesley, Michael. "APEC's Mid-Life Crisis? The Rise and Fall of Early Voluntary Sectoral Liberalization," *Pacific Affairs* 74, no. 2 (Summer 2001), pp. 185–204.

———, ed. *The Regional Organizations of the Asia-Pacific: Exploring Institutional Change.* Basingstoke: Palgrave Macmillan, 2003.

Whiting, Allen S. "China and Japan: Politics Versus Economics," *Annals of the American Academy of Political and Social Science* 519 (January 1992), pp. 39–51.

———. *China Eyes Japan.* Berkeley: University of California Press, 1989.

Wit, Joel S., Daniel B. Poneman, and Robert L. Gallucci. *Going Critical: The First North Korean Nuclear Crisis.* Washington, DC: Brookings Institution Press, 2004.

Woon, Eden Y. "Chinese Arms Sales and US-China Military Relations," *Asian Survey* 29, no. 6 (June 1989), pp. 601–618.

Wu, Yu-Shan. "Taiwan in 2001: Stalemated on All Fronts," *Asian Survey* 42, no. 1 (January/February 2002), pp. 29–38.

Yahuda, Michael. *The International Politics of the Asia-Pacific,* 2nd and revised ed. London: RoutledgeCurzon, 2004.

———. "Sino-American Relations," in Gerald Segal, ed., *Chinese Politics and Foreign Policy Reform.* London: Kegan Paul International, for the Royal Institute of International Affairs, 1990, pp. 180–194.

Zagoria, Donald S., ed. *Breaking the China-Taiwan Impasse.* Westport, CT: Praeger, 2003.

Zeiler, Thomas W. "Business Is War in US-Japanese Economic Relations, 1977–2001," in Akira Iriye and Robert A. Wampler, ed. *Partnership: The United States and Japan 1951–2001.* Tokyo: Kodansha International, 2001, pp. 223–248.

Zhang Yunling. "Emerging New East Asian Regionalism," *Asia-Pacific Review* 12, no. 1 (2005), pp. 55–63.

Zhao, Quansheng. *Japanese Policymaking: The Politics Behind Politics: Informal Mechanisms and the Making of China Policy.* Westport, CT: Praeger, 1993.

Zhao, Suisheng, ed. *Chinese Foreign Policy: Pragmatism and Strategic Behavior.* Armonk, NY: M.E. Sharpe, 2004.

Zheng, Yongnian. *Discovering Chinese Nationalism in China: Modernization, Identity, and International Relations.* Cambridge: Cambridge University Press, 1999.

Index

353

French-Viet Minh conflict, 13; HIV/AIDS, 226; Japanese relations, 94, 215, 223; Laotian relations, 220–221; as part of Southeast Asia, 7; political system, 19, 219; South China Sea territorial disputes, 69, 215–216; Thai relations, 219, 221; as Third World country, 21; unification of, 15, 33; US relations. *See also* Third Indochina War (1978–1991)

Vietnam War: as attempt to impose Western values, 36; Australian role, 281; Chinese policy, 68; ending of, 15, 17, 33, 281–282; Japanese role, 78, 102; Sino-Soviet conflict, 14; Sino-US conflict in, 13; and two-China policy, 166

Wa (people), 17

Wahid, Abdurrahman: Aceh conflict, 247; administration of, 239–241; as NU leader, 237; West Papua conflict, 249, 263*n49*

Waltz, Kenneth, 3

War on terror: Afghanistan War, 45–46, 70, 108, 127, 287; APEC response, 46, 127, 305; Australian role, 287–288; Central Asian role, 276; Chinese role, 173; Indonesia as focus in, 204, 210, 242–243, 254–255, 260–261, 288; international cooperation in, 46; Japanese-US cooperation in, 108; Philippines as focus in, 204, 210, 214; US strategy for, 39, 45, 47. *See also* Iraq War; September 11 attacks

Washington Conference (1921–1922), 32

Weapons of mass destruction (WMD), 46–48, 128–130

Weinberger, Caspar, 117

Wen Jiabao, 173

Western civilization, 23

Western Europe, 244

West New Guinea, 234–235, 281

West Papua: Dutch rule in, 234–235; future of, 326; IDPs/refugees from, 225, 257; name changes in, 263*n49;* separatism, 17, 248–250, 258–259, 326; transfer to Indonesia of, 235, 248, 281; under the New Order, 237

White Australia Policy, 279–280, 283

White Russian forces, 269

Whitlam, Gough, 282

Wiranto, Gen., 238–243, 246

Wolferen, Karel van, 110

Wolfowitz, Paul, 126

World Bank: Chinese membership, 63, 70; development loans in Asia Pacific, 314; HIV/AIDS, 228; Japanese membership, 90

World Bank Group, 310

World government, 316–317

World Health Organization (WHO), 171, 228, 310, 314

World Organization for Animal Health (OIE), 315

World product shares by region, 24, 27*n16*

World Trade Organization (WTO): Australian role, 290; Chinese membership, 63, 70, 130, 135; Doha Round, 313; establishment of, 304; global multilateralism through, 308; Japan-US differences in, 111; Japanese membership, 90; Taiwanese membership, 168; as UN related organization, 310, 313

World War I, 32, 76

World War II, 32, 76–77, 94, 181, 270

Xinjiang: missile-monitoring station in, 117; Russian influence in, 68; Uighur separatism, 46, 57, 65, 70, 127, 139, 275; US human rights concerns in, 137–138

Yakut (people), 268–269

Yakut Rebellion (1642), 269

Yasukuni Shrine, 147, 154

Yeltsin, Boris, 266, 272, 274–275

Yongbyon, 188–189, 191

Yoshida Doctrine, 14, 78–79, 91, 98, 102, 112

Yoshida Shigeru, 78

Yoshio Sakurauchi, 110

Yudhoyono, Susilo Bambang, 238–239, 241, 243–244, 248, 260, 288

Yugoslavia, 125

Zhao Quansheng, 60

Zhao Ziyang, 119

Zhu Rongji, 135

Zoellick, Robert, 47, 112

Zoku, 84

About the Book

I n this thorough, analytical introduction to Asia Pacific's dynamic role in contemporary world politics, Derek McDougall focuses on the region's major state actors—China, Japan, and the United States—as well as on the conflicts involving Taiwan and Korea, developments in Southeast Asia, and the influences of Russia, Australia, and a range of international organizations.

McDougall covers a broad canvas, considering issues of security broadly defined, international political economy, human rights, development, health, drug trafficking, crime, refugees, and the environment. Following the model of his earlier *The International Politics of the New Asia Pacific,* he provides an accessible, timely assessment of the key elements in the international politics of the Asia Pacific region today.

Derek McDougall is associate professor in politics at the University of Melbourne. His numerous publications include *Studies in International Relations* and *Historical Dictionary of International Organizations in Asia and the Pacific.*